Managing Human Resources for Environmental Sustainability

Environmental Sustainability in the Production of This Volume

Recognizing our responsibility to the environment, and in concert with our sustainability objectives, Wiley selects and works with suppliers that utilize the highest standards of sustainable, clean, and efficient production. For example, John Wiley and Sons, Inc., and its product imprints recognize our responsibility to source paper from global suppliers who demonstrate and document their commitment to environmental and human well-being.

In the production of this book, the following environmentally responsible choices were made.

Paper: The paper in this book was chosen for its light weight characteristic, produced by a high yield thermomechanical pulping process that utilizes as much as 80% of the harvested tree, and brightened using an elemental chlorine free bleaching process. It reduces the amount of forest wood required to produce this book, reduces product weight and thus production and transportation energy requirements. The paper supplier's chain-of-custody in fiber sourcing is certified by the globally recognized Programme for the Endorsement of Forest Certification (PEFC), the Forest Stewardship Council (FSC), and the Sustainable Forestry Initiative (SFI) for the procurement, use, and replenishment of responsibly managed paper.

Ink: This book is printed with inks that include vegetable based (soy) ink, reducing the amount of petroleum required.

Cover/jacket stock: Cover and jacket stocks contain 10% post-consumer recycled fiber.

Binding glues: A mixture of cold melt (aqueous based) and hot melt glue (thermoplastic adhesives) were used in the binding of this book, making the book both durable and more environmentally sustainable. Cold melt glues are water soluble and therefore reduce the environmental impact of the binding process.

Environmental sustainability of manufacturing process: The manufacturing plants producing this book have implemented quality programs that reduce emissions and recover for reuse or recycling every material possible, including different types of papers, unused inks and cartridges, adhesives, and used printing plates, among others.

The Professional Practice Series

The Professional Practice Series is sponsored by The Society for Industrial and Organizational Psychology, Inc. (SIOP). The series was launched in 1988 to provide industrial and organizational psychologists, organizational scientists and practitioners, human resources professionals, managers, executives, and those interested in organizational behavior and performance with volumes that are insightful, current, informative, and relevant to *organizational practice*. The volumes in the Professional Practice Series are guided by five tenets designed to enhance future organizational practice:

1. Focus on practice, but grounded in science
2. Translate organizational science into practice by generating guidelines, principles, and lessons learned that can shape and guide practice
3. Showcase the application of industrial and organizational psychology to solve problems
4. Document and demonstrate best industrial and organizational-based practices
5. Stimulate research needed to guide future organizational practice

The volumes seek to inform those interested in practice with guidance, insights, and advice on how to apply the concepts, findings, methods, and tools derived from industrial and organizational psychology to solve human-related organizational problems.

Implementing Organizational Interventions
Jerry W. Hedge, Elaine D. Pulakos, Editors

Organization Development
Janine Waclawski, Allan H. Church, Editors

Creating, Implementing, and Managing Effective Training and Development
Kurt Kraiger, Editor

The 21st Century Executive: Innovative Practices for Building Leadership at the Top
Rob Silzer, Editor

Managing Selection in Changing Organizations
Jerard F. Kehoe, Editor

Evolving Practices in Human Resource Management
Allen I. Kraut, Abraham K. Korman, Editors

Individual Psychological Assessment: Predicting Behavior in Organizational Settings
Richard Jeanneret, Rob Silzer, Editors

Performance Appraisal
James W. Smither, Editor

Organizational Surveys
Allen I. Kraut, Editor

Employees, Careers, and Job Creating
Manuel London, Editor

Published by Guilford Press

Diagnosis for Organizational Change
Ann Howard and Associates

Human Dilemmas in Work Organizations
Abraham K. Korman and Associates

Diversity in the Workplace
Susan E. Jackson and Associates

Working with Organizations and Their People
Douglas W. Bray and Associates

Managing Human Resources for Environmental Sustainability

The Professional Practice Series

Managing Human Resources for Environmental Sustainability

Susan E. Jackson

Deniz S. Ones

Stephan Dilchert

Editors

Foreword by Allen I. Kraut

JOSSEY-BASS
A Wiley Imprint
www.josseybass.com

Published by Jossey-Bass
A Wiley Imprint
One Montgomery Street, Suite 1200, San Francisco, CA 94104-4594
www.josseybass.com

For additional copies/bulk purchases of this book in the U.S. please contact 800-274-4434.

Jossey-Bass books and products are available through most bookstores. To contact Jossey-Bass directly call our Customer Care Department within the U.S. at 800-274-4434, outside the U.S. at 317-572-3985, fax 317-572-4002, or visit www. josseybass.com.

Wiley publishes in a variety of print and electronic formats and by print-on-demand. Some material included with standard print versions of this book may not be included in e-books or in print-on-demand. If this book refers to media such as a CD, DVD, or flash drive that is not included in the version you purchased, you may download this material at http://booksupport.wiley.com. For more information about Wiley products, visit www.wiley.com.

Cover images © Getty. Top two RM. Bottom RF.

Library of Congress Cataloging-in-Publication Data
Managing human resources for environmental sustainability / Susan E. Jackson, Deniz S. Ones, Stephan Dilchert, editors ; foreword by Allen I. Kraut.
    p. cm. – (The professional practice series)
    Includes index.
    ISBN 978-0-470-88720-2 (cloth); 978-1-118-22107-5 (ebk.); 978-1-118-23483-9 (ebk.); 978-1-118-25945-0 (ebk.)
    1. Management–Environmental aspects.   2. Personnel management–Environmental aspects.   3. Sustainable development–Management.   4. Industries–Environmental aspects.   I. Jackson, Susan E.   II. Ones, Deniz S., 1965-   III. Dilchert, Stephan, 1980-
    HD30.255.M337 2012
    658.3'01–dc23

Printed in the United States of America

PB Printing   10 9 8 7 6 5 4 3 2 1

Contents

Foreword
Allen I. Kraut

Rarely are there new developments that are true "game-changers" in the fields of I-O psychology and human resource management; perhaps no more than one in a decade. But the topic of this book, making organizations "green," tells us about one of those rare changes that is unfolding right now. Nothing could be more useful to practitioners and researchers in HRM, in I-O, and organization development than a solid understanding of this shift, as delivered in this book.

The topic, how to conduct organizational operations in ways that are environmentally friendly and sustainable, may still be new to most professionals in these fields. Its growth and development is so fresh in ideas and so powerful that it may be described as a hugely innovative, even revolutionary movement. This new way of thinking and acting marks an enormous sea change in how we deal with many issues that affect our lives daily at work and in the long term as well.

A Slow Revolution

In scope and impact, it reminds me of the U.S. Civil Rights movement in the 1960s, which seemed so extraordinary at the time. I recall that "before and after" vividly, as I began my professional life about then. The "before" included an Army stint in the state of Georgia. While Army life in Fort Benning was not structured by race, just outside the gates there was a stark and distasteful view of a racially segregated nation. Public accommodations, such as restaurants and hotels, were kept separately for so-called white and colored. So too were schools and even the restrooms in gasoline stations. It seems hard to imagine all that now.

When Civil Rights laws took effect in the mid-1960s, the "after" included huge changes in our employment practices. How we recruited, selected, trained, and rewarded employees were forever changed. Today we take for granted many practices that began to change then. (As one small example, no longer do we find "Help Wanted" notices split into "Male" and "Female" sections.)

In the coming decades, I believe we will look back at the current era as the start of one of those rare historic shifts that has major long-lasting impacts on our field. That shift is the recognition and relevance of environmental sustainability. I believe *this book will be seen as a watershed event, and its content will be a touchstone for many practitioners.*

Of particular interest is the diverse genesis of this movement. It is impelled by assorted sources, not just legislative, and many of them are just out of sight to everyday observers. As Susan Jackson writes in her introductory chapter, "Portrait of a Slow Revolution Toward Environmental Sustainability," several forces have been building over the last few decades.

There has been the attention given to disastrous trends and events in air and water pollution and nuclear accidents. The impact of global climate change has also made headlines. The United Nations' efforts and the Kyoto protocol of 1997, now ratified by 197 nations, have involved many governments. In the meantime, several international agencies have developed standards to measure and report environmental performance, and some of these standards are now being used by leading companies.

Providing Useful Tools

Our troika of editors, Susan Jackson, Deniz Ones, and Stephan Dilchert, are pioneers in their research, understanding, and writing about this new field of environmental sustainability in organizations. Their research is the product of innovative and clear thinking. Best of all, their writing is lucid, engaging, and trail-blazing.

For example, Deniz Ones and Stephan Dilchert provide us in one chapter with an original and data-based taxonomy of employee green behaviors. This model of the types of employee actions that contribute to environmental sustainability can help practitioners to think conceptually about just what employees do and can help in the measurement of such behaviors. They also expand their discussion of relevant tools in another chapter devoted to measuring environmental sustainability performance at the level of the employee, organization, or nation.

The choice of chapter contributors and use of case studies are especially valuable aspects of this volume. The chapter authors are knowledgeable and at the forefront of work in this field. For example, in one chapter we learn from the results of a recent survey of 728 human resource professionals just what their organizations are doing in green practices and how to recruit and socialize new employees, who are more apt to engage in appropriate environmental behaviors.

The chapter contributors also represent a global cast of researchers and practitioners in environmental sustainability. This is evident in the eight case studies that show how environmentally sustainable practices are being implemented in different organizations. The settings range from the U.S. to Uganda and Germany, and to the United Kingdom's McDonald's operation. It includes the case of Procter & Gamble's global survey of employees' green attitudes and behavior in eighty countries.

The environmental sustainability actions of many organizations may have once seemed merely public relations gestures or part of a morally commendable aspect of corporate social responsibility. Now such actions seem more likely to become an organizational way of life based on profit as well as principles of good governance, undergirded by law. As one contributor tells us, even the financial publisher Dow Jones has developed an environmental practices index to help assess green practices that "create shareholder value."

As with many other environmental changes, those organizations that adapt the best and fastest will reap the greatest gains. Those firms will be able to select and train the most suitable people early, set desirable patterns of behavior, and take proper credit for it—which may be another way of saying that the needed changes will not be easy, but they are likely to be worthwhile.

In moving our fields forward, we should be most grateful to our editors, Susan, Deniz, and Stephan, for imagining and producing this wonderful volume. We are indebted to them and to their outstanding set of chapter contributors. When this book was first proposed, the Professional Practice Series Editorial Board was enthusiastic and hopeful. The board's endorsement has been amply repaid by the final product. I believe this volume richly deserves the long shelf life I predict for it.

Rye, New York   ALLEN I. KRAUT, Series Editor
December 1, 2011

Preface

We were delighted when the Society for Industrial and Organizational Psychology (SIOP) gave us the opportunity to prepare this edited volume on environmental sustainability in organizations. As concerns about environmental degradation are becoming increasingly salient in all domains of life, businesses face increasing pressure from their stakeholders—governments, shareholders, customers, and employees—to adopt environmentally friendly policies and practices. Organizational efforts in this domain, however, typically focus on strategic questions, technological contributions, public policy linkages, or marketing considerations. Yet, employees and other organizational members are pivotal to all organizational initiatives. This volume was created to draw our attention to the growing number of *workforce issues* that relate to environmental sustainability.

Increasingly, industrial and organizational (I-O) psychologists and human resources practitioners are interested in the topic of environmental sustainability. Starting in 2010, a large number of SIOP sessions on the topic have attracted sizeable audiences. The 2011 day-long Theme Track at the annual SIOP conference and the 2012 SIOP Leading Edge Consortium provided further evidence that our field has recognized environmental sustainability as an important topic of scientific inquiry and applied psychological practice. At the same time, universities are increasingly offering workshops, courses, and even majors on environmental sustainability. Discussions of environmental issues are being incorporated into existing I-O psychology and HRM courses. As greater numbers of companies continue to adopt environmental goals, employees have to contribute in various ways to make sustainability in organizations a reality. I-O psychologists who work in industry as well as HR managers need to—at the very least—familiarize themselves with the issues in this domain. Moreover, we believe that "green" transformations of organizations are simply not possible without the involvement of I-O psychologists who will need to (re)define job requirements and design approaches to recruit, select, train, develop, manage, motivate, lead, and reward the future workforces of environmentally sustainable organizations.

This volume reflects diverse perspectives arising from the breadth of views and experiences represented. The contributing authors and organizations are international, from developed and emerging economies, spanning a variety of industries, and represent a mix of applied and academic backgrounds. The chapters and case studies aim to highlight the central role of employees, I-O psychologists, and human resource management in achieving environmental sustainability goals in applied organizational settings. In the field, many practitioners are already involved in the creation and implementation of initiatives with positive environmental impact. Yet, there is little empirical research, especially at the individual level of analysis, in our academic journals that documents and examines the green revolution transforming workforces and workplaces globally. This is an area in which practice is leading research.

Editing this volume was a rewarding experience for us, as it provided the opportunity to observe an evolving area within our profession and learn from the contributing authors. We are thankful for the support of several individuals. Allen Kraut, the SIOP Practice Series editor, was a strong advocate from the very beginning. His understanding of the strategic importance of HR in achieving environmental sustainability was much appreciated. Eduardo Salas, president of SIOP when this book was initiated, was also unwavering in his support of this project and related endeavors (the 2011 Theme Track and 2012 Leading Edge Consortium). Finally, we appreciated the support we received from our colleagues and students at Rutgers University, Baruch College, and the University of Minnesota.

We look forward to this book spurring future HR practice and psychological research on environmental sustainability in work settings.

December 2011   Deniz S. Ones
                                                       Stephan Dilchert
                                                        Susan E. Jackson

The Editors

Susan E. Jackson is Distinguished Professor of Human Resource Management, School of Management and Labor Relations, Rutgers University, and Research Fellow, Lorange Institute of Business, Zürich. She earned a Ph.D. in social and organizational psychology from the University of California–Berkeley. She is a Fellow of the Society for Industrial and Organizational Psychology, the Association for Psychological Science, and the Academy of Management, where she is past president. Her recent interest in environmental sustainability is an extension of her prior research on strategic HRM, work team effectiveness, and knowledge management, which has appeared in numerous scholarly journals. She is an author/editor of several books, including *Managing Human Resources* (11th ed., with R. S. Schuler and S. Werner), two SIOP-sponsored volumes—*Managing Knowledge for Sustained Competitive Advantage: Designing Strategies for Effective Human Resource Management* (with M. A. Hitt and A. DeNisi) and *Diversity in the Workplace: Human Resources Initiatives*. She also manages www.greenHRM.org, a website providing free resources for students, scholars, and practitioners interested in environmental sustainability and workforce management. Email: sjackson@smlr.rutgers.edu

Deniz S. Ones is the Hellervik Professor of Industrial Psychology and a Distinguished McKnight Professor at the University of Minnesota. Ones received her Ph.D. from the University of Iowa. Her research focuses on individual differences (personality, cognitive ability, job performance, counterproductive work behaviors, employee green behaviors) in work settings. She has received numerous prestigious awards for her research on individual differences in employee staffing, among them the 1998 Ernest J. McCormick Award for Distinguished Early Career Contributions from the Society for Industrial and Organizational Psychology (SIOP), as well as the 2003 Cattell Early Career Research Award from the Society for Multivariate Experimental Psychology. Ones also received the Award for Professional Contributions and Service to Testing from the Association of Test Publishers. She is a Fellow of the Association for Psychological Science and the American Psychological Association (Divisions 5 and 14–SIOP), for which she also chaired the Committee on Psychological Testing and Assessment (CPTA). Previously, she co-edited the best-selling, two-volume *Handbook of Industrial, Work and Organizational Psychology* (2001) and served as an editor-in-chief of the *International Journal of Selection and Assessment* and associate editor of the *Journal of Personnel Psychology*. Ones serves or has served on editorial boards of a dozen journals in applied and general psychology. She has also edited special issues of several journals devoted to personality variables, use of cognitive ability in employee selection, and counterproductive work behaviors. Recently, she has co-chaired the 2011 SIOP Theme Track on Environmental Sustainability and is the science co-chair of the 2012 SIOP Leading Edge Consortium on the same topic. Email: deniz.s.ones-1@tc.umn.edu

Stephan Dilchert is an assistant professor of management at the Zicklin School of Business, Baruch College, City University of New York. He received his Ph.D. in industrial and organizational psychology from the University of Minnesota. His dissertation research on creativity was recognized with the Meredith P. Crawford Fellowship from the Human Resources Research Organization, the Best Dissertation Award from the University of Minnesota, and the S. Rains Wallace Award from the Society for Industrial and Organizational Psychology. His work has been published in the *Journal of Applied Psychology, Personnel Psychology, Human Performance*, and *International Journal of Selection and Assessment*, among others. Dilchert serves on two editorial boards, has chaired the 2011 SIOP Theme Track on Environmental Sustainability, and is the science co-chair of the 2012 SIOP Leading Edge Consortium on the same topic. He teaches human resource management on the master's and doctoral level and an MBA course in sustainable organizational behavior. Email: stephan.dilchert@baruch.cuny.edu

The Authors

Stefan Ambec is an INRA researcher at Toulouse School of Economics, member of LERNA, a research center in environmental economics and natural resources, and director of the master's program in environmental and natural resources economics. He is also a visiting professor at the University of Gothenburg. He holds a Ph.D. in economics from the University of Montreal. His research focuses on the economic impact of innovations, environmental regulations, and on natural resource management. His papers have been published in various journals, including *Academy of Management Perspectives, Journal of Economic Theory, Games and Economic Behavior, American Journal of Agricultural Economics, Social Choice and Welfare,* and *Journal of Development Economics.* Email: stefan.ambec@toulouse.inra.fr

Serafin Bäbler holds a master's degree in economics from the University of Zürich. He published his master's thesis on the topic of human resource management with focus on environmental sustainability in the strategic context of a firm. He has also conducted field research with Swiss companies that are leaders in environmental sustainability. During his studies, he led several research project teams in the area of human resource management. His applied expertise, which he acquired in the telecommunications industry in several European countries, is in management for transition and change projects. Email: serafin. baebler@bluewin.ch

Talya N. Bauer is the Cameron Professor of Management at Portland State University. She earned her Ph.D. at Purdue University. Bauer is an award-winning teacher and researcher, SIOP Fellow, and Google Visiting Scholar. She conducts research about relationships at work. More specifically, she works in the areas of new hire on-boarding, recruitment, selection, over-qualification, mentoring, and leadership, which have resulted in numerous journal publications published in outlets such as the *Academy of Management Journal, Academy of Learning and Education Journal, Journal of Applied Psychology, Journal of Management,* and *Personnel Psychology.* She has acted as a consultant for dozens of government, Fortune 1000, and start-up organizations. Bauer is involved in professional organizations and conferences at the national level and serves on elected positions such as the Human Resource Management Executive Committee of the Academy of Management and member at large for the Society for Industrial and Organizational Psychology. Bauer is a past editor of the *Journal of Management.* In addition, she has also served on the editorial boards for the *Journal of Applied Psychology, Personnel Psychology,* and *Journal of Management.* Email: talyab@sba.pdx.edu

Andrew Biga is senior manager of leadership development for Procter & Gamble. He leads global talent management, including strategic succession planning through design and delivery of automated talent solutions. His responsibilities also include talent tracking using global KPIs to ensure a robust and diverse leadership pipeline. Biga completed his Ph.D. in industrial and organizational psychology from the University of South Florida. Email: biga.a@pg.com

Ernst A. Brugger is the president of BHP–Brugger and Partners Ltd., a consulting firm specialized in sustainability strategies. He is also chairman of the Sustainable Performance Group, Switzerland's largest sustainability fund, chairman of SV Group, chairman of Precious Woods Holding Ltd., chairman of Blue-Orchard, as well as a member of the board of directors of other organizations (including Trüb AG., BG Bonnard & Gardel Holding S.A., and the World Microfinance Forum Geneva). He is an honorary member of the International Committee of the Red Cross and a part-time professor at the University of Zürich. Over the last twenty-five years, he has been a consultant to businesses and institutions in Europe, Latin America, Africa, and Asia. In his role as co-founder and CEO of The Sustainability Forum Zürich and in his project work he advocates the implementation of long-term strategy, sustainability, and good governance in business and politics. Email: ernst.brugger@bruggerconsulting.ch

Jürgen Deller is a professor of organizational psychology and founding speaker of the Institute for Strategic HR Management Research and Development (SMARD) at Leuphana University of Lüneburg, Germany. He received his Ph.D. from Helmut-Schmidt University in Hamburg, Germany. His research interests include sustainability, especially in the context of the human resources function, ageing issues, such as consequences of the demographic change for management and human resources, international human resource management, for instance, expatriation and repatriation, and knowledge transfer. He has published on sustainability, the ageing workforce, bridge employment (silver work), personnel selection, management development, and international human resources. Before he joined academia, Deller worked for the corporate headquarters of Daimler-Benz group, Stuttgart, later with DaimlerChrysler Services (debis) AG, Berlin, as senior human resources manager responsible for the human resources board member's office and as head of Corporate Leadership Development IT Services. Email: deller@leuphana.de

Susan D'Mello is an industrial and organizational psychology Ph.D. student at the University of Minnesota and currently also works as a research associate for Kenexa's High Performance Institute. D'Mello has been involved in a variety of research streams regarding environmental sustainability at both the employee and organizational level and has presented her research at several professional conferences. Her other research areas include gender and disability bias in workplace decision making, workplace stress, organizational climate, and presidential job experience. Email: dmell002@umn.edu

Anne Doyle Oudersluys is the brand manager of global sustainability at Procter & Gamble. She joined P&G after graduating from Harvard College in 2004. Consistent with her passion for the environment and social responsibility issues, she is responsible for sustainability employee engagement for P&G's 127,000 employees, which includes educating and enabling employees to incorporate sustainability into their jobs. She also leads global sustainability communications for the company, setting communications strategy, and managing P&G's annual sustainability report. Oudersluys is also responsible for marketing P&G's corporate social responsibility programs. Email: doyle.at@pg.com

Cathy L. Z. DuBois is an associate professor at Kent State University, where she teaches human resource management and sustainability. Her sustainability research focuses on the roles of sustainability managers and human resource management in embedding sustainability within organizations, motivating sustainability behavior change, and sustainable work design. She is an active participant in the Association for the Advancement of Sustainability in Higher Education (AASHE) and serves as a member of the AASHE Advisory Council and as a STARS (Sustainability Tracking, Assessment, and Rating System) technical advisor. DuBois also participates in a number of sustainability professional groups and consults in sustainability and HRM issues. A winner of numerous teaching awards, she also teaches sustainability at ESC Rennes School of Business, France, and presents at workshops on integrating sustainability across the curriculum. She also publishes articles in a variety of HRM areas, highlighting a range of workplace gender issues and e-learning. Her work has been published in the *Journal of Applied Psychology, Personnel Psychology,* the *Academy of Management Review,* and *Psychology of Women Quarterly,* among others. Email: cdubois@kent.edu

Berrin Erdogan is Express Employment Professionals Professor of Management at Portland State University School of Business and is an affiliated faculty in the Industrial and Organizational Psychology Program. She earned her Ph.D. at the University of Illinois at Chicago. Erdogan regularly teaches classes in Athens Laboratory of Business Administration (Athens, Greece) and Koç University (Istanbul, Turkey), where she teaches courses related to organizational behavior and human resource management at undergraduate and graduate levels. As a researcher, Erdogan studies how organizations can create an engaged and motivated workforce and increase employee retention through a focus on fairness in their human resource practices as well as through leadership, organizational culture, and organizational climate. Erdogan is the recipient of the 2008 Western Academy of Management Ascendant Scholar award. Her work has been published in journals, including *Academy of Management Journal, Journal of Applied Psychology*, and *Personnel Psychology*; she also co-authored two widely used textbooks, *Organizational Behavior* and *Principles of Management*. Erdogan serves on the editorial boards of *Journal of Applied Psychology, Journal of Management, Journal of Organizational Behavior*, and *Personnel Psychology*. Email: berrine@sba.pdx.edu

Evren Esen is manager of SHRM's Survey Research Center and oversees the production of quantitative and qualitative research on workplace topics, human capital analytics, and other human resource topics. These data are used by HR and business leaders to improve workforce dynamics and drive strategic business decisions. She also manages SHRM's Customized Research Services, which specialize in conducting research for clients from academic institutions, associations, and non-profits, as well as corporate and government entities. Esen leads SHRM's People InSight service, an employee job satisfaction and engagement solution through which SHRM conducts employee surveys for small- to mid-sized organizations. She has worked at SHRM for nine years and possesses an in-depth understanding of HR issues, particularly in the areas of compensation, benefits, diversity, and employee job satisfaction. Prior to joining SHRM, Esen worked as a researcher and evaluator of federally funded community-based programs. She also worked as an instructor of psychology and sociology at Bilkent University in Ankara, Turkey. Esen holds a master's degree in clinical social work. Email: evren.esen@shrm.org

Shawn Fegley has served as a survey research analyst in the Survey Research Center at the Society for Human Resource Management (SHRM) for the past six years. Fegley currently serves as a project lead for developing quantitative and qualitative research on workforce topics, human capital analytics, and research related to topics to improve workforce dynamics and drive strategic business decisions. This includes SHRM's annual Employee Benefits Research Report and quantitative research on the topics of compensation, diversity and inclusion, social media, staffing management, and sustainability. He was also responsible for overseeing the launch of SHRM's Compensation Data Center. Prior to joining SHRM, Fegley worked as the market research manager at Goldhaber Research Associates, a full-service international research firm specializing in market research, national public opinion polling, and warning label and litigation research. At Goldhaber Research Associates, Fegley oversaw all the day-to-day operations of the Market and Survey Research Department. He received his undergraduate degree from the University of Buffalo. Email: shawn.fegley@shrm.org

Robert E. Gibby is senior manager of HR research and analytics for Procter & Gamble, headquartered in Cincinnati, Ohio. In this role, he leads a team of industrial and organizational psychologists and HR professionals to deliver HR analytics systems and capability, external selection and assessment, and the annual engagement survey for the company. He also has responsibility for developing and managing relationships with external partners in industry and academia to define best practice and bring in new insights. Gibby joined P&G in 2004 and completed his Ph.D. in industrial and organizational psychology from Bowling Green State University the same year. Outside P&G, he serves as a board member for Northern Kentucky University's master's of industrial and organizational psychology program, where he has taught undergraduate and graduate courses. He serves as an editorial board member of the *Journal of Personnel Psychology* and actively contributes to the field through other board and council memberships, book chapter and journal publications, and speaking engagements. Email: gibby.re@pg.com

Julie Haddock-Millar is a lecturer of human resource management and development at Middlesex University's business school and a chartered member of the Chartered Institute of Personnel and Development (CIPD). Haddock-Millar is the program leader for the postgraduate certificate, diploma, and M.A. in further education sector management practice and module leader for strategic human resource management for the master's in human resource management and the master's in human resource development. Her research interests include green HRD, mentoring, coaching, employability, and professional practice. Haddock-Millar is currently facilitating the organization development of Middlesex University Business School, developing, implementing, and evaluating the new employability and professional development strategy. She founded the Middlesex University Mentoring Network and is currently working with the United Kingdom Cabinet Office and First Division Association to develop a mentoring program for fast stream civil servants and undergraduate students. Email: j.haddock@mdx.ac.uk

Lewis Hollweg is CEO of Batrus Hollweg International, a leading talent management consulting firm specializing in customized human capital solutions for selecting, developing, and retaining top talent. Throughout his career, he has focused on understanding the cornerstones driving the development of peak performing individuals and teams. His background includes the development of executive assessment systems. He has interviewed, assessed, and coached thousands of senior leaders across almost every major industry. He is skilled in individual executive coaching and facilitating team change efforts. Hollweg received his B.A. from the University of Texas at Austin, his M.A. from Southern Methodist University, and a Ph.D. from Texas Christian University. He has maintained both a strong clinical education and a deep quantitative background and is licensed and certified in the State of Texas. Hollweg is an active member of the American Psychological Association and the Society for Industrial and Organizational Psychology. Email: lhollweg@batrushollweg.com

Leaetta M. Hough is founder and president of the Dunnette Group, Ltd., past president of the Federation of Behavioral and Brain Sciences (FABBS; a coalition of twenty-two scientific societies), past president of the Society for Industrial and Organizational Psychology (SIOP), and co-editor of the four-volume *Handbook of Industrial & Organizational Psychology*. She is a Fellow of SIOP, the Association for Psychological Science (APS), the American Psychological Association (APA) and its Division 5–Evaluation, Measurement, and Statistics. Hough has helped shape the science of I-O psychology as well as the practice of I-O psychology in the workplace, especially in the area of personnel selection. Email: leaetta@msn.com

Kevin Impelman is the manager of the Research Institute at Batrus Hollweg International, where he provides thought leadership, develops innovative products/services, and advises clients on best practices in talent management. He also designs and manages projects addressing talent assessment and strategy, including the development and implementation of customized selection systems for all levels of the organization. His research interests include personality assessment, technological advances in selection, integrity, and counterproductive behavior, and executive assessment. Impelman received his Ph.D. and an M.S. in industrial and organizational psychology from the University of North Texas and his B.A. in psychology from Southern Methodist University; he is a licensed psychologist in the state of Texas. Impelman is a member of the Society for Industrial and Organizational Psychology, the Society for Human Resource Management, and the American Psychological Association. Email: kimpelman@ batrushollweg.com

Holly R. Johnson is vice president of human resources and global education at Aveda Corporation. In this role, she provides strategic leadership of Aveda's global education and human resources. In her role for education, she provides leadership and oversight of four business areas: technical, retail, field sales, and employee development programs. Responsibilities for human resources include administration of employee management and employee services. She is a member of the Aveda Stewardship Team, direct reports of the president, and Brand Equity Stewardship Team. She contributes to the business decisions of the corporation and ensures the protection of the brand equity. Johnson has been with Aveda for eighteen years. Aveda is known industry-wide for its strong focus on environmental leadership and responsibility. Prior to Aveda, Johnson worked for ITT Financial for fifteen years. She actively participates in Aveda's mission-related activities, such as Earth Month events, and cares for the world she in lives in by volunteering at outside organizations such as Feed My Starving Children and the Backpack Program. E-mail: hjohnson@ aveda.com

Rachael M. Klein is a Ph.D. student in industrial and organizational psychology at the University of Minnesota. She graduated magna cum laude from Carleton College with a degree in psychology. Her research focuses on assessing employee motives for engaging in environmentally responsible and irresponsible behavior, as well as measuring and promoting environmental sustainability within organizations. She also does work on personnel selection, decision making, and leadership. Klein's research has been supported by a National Science Foundation Graduate Research Fellowship and a University of Minnesota Graduate School Fellowship. She has presented numerous talks and posters at professional conferences and was a member of the planning committee for the 2011 SIOP Theme Track on Environmental Sustainability. Email: klein674@umn.edu

Allen I. Kraut, Series Editor for the SIOP Professional Practices Series, is Professor Emeritus of Management at Baruch College, City University of New York, which he joined in 1989. For much of his professional career, he worked at the IBM Corporation, where he held managerial posts in personnel research and management development, until leaving in 1989. In 1995, he received the SIOP's Distinguished Professional Contributions Award, recognizing his work in advancing the usefulness of organizational surveys. In 1996, Jossey-Bass published *Organizational Surveys: Tools for Assessment and Change*, by Allen Kraut and Associates. His latest book, *Getting Action from Organizational Surveys: New Concepts, Technologies, and Applications*, is a 2006 publication of Jossey-Bass.

Paul Lanoie is a professor and the associate director for academic affairs and strategic planning at HEC Montreal. He holds a Ph.D. in economics from Queen's University in Kingston, Canada. His research focuses on the different impacts of environmental policies on the firm (its innovation, its productivity, its environmental performance, and so forth). He is also interested in the different ways firms can reconcile their environmental and financial performances. He has published in journals such as *Academy of Management Perspectives, Journal of Environmental Economics and Management, Ecological Economics, Journal of Human Resources,* and *Journal of Risk and Uncertainty.* Email: paul.lanoie@hec.ca

Daniel Manitsky is a management consultant affiliated with the Rapid Results Institute. He specializes in performance improvement projects within public, non-profit, and public-private organizations. Manitsky holds an MPA from New York University's Wagner School of Public Service and graduated magna cum laude from the University of Illinois with a dual B.A. in sociology and political science. Manitsky has worked in fifteen countries in Africa and the Middle East, contributing managerial training and business process redesign services to large-scale reform efforts. Additionally, he has supported health, education, and community development projects and facilitated several innovative public private partnerships in Africa. Prior to becoming a consultant, Manitsky worked as a health education specialist with the Peace Corps in El Salvador. During this time he worked with USAID, Salvadoran government officials, and NGOs to coordinate reconstruction aid following a series of earthquakes. Email: dmanitsky@ rapidresults.org

A. Silke McCance is manager–employee and organization research and sensing within the Leadership Development Group at Procter & Gamble in Cincinnati, Ohio. She owns the global corporate survey program that is delivered annually to over 127,000 employees, in more than eighty countries, in more than twenty languages, and analyzed using advanced analysis (factor analysis, IRT, SEM, LGCM, text analysis). In addition, she has global ownership of all external selection and assessment tools and systems used at P&G, including candidate reactions, job analysis/competency modeling, development, deployment, maintenance, training, and legal consultation/audit support. McCance received her Ph.D. in industrial and organizational psychology from the University of Illinois at Urbana-Champaign. Before joining P&G in June 2010, she worked as a consultant in both the public and private sector, where her experience included conducting job analysis; designing, administering, and serving as certified assessor for a developmental assessment center; and developing and validating work simulation tests. Email: mccance.a@pg.com

Jessica R. Mesmer-Magnus is an associate professor of management in the Cameron School of Business at the University of

North Carolina–Wilmington. She earned her Ph.D. in industrial and organizational psychology at Florida International University. Prior to her doctoral coursework, she worked as an HR manager and consultant for a national environmental engineering consulting firm, where her role included managing HR sustainability initiatives. Her research interests include social responsibility, whistleblower behavior and retaliation, team cognition and dynamics, and work-family conflict. Her research has been published in various peer-reviewed outlets, including *Journal of Applied Psychology, Organizational Behavior and Human Decision Processes, Human Resource Management Review, Journal of Business Ethics, Journal of Vocational Behavior, Organizational Psychology Review,* and *Human Performance.* In the past two years, Mesmer-Magnus has served as a consultant for several research projects on virtual organizations sponsored by the National Science Foundation. Email: magnusj@uncw.edu

Derek Miles is a professor of human resource development at Middlesex University, a chartered companion of the Chartered Institute of Personnel and Development (CIPD), and was formerly the director of global learning for Save the Children, UK. Miles has served as chair of the executive board of CIPD and president of the International Federation of Training and Development Organizations. He is the program leader for the master's in human resource management and the master's in international human resource management. He leads the university's research in HRD, undertakes consultancy internationally, and provides leadership and support to faculty, staff, and curriculum development in areas such as strategic human resource development, leadership, and organizational design. Email: d.miles@mdx.ac.uk

Kristin Miller is executive director, human resources, at Aveda Corporation. She and her team are responsible for recruiting and generalist support for the corporate, sales, retail, and supply chain functions at Aveda. She has supported Aveda's mission of environmental and social responsibility by volunteering at Families Moving Forward, Feed My Starving Children, and Earth Month events. She holds a degree in psychology from Governor's State University and is a senior professional in human resources (SPHR).

Miller has worked at Aveda for thirteen years. Before joining Aveda, she held human resource generalists positions at Baker & Taylor and the Metropolitan Council. E-mail: kmiller@aveda.com

Michael Müller-Camen is a professor of human resource management at Wirtschaftsuniversität, Vienna, Austria, and a professor of international human resource management at Middlesex University's business school. His research interests include sustainable, green, and international HRM and age management. Müller-Camen has published more than forty-five articles and book chapters and the textbook *Human Resource Management: A Case Study Approach* (with R. Croucher and S. Leigh, 2008). He recently edited a special issue of *Zeitschrift für Personalforschung* (*Journal of Research in Human Resource Management*) on green HRM (with S. Jackson, C. Jabbour, and D. Renwick). Email: m.muller-camen@mdx.ac.uk

John P. Muros is a senior HR research consultant with AT&T. He advises internal clients on selection testing, structured interviewing, surveys, and other human resource-related research projects. In previous roles, he has consulted with a diverse range of clients, including private industry, federal and state governments, and military and law enforcement organizations. Muros holds a Ph.D. in industrial and organizational psychology from the University of Minnesota. He received his B.A. in psychology and a B.S. in communication studies from the University of Texas at Austin. He is an active member of the Society for Industrial and Organizational Psychology, the American Psychological Association, and the Association for Psychological Science. His research has been published in top-tier journals, and he has been invited to present frequently at professional conferences. Email: john.muros@att.com

Patrice Murphy is a senior partner at Schaffer Consulting. Her practice focuses on the dynamics of top-to-bottom transformation, including leadership effectiveness, creating the conditions for breakthrough performance, and front-line employee engagement. Murphy holds an undergraduate degree with honors in political science and an MBA with distinction from the University of Melbourne. She also received a master's of labor law and relations degree from the University of Sydney and a Ph.D. in management and organizational behavior from New York University. Murphy is an expert in the Rapid Results Approach and the WorkOut methodology and uses them both globally to execute strategy. Her clients are leading corporations in sectors as varied as pharmaceuticals (Merck, Pfizer, Bausch & Lomb), financial services (Citigroup, Lloyds, Zurich, Fannie Mae), and technology (McKesson, the MITRE Corporation). Murphy teaches and writes on leadership development, performance management, and organizational change and has spoken on these topics at national and regional conferences. Her writing has contributed to books, including *The GE WorkOut* (2002) and *The Change Handbook* (2007), as well as online articles in *IndustryWeek.com*, *TalentMgt.com*, and *ODSeasonings*. Email: pmurphy@schafferresults.com

Robert C. Muschewske received a Ph.D. with an emphasis in counseling psychology from the University of Nebraska in 1969. Following service as an Army psychologist with the rank of captain, Muschewske embarked on a thirty-seven-year career as a partner with three international management consulting firms: the Hay Group, A.T. Kearney, and Personnel Decisions International. He has specialized in working with boards of directors and top management on sensitive issues relating to the assessment, selection, development, coaching, and positioning of key executives, especially chief executive officers. In recent years his work has also focused on assisting boards of directors to evaluate their own effectiveness. Email: rmuschewske@comcast.net

Kevin J. Nilan works in 3M's Measurement Center of Expertise. Most recently he has been managing the company's business unit employee opinion survey practice. Additionally, he is responsible for the company's employment testing practices outside the United States, he oversees the company's 360 efforts, and in 2011 he has been working with HR business partners on employee retention challenges throughout the globe. Nilan completed his Ph.D. in industrial and organizational psychology under the direction of Milton Hakel at The Ohio State University. In the area of sustainability, Nilan and the 3M Measurement Center of Expertise have been especially helpful in providing the employee data included in the company's documentation submitted to outside agencies (for example, the Dow Jones Sustainability Index) addressing the company's actions. At the 2011 SIOP conference, Nilan (with Karen Paul) presented the 3M story during a sustainability symposium. 3M is well recognized externally for strong historical leadership in sustainability. The company was selected as a member of the 2011/2012 Dow Jones Sustainability Index, a global stock index that recognizes and tracks the performance of leading sustainability-driven companies worldwide. Nilan has been at 3M for twenty-four years and previously served as vice president and partner at MDA Leadership Consulting. Email: kjnilan1@mmm.com

Karen B. Paul currently leads global HR measurement for 3M. Her focus in this role is to lead the Measurement Center of Expertise in support of global, regional, and local business needs. She is responsible for the creation and execution of global strategy for executive assessment and coaching, testing and assessment, engagement and retention, and organizational survey research. She received her Ph.D. in industrial and organizational psychology from Bowling Green State University. Paul has been with 3M for eighteen years and has held both specialist and generalist assignments within 3M. 3M is well recognized externally for strong historical leadership in sustainability, awarded ENERGY STAR "Sustained Excellence" Award for an industry-leading seventh consecutive year as well as the 2011 Green to Gold and ranking as number 2 in 2011 as Best Global Green Brands by Interbrand. Paul was asked to represent HR as a member of 3M's Corporate Sustainability Strategy Working Group to more closely tie employee engagement and sustainability at 3M. Email: kbpaul1@mmm.com

Laura Quinn is the portfolio manager for the Groups, Teams, and Organizational Leadership Practice at the Center for Creative Leadership. In this role, Quinn is responsible for the global implementation of the Developing the Strategic Leader Program and the Transforming Your Organization service. She also manages the capability development and content areas of the Center's talent, strategy, and culture work. Quinn is the Center's subject-matter expert on leadership and corporate social responsibility and sustainability. She manages the Center's research on this topic and is active in many networks and projects in this field. Quinn has a Ph.D. in organizational communication and leadership from the University of Texas at Austin, an M.A. in communication and a B.A. in business from the University of Colorado, Boulder. Her academic work has been recognized and published in the *Journal of Management Communication, Journal of Corporate Governance,* and *Business Communication Quarterly.* She also co-authored the chapter on globally responsible leadership in the Center's *Handbook of Leadership Development.* Email: quinnl@ccl.org

Mark J. Schmit is the vice president of research for the Society for Human Resource Management (SHRM). In this capacity he directs, oversees, and leads the association's research activities. He earned a Ph.D. in industrial and organizational psychology from Bowling Green State University. Prior to joining SHRM, Schmit served as an expert witness and consultant representing the field of industrial and organizational psychology in employment discrimination litigation. He has more than twenty-five years of experience in the field of human resources and has also been an academic, applied researcher, HR generalist, and internal and external consultant to both public and private organizations. He has developed recruitment, selection, promotion, performance management, organizational effectiveness/development tools, and systems for numerous organizations. Schmit has published more than twenty-five professional journal articles and book chapters and delivered more than fifty presentations at professional meetings on HR and industrial and organizational psychology topics. He is a Fellow of both the Society for Industrial and Organizational Psychology and the American Psychological Association. He is also a certified Senior Professional in Human Resources (SPHR). Email: mark.schmit@shrm.org

Theresa Schnieders studied business psychology, management, and human resources at Leuphana University of Lüneburg,

Germany, and the University of Queensland, Australia. She holds
a B.Sc. and an M.A. degree. Her academic work has focused on
international and strategic HR, HR development, and sustainable
HR management. Viewing HR as a key value proposition in the
business environment, she now works in HR development at RWE
IT GmbH, part of German energy provider RWE AG. Email:
theresa.schnieders@web.de

Jennifer Schramm is manager of the Workplace Trends and Fore-
casting program at the Society for Human Resource Management
(SHRM), where she manages SHRM's research on labor market
and workforce issues. This includes the SHRM Leading Indicators
of National Employment®—a set of monthly national employment indices—and the *SHRM Jobs Outlook* report. She writes the
monthly Future Focus column appearing in *HR Magazine,* is
the author of the *SHRM Workplace Forecast,* and is a co-author of
2015: Scenarios for the Future of Human Resource Management. Prior
to joining SHRM, Schramm worked as a research and policy
advisor specializing in workforce development for the Chartered
Institute of Personnel and Development (CIPD) in London, UK,
where she was also executive board member of the European
Training and Development Federation, UK steering committee,
member of the European Commission's Training of Trainers
Network, and UK representative for the European Commission's
Center for the Development of Vocational Education and Training. Before this she was a research manager of the Employment
Policy Institute, a London-based employment and economics
think tank. She received her master's degree in social and political
science from the University of Cambridge, UK, and her undergraduate degree from the University of Michigan, Ann Arbor. She
is also a certified Global Professional in Human Resources
(GPHR). Email: jennifer.schramm@shrm.org

Bruno Staffelbach holds a chair of business administration and
human resource management at the University of Zürich. He
holds a master's degree in economics, a doctorate in business
administration, and a postdoctoral qualification in management
and ethics. He has published and edited ten books and ninety

papers, mainly on strategic human resource management, management ethics, personnel and military economics, human relations, and the history of economic thinking. Previously, Staffelbach has held teaching positions at the University of Fribourg and the University of Applied Sciences in Lucerne. From 1992 to 2000, he was the director of the Executive Education Program, and until 2010 he headed the Institute for Strategy and Business Economics at the University of Zürich. In addition to his career in academia, Staffelbach served as commander and general staff officer on different levels in the Swiss Armed Forces, where he was Brigadier General and Commander of an infantry brigade from 2004 to 2008. He is a member of the boards of various organizations, vice president of the University Council of the University of Lucerne, and former president of the Executive MBA Program at the University of Zürich. He was elected a member of the International Committee of the Red Cross in 2010. Email: bruno.staffelbach@business.uzh.ch

Sully Taylor is a professor of human resource management at Portland State University and director of International Programs in the school. She has also served as director of the Master of International Management Program and as associate dean for graduate programs and regularly teaches at the Instituto de Empresa, Madrid, Spain. Taylor earned her Ph.D. at the University of Washington. She served as chair of the International Management Division of the Academy of Management. Taylor teaches international management, global human resource management, and sustainable HRM. Her research interests include international human resource management, organizational social capital in MNCs, and sustainable HRM. Taylor has consulted or provided training for a number of firms, including Intel, Hewlett-Packard, Tellabs, NEC America, and Boeing. She has published in such journals as *Academy of Management Review, Journal of International Business Studies,* and *Journal of Organizational Behavior* and has written a number of book chapters. With Nancy Napier, she wrote a book entitled *Western Women Working in Japan: Breaking Corporate Barriers.* She also serves on several editorial boards. Taylor has received two Fulbright awards and was named an ascendant scholar by the Western Academy of Management. Email: sullyt@sba.pdx.edu

Angela Titzrath has held several top management positions at Daimler AG, Germany, over the last twenty years. She studied business economics and Roman literature in Germany, Italy, and Portugal, and holds an M.A. degree from Ruhr-University, Bochum, Germany. Her professional career included senior management positions in financial services, sales and marketing, purchasing, production, and HR in Germany, Italy, Spain, and North America before she took over as vice president, executive development management, at Daimler AG in 2006. In that role, Titzrath was responsible for human resources development, placement, and staffing of Daimler AG's global top management. Her responsibilities included employer branding, marketing, expatriate management, and the corporate academy. In 2011, she joined the board of Daimler Buses, the world's largest bus manufacturer with a global reach, where she was responsible for global sales, marketing, and after sales. In May 2012, Tietzrath joined Deutsche Post DHL as the group's board member for personnel and labor director. With about 470,000 employees in more than two hundred countries and territories, the group forms a global network focused on service, quality, and sustainability, with programs in the areas of climate protection, disaster relief, and education.

Alan J. Tomassetti is a Ph.D. student at George Mason University in the industrial and organizational psychology program. He graduated summa cum laude with a bachelor's degree in psychology from Saint Louis University, where he was named to the Phi Beta Kappa national honor society. In 2011, he worked as a summer intern at the Society for Human Resource Management (SHRM). While at SHRM, Tomassetti aided in creating several reports on a variety of topics, including diversity in the cable industry and the development of human resource professionals. His research interests include discretionary problem solving in ill-defined domains and factors affected by situational strength, among other topics. Email: atomasse@gmu.edu

Ellen Van Velsor is a senior fellow at the Center for Creative Leadership headquarters in Greensboro, North Carolina. She holds a B.A. in sociology from SUNY–Stony Brook, an M.A. and Ph.D. in sociology from the University of Florida, and has completed a postdoctoral fellowship at the Center for the Study of Aging and Human Development at Duke University. Van Velsor is co-editor of the Center for Creative Leadership's *Handbook of Leadership Development* (1998, 2003, 2010) and co-author of *Breaking the Glass Ceiling: Can Women Reach the Top of America's Largest Corporations?* (1987, 1991). She has authored numerous book chapters, articles, and reports, including "Leadership Development as a Support to Ethical Action in Organizations" (*Journal of Management Development,* 2008), "A Complexity Perspective on Leadership Development" (Uhl-Bien & Marion, 2007), "Experiential Learning Through Simulation" (Silberman, 2007), "Developing Organizational Capacity for Leadership" (Hooijberg, Hunt, & Antonokis, 2007), and "Constructive-Developmental Coaching" (Ting & Scisco, 2006). Her current research focuses on leadership practices and processes related to corporate social responsibility in global organizations. Email: vanvelsor@ccl.org

Chockalingam (Vish) Viswesvaran is a professor of psychology at Florida International University, Miami. He earned his Ph.D. at the University of Iowa. Viswesvaran serves or has served on the editorial boards of *Journal of Applied Psychology, Educational and Psychological Measurement, Journal of Personnel Psychology, Journal of Work and Organizational Psychology, Personnel Psychology,* and *Journal of Organizational Behavior.* He was the associate editor of the *International Journal of Selection and Assessment* from 2001 to 2006 and is currently serving as its editor. He is also past chair of the American Psychological Association's (APA) Committee on Psychological Tests and Assessments. Viswesvaran is a fellow of the APA (Divisions 5 and 14–SIOP) and the Association for Psychological Science. He has studied the effects of social responsibility, whistle blowing, and organizational justice on employee behaviors and has co-edited the two-volume *Handbook of Industrial, Work and Organizational Psychology,* a special issue of the *International Journal of Selection and Assessment* on the role of technology on staffing, and a special issue of *Human Performance* on use of cognitive ability tests. Email: vish@fiu.edu

Brenton M. Wiernik is a student of industrial and organizational psychology at the University of Minnesota. His research interests focus on the measurement, prediction, and promotion of environmental sustainability in organizations, which he has been conducting research on since joining the University of Minnesota in 2008. His work has been featured in numerous conference presentations, and he has consulted on environmental sustainability for several non-profit organizations. Brenton also has active research programs in the areas of personality, assessment method fairness, and teacher effectiveness. Email: wiern001@umn.edu

Part One

The Imperative for Environmental Sustainability

Chapters in Part One describe the larger context that creates the imperative for organizations to invest in activities to achieve environmental sustainability, providing a foundation for human resource (HR) and organization development (OD) professionals who are expected to assist in achieving their organizations' environmental goals. Topics covered include some of the key historical events that stimulated government regulation, as well as the current business trends stimulating organizations to begin measuring and improving their environmental performance.

Chapter 1, "Portrait of a Slow Revolution Toward Environmental Sustainability," by Susan E. Jackson, presents a brief historical overview of the evolving environmental revolution. In addition to reminding readers of a few key events that heightened the public's concern about environmental issues, this chapter introduces several of the regulations, international agreements, and environmental performance metrics that are referred to in subsequent chapters.

Chapter 2, "The Strategic Importance of Environmental Sustainability," by Stefan Ambec and Paul Lanoie, presents the business perspective. The authors summarize the accumulating theoretical arguments and empirical evidence that support the assertion that improving environmental performance can be profitable for firms. Specifically, they describe the following means through which firms can enjoy a competitive advantage by improving environmental performance: improving the environmental quality of a product to increase demand and, therefore, revenues; complying with environmental regulations through the adoption of greener technology; implementing organizational changes such as the adoption of environmental management systems (EMS); gaining access to financial capital as a result of positive environmental performance; and gaining access to human capital as a result of establishing a positive environmental reputation. To illustrate these effects, Ambec and Lanoie describe several examples of firms that have used these green strategies successfully.

Chapter 3, "The Role of Strategic Context in Environmental Sustainability Initiatives: Three Case Studies," by Bruno Staffelbach, Ernst Brugger, and Serafin Bäbler, illustrates how the strategic context in which environmental sustainability initiatives are pursued can influence the roles and activities of HR departments. The authors present a simple framework for describing three different types of corporate environmental strategies and then illustrate how these different types of strategies can influence the involvement of various HR functions. Using three examples of Swiss firms in health care and manufacturing industries, they analyze the interactions of the HR roles and the strategic backgrounds of the initiatives and discuss the lessons learned.

Chapter 4, "Human Resource Management Efforts for Environmental Sustainability: A Survey of Organizations," by Mark Schmit, Shawn Fegley, Evren Esen, Jennifer Schramm, and Alan Tomassetti, describes results from the SHRM Sustainability Survey of Human Resource Professionals. Topics discussed in this chapter include the meaning of "sustainability" as it is used across organizations, the organizational reasons for investing in sustainability, the people involved in creating and implementing sustainability policies and strategies, corporate outreach activities related to sustainability, and the metrics organizations use to monitor the effectiveness of their sustainability efforts.

CHAPTER ONE

Portrait of a Slow Revolution Toward Environmental Sustainability

Susan E. Jackson

Deep-rooted respect and reverence toward the natural environment is evident in many religions and ancient cultural traditions worldwide (see Dudley, Higgins-Zogib, & Mansourian, 2005). As early as the 13th century, landscapes such as Mongolia's Bogd Khan Uul Strictly Protected Area, which is perhaps the world's oldest national park, have been revered as holy and protected from the influence of human activity. Yet concerns about the relationship between industrial activity and environmental degradation are fairly recent. Such concerns began to draw attention from scholars and philosophers during the age of enlightenment, and grew more salient as the Industrial Revolution changed where and how people lived. As large cities became established, political economists began arguing over the question of how much population growth could be supported through increasing economic development. By the time the world's human population reached one billion people in approximately 1820, Thomas Walter Malthus had written several persuasive and widely read essays questioning the widely held assumption that Earth's resources were sufficient to support continuing population growth. As early as the 1850s, the destruction of California's virgin forests led philosopher and poet James Russell Longfellow to call for a society dedicated to

3

protecting trees. Also during this era, Henry David Thoreau experimented with living in near isolation in rural surroundings near Walden Pond and wrote passionately about the dehumanizing influence of industrialization and the spiritual value of living close to nature.

By the end of the 19th century, far-sighted politicians began taking actions to safeguard pristine landscapes. In 1864, the U.S. federal government granted the State of California permission to create a small park as a means of protecting old-growth trees in the Yosemite Valley. A few years later, in 1872, President Ulysses S. Grant signed the Yellowstone Act, creating America's first national park. Since then, more than eighty million acres of natural landscapes and historic sites in the United States have been partially protected from commercial development.

Despite the success of early efforts at environmental preservation and conservation, however, the environmental rights and responsibilities of governmental institutions and business organizations continue to be disputed. At the heart of such disputes are disagreements over issues such as how to balance the costs and benefits of industrial development, the value of preserving biodiversity, and beliefs about the best means of managing wilderness areas.

Throughout the 20th century, public concern over environmental issues waxed and waned, as other economic and political issues with more obvious and immediate consequences vied successfully for the public's attention. Two world wars and the Great Depression commanded public attention for the first half of the 20th century. Then, shortly after World War II ended, environmental disasters around the world reawakened concerns about the effects of industrialization on our environment. Each of these disasters made people more aware of harmful pollutants that befouled the air they were breathing and the water they were drinking.

Problems of Pollution

Air Pollution

Donora, Pennsylvania, is a small town near Pittsburgh. In 1948, an unusual air inversion trapped polluted air from nearby steel mills and held it over the town for five days. Among the pollutants emitted during the steel production process were poisonous gases, including sulfuric acid, nitrogen dioxide, and fluorine. In this small town of fourteen thousand people, six thousand became ill, and twenty deaths were attributed to the smog that blanketed the town.

A few years later, in 1952, London was submerged in lethal smog that darkened the city for five days. An unusual weather pattern caused high concentrations of coal dust and tar particles from home and industrial energy use to become trapped in the city's air. In one week, an estimated three to four thousand people died from respiratory infections and asphyxiation caused by inhaling the pollutants. As a result of London's tragedy, Parliament enacted Britain's Clean Air Act in 1956. The United States moved more slowly. In 1963, Congress passed legislation to study air pollution. In 1970, they passed the Clean Air Act that governs industrial pollution today and established the Environmental Protection Agency (EPA) to administer that law.

Water Pollution

By the 1970s, other environmental disasters had heightened awareness of other health problems caused by environmental degradation. Among the most prominent disasters was the Love Canal tragedy. Love Canal was a neighborhood in Niagara Falls, New York, that was named after William Love, who had dug a canal there early in the 20th century. When the canal project failed economically, the canal ditch became the dumping site for a chemical company's industrial waste. Eventually, the chemical company closed its factory, covered over the waste site, and sold the property to the city for $1. Soon, a developer acquired the site and built a new community of about one hundred homes and a school. The former dumping ground became home to dozens of families. But eventually an unusually heavy downpour of rain dislodged the waste, and the evidence of industrial pollution became visible to everyone. Corroded barrels surfaced around the neighborhood and pools of residue formed in people's yards. Toxins seeped into the community water supply and leached into the ground soil. When the community health records were examined, they revealed unusually high numbers of miscarriages and birth defects. Children who grew up and attended schools in the neighborhood suffered maladies such as chromosome damage, seizures, eye irritation, and skin rashes (National Research Council, 1991).

The Love Canal tragedy focused public attention on the health hazards of industrial pollution, which had been largely unregulated during a century of rapid industrialization. On April 22, 1970, the American public's growing concern became evident when an estimated twenty million people participated in the first Earth Day. The brainchild of U.S. Senator Gaylord Nelson of Wisconsin, Earth Day was designed as a teach-in and modeled after the anti-Vietnam War demonstrations that had been taking place around the country. The first Earth Day is sometimes given credit as being the event that spearheaded the modern environmental movement due in part to the fact that the U.S. Clean Water Act of 1970 was passed by Congress, which also established the Environmental Protection Agency that same year (Roach, 2010). Within two years, Congress also passed the Clean Water Act of 1972, which provides financial resources to assist in the construction of municipal waste treatment facilities and seeks to protect all of the nation's surface water from harmful pollutants.

Perhaps because pollution of our air and water is relatively evident and its consequences are difficult to ignore, the American public supported regulations such as the Clean Air Act of 1970 and the Clean Water Act of 1972—laws that are generally acknowledged to be examples of successful government interventions. They provide clear rules about what constitutes unacceptable industrial action, and they account for significant, measureable improvement in the quality of our air and water.

Nuclear Accidents

Several nuclear plant disasters also have served to remind people of the need to be vigilant about environmental protection. Nuclear disasters, and fear of such disasters, have heightened public awareness of the potentially harmful consequences of modern industrial technologies.

The most serious nuclear incident in the United States to date occurred in 1979 at Three Mile Island, a nuclear power plant near Middletown, Pennsylvania. Since then, far more serious accidents have occurred in the Ukraine at the Chernobyl nuclear power plants and in Japan at the Fukushima Daiichi power plant.

Three Mile Island Incident

The incident at Three Mile Island in 1979 occurred as a consequence of multiple design problems, mechanical failures, and human errors. Their combined effect resulted in significant damage to one of the plant's nuclear reactor cores, causing small amounts of radioactivity to be released into the surrounding area. The Three Mile Island incident unfolded over a period of several days, during which fear and uncertainty reigned. Two days after the problems began, Pennsylvania's governor ordered the evacuation of preschool children and pregnant women within a five-mile radius of the plant. People living within a ten-mile radius were advised to stay inside and shut their windows. The incident was resolved within a week, and most evacuees had returned to their homes at that time.

There were no deaths or serious injuries as a result of the incident at Three Mile Island. Plant workers and members of nearby communities remained safe, and subsequent studies indicated that their exposure to radiation was very small. Nevertheless, it was clear that changes were needed to ensure that nuclear power plants would operate safely in the future. The lessons learned led to major changes in emergency response planning, training, human factors engineering, and radiation safety protection, among other aspects of nuclear power plant operations, and the U.S. Nuclear Regulatory Commission, which is responsible for ensuring the public is protected from exposure to unsafe nuclear radiation, stepped up its oversight activities (U.S. Nuclear Regulatory Commission, 2002).

Chernobyl Disaster

In 1986, an explosion and fire at the Chernobyl nuclear power plant released radioactive material into the atmosphere, resulting in widespread contamination across the USSR and Europe. An estimated five million people lived in the contaminated area, and of those about 10 percent were eventually evacuated. During the accident, approximately one thousand workers were exposed to high levels of radiation, resulting in twenty-eight deaths from acute radiation poisoning and an unknown number of deaths and illnesses from exposure to lower doses of radiation during subsequent years. Plant and animal populations within thirty kilometers of the explosion—an area now referred to as the Exclusion Zone—suffered from increased deaths and decreased reproduction.

The long-term environmental effects of the Chernobyl explosion have been substantial. The urban areas near the reactor were heavily contaminated and rapidly evacuated. Food sources were contaminated with radioactive iodine for several months after the accident, exposing the population to a major source of cancer. Concern over contamination from longer-lived radioactive materials—which have been detected in Scandinavia's reindeer and remain concentrated in some lakes—will continue to be a source of concern throughout the region for several decades.

Even after twenty-five years, estimates of Chernobyl's health effects on humans vary greatly, with estimates of deaths due to radiation exposure ranging from four to nine hundred thousand (Chernobyl Forum, 2006; Taylor, 2011). At least six thousand people have developed thyroid cancer attributable to the accident. Among the surviving recovery workers, elevated incidents of leukemia and cataracts have been observed. High levels of nervous system diseases, cardiovascular disease, and gastrointestinal diseases have all been observed in those exposed to radiation released from Chernobyl (United Nations Scientific Committee on the Effects of Atomic Radiation, 2008).

Fukushima Daiichi

As of this writing, the most recent nuclear accident had taken place in Japan caused by a tsunami that damaged six nuclear reactors at the Fukushima Daiichi site in 2011. For weeks, the world watched as Japan struggled to prevent the discharge of massive amounts of radiation. Months later, reports that radiation contaminated beef was appearing in food markets reminded us that it will be many years before we understand the full extent of damage caused by the Fukushima nuclear disaster.

Currently, the United States gets 20 percent of its energy from 104 nuclear power plants. In many developing economies, reliance on nuclear power is expected to grow considerably in the future because it offers a clean alternative to fossil fuel. Meanwhile, many developed countries oppose nuclear power, and some are making plans to close existing reactors, deeming them too dangerous. As the Chernobyl and Fukushima disasters remind us, the potential benefits of nuclear power must be weighed against the considerable risks associated with such technology. Employers, employees, and customers are all affected by decisions concerning which sources of energy to rely on and how to manage the risks associated with each energy source.

Climate Change (a.k.a. Global Warming)

Today, the environmental issue attracting the most attention is climate change, which is also referred to as "global warming." Climate is a general term that refers to temperatures, precipitation, and wind. Among the scientific community, there is widespread agreement that the earth's climate has changed substantially during the past 150 years, and continues to do so at an accelerating rate. In particular, the earth's atmosphere is getting hotter as so-called greenhouse gases become more concentrated and trap heat that previously escaped Earth's gravitational pull. Greenhouse gases such as carbon dioxide (CO_2), methane (CH_4), and nitrous oxide (N_2O) are associated with human activities such as the burning of fossil fuels, farming, and industrial production activities. Global warming, in turn, results in weather-related consequences such as more frequent and severe storms, droughts, and floods, as well as the rapid melting of glaciers and rising sea levels.

Given the nature of global climate change, success in addressing the problem will require that the world's largest producers of greenhouse gases take action to reduce their own output, that is, their carbon footprints. In response to the accumulating scientific evidence concerning climate change (see Huber & Gulledge, 2011), governments around the world have enacted policies intended to address climate change and curb the environmental damage from industrial activities that contribute to it. In the United States, policymakers have reached no consensus about the causes and likely consequences of climate change, and there have been no significant government interventions aimed at addressing this issue. Nevertheless, the globalization of business activities means that most large organizations have operations outside the United States that subject them to tightening environmental regulations.

United Nations

Many international efforts to address environmental concerns are rooted in the United Nations' Environment Programme (UNEP), which was established in 1992 following recommendations that arose during that year's Conference on the Human Environment held in Rio de Janeiro. Perhaps the most familiar UNEP-sponsored activity is sponsorship of the United Nations Conferences on Environment and Development. Now commonly referred to as the "Earth Summits," the goal of these international meetings has been to persuade governments to recognize and exercise their responsibility for preserving and enhancing the human environment.

Kyoto Protocol

The most significant Earth Summit to date took place in 1997, when the so-called Kyoto Protocol was adopted. As of 2011, 193 countries had ratified the Kyoto Protocol, thereby committing to reducing several greenhouse gases that contribute to global warming and climate change against targets set for 2012, when the Kyoto Protocol was scheduled to expire.

Notably, the United States was not a signatory of the Kyoto Protocol. However, several state governments acted independently of the U.S. Congress to begin addressing the causes of climate change at the local level. For example, the Regional Greenhouse Gas Initiative (RGGI) is a collaborative effort of nine Northeast and Mid-Atlantic American states. RGGI is the first regional, market-based "cap-and-trade"–style agreement adopted to reduce the greenhouse gases that contribute to climate change. The participating states capped their CO_2 emissions and pledged to achieve a 10 percent reduction in CO_2 emissions from the power sector by 2018. The program is designed to increase energy efficiency and speed the transition away from fossil fuels toward greater reliance on renewable, clean energy.

Several large U.S. corporations also have voluntarily taken steps to improve their environmental performance. Stricter international regulations are one reason American corporations—many with global operations—take such "voluntary" actions. Increasingly, investors also are pressuring companies to improve their environmental performance as part of a broader desire to encourage businesses to balance their drive for profitability with a concern for social responsibility and sustainable development. These external pressures for companies to become environmentally sustainable are described next.

Business Accountability for Environmental Impact

Companies that seek to establish themselves as environmentally sustainable can do so by documenting their environmental management processes and providing environmental performance data. Wall Street analysts, management consulting companies, and business media are all becoming involved in the rating and ranking of companies based on their environmental performance. Thus, it appears that a consensus is beginning to form around the need to protect the natural environment from the harmful effects of some industrial activities. Recent surveys of executives worldwide show that environmental issues such as climate change, energy efficiency, biodiversity, and pollution are recognized as important business issues that can present both threats and opportunities (see McKinsey & Company, 2010, 2011).

Assessing the environmental impact of industrial activities is not easy. The natural environment is a complex biological system comprised of many interconnected elements and dynamic forces, in which small changes can have surprising large consequences. The release of seemingly small quantities of chemical pollutants into the air has resulted in global climate change. The release of seemingly small quantities of chemical pollutants into rivers and streams changed the acidity levels of the oceans. Small increases in the average temperature during a growing season can have significant effects on agricultural productivity and food supplies. Small increases in the acidity of seawater can result in the collapse of fish populations, which are a major source of protein for human populations around the world. On the positive side, the global ecosystem also has a regenerative capacity, so small corrective actions taken at the right time may result in significant improvement in the health of the entire system.

During the past decade, several standardized methods for reporting such data have become widely accepted. These include the ISO 14000 series of certifications, EMAS certification, the Global Reporting Initiative (GRI) Index, and the SAM Corporate Sustainability Index.

ISO 14001

Following the 1992 Earth Summit in Rio, the International Organization for Standardization (ISO) created a study group to determine how the environmental standards that were discussed at the meeting could be assessed. Subsequently, they developed the 14000 series of certifications for environmental management, anchored by ISO 14001. The certification criteria provide guidelines for developing and implementing environmental management systems, for securing third-party auditors to review and verify a company's environmental management practices, setting performance targets, monitoring the Environmental Management System, and addressing life cycle issues. As is true of all ISO certifications, companies seek ISO 14000 certifications voluntarily. However, as environmental concerns have grown, an increasing number of companies have begun to require ISO 14000 certification for their suppliers. Two major advantages of ISO 14000 certifications are that they make it possible to meaningfully compare companies on a set of fixed standards and they require third-party verification.

Eco-Management and Audit Scheme (EMAS)

In 1995, the European Commission established the Eco-Management and Audit Scheme as a way to help companies voluntarily manage their environmental performance. To achieve EMAS certification, a company must establish that it has developed a written policy stating its commitment to the environment, has conducted environmental impact reviews and conducts regular environmental audits, has specified programmatic actions that are to be taken, has put a management system in place to implement the environment program, produces a report summarizing its environmental performance, and uses a third party to verify that its report is accurate. In 2011, approximately eight thousand companies throughout Europe were EMAS certified.

Global Reporting Initiative (GRI) Index

The Global Reporting Initiative is a non-profit, network-based organization headquartered in Amsterdam and dedicated to the "mainstreaming of disclosure on environmental, social, and governance performance" (Global Reporting Initiative, 2011). The criteria used for the GRI Index were developed in a collaborative effort that involved a variety of stakeholders. Participants included representatives from business and government, labor groups, and academic institutions' professional associations. Among other things, the data requested include descriptions of how a company manages environmental issues and its objective performance on a variety of metrics.

Participation in the GRI reporting process is voluntary; nevertheless, during the past decade, the proportion of large firms participating has increased steadily. Today, almost all Global 500 firms and most S&P 500 firms assess their environmental performance using portions of the GRI Index, and many companies disclose this information to the public on their company websites. Currently, the consulting firm PricewaterhouseCoopers uses the GRI Index to produce a suite of reports that compare companies in various regions and sectors (PricewaterhouseCoopers, 2009, 2010, 2011).

SAM Corporate Sustainability Index

The SAM Corporate Sustainability Index is similar to the GRI Index in content, but it is a product of the Sustainable Asset

Management (SAM) group, which is an independent company that provides investment advice to private and institutional clients. Each year, the world's 2,500 largest companies are invited to provide data for use as input into the SAM Corporate Sustainability Index. SAM analyzes the results and uses them in a variety of ways. Participating companies can use SAM reports as a source of benchmarking data to judge how well the company is doing compared to competitors. Investors can use the results to evaluate whether a company meets their expectations for corporate responsibility. The extensive set of Dow Jones Sustainability Indexes, which identify environmentally responsible companies in a variety of regions and industry sectors, uses the SAM reports as one of its primary criteria.

FTSE4GOOD Index

The FTSE4Good Index is another similar effort. Firms provide data to FTSE using a standard framework, and those data are used to produce a series of FTSE4Good reports and indexes for investors who want to invest selectively in companies on the London Stock Exchange that have been screened for acceptable environmental performance.

Apparently, many top executives and their boards of directors consider environmental issues to be too important to ignore. Indeed, many of them realize there are significant business opportunities associated with the changing attitudes of investors, consumers, and other stakeholders. Rather than simply comply with environmental regulations as necessary, organizations are taking steps to ensure that their efforts to improve the financial bottom line are environmentally responsible. And a few organizations realize that financially attractive new business opportunities await those companies that choose to be leaders as the world moves toward environmental sustainability.

Sustainable Development and Corporate Social Responsibility

With the exception of the ISO 14000 standards, each of the sustainability indicators just described includes environmental sustainability as one element in a broader framework for assessing sustainability and/or corporate social responsibility (CSR). All of these frameworks are grounded in a philosophical view of corporations as entities that are accountable not only to investors but also to other stakeholders, including employees and the broader community. This perspective is sometimes referred to as the "triple bottom line" or "people, planet, and profits."

The expectation that corporations should operate with a view toward the consequences of their actions for future generations— that is, being "sustainable"—is another layer of complexity. Corporate critics have bemoaned the short-term, financial focus of company executives for many decades, but it was not until 1987 that an alternative approach was clearly articulated and given a memorable label—namely, "sustainable development." In 1987, a committee of the United Nations produced a report titled, "Our Common Future," in which they defined sustainable development as follows (see Chapter 2, available at www.un-documents.net/ocf-02.htm):

> "Sustainable development is development that meets the needs of the present without compromising the ability of future generations to meet their own needs. It contains within it two key concepts:
>
> - the concept of 'needs', in particular the essential needs of the world's poor, to which overriding priority should be given; and
>
> - the idea of limitations imposed by the state of technology and social organization on the environment's ability to meet present and future needs.
>
> ". . . In essence, sustainable development is a process of change in which the exploitation of resources, the direction of investments, the orientation of technological development, and institutional change are all in harmony and enhance both current and future potential to meet human needs and aspirations." (Brundtland, 1987)

The UN report that defined sustainable development is often referred to as the "Brundtland Report," after Gro Harlem Brundtland, who was the committee's chairwoman. This committee's report provided an extensive set of principles for achieving sustainable development, and these principles serve as the foundation for many approaches to measuring sustainability. The principle of most relevance to the topic of this volume is the principle of Merging Environment and Economics in Decision Making. This principle asserts that sustainable development and economic development and growth must be addressed together in an integrated manner; they cannot be dealt with separately. Further, the committee argued, economic growth and environmental protection could be pursued in concert; they were not necessarily in opposition. Thus, for example, increasing efficiency in the use of energy and raw materials serves both to reduce costs and to preserve ecological resources.

While the focus of this volume is on environmental sustainability, readers will discover that many of the companies we highlight pursue environmental objectives in the context of sustainability broadly defined. Indeed, the growing popularity of initiatives to address the broader concerns about sustainable development and corporate social responsibility may be partly responsible for the recent greening of human resource management scholarship and practice.

The Role of Human Resource Management in Achieving Environmental Sustainability

The authors of the chapters in this volume discuss and illustrate the many human resource management implications associated with this growing recognition that environmental sustainability should be included among a firm's several longer-term business objectives. They provide examples of how firms in a variety of industries and several different countries are addressing environmental threats and the business opportunities they sometimes create. Depending on an organization's specific objectives, a variety of human resource management practices may be relevant, including adding "green" jobs and adding "green" duties to existing jobs, recruitment and selection, training and development, performance management, compensation, employee communications, monitoring employee attitudes, and so on (see SHRM, 2011). After reading this volume, you will have a better understanding of the reasoning that has led some firms to take a proactive stance in addressing environmental issues. Briefly, the volume proceeds as follows:

Chapters in Part One describe the larger context that creates the imperative for organizations to invest in activities to achieve environmental sustainability, providing a foundation for human resource (HR) and organization development (OD) professionals who are expected to assist in achieving their organizations' environmental goals. Topics covered include some of the key historical events that stimulated government regulation as well as the current business trends stimulating businesses to begin measuring and improving their environmental performance.

Part Two seeks to inform readers of the most recent empirical research relevant to understanding environmentally friendly behavior in work settings. Here readers will learn about several measurement tools that are available for use in assessing environmental behaviors and related attitudes, and they also will find reviews of the small but growing body of evidence concerning practices that can influence employees' environmental attitudes and behaviors.

Part Three describes some of the challenges and successes experienced by HR and OD professionals in organizations that are actively pursuing environmental sustainability. Case studies of companies such as Procter & Gamble, 3M, Daimler, Sherwin-Williams, McDonald's UK, and many others offer valuable insights about managing environmental initiatives at various stages of maturity.

Part Four concludes the volume by describing several implications for practicing HR and OD professionals as well as scholars who are interested in pursuing new research on the important topic of managing human resources for environmental sustainability. These chapters will be of interest to readers who might be wondering about the potential personal and professional implications of environmental sustainability in the workplace.

Conclusion

During the past two centuries, an Industrial Revolution profoundly changed the patterns of resource extraction, use, and waste by humans. At the same time, the human population has grown at exponential rates. The interdependency between the health of the planet and the health and prosperity of our human population has slowly become evident, so now the calls for attending to this fragile relationship are growing louder. Even as governments and individual members of society disagree about the urgency of environmental issues, many companies have concluded that they must take actions to satisfy customers, investors, and employees who expect businesses to embrace their environmental responsibilities for the common good of people and the planet. Regardless of the reasons behind an organization's environmental initiatives—whether to satisfy customers, comply with regulations, reduce costs, and/or promote corporate social responsibility—professionals and scholars in the fields of human resource management and organization development are being handed duties related to the design, implementation, monitoring, and evaluation of workforce interventions to support those environmental initiatives.

In preparing this volume, the editors sought to create a resource for HR and OD professionals and scholars seeking to deepen their own knowledge about the slow but transformative environmental revolution and motivate them to learn from the pioneering efforts underway at leading-edge organizations. Through greater awareness and more widespread sharing of knowledge within the profession, the contribution of our field to the success of this slow revolution is sure to be enhanced.

Bibliography

Brundtland, G. (1987). *Our common future: The World Commission on Environment and Development.* Oxford: Oxford University Press. Retrieved from www.un-documents.net/wced-ocf.htm.

Dudley, N., Higgins-Zogib, L., & Mansourian, S. (2005). *Beyond belief: Linking faiths and protected areas to support biodiversity conservation.* Washington, DC: World Wide Fund for Nature.

Chernobyl Forum. (2006). *Chernobyl's legacy: Health, environmental, and socio-economic impacts and recommendations to the governments of Belarus, the Russian Federation and Ukraine* (2nd rev ed.). Vienna, Austria: International Atomic Energy Agency.

Global Reporting Initiative. (2011). About GRI: Funding. Quoted from www.globalreporting.org/AboutGRI/Funding/

Huber, D. G., & Gulledge, J. (2011). *Extreme weather and climate change: Understanding the link, managing the risk.* Arlington, VA: Pew Center on Global Climate Change.

Malthus, T. R. (1798). *An essay on the principle of population (Oxford World's Classics).* Oxford, UK: Oxford University Press.

McKinsey & Company. (2008, February). A McKinsey global survey. *McKinsey Quarterly,* www.mckinseyquarterly.com.

McKinsey & Company. (2010, April). The next environmental issue for business: McKinsey Global Survey results. *McKinsey Quarterly,* www.mckinseyquarterly.com.

McKinsey & Company. (2011, October). The business of sustainability: McKinsey Global Survey results. *McKinsey Quarterly,* www.mckinseyquarterly.com.

National Research Council. (1991). *Environmental epidemiology, Vol. 1: Public health and hazardous wastes.* Washington, DC: National Academy Press.

PricewaterhouseCoopers. (2009). *Carbon Disclosure Project 2009: Global 500 report.* Accessed at www.pwc.com/gx/en/carbon-disclosure -project/pdf/CDP-2009-Global-500.pdf.

PricewaterhouseCoopers. (2010). *Carbon Disclosure Project 2010: S&P 500 report.* Accessed at www.pwc.com/en_US/us/corporate -sustainability-climate-change/assets/carbon-disclosure-project -2010.pdf.

PricewaterhouseCoopers. (2011). *CDP Global 500 report 2011: Accelerating low carbon growth.* www.cdproject.net/CDPResults/CDP-G500-2011 -Report.pdf.

Roach, J. (2010). Earth day facts: When it is, how it began, what to do. *National Geographic News,* April 6. Accessed at http://news .nationalgeographic.com/news/2009/04/090421-earth-day-facts/

SHRM. (2011). *Advancing sustainability: HR's role. A research report by the Society for Human Resource Management, BSR, and Aurosoorya.* Accessed at www.shrm.org/Research/SurveyFindings/Articles/ Pages/AdvancingSustainabilityHR%E2%80%99sRole.aspx.

Taylor, A. (2011). The Chernobyl disaster: 25 years ago. *The Atlantic,* March 23, 2011.

Thoreau, H. D. (1854). *Walden, Or Life in the Woods.* Boston, MA: Tichnor and Fields.

United Nations Scientific Committee on the Effects of Atomic Radiation. (2008). *Sources and effects of ionizing radiation: Volume II.* New York: United Nations.

U.S. Nuclear Regulatory Commission. (2002). Accident at Three Mile Island. *Almanac of Policy Issues* accessed at www.policyalmanac.org/

World Commission on Environment and Development. (1987). Our common future. United Nations Report accessed at www.un -documents.net/wced-ocf.htm.

CHAPTER TWO

The Strategic Importance of Environmental Sustainability

Stefan Ambec
and Paul Lanoie

Production activities often harm the environment through the emission of pollutants or the use of natural resources such as fossil energy, water, fisheries, or forests. It is generally admitted that protecting the environment entails supplementary costs to firms that may erode their productivity. It may require switching to less polluting but more expensive methods such as low sulphur content coal. It may divert capital investment from productivity improvement to the adoption of cleaning devices (such as buffers) or of less polluting but more costly technologies (such as renewable sources of energy). As put forward by Friedman (1970), environmental concerns divert managers from their main responsibility, which should be the maximization of profits.

Yet this antagonism between environmental protection and business performance has been recently challenged by many scientists and practitioners. In particular, Michael Porter has argued that well-designed environmental policies can enhance innovation, which may lead to a productivity improvement that may offset the costs of complying with these policies (Porter, 1991;

We gratefully acknowledge financial support from INRA and the chair on Sustainable Finance and Responsible Investments.

Porter & van der Linde, 1995). This argument is often referred to as the Porter hypothesis. Moreover, the traditional paradigm fails to explain why corporate environmentalism became so popular among firms. If profit-maximizing firms freely adopt environmental management procedures such as ISO 14000, being greener can be beneficial for firms. More and more case studies provide evidence of green strategies that have led to an improvement of both the environmental and the economic performance of firms. A growing literature in economics provides theoretical arguments and empirical evidence that environmental and economic performance are not always antagonistic, but can indeed be complementary. In this chapter, we survey this literature. We review the main economic arguments that explain why improving environmental performance can be profitable for firms. We also review the empirical evidence and provide illustrative examples of successful green strategies.

In the remainder of this chapter, we distinguish among five different ways for firms to enjoy a competitive advantage by improving environmental performance. These are (1) improving the environmental quality of a product and thereby increasing demand and revenues; (2) complying with environmental regulations through the adoption of greener technology; (3) changing management and business practices, for example, by adopting an environmental management system (EMS); (4) gaining access to needed financial capital; and (5) gaining access to better quality human capital.

Increasing Demand for Products and Services

Firms might reduce their negative impact on the environment by improving the environmental quality of their products. They might use less polluting inputs (for example, less pesticide or other harmful chemicals). They might use renewable sources of energy. They might adopt sustainable production procedures (for example, replant forests after harvesting or use fishing practices less damaging for ecosystems). They might make their product easier to recycle. They are sometimes forced to do so when governments set more stringent standards. Yet, in many cases, firms go beyond minimal standards of environmental quality.

For this strategy to be profitable, at least one of the two following conditions is required. The first necessary condition is a generous environmental policy that rewards the environmental quality of products beyond the legal standard. In practice, governments not only use the minimal standard stick to reduce the environmental impacts of products, but they also use carrots such as subsidies. Firms obviously make money by harvesting these subsidies. An example is the feed-in tariffs for electricity produced from renewable sources of energy that assigns a premium price for electricity generated from solar and wind power. Designed to encourage the adoption of renewable sources of energy, it is in place in many countries, including Australia, France, Germany, and Spain, as well as in some U.S. states. Another example is the American government's support for bio-energy through subsidies to corn-based ethanol. Thanks to generous tax credits for the bio-fuel industry, corn producers found a new market for their crops. Consequently, the share of U.S. corn production that is allocated to ethanol increased to one-third in 2008. Such subsidies contributed to the increase in corn prices and U.S. corn yields during the last three decades (Environmental Protection Agency, 2010; U.S. Department of Agriculture, 2007).

The second necessary ingredient is some green purchasing by consumers. Consumers who express their environmental consciousness in their purchasing are willing to pay more for the same product when it is of higher environmental quality. In economic terms, environmental quality is a vertical differentiation strategy used by firms to attract those green consumers who are sensitive to the environmental quality of a product. It helps firms to move away from price-based competition that erodes profit. It allows them to increase revenues by exploiting the market niche of green consumers. An example of such successful vertical differentiation strategy on environmental quality is CIBACRON LS, a bioreactive dye commercialized by the Swiss chemical company Ciba-Geigy in the mid-1990s. This new dye had a higher fixation rate, which meant that less dye was required to color textiles. In turn, this meant that rinsing was simpler and less expensive, and that firms' wastewater treatment costs could be lower. In other words, this dye helped Ciba's clients reduce their environmental cost. The dye was a commercial success in spite of a higher price (Reinhardt, 1999).

Firms can signal the higher environmental quality of their products through certification and labeling. Examples include the Forest Stewardship Council (FSC) certificate for wood produced from sustainable managed forests, the Marine Stewardship Council (MSC) certificate for seafood harvested using sustainable fishing procedures, the Ecolabel launched by the European Union, and the organic food accreditation from the U.S. Department of Agriculture.

The final consumers are not the only ones to value the environmental attributes of products. Private companies often take steps to green their supply chain. For instance, production plants involved in the ISO 14001 certification procedure commit to use environmental performance as criteria for selecting their suppliers. In a sample of four thousand facilities in seven OECD countries, Johnstone, Glachant, Serravalle, Reidinger, and Scapecchi (2007) found that 43 percent assess their suppliers' environmental performance. Governments also favor products and suppliers with better environmental performance through green public purchasing policies. In the U.S., the *Federal Acquisition Regulations* provide detailed rules governing procurement by all federal agencies. For instance, these rules specify that the Environmental Protection Agency (EPA) has to prepare guidelines on the availability, sources, and potential uses of recovered materials and associated products, including solid waste management services, and require federal agencies themselves to develop and implement affirmative procurement programs for EPA-designated products (Kunzik, 2003, p. 203).

Improving Productivity When Complying with Regulations

Technological innovation is central to the Porter hypothesis. It is a necessary but not sufficient condition for more stringent environmental regulations to be profitable. Porter and van der Linde (1995) describe several cases studies of successful innovation strategies following environmental regulations. In these cases, firms complied with more stringent regulations by improving their technology at a cost that was more than offset by the gain of productivity.

As we have already noted, the so-called Porter hypothesis suggests that firms can benefit from governmental regulations that place restrictions on the environmental impacts of their production processes. Several empirical studies have assessed the validity of the Porter hypothesis. Most studies find a positive although sometimes weak relationship between more stringent environmental policies and innovation measured by investment in R&D and new technologies or successful patent applications (see Ambec & Lanoie, 2007, for a review).

Another strand of the literature estimates the impact of environmental regulations on productivity. These studies usually find a negative relationship (Jaffe, Peterson, Portney, & Stavins, 1995), although in some cases, more stringent regulations are not found to be associated with lower productivity (Alpay, Buccola, & Kerkvliet, 2002; Berman & Bui, 2001). Lanoie, Laurent-Lucchetti, Johnstone, and Ambec (2011) tested the impact of stringent environmental regulations on environmental R&D and subsequent business performance using a survey of four thousand OECD production plants. They found that environmental regulation stringency affects investment in environmental innovation positively, consistent with the Porter hypothesis. Nevertheless, the net impact of environmental regulations on business performance was found to be negative.

More stringent environmental regulation is not always a premise for improving the environmental performance of production technologies. For example, many firms innovate to reduce their pollution impact for other reasons than regulation compliance. One is that the productivity of the production process is sometimes complementary with environmental performance. Improving the energy efficiency leads both to an increase of productivity through a reduction of energy inputs and to improved environmental performance. It is easy to find cases in which the initial cost of reducing energy uses is more than offset by the benefit. As one example, in a study of thirty-three green buildings, Kats (2003) found that the financial benefit of green design was more than ten times the additional cost associated with building green (see also Lanoie & Tanguay, 2000 and 2004 for more examples).

Finally, firms can take advantage of cleaner technologies by exploiting them to diversify and expand the business. For instance, many electricity producers diversified their activity from thermal, hydro, and nuclear power to also include wind and solar power. Firms can also sell the new technology to their competitors or to other sectors. As mentioned above, Ciba-Geigy patented its new Cibacron LS dye that could be sold to other companies under licensing agreements. Subsequently, Ciba bought Allied Colloids Group, a UK manufacturer of water treatment additives, which was the first step in creating its environmental division and thus diversifying its activities to the so-called eco-industry.

Changing Management and Business Practices

Environmental concerns have an impact on the management of production and business practices. A first step of corporate environmentalism is often the implementation of an environmental management system, such as the popular ISO 14000 certification or the European Eco-Management and Audit Scheme (EMAS). The 14000 procedure from the International Organization for Standardization (ISO) specifies practices to measure and improve the firm's environmental impact. It requires, among other things, establishing a system for green accountability, training employees in the principles of sustainable development, rewarding employees based on their environmental performance, and creating a position in the management hierarchy with responsibility for addressing environmental issues. Firms may implement such procedures for reasons that are not directly related to meeting productivity goals. Nevertheless, implementation of the ISO 14000 procedures may have the consequence of enhancing firm performance. When implementing ISO 14000 certification, firms often have to review their production processes to identify their main environmental impacts; in the process, they may discover other ways to improve productivity. For example, a GM plant in Detroit, while devising a monitoring system of its energy use for ISO, realized that a lot of energy was wasted at night and during weekends.

With minor changes in procedures, they saved more than $250,000 per year (Ambec & Lanoie, 2008).

Improving environmental performance may also require changing business relationships with partners up and down the supply chain—that is, with suppliers and distributors. The ISO 14000 certification prescribes that one select suppliers according to the environmental performance of their products. More generally, firms should consider environmental issues when they negotiate with suppliers. Walker (2008) reports the case of Herman Miller, a furniture firm, that has improved the environmental quality of its office chairs by coordinating the design of the inputs with suppliers. All components of the chairs were analyzed and modified to reduce environmental impact. The company found ways to reduce energy use during transportation, waste due to packaging, and the use of toxins during their lifecycle from production to disposal. Moving up the supply chain, Herman Miller launched a procedure to measure the environmental quality of the suppliers' products and then convinced them to improve it. The firm had to go far away along the supply chain, contacting suppliers of the suppliers.

Access to Financial Capital

Another means through which improving environmental performance can contribute to firm performance is by lowering the cost of financial capital. First, greener firms might levy more funds in financial markets by attracting socially responsible investments. Socially responsible investors care not only about the return of their investment, but also about social and environmental criteria. For green fund managers, good social and environmental performance might somehow compensate for lower returns on investment. Socially responsible investment (SRI) is a growing phenomenon. In the United States, assets invested in SRI funds increased by 325 percent from $639 billion in 1995 to $2.7 trillion in 2007. Europe experienced a similar increase of SRI funds during the last decade. The total SRI assets in a set of thirteen European countries surveyed by Eurodif have reached €2.665 trillion in 2007 and represent as much as 17.5 percent of the asset management industry. Some empirical studies estimate whether

SRI funds (or indices) exhibit different financial performance from standard funds. Of the sixteen studies summarized by Ambec and Lanoie (2007), eleven concluded that there was no statistical difference in the returns to investors for the two types of funds. Five of the studies found that SRI funds outperformed conventional ones.

Second, a firm's good environmental performance might also contribute to better relationships with lending institutions. Most banks now have a team of experts to evaluate the environmental performance of possible borrowers, in particular the size of potential liabilities owing to contaminated assets. Furthermore, around forty international banks have now adopted the Equator Principles to make sure that the projects they finance are developed in a manner that is socially responsible and reflects sound environmental management practices.

Third, a good environmental performance record can be a signal of good financial performance. There is evidence that shareholders are influenced by information about the environmental performance of companies, and their reactions can be reflected on the stock market. These movements may, in turn, influence the cost of capital. A large number of empirical studies have analyzed stock market reactions to news about environmental performance. Sometimes the events considered are negative news, such as information about illegal spills, prosecutions, fines, or emission data related to the American Toxics Release Inventory (TRI). Some studies also considered the effects of positive news, such as information on environmental awards. All of the studies surveyed in Ambec and Lanoie (2007) show that stock markets react significantly to good or bad environmental news. More recently, Krüger (2009) analyzed the impact of both positive and negative incidents related to corporate social responsibility (environmental incidents being one of them) reported by newspapers, non-governmental organizations, or regulatory authorities on shareholder value. He found that reported negative incidents on product safety—including harm suffered by communities and employees—strongly reduced stock market returns. On the other hand, positive news about the use of environmentally friendly materials in the production process had a positive impact. Reports concerning the use of clean energy and pollution reduction had no apparent consequences for stock market returns.

In the empirical literature, we also find estimates of the impact of better environmental performance on financial performance at the firm or industry level. Different measures of economic performance (Tobin's Q^1, return on assets, return on sales, return on equity) and environmental performance (TRI emissions, ISO 14001 certification, the adoption of other international environmental standards) have been considered. Ambec and Lanoie (2007) reviewed twelve of these studies. Nine of them found that better environmental performance was associated with better economic performance. Two studies found no impact, while one concluded that a negative relationship exists.

Access to Human Capital

Improving environmental performance may also impact the cost of labor through two channels. First, it can help to attract better and more productive workers at a lower cost. Second, it may foster employees' productivity by improving workforce motivation and by reducing accidents, illnesses, absenteeism, recruitment, and turnover. A survey of Stanford MBAs in 2004 found that 97 percent of them were willing to forgo 14 percent (on average) of their expected income to work for an organization with a better reputation for corporate social responsibility (Ambec & Lanoie, 2008). Thus, it appears that greener firms can offer to pay a lower wage and still attract the most productive workers. Saving on labor costs may more than compensate the cost of improving environmental performance. Being green is then a strategy to obtain a competitive advantage in the labor market. As stated by two Ciba-Geigy managers:

> "An improved image of the company results in an improved
> atmosphere in the workplace and hence in higher
> productivity . . . People who feel proud of the company for which

---

[1]Tobin's Q is the ratio of the market value of a firm divided by its replacement cost.

they work not only perform better on the job, but also become ambassadors for the company with their friends and relatives, enhancing good will and leading to a virtuous circle of good repute. Of course, this is impossible to quantify, but it seems clear that it is true. . . . This is especially important in recruiting talented young scientists, managers, and engineers, many of whom . . . simply would not work for a company with a poor social and environmental reputation. . . . No one wants to work for a dodgy company, and the brightest people obviously have a choice." (Reinhardt, 1999, p. 11)

On the motivation effect, De Backer (1999) provides anecdotal evidence that ISO 14000 certification has positive effects on employees' morale and productivity, much more than ISO 9000 certification (for quality). Even if the argument is fairly compelling, to our knowledge there is no direct empirical evidence supporting it. Yet its economic rationale can be understood in the lights of the behavioral economic literature. According to Benabou and Tirole (2010), individuals' behaviors are often motivated by their social identities and self-images. People contribute to charity or protect the environment to maintain positive self-images and because they are pressed by the others to do so. Self-image induces workers to conform to the corporate culture through social norms and practices. A more responsible corporate culture leads to more responsible norms and working practices. In the same vein, Kandel and Lazear (1992) argue that peer pressure makes workers conform to some cooperation norms and reduces free riding within companies. Feelings such as shame or guilt, as well as peer monitoring and sanctions, provide incentives to cooperate in work teams. Firms that develop a reputation of contribution to environmental protection and cooperating in efforts to reduce pollution signal a high cooperation norm that is transmitted to workers. Conversely, environmentally conscious employees might transmit a behavioral norm of environmental protection to top managers. Indirect evidence from survey research indicates that companies are aiming at better environmental performance to improve the satisfaction of their employees and unions. For instance, Henriques and Sadorsky (2007) found that pressure from employees was a significant determinant of a firm's commitment to better environment performance (for example, implementation of an environmental management system).

Conclusion

The conventional wisdom about environmental protection is that it comes as an extra burden for companies—a burden that is often imposed by government. However, during the last decade, this paradigm has been challenged by a number of analysts who argue that improving a company's environmental performance can be associated with better economic performance, for a variety of reasons. We described five of these reasons: (1) more environmentally oriented products may allow a firm to reach new clients; (2) innovation induced by environmental regulations may reduce operating costs; (3) the adoption of EMS may stimulate organizational changes that improve firm performance; (4) better environmental performance may improve a firm's access to financial capital and thus reduce its costs; and (5) better environmental performance may improve its access to human capital, and thus lower its labor costs.

We do not intend to suggest that a reduction of pollution is *always* accompanied by better financial performance. Rather, we have argued that the expenses incurred to reduce pollution can be partly or completely offset by gains made elsewhere. As one can see, the set of opportunities is quite large and could pertain to firms of different sizes in many different sectors.

There are many possible means through which efforts to improve environmental performance can result in improved firm performance. Nevertheless, we recognize that there are probably diminishing returns. Concerning cost-reducing opportunities, it is likely that there is some obvious low-hanging fruit, but that greater effort is required once this fruit has been harvested. Similarly, the sales-enhancing potential of environmental performance improvements is probably limited by consumers' willingness to pay for environment-friendly products. On the other hand, many of the trends we have described in this chapter are likely to become increasingly important in the future, among them green consumerism, socially responsible investing, and employees wishing to work for green companies.

Furthermore, it is possible that some of the positive consequences of improved environmental performance become apparent only over long periods of time. Many costs occur in the short term (for example, green buildings, extra cost for the purchase of a hybrid car), but the associated benefits are uncertain and may arise only in the longer term. Owing to this temporal asymmetry in the distribution of costs and revenues, the period over which the economic impact is examined has a considerable effect on the outcome of the examination. In most cases, the smaller the discount rate and the longer the time period considered, the more win-win situations there are. Managers focusing on short-term returns for impatient shareholders are thus less likely to identify profitable opportunities.

As we saw, the evidence of a link between better environmental performance and lower labor costs remains fairly anecdotal. In order to establish such a link, more research is needed. Future studies could examine relationships between adoption of environmental management systems and outcomes such as recruiting effectiveness, turnover rates, absenteeism, and pay levels. In addition, even if labor costs are not lower for firms that lead their industries in environmental practices, it is possible that other benefits accrue to these firms, such as the ability to attract more talented and innovative employees and to keep these employees more engaged and satisfied over longer periods of time.

Bibliography

Alpay, E., Buccola, S., & Kerkvliet, J. (2002). Productivity growth and environmental regulation in Mexican and U.S. food manufacturing. *American Journal of Agricultural Economics, 84*(4), 887–901.

Ambec, S., & Barla, P. (2002). A theoretical foundation of the Porter hypothesis. *Economics Letters, 75*(3), 355–360.

Ambec, S., & Barla, P. (2005). Quand la réglementation environnementale profite aux pollueurs. Survol des fondements théoriques de l'hypothèse de Porter. *L'Actualité économique.* www.ecn.ulaval.ca/w3/recherche/cahiers/2005/0504.pdf.

Ambec, S., & Barla, P. (2006). Can environmental regulations be good for business? An assessment of the Porter hypothesis. *Energy Studies Review, 14*(2), 42–62.

Ambec, S., & Lanoie, P. (2007). When and why does it pay to be green? HEC Montreal Discussion Paper IEA-07-04. www.hec.ca/iea/cahiers/2007/iea0704_planoie.pdf.

Ambec, S., & Lanoie, P. (2008). Does it pay to be green? A systematic overview. *Academy of Management Perspectives, 22*(4), 45–62.

Anton, W. R., Deltas, G., & Khanna, M. (2004). Incentives for environmental self-regulation and implications for environmental performance. *Journal of Environmental Economics and Management, 48*, 632–654.

Arimura, T., Hibiki, A., & Johnstone, N. (2007). An empirical study of environmental R&D: What encourages facilities to be environmentally innovative? In N. Johnstone (Ed.), *Environmental policy and corporate behaviour.* Cheltenham, UK: Edward Elgar in association with OECD, pp. 142–173.

Barla, P. (2007). ISO 14001 certification and environmental performance in Quebec's pulp and paper industry. *Journal of Environmental Economics and Management, 53*(3), 291–306.

Benabou, R., & Tirole, J. (2010). Individual and corporate social responsibility. *Economica, 77*(305), 1–19.

Berman, E., & Bui, L. T. M. (2001). Environmental regulation and productivity: Evidence from oil refineries. *The Review of Economics and Statistics, 83*(3), 498–510.

Bracke, R., Verbeke, T., & Dejonckheere, V. (2008). What determines the decision to implement EMAS? A European firm-level study. *Environmental and Resource Economics, 41*, 499–518.

Brekke, K. A., & Nyborg, K. (2008). Attracting responsible employees: Green production as labor market screening. *Resource and Energy Economics, 30*(4), 509–526.

Dasgupta, S., Hettige, H., & Wheeler, D. (2000). What improves environmental compliance? Evidence from Mexican industry. *Journal of Environmental Economics and Management, 39*, 39–66.

De Backer, P. (1999). L'impact économique et l'efficacité environnementale de la certification ISO 14001/EMAS des entreprises industrielles. ADEME consulting report.

Environmental Protection Agency. (2010). *Renewable fuel standard program regulatory impact analysis.* Washington, DC: U.S. Environmental Protection Agency.

Friedman, M. (1970, September 13). The social responsibility of business is to increase its profits. *New York Times Magazine,* p. 33.

Greaker, M. (2003). Strategic environmental policy: Eco-dumping or a green strategy? *Journal of Environmental Economics and Management, 45*(3), 692–707.

Henriques, I., & Sadorsky, P. (2007). Environmental management and practices: An international perspective. In N. Johnstone (Ed.), *Environmental policy and corporate behaviour.* Cheltenham. UK: Edward Elgar in association with OECD.

Jaffe, A. B., Peterson, S. R., Portney, P. R., & Stavins, R. N. (1995). Environmental regulation and the competitiveness of U.S. manufacturing: What does the evidence tell us? *Journal of Economic Literature, 33*(1), 132–163.

Jaffe, A. B, Newell, R. G., & Stavins, R. N. (2004). A tale of two market failures: Technology and environmental policy. Resource for the Future discussion paper (RFF DP 04-38).

Johnstone, N., Serravalle, C., Scapecchi, P., & Labonne, J. (2007). Public environmental policy and corporate behaviour: Project background, Overview of the data and summary results. In N. Johnstone (Ed.), *Environmental policy and corporate behaviour.* Cheltenham, UK: Edward Elgar in association with OECD, pp. 1–33.

Johnstone, N., Glachant, M., Serravalle, C., Reidinger, N., & Scapecchi, P. (2007). Many a slip twixt the cup and the lip: Direct and indirect public policy incentives to improve corporate environmental performance. In N. Johnstone (Ed.), *Environmental policy and corporate behaviour.* Cheltenham, UK: Edward Elgar, pp. 88–141.

Kandel, E., & Lazear, E. P. (1992). Peer pressure and partnership. *Journal of Political Economics, 100*(4), 801–817.

Kats, G. H. (2003). *Green building costs and financial benefits.* Boston, MA: Technology Collaborative. Retrieved from www.mtpc.org/

Krüger, P. (2009). Stakeholder information and shareholder value. Unpublished manuscript. Toulouse School of Economics, Toulouse, France.

Kunzik, P. (2003). National procurement regimes and the scope for the inclusion of environmental factors in public procurement. In OECD, *The environmental performance of public procurement: Issues of policy coherence* (pp. 193–220). Paris: OECD.

Lankoski, L. (2006). Environmental and economic performance: The basic links. In S. Schaltegger & M. Wagner (Eds.), *Managing the business case for sustainability* (pp. 32–46). Sheffield, UK: Greenleaf Publishing.

Lanoie, P., & Tanguay, G. (2000). Factors leading to green profitability: Ten case studies. *Greener Management International, 31,* 39–50.

Lanoie, P., & Tanguay, G. (2004). Dix exemples de rentabilité verte. *Risque et management international, 3,* 85–106.

Lanoie, P., Laurent-Lucchetti, J., Johnstone, N., & Ambec S. (2011). Environmental policy, innovation and performance: New insights on the Porter Hypothesis. *Journal of Economics and Management Strategy, 20*(3), 803–841.

Mohr, R. D. (2002). Technical change, external economies, and the Porter hypothesis. *Journal of Environmental Economics and Management, 43*(1), 158–168.

Nakamura, M., Takahashi, T., & Vertinsky, I. (2001). Why Japanese firms choose to certify: A study of managerial responses to environmental issues. *Journal of Environmental Economics and Management, 42,* 23–52.

Nishitani, K. (2009). An empirical study of the initial adoption of ISO 14001 in Japanese manufacturing firms. *Ecological Economics, 68,* 669–679.

Palmer, K., Oates, W. E., & Portney, P. R. (1995). Tightening environmental standards: The benefit-cost or the no-cost paradigm? *Journal of Economic Perspectives, 9*(4), 119–132.

Porter, M. E. (1991). America's green strategy. *Scientific American, 264*(4), 168.

Porter, M. E., & van der Linde, C. (1995). Toward a new conception of the environment-competitiveness relationship. *Journal of Economic Perspectives, 9*(4), 97–118.

Reinhardt, F. L. (1999). *Ciba Specialty Chemicals.* Cambridge, MA: Harvard Business School Press. Case Study No. 9-799-086.

Simpson, D., & Bradford, R. L. (1996). Taxing variable cost: Environmental regulation as industrial policy. *Journal of Environmental Economics and Management, 30*(3), 282–300.

U.S. Department of Agriculture. (2007). *An analysis of the effects of an expansion in biofuel demand on U.S. agriculture.* Washington, DC: U.S. Department of Agriculture.

Walker, B. (2008). You are only as green as your supply chain. *Harvard Business Review,* www.hbrgreen.org/2008/02/you_are_only_as_green_as_your.html.

Walley, N., & Whitehead, B. (1994). It's not easy being green. *Harvard Business Review, 72*(3), 46–52.

CHAPTER THREE

The Role of Strategic Context in Environmental Sustainability Initiatives
Three Case Studies

Bruno Staffelbach,
Ernst A. Brugger,
and Serafin Bäbler

Companies utilize different strategies toward sustainable business models (Delmas & Montes-Sancho, 2010; Kolk & Mauser, 2002). Some companies see "green" as a threat, while others recognize "green" as an opportunity. The diversity of sustainable strategies leads to diverse requirements for business functions. The role of human resource management (HRM) is especially dependent on strategic decisions and is influenced by a firm's corporate strategy (Campbell, 2007). This chapter will examine the potential influences of the strategic background of an environmentally sustainable initiative on the roles played by the HR department and the activities that may be incorporated into the environmental initiative.

We will outline and describe a framework for different types of corporate environmental strategies. The framework distinguishes among three types of strategies. Different approaches toward environmental sustainability will be acknowledged, but these approaches will remain unaddressed here. The term "sustainability" will primarily refer to environmental sustainability. A "type B" business strategy is defined as one in which environmental concerns are an integral part. Corporate strategies in which environmental issues are seen as potential risks that must be mitigated will be described as "type A." Situations in which both types of environmental strategies are used are presented as a hybrid of type A and type B strategies. Given the strategic background of the firm, initiatives can be classified by the HR activities involved. Based on these HR activities, the roles of the respective HR functions can be assessed. The different strategies, the HR activities, and the roles of HR can be arranged into a cube, which serves as the guiding framework.

As a next step, we will analyze three initiatives from three Swiss firms and study the interactions between the strategic background of the initiatives and the HR functions. The first example is an initiative of a firm that follows a type A strategy. The other two cases describe initiatives that follow a type B strategy and a hybrid strategy, respectively. The case studies are based on qualitative research methods, including semi-structured interviews with the executives and senior managers of each company. During the research process, the strategic backgrounds of the companies will be identified and discussed, and one specific initiative will be described in more detail.

The last section will analyze the interactions of the HR roles and the strategic backgrounds of the initiatives and will outline the implications and lessons learned from the case studies. In addition, we will describe areas for potential future research.

Conceptual Framework

Companies must outline the impact of environmental matters on their corporate strategies. Environmental issues do not necessarily influence all companies in the same way. Executives addressing environmental issues must adapt their corporate strategy to existing environmental requirements. Drivers for the evolution toward an environmentally friendly strategy are numerous and differ across both markets and industries.

This section aims to describe the underlying conceptual framework used to assess and discuss an environmental initiative in its strategic context. The framework will elaborate a three-dimensional cube that allows initiatives to be rated according to the three axes: type of strategy, HR activities, and role of HR. The illustration below shows the cube with its dimensions labeled accordingly.

In the following sections, the three dimensions will be described in more detail. Moreover, we will describe the aforementioned three types of corporate environmental strategies, which comprise the horizontal axis of the cube shown in Figure 3.1. The second section explains the vertical axis, which is composed of the HR activities. Last, the third dimension, which lists the different roles that can be fulfilled by the HR functions, will be explained.

Figure 3.1. Typology of Corporate Environmental Strategies and Corresponding Initiatives

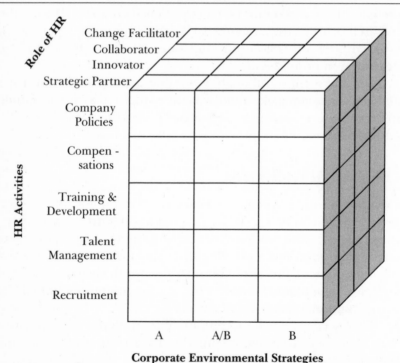

Corporate Environmental Strategies

Corporate Environmental Strategies

According to Nidumolu, Prahalad, and Rangaswami (2009), Delmas and Montes-Sancho (2010), and Porter and Kramer (2006), the most frequently cited factors driving evolution toward a sustainable corporate strategy are the following:

- Emerging regulations from the government
- Consumer pressure from the market
- A sense of social responsibility
- Increased competitiveness stemming from new environmental initiatives

Over the last few decades, environmental issues have become an increasingly political matter. Because of public pressure, recent natural crises, and findings by the scientific community, environmental sustainability has become a topic of debates in congresses and governmental administrations all over the world. In addition, the number of environmental regulations and policies implemented by governments is continually rising at the international, national, and industrial levels.

Thus, not all companies face the same regulations, market pressures, or opportunities to generate competitive advantages by incorporating green strategies. Moreover, personal perceptions of the importance of environmental problems differ among executives. Consequently, the impact of environmental issues on corporate strategy can differ by company.

A type A initiative views environmental issues as a threat to the company. As a result, a company adopting a type A initiative enacts a corporate control strategy to mitigate potential risks in the areas in which environmental issues may arise. The company does so by utilizing a compliance strategy (Lubin & Esty, 2010). According to Jabbour, Santos, and Nagano (2010), this strategy is designed to mitigate the negative effects stemming from business activities. If the company adheres to the regulation or the compliance standard, then the risk will appear to be neutralized. Type A strategies may be motivated by the need to comply with existing regulations or standards. Furthermore, the company may aim to achieve cost savings by mitigating greenhouse gas emissions, removing wastewater, or disposing of waste materials.

By implementing a corresponding initiative, a company might expect the following:

- Hands-on solutions to mitigate negative effects on costs
- Achieving compliance with regulations and standards
- Improvements in specific environmental key performance indicators (KPIs), such as greenhouse gas emissions

The scope is therefore circumscribed by a specific problem or risk. Lubin and Esty (2010) describe these initiatives as mirroring the look and feel of tactical programs in different areas of the firm. Within the initiatives, solutions depend on problem identification and dedicated problem solving, and roles and responsibilities are also organized in this manner. The target is set by a central authority, and units execute the initiative. From a leadership point of view, this process might be considered transactional rather than transformational (Brass & Riggio, 2006).

If the company follows a type B strategy, then the organization will focus on an entrepreneurial approach to resolve environmental matters. Confronting environmental issues is seen as an opportunity. The company is willing to radically change its value chain and core beliefs.

Type B initiatives address the need to transform a company into an environmentally friendly business. Compliance requires that minimum requirements be satisfied. However, type B strategies typically achieve much more than the minimum level of compliance required by stakeholders. In this case, a company is willing to rethink current processes and working methods as it seeks to establish a sophisticated, environmentally friendly policy. In terms of financial figures, type B initiatives focus on improving long-term profitability. Because significant transformations only occur with changes to the mindsets of the employees and management, increased awareness may be necessary for companies following type B strategies.

The corresponding objectives of a type B initiative are therefore composed of two levels. First, the objective is to bring the company one step closer to an environmentally friendly business policy and process. Second, companies will seek to increase the understanding and relevance of environmental matters at the employee level. In other words, the objectives can rely on hard factors to improve the relevant KPIs or the financial bottom line while simultaneously utilizing soft factors. Type B initiatives also seek to improve employee commitment, trust, and motivation.

The typical scope and context of a type B initiative is much wider and more extensive than for a type A initiative. The successful transformation of a company can only be achieved when the entire value chain, including all primary and support functions, is involved. Doing so requires an integrated view of the company and an expanded scope for the initiative. Such transformations can be realized by aligning projects throughout the company and integrating the support functions with the initiative.

For a type B initiative, it is crucial to bring the stakeholders together and to integrate them into the process from the very beginning. Planning, target setting, and execution should be conducted together to benefit from interaction effects. The process of developing and conducting a type B initiative consists of an iterative process of revision, experimentation, and innovation toward an environmentally sustainable business. In constructing the initiative, the leadership style conforms to a transformational rather than a transactional style (Brass & Riggio, 2006).

In diversified companies, different divisions of the company can follow other corporate environmental strategies. If one business unit maintains the old production technologies and products and another division reengineers, innovates, and creates new business opportunities, the company must manage different environmental strategies. This situation may occur if long investment cycles prevent the management from responding proactively to environmental matters.

As a result, the objectives of the environmental initiatives may vary between the business units. The different initiatives across the company create distinctive subcultures and understandings of environmental issues. Consequently, "parallel worlds" will be created in environmental management, and two different approaches to environmental sustainability will exist within the same company.

The three types of strategies comprise the horizontal axis of the framework (that is, the aforementioned cube).

Human Resource Management Activities in Environmental Initiatives

A number of studies have shown the range of HRM practices that can contribute to the successful implementation of a firm's corporate strategy. Huselid (1995) states that selection processes, an incentive compensation system, performance management systems, and employee involvement and training processes are central to a company's success.

A subset of environmental management includes the activities that are crucial for the development and execution of environmental initiatives. To aggregate these elements, a literature review has been conducted (Glavas, Senge, & Cooperrider, 2010; Lai, Cheng, & Tang, 2010; Porter & Kramer, 2006; Shari, 2010; Wirtenberg, Harmon, Russell, & Fairfield, 2007). The following overview of HRM practices reflects the six most-cited topics relevant to this study. The subset covers five areas relevant to HRM activities. The illustration of the cube has shown the relevant HRM activities, which include employee training and development, HR company policies, recruitment, individual compensation, and talent management.

HR policies include written regulations for the employees of the firm. Typical regulations include a code of conduct or behavioral guidelines with respect to environmental matters. A code of conduct advises employees on how to act with respect to environmental, social, and legal issues. With the rollout of an initiative, the written policies must be expanded, adjusted, or emphasized.

Another important practice is individual compensation or performance appraisals. A variety of research has shown why compensation constitutes a strategic element of HRM practices (Huselid, Jackson, & Schuler, 1997). Compensation focuses and adjusts organizational objectives by setting personal targets for employees.

Training is the preferred practice for changing the skills, knowledge, and behavior of employees. Because an initiative often targets improvement in these areas, training and development are carefully considered with regard to the objectives of an initiative.

Talent management practices are also important for environmental initiatives. Talent management, in this context, defines the types of employees who are considered high performers and therefore potential candidates for promotion. As the values and objectives of the organization change, the criteria for talent may be influenced as well. Therefore, the practice of talent management is assigned as an area of interest.

Finally, recruiting guidelines and regulations play a significant role in environmental initiatives. These guidelines determine who will be hired. The qualities and competence of a candidate are assessed to determine the likelihood of his or her success at a company. Any changes resulting from an initiative will alter the desired skills of the employees, and, as a result, the requirements for entry into the company must be adjusted.

The five areas presented here have been identified as relevant to assessing the interactions between environmental initiatives and the HRM.

Roles of Human Resource Management

The scientific community of "role theorists" (Ashforth, 2001) understands an organization as composed of a system of roles. Role players share and distribute information on the activities expected of organization members. To develop and execute an initiative, several parts of the company must contribute. The previous section reviewed the most important HRM practices with regard to environmental initiatives. Defined organizational units (that is, functions) execute these practices. The functions act within a network to contribute to the environmental initiative. The aim of this section is to construct a framework for the different roles assumed by the different functions during the development and execution process of an initiative.

Schuler, Jackson, and Storey (2001) propose a framework for the generic roles that can be adopted by HR functions. The framework was originally developed to explain the interaction processes between HRM and business functions. Table 3.1 depicts four roles, each of which reflects a different level of involvement.

Table 3.1. The Key Roles and Responsibilities for HR Professionals

Possible Roles	Responsibilities of the Roles
Strategic Partner	Understands the business model of the corporation including strategies in a global context Encourages the dialogue across multiple stakeholders, including employees, customers, shareholders, and society Shares with managers the strategies, the value of human resources, and the consequences of managing people effectively
Innovator	Enables the organization to develop a learning culture Finds new approaches to leading and directing people and does not just copy what others are doing
Collaborator	Understands how to build win-win situations Cooperates and supports Works task-oriented across internal and external organizational constraints
Change Facilitator	Is aware of the need for change and creates favorable conditions in the organization for it Helps lead changes in strategy Energizes others for the desired change

Adapted from Schuler, Jackson, and Storey, 2001.

These roles can be applied to the context of environmental initiatives. The strategic partner brings together all of the relevant stakeholders for the initiative and steers the process. The innovator contributes special knowledge on environmental aspects to the initiative. This knowledge includes the ability to train and educate dedicated units of the company for an initiative. The collaborator takes an active part in the development and execution of the initiatives by bringing together the specific competences of each function. The change facilitator supervises the execution of the initiative.

This framework provides the model for analyzing the contributions of several functions in the case studies, as shown in the next section.

Cases Studies: Experiences from Swiss Firms

Based on case studies of three Swiss firms, the objective of the empirical part of this study is to illustrate the interdependence of the environmental strategies and the roles of the HR functions in the corresponding initiatives. Therefore, the research will address the following two questions: What were the roles of the HR functions in the development and execution of environmental initiatives? and What were the lessons necessary to derive normative statements about the interactions between environmental strategies and the roles played by the HR functions? The following section will describe the methodology, sample, and structure of the case studies.

With regard to methodology, the case studies were developed through qualitative research methods. First, extended desk research provided the fundamental information about each company and each initiative. Annual reports, market communications, and internal briefing documents were analyzed to provide the basic information about each case. Second, the findings were assessed and expanded through qualitative interviews with senior management and executives overseeing environmental sustainability in each company. The research resulted in a description of the corporate environmental strategy of each firm, which will be assessed in the theoretical model presented later in this chapter. Additionally, one specific initiative that is representative of each firm's individual strategy will be analyzed in more detail. This analysis will focus specifically on the roles of the HR functions involved in the initiative. In the concluding part of this section, the lessons learned from each of the cases will be discussed in the strategic context of each company.

All three companies in the case studies are headquartered in Switzerland and operate in the international market, either by having production sites abroad or by serving the European or worldwide markets with their products or services. Only companies that have shown a positive commitment to environmental sustainability were considered. The firms were required to have defined an explicit environmental strategy and implemented environmental initiatives. The first case shows the initiative of a pharmaceutical company that developed an environmental code of conduct through employee participation and increased its staff's sensitivity to environmental issues. The second case shows the training initiative of a company in the materials industry. The initiative succeeded in enhancing the employees' knowledge and motivation, which was necessary for a deep corporate transformation to a green business model. The third case describes the initiative of a company in the cement industry. Although cement production cannot undergo drastic environmental improvements, the company managed to reduce traditional energy consumption by utilizing a waste management solution that contributed to cost savings in energy and, at the same time, helped the local communities dispose of its litter.

The case studies follow the same structure. First, each company is presented and the environmental sustainability strategy of each firm is explained to provide the context for each case. Second, the scope of the specific initiative is explicated in more detail. In other words, the HR functions affected by the initiative are outlined, and the roles of the HR functions are described. Finally, the results and achievements of the initiative are presented.

Case Study 1: Galenica's Environmental Code of Conduct

The Galenica group is an international company operating in the health care industry. Its headquarters are in Bern, Switzerland. The firm was founded in 1927 as a pharmaceutical wholesaler. Today, the company employs approximately 1,100 people and is listed on the Swiss stock exchange. Over the years, Galenica has developed into a highly diversified health care provider serving different business sectors, including pharmaceutical manufacturing, logistics services, pharmaceutical retail services, and special pharmaceutical IT services.

Galenica is following a far-reaching sustainability strategy, and it takes the impact of its business on the environment seriously. Whenever possible, environmental aspects are considered in the planning and execution of its business actions. For example, Galenica has managed to reduce energy consumption by adjusting a building's climate control system. By installing motion sensors in the facilities, Galenica has achieved energy savings. Galenica has also distributed waste-handling guidelines to its employees to teach them how to prevent unnecessary waste in the offices and avoid recycling mistakes. At some sites, Galenica has coordinated carpools to the next public transport station to prevent unnecessary car and taxi use. Additionally, the management has maintained close connections with the city authorities to arrange bus stations close to the Galenica buildings and attractive time schedules. Furthermore, Galenica has attempted to purchase only vehicles with excellent emission standards.

Overall, Galenica's environmental strategy, which has focused on slight improvements to their core processes, reflects the type A strategy presented in this chapter. "Our employees act 'green' in their day-to-day behavior. All we need is to gather their effort and make it visible," said Mr. Henzi, the head of the legal department, who is responsible for sustainability at the Galenica group. These efforts are reported regularly in the sustainability report, which is an integral part of the annual report and follows the GRI 3.0 standard.

Here we highlight Galenica's effort to develop and establish a code of conduct at a company site in Niderbipp, Switzerland. This operations center is part of Galexis, a subsidiary of the Galenica logistics and retail division. The site was established during 2008 and 2009. The primary purpose of the initiative was to gather and establish hands-on regulations to achieve cost savings in terms of energy costs, water consumption, and waste production. Furthermore, the initiative was intended to raise employees' awareness regarding this topic. All employees were informed of the initiative and asked to submit ideas on environmental improvement possibilities to a postbox. A lottery created incentives for participation. Every input was automatically accompanied by a ticket for a lottery drawing in which the employees could win up to $1,000. The deadline for submission was limited to approximately three months after the announcement.

To assess the HR activities and the role of the HR functions in this initiative, we focus on the theoretical framework in Figure

Figure 3.2. Gelenica's Initiative in the Framework

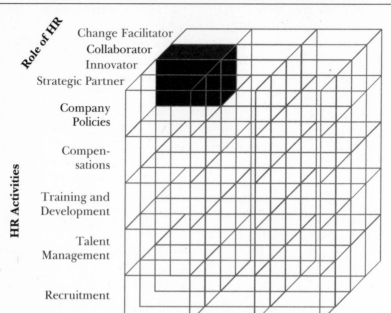

3.1. On one axis, the framework defines the generic strategies for environmental sustainability. As explained earlier, Galenica mostly qualifies as a type A environmental strategy. Therefore, this initiative is located on the strategic background of the left column in the cube (see Figure 3.2). To assess the role of HR, we analyzed the division of duties within this initiative. In the process of developing and conducting the initiative, the local employee representative committee at the production site took over the role of strategic partner of the initiative. With the help of the local management, the committee established the initiative, communicated with the stakeholders, and steered the process. Specialized units such as process management supported the initiative with their specific knowledge. HR assumed its respective functions and provided support where necessary, but did not assume a leadership position. The initiative and responsibility were placed with the local employee representative committee and the local management. Applying this information to the framework of Figure 3.1, we find that the initiative operated in the area of "HR activity company policies," and HR played the role of "collaborator" in the initiative.

The commitment to the initiative was high across the whole production site. During the three-month period, 160 ideas were submitted. Some teams conducted workshops to develop ideas for the postbox. Finally, approximately sixty ideas were compiled in the final document of the environmental code of conduct. The regulations included rules such as the handling of computers and printers. By making simple changes to the monitor settings, the entire company was able to save a significant amount of energy; by adjusting the management of printers, less paper was used for printouts. The code of conduct included additional guidelines for the purchasing of new cars, requiring only cars with guarantees of high energy efficiency to be purchased. In the section on facility management, the document prescribed rules for heating and lightning in the company building to save energy. Overall, the environmental code of conduct created guidelines for environmentally friendly behavior based on a participatory process in which ideas were collected from the employees. By following this process, Galenica was able to create a document with high credibility among the employees and, at the same time, to save energy and reduce costs.

Case Study 2: Geberit's Initiative for Environmental Training and Development

The Geberit group produces and sells sanitary products and technologies in over one hundred countries. The headquarters is located in Rapperswil-Jona, Switzerland. Geberit was founded in 1874 and garnered approximately 2.2 billion Swiss francs in revenue in 2009. In the same year, the Geberit group employed approximately 5,600 people in sixty-seven countries. The product portfolio of the Geberit group consists of sanitary materials, including cistern systems, faucets and flushing systems, waste fittings, traps, and accordion piping systems. The group is listed on the Swiss stock exchange and is publicly owned. Geberit follows an extensive sustainability strategy that primarily covers two areas. First, Geberit aims to develop and provide sustainable products for the market. Second, Geberit aims to demonstrate sustainable business behavior toward all stakeholders. Therefore, sustainability is emphasized in all business actions with the goal of continually transforming the character of the business. Environmental concerns are considered a possible risk to be mitigated as well as a challenge to create new and innovative ways of raising the value of the company. In terms of sustainability reporting, Geberit has completely adapted to the GRI 3.0 standard (A+ adaptor). The sustainability policy and the transparent reporting standards have also had a positive impact on Geberit as an investment opportunity. Over the last few years, Geberit has developed into an interesting stock for investors sensitive to environmentally friendly behavior. The stock of the company is currently listed in the Dow Jones Sustainability Index (DJSI) (SAM, 2010).

Geberit has conducted a number of environmental initiatives, including waste and water reduction and energy efficiency programs. Specifically, Geberit has worked to raise sustainability awareness among its employees by developing and conducting sustainability training sessions.

These training sessions are the focus of this case study. For the last three years, Geberit has conducted an extensive environmental and recycling training program at the production site in Rapperswil-Jona. This initiative was designed to raise awareness of sustainability and to show how sustainability affects the daily work of the employees. Although the topic of sustainability was quite important to Geberit managers, the employees lacked understanding of the impact of sustainability on their daily work. This initiative sought to build an integral understanding of environmental sustainability among employees.

We will now describe this initiative within the cube framework. According to the description of Geberit's sustainability strategy, the company integrates environmental sustainability into its core business strategy, which could be described as a type B strategy. Therefore, the case is placed in the type B strategy column in Figure 3.3. HR activities affected by the initiative are mainly in the fields of HR training and development, although compensation and company policies are also ultimately involved in the

Figure 3.3. Geberit's Initiative in the Framework

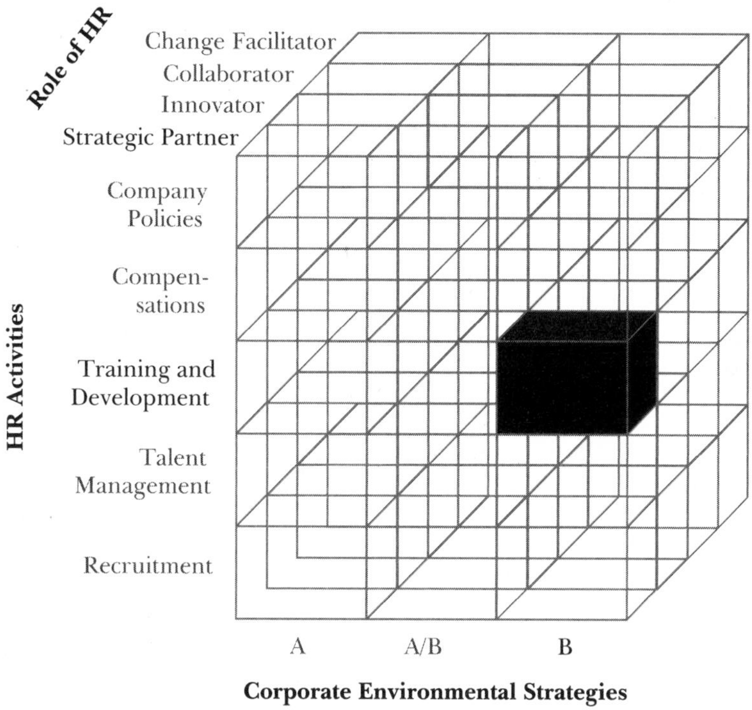

Corporate Environmental Strategies

initiative. However, the central focus is in the field of training and development. The conception and rollout of the initiative were organized in such a way that the local responsible manager for training and development played the role of the strategic partner. He coordinated the stakeholders, steered the content, and executed the training in close collaboration with the group function for sustainability and the local management. After applying this information, we find that HR fulfills the role of strategic partner in the initiative. Overall, the cube summarizes the three levels and describes the relationship among strategy, HR activities, and the role assumed by HR in the figure.

The initiative was rolled out in small group training sessions consisting of four to eight people. These sessions were aligned with employee shifts and usually took place before or after the shifts for approximately one hour. The training was divided into two major parts. In the first part, overall awareness of the topic was increased. In the second part, the newly acquired information was put into practice and applied to the specific tasks of the employees. "In our view, it is essential that our employees have a deep understanding of the materials they are working with and how and why things can be recycled," said Mr. Wydler, head of technical training.

The initiative had a concrete impact on the company on two different levels. On one hand, the amount of special waste and the number of recycling mistakes were reduced. On the other hand, the policy had a strong impact on the social skills of the employees. "We recognized an eminent reduction of recycling mistakes and, therefore, achieved cost savings by avoiding extra recycling work," Mr. Wydler said. By integrating the environmental training into the overall training program, Geberit managed to integrate environmental awareness smoothly into the mindset of its employees.

Case Study 3: Holcim's Initiative for Alternative Energies

The Holcim Group produces building materials for construction work and delivers related services. Its main products are cement and cement aggregates such as gravel. The company, founded in 1912, has its headquarters in Zurich, Switzerland. The production sites and the key markets are spread around the world. Holcim maintains local units in more than seventy countries across all continents. In 2009, Holcim employed approximately eighty thousand people. As the nature of Holcim's business activities might imply, environmental challenges exert a significant influence on Holcim's business strategy. The extraction of natural resources for cement production affects the environment at the quarry sites, and the cement production process itself requires a huge amount of energy. The traditional energy sources most commonly used are coal, heavy fuel oil, or gas. Thus, environmental sustainability and fossil fuel independence play integral roles in the corporate strategy of the Holcim group (Holcim, 2008). In this context, the case study examines the Holcim group's initiative to increasingly substitute alternative energies for traditional fossil fuels in the cement production process.

To understand the initiative in the context of Holcim's market situation, the following section will explain the most important parts of Holcim's environmental strategy. Sustainable development, which consists of environmental performance, economic growth, and social responsibility, is well embedded in the overall strategy of the company. But what does sustainable development mean for a business in which huge investments must be made in heavy assets and the production of cement consumes significant energy and natural resources?

Although improving environmental performance is not easy under these circumstances, Holcim developed and implemented an environmental strategy in different fields of the company. Holcim represents a company in which both types of strategies, A and B, are reflected in the overall environmental policy. On the one hand, cement production technology creates an unavoidable amount of greenhouse gas emissions. Environmental damage can only be mitigated, which suggests a type A strategy. On the other hand, Holcim has strived to create new business models around the cement process that, for example, could increase the resource efficiency or substitute traditional energy with alternative energy, as the case study will outline.

Holcim reported its efforts in a sustainability report (Holcim, 2010). This report was compiled according to the GRI 3.0 standard and achieved an adaptation level of A+, which represents the highest level of sustainability attainable. As a result, Holcim stock has been listed in the DJSI and FTSE4 Good Sustainability Index (Holcim, 2010).

In this case study, Holcim was seeking ways to substitute for traditional energy sources in the cement-making process. Thus, the idea of "co-processing" was born. Co-processing is based on the principles of industrial ecology and involves the usage of waste materials in energy-intensive industries as raw materials and/or sources of energy. These waste materials replace natural resources (material recycling) and fossil fuels, such as coal, petroleum, and gas (energy recovery). By using waste as a source of energy, Holcim was able to create a win-win situation for the local community and the company; the sound treatment of waste helped the local community increase its living standards and helped Holcim to replace part of its fossil fuels. Because of the success of co-processing, Holcim decided to steadily increase its usage of waste as a source of energy. Waste co-processing was a completely new field for the Holcim sites and required additional skills, processes, and equipment. Because the required skills differed significantly from the company's existing skills, people had to be recruited externally from the labor market. With these people's cooperation, co-processing could be implemented. After the implementation of co-processing, the company was split into two parts that differed slightly in both technological and cultural terms. The company now contained not only the traditional production technology for cement products, but also the new waste solution for alternative energy production. However, the two parts needed to collaborate closely, which required them to act as one company. Therefore, each part had to continuously interact with and communicate its needs to the other part of the company.

In the cube, the Holcim initiative might be placed in the position depicted in Figure 3.4. According to the Holcim environmental strategy, which has been identified as a hybrid type of strategy, the initiative should take place in the middle column of the cube. Two HR activities are included. First, as the company hires new people, the recruitment activities are included in the initiative. Second, to achieve the smooth integration of the new waste management division into the company, the initiative requires a significant amount of managerial attention. Holcim chose to raise awareness of the new section by including the waste management division in the career paths of the managers. Hence, the waste solution process enriched the management horizon within the company and became an important opportunity to show leadership skills. The initiative can therefore be seen as a talent management opportunity for local management in which HR acts as a strategic partner.

In 2010, the Holcim Group replaced approximately 12 percent of its thermal energy needs with alternative energies, and the individual plants replaced approximately 75 percent of their energy needs with alternative energies. Holcim is now

Figure 3.4. Holcim's Initiative in the Framework

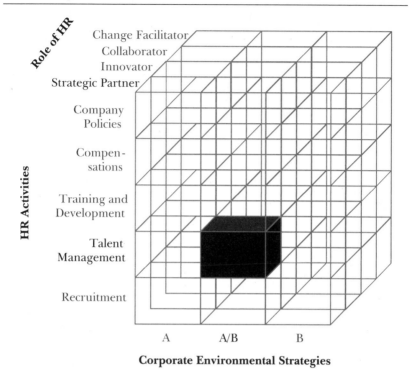

Corporate Environmental Strategies

successfully applying this strategy in more than forty countries around the world.

Conclusion and Lessons Learned

In the first section, we will reflect on the conclusions and lessons learned from the case studies. Then we will derive general implications from the research. Each case will be discussed, with a focus on the critical success factors of the initiative in each context and the areas that could be improved in future research.

Lessons Learned from the Case Studies

The Galenica case study presented an example of a type A environmental strategy. From discussions with several interview partners, we derived the following three criteria for successfully implementing such an initiative. First, the initiative was successful because of the positive effects of employee participation. When an initiative is founded on an employee level, the motivation for pursuing environmental sustainability is much higher than the motivation that may be achieved through a top-down initiative. Therefore, the role of HRM must be to encourage employee participation in the formation of a sustainability strategy. Second, the effort exerted by top management showed the employees that the initiative must be taken seriously and ensured strong participation rates from the employees in the project. Thus, HRM must ensure that the management is committed to provide the initiative with the necessary motivational power. Third, Galenica recognized the importance of supporting and guiding the initiative with expert knowledge from the central site. Employees were coached on financial planning and project scheduling processes. Therefore, HRM must ensure the management provides guidance, which in this case was administered by the process management function of Galenica. Overall, in this situation, HRM must focus on encouraging employee participation and providing conditions conducive to executing the initiative by ensuring management support and guidance.

The Geberit case study outlined an extensive environmental training initiative based on a type B environmental strategy. Because training represents a core competence of HRM, the HR function for training must reflect the role of a strategic partner. HRM must bring together all necessary stakeholders for the training and establish a common understanding of the objectives and content. Especially during the development and the early implementation phases of the initiative, it is crucial to compile necessary knowledge, particularly regarding the alignment between the support functions and the business unit. It is also mandatory to show the relevance of sustainability to the respective jobs and tasks. As sustainability training is integrated into the overall employee education process, sustainability will be recognized as an integral part of the company's strategy and values.

The alternative energy initiative of the Holcim group is a hybrid environmental strategy. The company maintained standard industry technologies but implemented them in parallel environmental business models, bringing HRM into a new position. The initiative primarily affected three areas. First, the setup of the new business model required different skills and new resources, which could be achieved by training existing employees. In this case, the required knowledge was unique, so new talent with specialized knowledge was recruited from the labor market. HRM provided a major contribution to the setup of the new business model by recruiting talent. Additionally, HRM functions were asked to take over the strategic responsibility of establishing a corporate culture of coexistence and cooperation at the employee level. At the management level, the company was understood as one joint factory and not as two separate divisions. As a result, HRM had to ensure that knowledge transfer took place between the two cultures through employee training and management exchange. Here, HRM functions had to ensure that the company was understood at the management level as a joint factory.

General Implications and Conclusion

This final section will focus on the implications of the research. The cube framework can assess environmental initiatives by examining the interactions among corporate environmental strategy, the HR activities involved, and the roles played by the HR department within the initiative. The application of the framework to the case studies has shown that initiatives operate in different fields of the cube framework, depending on the nature of the initiative and the underlying strategy of the firm. Generally speaking, three implications can be derived from the development and application of the framework to practice.

First, understanding environmental initiatives requires an understanding of the respective strategic background of each firm. The needs addressed by the initiative differ significantly depending on whether the firm follows a deep transformational green strategy or a risk mitigation strategy. The type A strategy describes a corporate risk mitigation and control strategy, where environmental issues are seen as a threat. The type B strategy views environmental matters as an entrepreneurial opportunity to create new environmentally friendly business models. If aspects of type A and B appear at the same time, then a hybrid strategy will result. In this case, the old and new business models must coexist. The different strategies lead to type A, type B, or hybrid initiatives. The strategy of the firm has an impact on the HR activities involved.

Second, the HR activities involved depend on the strategic context of the firm. From a theoretical point of view, training and development via organizational transformation with the goal of greater understanding of environmental issues are more critical for type B and hybrid strategies because knowledge and awareness of the environmental issues must be implemented on a transformational level. However, policies and control systems appear to be the focus of type B strategies, where risk mitigation is the overarching aim of the strategy. As a result, the three case studies also focused on different fields of HR activities.

Third, depending on the HR activities, the role of the HR department differs for each initiative. The HR functions can assume a range of possible roles. Type A initiatives require timely support from HR functions, management attention for the initiative, and central guidance for the execution process. Type B initiatives require a much higher level of involvement from the HR function because the company intends to establish a deep understanding of environmental matters. The company must go through a proper adaptation process, which involves a significant amount of effort in terms of training and restructuring. Because these initiatives operate mainly in the field of core HR activities such as training or talent management, the optimal role of HR is the strategic partner because of synergies, knowledge management, and efficiency advantages afforded by the position. HR activities such as employee development, individual compensation, and talent management are crucial in this situation. In the case of a hybrid initiative, the HR functions must balance the two divisions in terms of skill management, cultural understanding, and management development.

Considering all of these points, HR can drive and positively support initiatives by understanding the background of the underlying corporate environmental strategy and choosing its activities accordingly. With regard to its roles, HR must assume the strategic lead and partner position for the initiative wherever HR activities are the focus of the initiative. In doing so, HR functions are able to oversee an important part of the implementation of a company's environmental strategy.

The construction of the theoretical framework and its application to the three case studies illustrated the fundamental interactions among environmental strategy, HR activities, and the corresponding roles of HR. Although an initial set of implications for interdependence can be described from these results, further research is recommended to strengthen the results and to enrich the number of examples. This research did not identify which type of strategy is most successful, and the existence of different environmental strategies has been assumed. Therefore, comparisons between initiatives operating in different strategic columns are not recommended. However, the comparison of initiatives operating in similar strategic contexts and utilizing the same HR activities would be an area for future research. Similarly, the impact of different HR roles could be outlined.

Even without these comparisons, this research was able to describe and assess environmental initiatives within their strategic backgrounds and link them with their corresponding HR activities and the roles played by the HR functions. As a result, the HRM functions are able to contribute to the process toward environmental sustainability with regard to the strategic context of the firm.

References

Ashforth, B. E. (2001). *Role transitions in organizational life*. Mahwah, NJ: Lawrence Erlbaum Associates.

Brass, B. M., & Riggio, R. E. (2006). *Transformational leadership*. Mahwah, NJ: Lawrence Erlbaum Associates.

Campbell, J. L. (2007). Why would corporations behave in socially responsible ways? An institutional theory of corporate social responsibility. *Academy of Management Review, 32*, 946–967.

Delmas, M. A., & Montes-Sancho, M. J. (2010). Voluntary agreements to improve environmental quality: Symbolic and substantive cooperation. *Strategic Management Journal, 31*, 575–601.

Glavas, A., Senge, P., & Cooperrider, D. L. (2010). Building a green city on a blue lake: A model for building a local sustainable economy. *People & Strategy, 33*(1), 26–33.

Holcim. (2008). Fact sheet: Alternative fuels & raw materials (AFR). www .holcim.com/holcimweb/gc/CORP/uploads/Holcim_FactSheet _AFR_2008.pdf.

Holcim. (2010). *Annual report 2009.* www.holcim.com/holcimweb/gc/ CORP/uploads/AR_2009.pdf.

Huselid, M. A. (1995). The impact of human resource management practices on turnover, productivity, and corporate financial performance. *Academy of Management Journal, 38,* 635–672.

Huselid, M. A., Jackson, S. E., & Schuler, R. S. (1997). Technical and strategic human resource management effectiveness as determinants of firm performance. *Academy of Management Journal, 40,* 171–188.

Jabbour, C. J. C., Santos, F. C. A., & Nagano, M. S. (2010). Contributions of HRM throughout the stages of environmental management: Methodological triangulation applied to companies in Brazil. *International Journal of Human Resource Management, 21,* 1049–1089.

Kolk, A., & Mauser, A. (2002). The evolution of environmental management: From stage models to performance evaluation. *Business Strategy and the Environment, 11,* 14–31.

Lai, K., Cheng, T. C. E., & Tang, A. K. Y. (2010). Green retailing: Factors for success. *California Management Review, 52,* 6–31.

Lubin, D. A., & Esty, D. C. (2010). The big idea: The sustainability imperative. *Harvard Business Review, 88,* 42–50.

Nidumolu, R., Prahalad, C. K., & Rangaswami, M. R. (2009). Why sustainability is now the key driver of innovation. *Harvard Business Review, 87,* 56–64.

Porter, M. E., & Kramer, M. R. (2006). Strategy & society: The link between competitive advantage and corporate social responsibility. *Harvard Business Review, 84,* 78–92.

SAM. (2010). *The sustainability yearbook 2010.* www.sam-group.com/ htmld/yearbook/downloads/The_Sustainability_Yearbook_2010 _FINAL.pdf.

Schuler, R. S., Jackson, S. E., & Storey, J. (2001). HRM and its link with strategic management. In J. Storey (Ed.), *Human resource management: A critical text* (2nd ed.) (pp. 114–130). London: International Thomson.

Shari, A. (2010). Perspectives–Counterpoints. *People & Strategy, 33*(1), 14.

Wirtenberg, J., Harmon, J., Russell W. G., & Fairfield, K. (2007). HR's role in building a sustainable enterprise. *Human Resource Planning, 30,* 10–20.

CHAPTER FOUR

Human Resource Management Efforts for Environmental Sustainability

A Survey of Organizations

Mark J. Schmit,
Shawn Fegley,
Evren Esen,
Jennifer Schramm,
and Alan Tomassetti

Sustainability has become a bit of an ambiguous term in both the research and the applied world. To illustrate this point, a Business Source Complete search for "sustainability" yields 24,030 results from 1990 to 2011. That is roughly three articles a day being published on sustainability in some context. People are applying the idea (or at least the word) of sustainability to all facets of the world. There is environmental sustainability, corporate sustainability, sustainable accounting, sustainable investment, sustainable decision making, sustainable development, sustainable growth, sustainable consumption, and the list goes on. To speak as generally as possible, "sustainability" is a term created to describe the relationship that exists between human actions (usually this refers to economic or organizational developments) and global, both natural and manmade, ecology (Chiesa, Manzini, & Noci, 1999).

Given that litany of terms utilizing the idea of sustainability, it should come as no surprise that the concept of sustainability has been applied in a global sense. Most notably, when the United Nations (1992) declared, "It is in the hands of humanity to make development sustainable, that is to say, seek to meet the needs and aspirations of the present without compromising the ability of future generations to meet their own." That definition is almost maximally broad, including almost all aspects of life. This has led to sustainability being studied in many diverse areas such as economic, social, ecological, institutions, ethical, political, and more (Ciegis, Ramanauskiene, & Martinkus, 2009).

There are more than fifty definitions of sustainability, and there exists little ground upon which all of them can be easily compared (Faber, Jorna, & Van Engelen, 2005). While some focus on financial outcomes, others focus on cohesion, and still others focus on understanding sustainability as negotiated outcomes between a business and the world around it (Ciegis, Ramanauskiene, & Martinkus, 2009; Scerri & James, 2010).

The Dow Jones Sustainability Index, which measures companies' sustainability initiatives, defines corporate sustainability as "a business approach that creates long-term shareholder value by embracing opportunities and managing risks deriving from economic, environmental, and social developments." Most current work-related definitions (including SHRM's, "the commitment by organizations to balance financial performance with contributions to the quality of life of their employees, the society at large, and environmentally sensitive initiatives") revolve around three core elements: economic/organizational, environmental, and social. This definition looks beyond just one narrow view of sustainability and acknowledges that sustainability does not exist as a concrete concept with a single way to be achieved.

This conceptualization of sustainability is clearer than the nebulous idea put forth by the United Nations, but the measurement and elucidation of sustainability remain a veritable quagmire. There are multitudes of indexes, measurements, indicators, surveys, and models for qualifying or quantifying sustainability (for example, the Dow Jones Sustainability Index, 2011; see Tenuta, 2010, for more examples). Yet, without a clear paradigm for individuals and organizations to follow (luckily, one appears to be slowly emerging, as sustainability continues to receive attention in both research and applied domains), it is difficult to say when exactly a single organization has achieved sustainability.

There are numerous ways to engage in sustainability as an organization, and different strategies exist to attempt to achieve sustainability: focusing on meeting environmental and social legal regulations, focusing on external relationships, focusing on eco-friendly actions, and focusing holistically on sustainability within all business activities (Baumgartner & Ebner, 2010). Despite the nearly infinite ways to attempt to achieve sustainability, the majority of extant research supports the idea that there is a positive link between sustainability practices and a number of positive organizational outcomes, including what some view as the primary purpose or focus of business—increased corporate financial performance (Hahn, Figge, Pinkse, & Preuss, 2010; Orlitzky, Schmidt, & Rynes, 2003).

Given the ambiguity of the concept of sustainability and how it is practiced in organizations, the Society for Human Resource Management (SHRM) conducted a survey study of current sustainability practice in organizations (SHRM, 2011). We had several objectives in conducting this research. We wanted to (a) describe the state of organizations when it comes to sustainable practices, (b) quantitatively describe what individuals in organizations perceive sustainability to be (conceptual views and actual practices), (c) find out what motivates an organization to be sustainable, and (d) find out the role leadership plays in the sustainability of an organization. We report some of the results of the study in this chapter, providing a baseline of the role that human resource (HR) professionals play in the corporate sustainability realm.

Survey Study with Organizations

Study Methodology

The SHRM Sustainability Survey was conducted among HR professionals employed by organizations operating in the United States. A sample of HR professionals was randomly selected from SHRM's membership database, which included approximately 250,000 individual members at the time the poll was conducted. Only members who had not participated in a SHRM survey or poll in the last six months were included in the sampling frame.

Members who were students, consultants, academics, located internationally, or had no e-mail address on file were excluded from the sampling frame. In March 2010, an e-mail that included a hyperlink to the survey was sent to five thousand randomly selected SHRM members. Of these, 4,550 e-mails were successfully delivered to respondents, and 728 HR professionals responded, yielding a response rate of 16 percent. The survey was accessible for a period of eight weeks, and six e-mail reminders were sent to non-respondents in an effort to increase response rates. The final sample of HR professionals was generally representative of the SHRM membership population. The SHRM population of members is highly representative of the organizations in the United States that employ at least one HR professional. For interpretation for the results, the margin of error, using a 95 percent confidence interval, is plus or minus approximately 3 percentage points. The following sections of this chapter describe the results of the survey.

Defining Sustainability

As previously noted, the word "sustainability" is difficult to define since sustainability is a dynamic and evolving concept. As a result, this concept can take on many different meanings and represents different things to different people. The definition also varies within different contexts and is sometimes confused with other concepts such as corporate social responsibility. For the purpose of this study, sustainability was defined as the commitment by organizations to balance financial performance with contributions to the quality of life of their employees, the society at large, and environmentally sensitive initiatives. Companies were asked whether their organization had an approach for defining sustainability, and 68 percent of businesses responded affirmatively.

Who Is Engaging in Sustainable Workplace or Business Practices?

Sustainability is becoming an extremely popular topic in the business world. Regardless of company size or type of business, organizations are feeling the pressure from a range of stakeholders to engage in sustainability. Overall, 72 percent of organizations in the sample reported engaging in sustainable workplace or business practices.

Motivations for Investing in Sustainability

Organizations were asked to identify the main driver for their organizations' investment in sustainability. The key drivers were (1) contribution to society, (2) competitive financial advantage, (3) environmental considerations, (4) saving money on operational costs, and (5) health and safety considerations (see Table 4.1). Less frequently cited drivers included employee activism (4 percent), local/federal regulations (4 percent), market share improvement (4 percent), public/media relations strategy (4 percent), consumer activism/grassroots pressure (2 percent), internal activism (1 percent), local/federal incentives (1 percent) and recent corporate scandals (1 percent).

Sustainability is more likely to be accepted and adopted by stakeholders when it is woven into the organization's fabric. When asked about ways their organizations demonstrate their commitment to sustainability internally, 57 percent of respondents reported that sustainability is part of the organizational goals, 52 percent indicated that information about sustainability efforts is on their organization's intranet, and 51 percent include this information on their organization's external website (see Table 4.2).

Table 4.1. Drivers for the Investment in Sustainability

Top Five Drivers	Percentage
Contribution to society (e.g., good corporate citizenship)	39 percent
Competitive financial advantage	13 percent
Environmental considerations	12 percent
Saving money on operational costs	10 percent
Health and safety considerations	8 percent

Note: n = 411. Excludes organizations not engaging in sustainable workplace or business practices.

Source: *Advancing Sustainability: HR's Role* (SHRM, 2011).

Table 4.2. Methods Organizations Use to Demonstrate Commitment to Sustainability

Methods	Percentage
Sustainability is part of the organizational goals	57 percent
Includes information about sustainability efforts on your organization's intranet	52 percent
Includes information about sustainability efforts on your organization's website	51 percent
Sustainability commitment is included in the organization's mission	35 percent
Covers sustainability efforts in the organization's annual report	31 percent
Sustainability is linked to individual performance goals	16 percent
Issues a report dedicated exclusively to sustainability	15 percent
Sustainability seminars/training is mandatory	9 percent
Other	3 percent

Note: $n = 290$. Percentages do not total 100 percent due to multiple response options. Excludes organizations not engaging in sustainable workplace or business practices.

Source: *Advancing Sustainability: HR's Role* (SHRM, 2011).

Creating and Implementing the Sustainability Strategy: The Role of Leadership and Organizational Culture

Sustainability is a continual practice that is likely to succeed when it is incorporated into the company's strategic framework. In the survey, 52 percent of organizations engaging in sustainable workplace or business practices reported their organizations had a formal sustainability policy that included sustainable workplace goals and polices directly tied to the company's strategic planning process. Thirty-nine percent of companies reported they had an informal policy that had no accountability through their strategic planning process, but they strived to be environmentally and socially responsible. Only 9 percent of companies had no policy in place.

Table 4.3.   Groups Primarily Responsible for Creating Organizations' Sustainability Strategy

Group	Percentage
Senior Management Team	36 percent
CEO/President	22 percent
Employee Taskforce/Committee	12 percent
Board of Directors	9 percent
Dedicated Sustainability Department	8 percent
HR Department	6 percent
Public/Media Relations Department	2 percent
Finance Department	1 percent
Other	4 percent

Note: n = 395. Excludes organizations not engaging in sustainable workplace or business practices.

Source: *Advancing Sustainability: HR's Role* (SHRM, 2011).

Who is responsible for creating the sustainability strategy? The formation of a sustainability strategy varies by type of organization. Further, since there is no one-size-fits-all model to create a strategy, careful consideration should be used in this course of action. A company supporting sustainability can transform an organizational culture that encourages employees to value and engage in sustainability-related activities. As shown in Table 4.3, the largest percentage (36 percent) indicated that the senior management team was primarily responsible for creating the sustainability strategy in their organization. This was followed by the CEO/president (22 percent). Other areas primarily responsible for creating the sustainability strategy are employee taskforce/ committee (12 percent), board of directors (9 percent), dedicated sustainability department (8 percent), HR department (6 percent), public/media relations department (2 percent), and finance department (1 percent).

Implementation of a sustainability strategy can be a long process. To better understand which individual or group is most likely to lead the implementation efforts, the respondents were asked who is primarily responsible for implementing the strategy.

Table 4.4. Groups Primarily Responsible for Implementing Organizations' Sustainability Strategy

Group	Percentage
Senior Management Team	51 percent
HR Department	25 percent
CEO/President	23 percent
Employee Taskforce/Committee	18 percent
Dedicated Sustainability Department	12 percent
Board of Directors	8 percent
Finance Department	7 percent
Public/Media Relations Department	7 percent
All Employees	4 percent
Outside Consultant	*
Other	4 percent

Note: n = 390. * = Less than 1 percent. Percentages do not total 100 percent due to multiple response options. Excludes organizations not engaging in sustainable workplace or business practices.

Source: *Advancing Sustainability: HR's Role* (SHRM, 2011).

The top five responses were (1) senior management team, (2) HR department, (3) CEO/president, (4) employee taskforce/committee, and (5) dedicated sustainability department. These are detailed in Table 4.4.

The results from this survey revealed somewhat of a disconnect between HR's involvement in creating and implementing the sustainability strategy in their organizations. While HR was much less likely to be involved in the creation of strategic sustainability programs (6 percent), it was more involved in the implementation of strategy (25 percent). Sustainability is an issue that is good for business because it positively affects a company's culture, employees, customers, and brand proposition. It is a call to action for the HR profession to take a greater role in the strategic planning process and display leadership on this important topic.

Employees' View of Sustainability

Companies are unlikely to deliver the long-term sustainability benefits if employees are not engaged or do not recognize the advantages of their companies' initiatives. Programs that engage, inspire, and connect employees are vital to organizations trying to tap into the full potential of their sustainability outcomes. Organizations were asked how sustainability is viewed by different employee groups within their organizations. As shown in Table 4.5, the board of directors, C-suite, and executive-level employees were more likely to view sustainability as being "very important," compared with manager-level and non-managerial employees, who comprise the majority of the workforce in most organizations. These findings are consistent with research conducted in early 2010 that revealed an organization's commitment to

Table 4.5. Importance of Sustainability as a Business Practice by Organizational Group

Group	Very Important Percentage	Important Percentage	Unimportant Percentage	Very Unimportant Percentage
Board of Directors (n = 307)	49 percent	45 percent	5 percent	2 percent
C-suite and Executive-Level Employees (n = 378)	46 percent	49 percent	4 percent	1 percent
Manager-Level Employees (n = 389)	26 percent	64 percent	9 percent	1 percent
Non-Managerial Employees (n = 369)	17 percent	62 percent	19 percent	2 percent

Note: Excludes organizations that answered "not applicable" or "not sure" and those not engaged in sustainable workplace or business practices.

Source: *Advancing Sustainability: HR's Role* (SHRM, 2011).

corporate social responsibility and to a green workplace were rated by employees as two of the least important contributors to employee job satisfaction (SHRM, 2010). However, there is a growing sense that new generations of younger employers entering the workplace are more likely to value sustainability in the years ahead.

Because manager-level and non-managerial employees are less likely than their higher-level counterparts to be engaged in planning and implementing the sustainability strategy at their companies, they may be less likely to be engaged or interested in such initiatives. The findings suggest that if all levels of employees are able to participate in these activities, then their view toward sustainability may become more positive. HR will play a critical role in promoting this kind of broad employee involvement.

Leveraging Sustainability to Manage Talent

Sustainability programs can provide a vehicle for increasing job satisfaction and engaging current and new employees. Companies committed to aligning their sustainability and CSR strategies in ways to help deliver more effective recruitment strategies and outcomes reduce employee turnover, improve morale, and develop a leadership pipeline. Companies were asked to indicate the importance of their involvement in sustainability to attract, retain, and develop employees. As shown in Table 4.6, 49 percent of firms reported their involvement in sustainability was "very important" in creating a positive employer brand that attracts top talent, 40 percent reported it was "very important" in improving employee retention, and 39 percent indicated the involvement in sustainability was "very important" in developing the organization's leaders.

Sustainability Outreach Initiatives

Community outreach. Organizations were asked how they engage employees in volunteer community outreach initiatives related to sustainability. The top five responses were (1) recognize employee participation in volunteer programs, (2) provide company-sponsored volunteer events after work hours, (3) encour-

Table 4.6. Importance of Sustainability to Attract, Retain, and Develop Employees

Group	Very Important Percentage	Important Percentage	Unimportant Percentage	Very Unimportant Percentage
Creating a positive employer brand that attracts top talent ($n = 387$)	49 percent	40 percent	9 percent	1 percent
Improving employee retention ($n = 383$)	40 percent	45 percent	14 percent	1 percent
Developing the organization's leaders ($n = 375$)	33 percent	48 percent	17 percent	2 percent

Note: Excludes organizations that answered "not sure" and those not engaged in sustainable workplace or business practices.

Source: *Advancing Sustainability: HR's Role* (SHRM, 2011).

age senior management to participate in volunteer programs, (4) provide company-sponsored volunteer events during work hours, and (5) encourage employees to spearhead volunteer programs. These results are displayed in Table 4.7. Less frequently reported methods of engaging employees in community outreach initiatives included allowing employees to take a leave of absence to work for a volunteer organization or to help in relief efforts (33 percent), soliciting employee input when selecting or revising volunteer programs (31 percent), reflecting volunteer participation in performance reviews (16 percent), and providing paid leave for employees who participate in volunteer events (not company-sponsored) after work hours on their own time (11 percent).

Community outreach programs that engage employees can create passionate support for the organization's sustainability

Table 4.7. Top Five Methods of Involving or Engaging Employees

Method	Percentage
Recognize employee participation in volunteer programs	67 percent
Provide company-sponsored volunteer events after work hours (or on weekends)	48 percent
Encourage senior management to participate in volunteer programs	46 percent
Provide company-sponsored volunteer events during work hours	45 percent
Encourage employees to spearhead volunteer programs	44 percent

Note: $n = 330$. Excludes organizations not engaging in sustainable workplace or business practices.

Source: *Advancing Sustainability: HR's Role* (SHRM, 2011).

efforts and translate sustainability-related values into action. One of the fundamental keys to employee engagement is actually listening to the workforce. It is one thing for an executive to say, "We are listening to our workforce," but quite another thing to actively carry out what the employees want. HR can help engage employees in sustainable workplace or business practices by implementing a process to facilitate capturing those "wants" and how to allow employees to participate in executing that process.

Socially responsible activities. Today many companies are aware that socially responsible activities can improve their image among a wide range of stakeholders, including employees, customers, investors, and local communities. Socially responsible practices can include a broad range of activities, which can result in a more favorable image for a company while positively affecting its competitiveness and bottom line. Companies were asked in which socially responsible activities they participated. The top five reported practices were (1) donating/collecting money for local charities, (2) donating/collecting money for natural disasters, (3) supporting the community through company-sponsored volunteer projects, (4) considering the overall social impact of business decisions, and (5) partnering with environmentally friendly suppliers/companies. These results are displayed in Table 4.8.

Table 4.8. Participation in Socially Responsible Activities Related to Sustainability

Activities	Percentage
Donate/collect money for local charities	77 percent
Donate/collect money for natural disasters (for example, South-Asian tsunami, Hurricane Katrina, earthquakes)	58 percent
Support the community through company-sponsored volunteer projects	58 percent
Consider the overall social impact of business decisions	47 percent
Partner with environmentally friendly suppliers/companies	47 percent
Monitor the impact of business on the environment	46 percent
Partner with women- or minority-owned suppliers/companies	35 percent
Cause marketing/branding (aligning product or company marketing with a particular social cause)	29 percent
Monitor global fair labor standards/practices (such as child labor regulations, working conditions)	17 percent
Track sources of global raw materials/suppliers	11 percent

Note: n = 410. Percentages do not total 100 percent due to multiple response options. Excludes organizations not engaging in sustainable workplace or business practices.

Source: *Advancing Sustainability: HR's Role* (SHRM, 2011).

Other less frequently cited activities included monitoring the impact of business on the environment (46 percent), partnering with women- or minority-owned suppliers/companies (35 percent), cause marketing/branding (29 percent), monitoring global fair labor standards/practices (17 percent), and tracking sources of global raw materials/suppliers (11 percent).

Environmentally responsible practices. There is growing recognition that going green is not just good for the environment, but also can help the bottom line and be used as a means to engage employees. Respondents were asked to report the environmentally responsible activities that support their organizations' sustainable workplace practices. The top ten practices identified were (1) offering recycling program for office products (86 percent), (2) using virtual tools to conduct meetings (81 percent), (3) donating/discounting used office furniture (71 percent), (4) using energy-efficient lighting systems and equipment (69 percent), (5) partnering with environmentally friendly suppliers/companies (61 percent), (6) buying or leasing refurbished goods (59 percent), (7) encouraging employees to power down computers after a few minutes of inactivity (58 percent), (8) installing automatic shutoffs for equipment (58 percent), (9) minimizing water consumption by using water-conserving plumbing fixtures (53 percent), and (10) using supplies and materials more efficiently (55 percent). These and other less frequently cited environmentally responsible practices are displayed in Table 4.9.

As evidenced by the results, green practices have become mainstream and almost universal. The tools and resources are well-established, with many best practices to draw upon. However, if an organization's efforts are viewed as "greenwashing," primarily as a PR effort, or a practice that does not fit the culture, employees are unlikely to be engaged. To engage all levels of employees, employees need to be provided many examples of how what they do on a daily basis helps to meet the triple bottom line: people, profits and the environment/community.

Tracking and Measuring Sustainability Outcomes

Organizations should establish some performance metrics to measure the effectiveness of their sustainability initiatives. Determining a return on investment (ROI) from these initiatives is not easy, but it is not impossible to achieve. Still, only 39 percent of businesses reported calculating an ROI for their sustainability efforts. Among organizations calculating an ROI, 47 percent calculated a positive return on investment, 46 percent reported it was still too early to determine their ROI, 6 percent calculated a break-even point, and no organizations reported calculating a negative ROI.

Organizations were asked to identify the positive outcomes of their organizations' sustainability initiatives. The most frequently reported outcomes were (1) improved employee morale, (2)

Table 4.9. Environmentally Responsible Practices

Environmentally Responsible Practices	Percentage
Offering recycling program for office products	86 percent
Using virtual tools to conduct meetings	81 percent
Donating/discounting used office furniture	71 percent
Using energy-efficient lighting systems and equipment	69 percent
Partnering with environmentally friendly suppliers/ companies	61 percent
Buying or leasing refurbished goods	59 percent
Encouraging employees to power down computers after a few minutes of inactivity	58 percent
Installing automatic shutoff for equipment	58 percent
Using supplies and materials more efficiently	55 percent
Minimizing water consumption by using water-conserving plumbing fixtures	53 percent
Encouraging/promoting/providing car pooling for employees	49 percent
Minimizing pollution	46 percent
Promoting walking, biking, taking public transit instead of driving a vehicle	45 percent
Salvaging or reusing construction materials	39 percent
Selecting a location with public transit access	32 percent
Offering employees telecommuting to reduce environmental impact of commuting	36 percent
Offering incentives to employees for the use of mass transit	29 percent
Using recycled materials in the construction or remodeling of your building	26 percent
Buying hybrid vehicles for your fleets	15 percent
Buying alternative energy	11 percent
Installing solar panels on roof	9 percent
Buying carbon offsets	7 percent
Community garden where employees can grow their own produce	4 percent
Offering incentives to employees for the purchase of hybrid vehicles	4 percent
Using a green or living roof	4 percent

Note: ns = 364–395. Percentages do not total 100 percent due to multiple response options. Excludes organizations not engaging in sustainable workplace or business practices.

Source: *Advancing Sustainability: HR's Role* (SHRM, 2011).

Table 4.10. Positive Outcomes of Sustainability Initiatives

Positive Outcomes	Percentages
Improved employee morale	55 percent
More efficient business processes	43 percent
Stronger public image	43 percent
Increased employee loyalty	38 percent
Increased brand recognition	34 percent
Increased consumer/customer confidence	34 percent
Increased employee retention	33 percent
Position as an employer of choice	27 percent
Positive financial bottom line	25 percent
Increased workforce productivity	21 percent
Increased recruitment of top employees	17 percent
Improved product portfolio	13 percent
Other	2 percent

Note: n = 343. Percentages do not total 100 percent due to multiple response options. Excludes organizations not engaging in sustainable workplace or business practices.

Source: *Advancing Sustainability: HR's Role* (SHRM, 2011).

more efficient business processes, (3) stronger public image, (4) increased employee loyalty, (5) increased brand recognition, (6) increased consumer/customer confidence, (7) increased employee retention, (8) position as an employer of choice, (9) positive financial bottom line, and (10) increased workforce productivity (Table 4.10). Less frequently cited outcomes were increased recruitment of top employees (17 percent) and improved product portfolio (13 percent).

Barriers to Engaging in Sustainability

Organizations that do not engage in sustainable workplace or business practices reported the obstacles preventing them from implementing a plan. The top five obstacles were (1) costs of launching, (2) difficulty in measuring the return on investment, (3) lack of support from organization's leaders, (4) costs of main-

Table 4.11. Top Five Obstacles Preventing Organization from Utilizing Sustainable Workplace or Business Practices

Obstacles	Percentage
Costs of launching	38 percent
Difficult to measure the return on investment	35 percent
Lack of support from organization's leaders	34 percent
Costs of maintaining	31 percent
Lack of internal capacity or knowledge	30 percent

Note: n = 369. Excludes organizations engaging in sustainable workplace or business practices.

Source: *Advancing Sustainability: HR's Role* (SHRM, 2011).

taining, and (5) lack of internal capacity or knowledge. These results are displayed in Table 4.11. Other less frequently reported obstacles included: sustainably practices detract from primary business goals (21 percent), such practices are not yet mainstream, so there is no business advantage (18 percent), lack of interest among employees (14 percent), lack of shareholder support (5 percent), lack of interest among customers (4 percent), and lack of technological support (4 percent).

Sustainability is an issue that affects organizations in many ways. It affects an organization's culture, priorities, and the framework in which decisions are made. By ignoring sustainability, companies are missing an opportunity to broaden their scope of influence and may damage their brand equity. Companies that indicated they did not engage in sustainability were asked whether they had plans to launch any workplace or business practices within the next twelve months. The vast majority of companies reported they were not sure (43 percent) or had no plans to move into this area (52 percent). Of this group, only 5 percent of firms reported they had plans to launch sustainability initiatives within the next year.

Conclusions

An assortment of factors shape how organizations are looking at sustainability and the impact sustainability has on them. This report surveyed organizations to determine the impact sustainability has on areas of the business and examined companies from Stanford University Medical Center to Pfizer that utilize the potential of sustainability. How organizations think about what sustainability means for them varies based on many factors. Multinational organizations tend to think of sustainability in global terms, while smaller organizations can also make sustainability a priority with their efforts and activities focused locally. Understanding the factors that make sustainability work is the key to any company engaged in sustainability focused activities.

This research found that the human resource function is one of the key groups responsible for implementing a sustainability strategy in organizations. This is not surprising since sustainability is a people issue, which is important in shaping the organization's behavior and culture. It is for these and other reasons that the HR profession is and will continue to be an important component in the emergence and evolution of sustainability.

Bibliography

Baumgartner, R. J., & Ebner, D. (2010). Corporate sustainability strategies: Sustainability profiles and maturity levels. *Sustainable Development, 18*, 76–89.

Ciegis, R., Ramanauskiene, J., & Martinkus, B. (2009). The concept of sustainable development and its use for sustainability scenarios. *Inzinerine Ekonomika-Engineering Economics, 2*, 28–37.

Chiesa, V., Manzini, R., & Noci, G. (1999). Towards a sustainable view of the competitive system. *Long Range Planning, 32*, 519–530.

Dow Jones Sustainability Indexes. (2011). *Corporate sustainability.* Retrieved from www.sustainability-index.com/07_htmle/sustainability/corpsustainability.html.

Faber, N., Jorna, R. J., & Van Engelen, J. (2005). The sustainability of "sustainability": A study into the conceptual foundations of the notion of "sustainability." *Journal of Environmental Assessment Policy and Management, 7*, 1–33.

Grinde, J., & Khare, A. (2008). The ant, the grasshopper, and Schrodinger's cat: An exploration of concepts of sustainability. *Journal of Environmental Assessment Policy and Management, 10*, 115–141.

Hahn, T., Figge, F., Pinkse, J., & Preuss, L. (2010, May). Trade-offs in corporate sustainability: You can't have your cake and eat it. *Business Strategy and the Environment, 19*(4), 217–229.

Kiewiet, D. J., & Vos, J. F. J. (2007). Organizational sustainability: A case for formulating a tailor-made definition. *Journal of Environmental Assessment Policy and Management, 9,* 1–18.

Orlitzky, M., Schmidt, F. L., & Rynes, S. L. (2003). Corporate social and financial performance: A meta-analysis. *Organizational Studies, 24,* 403–441.

Scerri, A., & James, P. (2010). Accounting for sustainability: Combining qualitative and quantitative research in developing "indicators" of sustainability. *International Journal of Social Research Methodology, 13,* 41–53.

SHRM. (2010, June). *2010 employee job satisfaction: A survey report by SHRM.* Alexandria, VA: Society for Human Resource Management.

SHRM. (2011). *Advancing sustainability: HR's role.* Alexandria, VA: Society for Human Resource Management.

Tenuta, P. (2010). The measurement of sustainability. *Review of Business Research, 10,* 163–171.

United Nations. (1992). *The Rio declaration on environment and development.* Rio de Janeiro, Brazil.

Theoretical and Empirical Foundations to Guide Environmental Initiatives

The chapters in Part Two inform readers by describing recent empirical research intended to deepen our understanding of employee behaviors that arise in organizations pursuing environmental sustainability.

Chapter 5, "Employee Green Behaviors," by Deniz Ones and Stephan Dilchert, describes a model of employee green behaviors and summarizes empirical efforts that investigate the criterion domain of environmentally sustainable work performance. The chapter presents a taxonomy of environmentally friendly/destructive behaviors that employees engage in at work, describes the studies that were conducted to create the taxonomy, and discusses prevalence rates for behaviors in the taxonomy.

Chapter 6, "Demographic Characteristics and Employee Sustainability," by Rachael Klein, Susan D'Mello, and Brenton

Wiernik, summarizes research relating to the influence of demographic variables on individuals' sustainability attitudes, values, and behaviors. Findings from work settings are highlighted. The chapter can help human resource managers and practitioners understand how an employee's gender, age, educational level, and socioeconomic status may influence his or her environmentally relevant workplace behavior.

Chapter 7, titled "The Role of Commitment in Bridging the Gap Between Organizational Sustainability and Environmental Sustainability," by Jessica Mesmer-Magnus, Chockalingam Viswesvaran, and Brenton Wiernik, provides insights into the links between employee commitment and environmental sustainability. Different forms of commitment and sustainability are distinguished. The important role of employee commitment to organizationally sponsored sustainability initiatives (for example, green management programs, environmental sustainability initiatives, and so forth) are highlighted. Suggestions for engaging employees in environmental sustainability initiatives are provided.

Chapter 8, "Measuring and Improving Environmental Sustainability," by Stephan Dilchert and Deniz Ones, discusses the means by which environmental sustainability has been and can be measured at the individual and organizational levels. Several factors that can influence environmental outcomes for individuals, organizations, and economies are described, and the authors also provide a brief review of the effectiveness of various interventions for producing pro-environmental behavior.

Chapter 9, "Creating and Maintaining Environmentally Sustainable Organizations: Recruitment and On-Boarding," by Talya Bauer, Berrin Erdogan, and Sully Taylor, provides an overview of research and practice related to the issue of how recruitment and socialization can be used to facilitate the pursuit of environmental sustainability. Through their recruitment practices, employers can obtain the skills, attitudes, and behaviors needed to achieve their environmental goals, while also building their reputations. Subsequently, on-boarding activities and appropriate performance management practices can help further strengthen employees' understanding of and commitment to environmental sustainability. Based on their review of research and current practices,

Bauer, Erdogan, and Taylor provide useful checklists for effective recruitment and on-boarding in organizations striving for environmental sustainability.

Chapter 10, "Leadership and Environmental Sustainability," by Ellen Van Velsor and Laura Quinn, discusses the role of individual and collective beliefs and leadership practices for creating and sustaining environmentally responsible organizations. Individual and collective beliefs and leadership practices are viewed as key elements of organizational cultures that serve to establish the organization's direction, alignment, and commitment to sustainability. To foster an improved understanding of how to create an organizational culture that facilitates sustainable operations, products, and services, Van Velsor and Quinn explain some of the unique challenges associated with sustainability efforts, summarize and integrate recent conceptual frameworks, and describe findings from the Center for Creative Leadership's recent research.

CHAPTER FIVE

Employee Green Behaviors

Deniz S. Ones
and Stephan Dilchert

Environmental sustainability is a top-of-mind issue among organizational leaders (World Economic Forum, 2009), the world's scientists (National Academies of the G8+5, 2009), and the general population (National Geographic and Globescan, 2009). Yet, we know little about what constitutes environmentally friendly behaviors in occupational settings. Around the world, policymakers and organizations are trying to define and understand what it means to encourage and sustain a green workforce. Organizations are increasingly focusing on the "triple bottom line," recognizing the interconnectedness of economic performance (profits), people (social performance), and environmental performance (cf. Elkington, 1998). Strategic management concepts such as "embedded sustainability" highlight the benefits, virtues, and vitality of incorporating environmental, health, and social

Some of our research summarized in this chapter was supported by the Small Grants Program of the Society for Industrial and Organizational Psychology and a PSC-CUNY Award, jointly funded by the Professional Staff Congress and the City University of New York. We would like to thank the following individuals for their generous help in collecting data that contributed to research on the Green Five taxonomy: Brenton Wiernik, Rachael Klein, Susan D'Mello, Lauren Hill, and Sarah Semmel.

values into core business activities without compromising economic outcomes.

A better understanding of what constitutes environmentally friendly behaviors is essential at all stages of human resource management. In order to train workers for environmentally responsible performance, we need to first examine what such performance entails. In order to select new employees who will display environmentally sustainable behaviors, we need to know which individual characteristics relate to such behaviors. In order to manage organizational workforces, we need to know the nature of behaviors that lead to or detract from environmental sustainability.

The overall objective of this chapter is to describe individual variability in employee behaviors that relate to environmental sustainability in work settings. To achieve this goal, we first define a broad category of behaviors that we have come to refer to as employee green behaviors. Second, we then detail a taxonomy of employee green behaviors that is intended to describe the content of employee green behavior categories and define a construct of individual level environmental sustainability in work settings. Third, we address the connections between employee green behaviors and models of individual level performance. Fourth, we offer guidance on how the framework presented in this chapter can be used in human resources management practice and research applications. We conclude by addressing construct validity questions about the model of employee green behaviors.

Employee Green Behaviors Defined

Although individual behaviors that impact the environment have been studied by environmental psychologists for over half a century (such as littering, polluting, recycling, conserving, petitioning the government for environmental causes, use of public transportation), there has been little effort directed at studying such behaviors in work settings. Rather, environmental sustainability in work settings has mostly been studied at the *organizational* level. Yet, individuals working for the same organization differ in terms of their environmentally responsible behaviors. Even employees who perform the same job differ (that is, performance variability exists among them). Understanding how and why employees differ in terms of their behaviors that have an environmental impact should be of concern to organizations aiming to operate in environmentally sustainable ways, to societies at large aiming to address environmental problems, and ultimately to humanity aiming to sustain itself on this planet.

Regrettably, the handful of research studies and applications on environmental sustainability that have ventured from studying such behaviors in personal lives to studying them in work lives have focused on very specific applications (for example, Can we pay employees to take public transportation?) as well as only particular aspects of environmental sustainability (for example, participation in corporate recycling). Yet, these are single-item indicators of broader categories of environmental sustainability behaviors. Such single indicators may be too unreliable and too narrowly focused to be of use in building a scientific understanding of environmental sustainability behaviors of individuals. An overly specific definitional focus and idiosyncratic measures of pro-environmental behavior can hinder scientific understanding, knowledge accumulation, and useful prescriptions for application.

Each individual behavior directed at environmental sustainability should be a manifestation of general environmental sustainability among individuals. Employee green behaviors are defined as "scalable actions and behaviors that employees engage in that are linked with and contribute to or detract from environmental sustainability."

There are four features of this definition that should be highlighted. First, the focus is on *employees*. The enactors of green behaviors are employees and not organizations. Certainly, there is value in describing and modeling *organizational* variability in terms of environmental sustainability performance. However, our definition is directed at specifying a behavioral domain where there is *individual* variability. Members of the same organization display differences in their environmentally relevant behaviors. Organizational initiatives and actions stem from employees: organizational leaders institute organizational policies; organizational initiatives, including environmental initiatives, originate from employees and decision-makers. All organizational actions with an impact on environmental sustainability can be traced to organizational members. It is not the organization that acts or behaves, but rather it is employees who do.

Second, the definition of employee green behaviors presented here focuses on what employees actually *do* in connection with their activities at work. By focusing on actions and behaviors, the definition excludes outcomes and consequences that are not under the control of the employee. Environmental consequences of behaviors can be influenced to a great degree by the actions and behaviors of other employees and actions of a variety of groups (such as teams or departments), as well as external stakeholders (such as communities or governments), among others. Any definition of employee green behaviors should only include behaviors and outcomes under individuals' control; employees' green behaviors should reflect their own behavior.

Third, the definition specifies s*calable* actions and behaviors. That is, behaviors should be *measurable* in terms of their contribution to the goal of environmental sustainability. Different employees contribute at different levels to environmental sustainability goals. Employee green behaviors are synonymous with employee green performance and thus require an evaluative statement about the proficiency of each employee in relation to environmental sustainability. How much does a given employee contribute to environmental sustainability goals? This is a legitimate question that can be answered by assessing employee behaviors.

Fourth, the definition explicitly recognizes that not all behaviors that impact the environment are beneficial. Employee behaviors can also cause environmental harm, which reflects the well-recognized "dark side" of the construct. Both *beneficial* and *harmful behaviors* are included in the construct defined here. Employees can engage in behaviors that help the environment (for example, invent and use eco-friendly products, conserve energy) or they can refrain from engaging in such environmentally friendly acts. They can also actively perform actions that harm the environment (pollute, destroy ecosystems). By including both beneficial and harmful behaviors, the employee green behaviors spectrum encompasses: (1) engaging in helpful behaviors versus refraining from them, as well as (2) engaging in harmful behaviors versus refraining from them. This is a distinction that recognizes that both behaviors that need to be proactively pursued as well as those that need to be inhibited contribute to environmental sustainability.

Two features of the definition are notable by their absence. First, the definition does not specify whether the behaviors included are job or role behaviors (Ilgen & Hollenbeck, 1991). Employee green behaviors can be undertaken as part of tasks that employees perform in their organizationally sanctioned roles. Employee green behaviors can also be undertaken outside of formal duties and responsibilities, but in work settings nonetheless. Note that the absence of the job/role distinction means that employee green behaviors are not limited to green jobs (Milano, 2009). We will return to this point later in this chapter when we discuss employee green behaviors in light of existing models of job performance. The generality of the roles and jobs that the definition applies to has another consequence. Clearly, employee green behaviors are not limited only to green industries either.

Second, organizational goals are not an explicit feature of the definition. For organizations to be viable in the long term, environmental sustainability must necessarily be included as one of their goals. This is not only a value-driven, but also a logic-driven argument: If humanity does not survive in the face of resource shortages (for example, clean water and food supplies for nine billion individuals by 2050; see U.N. Department of Economic and Social Affairs, 2004) and environmental calamities (such as climate change and destruction of ecosystems), no organization will remain. Logically then, attaining the triple bottom line (economic, social, and environmental performance) should be among the goals of all business organizations. It is exceedingly clear that focusing only on economic performance can detract from environmental performance and therefore the long-term sustainability of organizations. Thus, when employees behave in ways that contribute to environmental sustainability, they directly or indirectly contribute to the organization's triple bottom line and hence to organizational sustainability.

A Content-Based Model of Employee Green Behavior: The Green Five Taxonomy

For most people, environmentally friendly behaviors start and end with the 3Rs. "Reduce, reuse, recycle" are important, but do not encompass the entire spectrum of green behaviors at work.

A taxonomy is essential for any behavioral domain before it can be better understood, modeled, and modified. In this vein, a taxonomy of employee green behaviors illuminates what it means to be green at work. It provides a framework of positive and negative employee behaviors that have an impact on the environment.

Over the past three years, we, along with our students and colleagues (Ones, 2011; Ones & Dilchert, 2009; 2010; Hill, Ones, Dilchert, Wiernik, Klein, & D'Mello, 2011), have built a taxonomy of employee green behaviors. This taxonomy is a model of classifying employee green behaviors into psychologically meaningful, functionally similar categories. Within the taxonomy, broader categories are successively organized further into substantively more homogeneous clusters, creating a multi-tiered, hierarchical model. At the apex of the hierarchy of employee green behaviors is "general green performance" (that is, general environmental sustainability performance at the individual employee level). Below this, major behavioral categories of employee green behaviors are (1) Working Sustainably, (2) Avoiding Harm, (3) Conserving, (4) Influencing Others, and (5) Taking Initiative. These meta-categories are subsumed under general green performance. In turn, each subsumes more finely distinguished categories.

The model was built in three stages. In the *development* phase, 1,299 critical incidents were obtained from 274 interviews with individuals holding 189 different types of jobs in 157 organizations across twenty U.S. industries. A modified critical incidents methodology was used. Employees were asked to describe behaviors they had observed co-workers perform that had an impact on the environment (either negatively or positively). The critical incidents were content analyzed and sorted by multiple raters following standard critical incidents approaches (Anderson & Wilson, 1997). Emerging categories of behaviors were then subjected to *confirmation* for their usefulness in correctly categorizing an entirely new set of critical incidents. For this purpose, 773 new critical incidents were obtained from 133 interviews with individuals holding ninety-seven different types of jobs in ninety-two organizations across sixteen U.S. industries. Finally, the *cross-cultural relevance and generalizability* of the resulting categories was tested using similar critical incidents data from Europe (Hill, Ones, Dilchert, Wiernik, Klein, & D'Mello, 2011).

The European critical incidents database contained 1,002 critical incidents, obtained from 208 interviews with individuals holding eighty-six different types of jobs in seventy organizations across fifteen industries. Fourteen European countries were represented in the sample: Belgium, Bulgaria, Czech Republic, Denmark, England, Finland, France, Germany, Greece, Ireland, Italy, Norway, Sweden, and Turkey.

These efforts led to sixteen functionally distinguishable behavioral categories with relatively homogeneous content. Across the three tests of the model (development, confirmation, and generalization), these categories could be successfully grouped into the five basic meta-categories.

The Green Five Taxonomy is depicted in Figure 5.1. To illustrate the range of employee green behaviors and their psychological meaning, we will describe each of the categories in turn.

Conserving

The functional core of this meta-category is avoiding wastefulness and thus preserving resources. This includes preservation of a wide spectrum of resources: water, energy, gas, and other natural resources. The psychological meaning of the meta-category can be described in terms of frugality or thrift. The category encompasses behaviors that have traditionally been described as the 3Rs (reduce, reuse, recycle). As De Young (1993) has stated, "a sustainable planet is not possible without patterns of conserving behavior" (p. 485), and employees' conserving behaviors contribute to sustaining the planet as well. Employees' conserving behaviors can further be distinguished into *Reducing Use, Reusing, Repurposing,* and *Recycling.* These behaviors aimed at minimizing waste can be further organized hierarchically

Figure 5.1. The Green Five Taxonomy

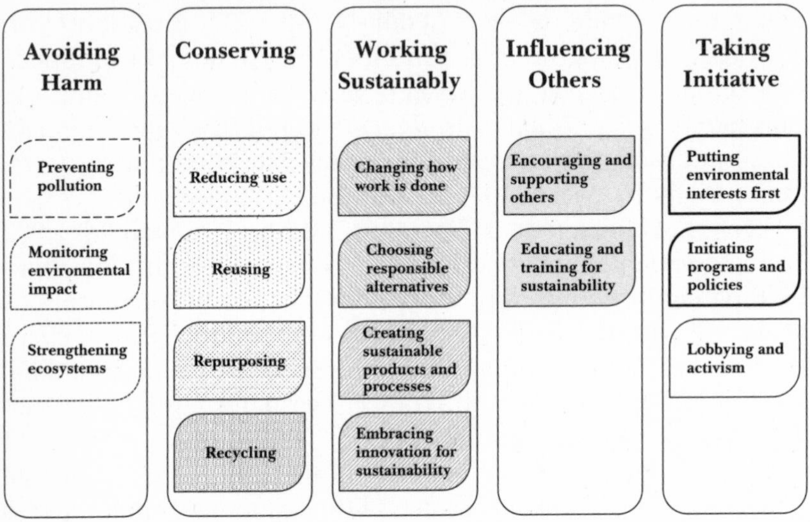

Avoiding Harm	Conserving	Working Sustainably	Influencing Others	Taking Initiative
Preventing pollution	Reducing use	Changing how work is done	Encouraging and supporting others	Putting environmental interests first
Monitoring environmental impact	Reusing	Choosing responsible alternatives	Educating and training for sustainability	Initiating programs and policies
Strengthening ecosystems	Repurposing	Creating sustainable products and processes		Lobbying and activism
	Recycling	Embracing innovation for sustainability		

according to their contribution to environmental sustainability. Across our three examinations of over three thousand critical incidents, employees appear to engage in these four major categories of conserving behaviors at differential rates. Table 5.1 lists these facets of Conserving and other components of the remaining Green Five meta-factors. The table provides example behaviors for each category, both positive (those that benefit environmental sustainability and need to be proactively pursued) and negative (those that negatively impact the environment and need to be inhibited).

Reducing the use of resources is the most responsible way to conserve, because it minimizes initial environmental impact. Reusing also reduces environmental impact, as it involves using the same resources or materials multiple times, rather than disposing of them after a single use. Repurposing, on the other hand, refers to using the same resources or materials multiple times for purposes other than those originally intended. Finally, recycling conserves the least resources and can only mitigate environmental impact, because it requires additional energy, raw materials, and the like (including fuel for transportation) and

Table 5.1. The Green Five Taxonomy and Examples of Positive and Negative Behaviors in Each Category

Green Five Category	Examples of Positive Incidents	Examples of Negative Incidents
Conserving		
Reducing use	Turning off lights when not needed; printing double sided	Using water excessively; leaving machinery running when not in use
Reusing	Reusing disposable plastic products	Relying on single-use, disposable products
Repurposing	Using modern garbage incinerator to heat building; diverting used cooking oil to make biodiesel	Throwing out surplus material that could be used for something else
Recycling	Recycling cans, bottles, paper	Failing to recycle (or separate trash) despite available containers
Working Sustainably		
Choosing responsible alternatives	Purchasing non-disposable equipment or supplies; using eco-friendly chemicals or natural ingredients in productions	Using raw materials from unsustainable sources
Changing how work is done	Optimizing shipping program to reduce air shipments	Knowingly relying on a work process that is not environmentally sustainable
Creating sustainable products and processes	Designing *new* product to substitute for environmentally unfriendly one; developing *new* manufacturing process with less environmental impact	

Continued

Table 5.1. Continued

Green Five Category	Examples of Positive Incidents	Examples of Negative Incidents
Embracing innovation for sustainability	Choosing virtual meetings (videoconferencing, online collaboration) instead of travel; purchasing hybrid cars for company	Insisting on computer printouts where paperless options are available
Avoiding Harm		
Pollution	Upgrading sewer collection system to prevent overflow and contamination of drinking water; treating hazardous waste properly	Improperly disposing of paint, oils, and other hazardous substances; contaminating soil by dumping harmful chemicals
Monitoring environmental impact	Monitoring emissions from operations; regularly testing groundwater and soil for contamination	Failing to follow up on cleanup effort after an accident or negative event
Strengthening ecosystems	Planting a "living roof" on a factory building; maintaining wildlife area around work facilities	Clear cutting unnecessarily
Influencing Others		
Educating and training for sustainability	Hiring a sustainability education coordinator; participating in courses on proper chemical handling	

Table 5.1. Continued

Green Five Category	Examples of Positive Incidents	Examples of Negative Incidents
Encouraging and supporting	Encouraging carpooling and providing benefit for it; asking co-workers to dress warmly instead of using space heaters	
Taking Initiative		
Initiating programs and policies	Starting a new environmental program; instituting a policy on reduced energy use	Stopping an environmental program for business reasons
Lobbying and activism	Pushing organization to disclose environmental record; arguing for environmental issues on board	
Putting environmental interests first	Not using air conditioners on hot days; turning down an environmentally unfriendly project	Not being willing to compromise own comfort or convenience to reduce energy or resource use

Note: Positive and negative examples of employee green behaviors are based on several critical incidents data collections described in the text. Missing examples in a given category are not an indication that such behaviors do not occur in work settings, but rather that illustrative examples for these categories were not reported in the interviews we conducted.

processing before resources can be recovered for further use. Hence, reducing use is the most desirable, and recycling the least desirable and environmentally sustainable option among Conserving categories.

About half of all behavioral incidents we have gathered through our research fall into the Conserving meta-factor. Interestingly, this was the case both in data originating from Europe and the U.S. Reducing use, followed by recycling, was by far the most frequently reported conserving behavior in both parts of the world.

Working Sustainably

This meta-category relates to the behaviors employees engage in to enhance the environmental sustainability of work products and processes. Naturally, these behaviors include performance on tasks that are job-specific (for example, an architect designing a building with low environmental impact), as well as those that contribute to organizational purpose and functioning more broadly (for example, an employee who redesigns a shipping program to reduce air shipments). The functional core of this meta-category involves adapting work products and processes to minimize their negative impact on the environment; its psychological core is adaptability.

There are two fundamental ways in which work can be adapted to make it more environmentally sustainable: (1) by focusing on currently available products and processes and (2) by creating, innovating, and adopting innovations. The four behavioral subcategories of Working Sustainably can be organized around these two themes. Both Choosing Responsible Alternatives and Changing How Work Is Done encompass employee behaviors that relate to existing products and processes. In the former case, employees choose environmentally friendlier products and processes among alternatives that are available to them. The latter refers to introducing a change to the way work is conducted to make it more environmentally friendly. The remaining two components of Working Sustainably go beyond simply changing products and processes by employing or creating something new: Creating Sustainable Products and Processes and Embracing Innovation for

Sustainability describe employee behaviors that involve creating, innovating, and adopting innovations that have a positive impact or mitigate environmental harm.

There are many ways for employees to contribute to their organizations' environmental sustainability through work products and processes. This involves making responsible choices, optimizing processes currently in use, creating new products and processes, and embracing and adopting environmentally friendly innovations. All of these behaviors lead to products and processes that are more environmentally sustainable than the status quo. Table 5.1 provides examples of behaviors for these categories. Both in our American and European data, the bulk of behavioral exemplars for Working Sustainability involved Choosing Responsible Alternatives.

Avoiding Harm

The two categories of employee green behaviors described so far involve employees performing actions that reflect (1) frugality/ thrift and (2) adaptability. The third category of employee green behaviors can be characterized as involving avoidance and inhibition of negative environmental behaviors.

The category of Avoiding Harm can perhaps be best understood when we consider that most economic activities have an impact on the natural environment. Ideally, such impact is small or naturally reverses over time (for example, cutting a single tree to produce a product made from wood). However, many economic activities, and the employee behaviors that enable them, cause lasting damage to the environment that may not be not self-healing. The negative pole of this category includes behaviors that *harm* the environment by diminishing the health of the Earth's ecosystems and disrupting natural biological, chemical, and physical processes that help the planet recover from distress. Viewed from their positive pole, behaviors that *help* the environment enhance the health of the Earth's ecosystems and aid natural biological, chemical, and physical processes that help the planet recover from distress. The functional core of this category involves helping maintain a healthy planet. Thus, behaviors that support the prevention of long-term harm, such as those performed to monitor one's environmental impact or to reverse damage to ecosystems, are included. Our psychological understanding of these behaviors is tied to the distinction between harming versus helping. At the core of these damaging behaviors might be a lack of cautiousness and self-control as well as a lack of responsibility and integrity. On the other hand, helping the natural environment would likely involve both altruism and responsibility.

Most of the behaviors included in this meta-category involve Polluting/Preventing Pollution. Employees can pollute the environment or perform behaviors that prevent or minimize pollution as the result of their work. The other two components can be viewed as supporting this primary one: Monitoring Environmental Impact and Strengthening Ecosystems. The former pertains to employees' informal scanning of the environment and formal measuring of relevant environmental variables to assess potential damage caused by their work activities. The latter includes employee behaviors that aim to strengthen various ecosystems to make up for or protect against potential damages caused by economic, industrial, and organizational activities (see Table 5.1 for examples).

Influencing Others

Although each employee's individual behaviors and contributions are important when moving toward environmental sustainability goals, economies of scale are needed to achieve sizable impact. For the former three categories of employee green behaviors, economies of scale and multiplier effects are assumed to occur through summation of effects of individual behaviors across those employees who engage in them. This does not consider how environmental sustainability behaviors or their effects can be disseminated by employees. The fourth meta-category of Influencing Others focuses on employee behaviors aimed at spreading sustainability behaviors to other individuals. It is the only category of the Green Five with explicit social underpinnings. Thus, the functional core of this meta-category is to exert influence. The associated psychological processes involve disseminating knowledge and encouraging and aiding behavioral change in others.

Typical employee behaviors from this domain include teaching, mentoring, leading, encouraging, and supporting.

Influencing others to be more environmentally friendly and responsible requires both Educating and Training for Sustainability and Encouraging and Supporting environmentally sustainable behaviors (see Table 5.1 for examples). The former category focuses on behaviors that facilitate the acquisition of declarative and procedural knowledge, among others. The latter refers to behaviors that involve persuasion, encouragement, and support to increase the environmental sustainability of others' behaviors. These behaviors can also target the propagation of green behaviors beyond other employees to other stakeholders, such as customers and communities at large.

Taking Initiative

The last meta-category of the Green Five is a proactive, entrepreneurial domain that involves a certain level of personal risk or sacrifice. It includes behaviors that break the mold and go against societal expectations. Willingness to forego certain benefits or suffer potential negative consequences is inherent in these behaviors. Taking Initiative behaviors serve the function of rejecting the (unsustainable) status quo. Psychologically, individuals who take initiative can be viewed as change agents (Frohman, 1999). Unlike Influencing Others, behaviors included in Taking Initiative may or may not be social in nature. These behaviors can be directed at Avoiding Harm, Working Sustainably, or Conservation. As such, Taking Initiative can be considered an instrumental behavioral category (that is, they describe *how* employees go about initiating and promoting environmentally relevant behaviors that might, based on their content, fall into other categories).

The entrepreneurial aspect of this behavioral domain is manifested in its component Initiating Programs and Policies. The programs and policies employees might initiate can address any aspect of environmental sustainability or domain of employee green behaviors. Initiating a program or policy involves creating or developing a new venture and thus requires some degree of risk taking and willingness to sacrifice (money, resources, or effort, for example). Lobbying and Activism is another behavioral cluster that is part of Taking Initiative. These behaviors involve standing up for environmental causes. Again, an element of risk is involved as Lobbying and Activism intends to change the status quo towards increased sustainability, without necessarily considering all possible outcomes to employees themselves. Overcoming organizational inertia and bucking the status quo requires courage. Putting Environmental Interests First is the third and final behavioral cluster of the Green Five Taking Initiative meta-factor. Behaviors that define Putting Environmental Interests First require self-sacrifice in the interest of the environment (for example, turning down profitable but harmful projects, inconveniencing oneself for an environmental benefit). Table 5.1 again provides examples of some relevant behavioral clusters.

The Green Five taxonomy described above is built on empirical evidence that the meta-categories and their components are conceptually distinguishable from one another. The similarity or dissimilarity of behavior content in terms of operational and psychological function is the driving force behind the established categories. However, measurement of the relevant behaviors among employees in organizational settings has led us to conclude that in most organizations, some of the Green Five categories are substantially correlated and thus give rise to a general green performance factor. Data from both self-reports and supervisory ratings have supported this notion (Dilchert & Ones, 2011). Yet, the Green Five and their components are correlated far from perfectly, raising the potential that employees can differentially contribute to environmental sustainability in organizations. However, those employees who successfully perform behaviors across the entire taxonomy are likely to contribute more to environmental sustainability than individuals who are less uniform in their behavioral engagement.

Uses of the Green Five Taxonomy in Human Resource Management

The Green Five Taxonomy offers an initial nomenclature to industrial and organizational psychologists and human resource practitioners that can be utilized by different users and for a variety of purposes. Having achieved more clarity about the behavioral domain of employee green behaviors, subsequent work can identify antecedent attributes (individual and situational) and the processes by which environmentally friendly behaviors can be promulgated throughout organizations. That is, the Green Five Taxonomy can be utilized to help organizations minimize their environmental impact and improve sustainability through recruitment, employee attraction, selection, training, performance management, and other HR interventions.

Uses in Recruitment

It has been firmly established that general corporate social responsibility (CSR) has a positive impact on employer attractiveness. Bauer, Erdogan, and Taylor (Chapter 9) summarize several surveys that indicate that CSR makes organizations more attractive to potential job applicants. They also point to several experimental studies that suggest that organizations' environmental stance might have a similar effect. However, field data on organizational environmental initiatives and employer attractiveness is sparse and has been discouraging so far. A survey conducted in 2003 among MBA students graduating from top U.S. and European business schools indicated that environmental sustainability was relatively low on their list of priorities (Montgomery & Ramus, 2007).

A more recent survey conducted among undergraduate business students in New Zealand (O'Rourke, 2010) investigated only the relative importance of environmental sustainability compared to organizational positions on diversity and community relations. In this survey, organizations' environmental concern was ranked slightly more highly in importance than diversity issues and notably higher than community relations. However, as issues of environmental sustainability are increasingly becoming top-of-mind issues among many global societies (National Geographic and Globescan, 2008, 2009), we can expect them to play an increasing role in employer attractiveness and thus organizational recruiting initiatives. Case studies of successful multinational corporations confirm this trend (Biga, Dilchert, McCance, Gibby, & Doyle, Chapter 17 in this volume; Deller, Schnieders, & Titzrath, Chapter 13 in this volume).

We postulate that environmental sustainability can play a more powerful role in recruiting efforts when organizations successfully link their own initiatives in this domain to job candidates' values and pro-environmental behaviors. People are attracted to employers who share values similar to their own (Highhouse, Hoffman, Greve, & Collins, 2002). However, it is difficult to communicate value congruence if organizations focus their green recruiting on *product-based* environmental initiatives (for example, by advertising the range of eco-friendly products they produce). Such a strategy might work to attract customers, but is less likely to persuade job seekers. Making an organization attractive from *the job applicant's point of view* means stressing environmental initiatives that are *people-based*. Opportunities to engage in different categories of the Green Five on the job may be differentially attractive to applicants. Furthermore, research on individual motives associated with Green Five behaviors (Klein, D'Mello, Ones, Dilchert, Hill, & Wiernik, 2010) can inform recruiting efforts as well.

Uses in Employee Selection

Organizations that intend to take an even more active pro-environmental stance might aim to not only align applicant preferences but actual work behaviors in this regard. Through applied personnel selection science, we can identify job candidates who are more likely to display high levels of job performance once hired. Industrial psychology has a long tradition of maximizing task performance, citizenship, or minimizing counterproductive behaviors of individuals hired in this way. When choosing and validating the correct assessment tools to serve as predictors in applied settings, it is crucial to align individual differences, traits, and dimensions of job performance based on appropriate models of each domain (Campbell, 1990). "Success is a many-faceted thing, and we need to relate the predictors to the different facets of success. This is a complex task and one not easy of fulfillment" (Thorndike, 1960, as cited in Dunnette, 1963). Our field has established those models for most predictor (such as cogntive abilities and personality, for example; cf. Ones, Dilchert, & Viswesvaran, 2012; Ones, Dilchert, Viswesvaran, & Judge, 2007) and performance domains (cf. Campbell, McCloy, Oppler, & Sager, 1993; Hoffman & Dilchert, 2012). These models have enabled progress both in terms of cumulating empirical knowledge on predictor-criterion relationships as well as applied prediction of employee behavior (Hogan & Holland, 2003).

The Green Five Taxonomy provides such a framework for the performance domain of employee green behaviors. With its help, we can conduct research on antecedents of specific dimensions of green performance and match them to existing predictors as well as develop new tools for their prediction. Those organizations willing to integrate environmental sustainability goals into the hiring process beyond simple recruiting can promote an environmentally friendly workforce by selecting employees who are more inclined to engage in the relevant behaviors on their own accord. Such HR interventions do not need to come at the cost of those targeted at maximizing core task performance (see Johnson & Miller, Chapter 14). We predict that, in the near future, more organizations will add components to their hiring processes that explicitly test for alignment with their respective environmental missions.

Uses in Motivating and Engaging Employees

The Green Five and the behavioral categories they encompass will also be helpful in identifying areas of employee green behaviors that could benefit from motivational interventions. With the help of the taxonomy, workforce surveys can determine the employee green behavior areas employees are least motivated in or where they perceive the largest roadblocks to incorporating environmental sustainability into their job routines. In addition, research has begun to explore how different motives determine positive and negative performance in each of the categories (Klein, D'Mello, Ones, Dilchert, Hill, & Wiernik, 2010; Klein, Ones, Dilchert, & Wiernik, 2011). As discussed above, the psychological processes that underlie performance in each category are different and subject to empirical identification. Hence, parallel to personnel selection, motivational interventions can be designed that selectively target sustainability areas that represent either priorities or current organizational weaknesses. Knowledge that links the Green Five and motivational information will be tremendously useful to organizations that are planning to design targeted interventions for their current workforce.

Uses in Employee Appraisals and Development

Regardless of whether performance appraisals are conducted for developmental (for example, training, feedback) or administrative purposes (for example, to determine salary increases, promotion, retention), measurement of employee performance must be grounded in established taxonomies of performance components. Identifying individual employees' strengths and weaknesses in terms of environmental performance, as well as conducting normative comparisons across different contributors, is only possible if our appraisal tools follow a framework that reflects the actual structure of employee green behaviors. Especially when providing developmental feedback, appraisals need to be framed in terms of employee *behavior*, in order to identify concrete areas for potential improvement. The employee green behavior model we have presented here can enable the design of the appropriate appraisal tools and developmental aids.

Even though performance in different categories of green behaviors is likely to be correlated due to common antecedents (for example, personality, attitudes, knowledge), employees are unlikely to display a wholly uniform pattern across behavioral domains. When evaluating employees' green performance for administrative purposes, the use of standardized tools that measure individual dimensions of employee green behaviors will allow for more differentiated assessment. Moreover, such tools can be used to evaluate employees' standing quantitatively and normatively. This, in turn, allows HR to compare levels of relevant behaviors to job and organizational requirements and identify gaps that might be addressed through training interventions. Knowledge of green behaviors (both declarative and procedural) is a necessary (but not sufficient) condition for green performance. Like any knowledge-based training, training for employee green behaviors will require an understanding of what it is that employees need to be taught. The Green Five provide one framework for developing interventions to increase organizational environmental sustainability through employee training.

Organizational Benchmarking

Similar to needs assessment on the individual employee level, organizational benchmarking can be conducted to keep a pulse on how an organization is doing in terms of employee green behaviors in the aggregate. That is, rather than taking a bird's-eye view of the environmental sustainability of manufacturing or general operations (for example, *Newsweek* magazine's annual "Green Rankings"), we can take a bird's-eye view of the employees' perspective. On average, how green are employees of organization X? Are employees in location A performing more greenly than in location B? More importantly, how does organization X fare compared to organization Y, or perhaps its industry average? And if it is trailing behind, what areas in particular need improvement? These and other questions can be addressed through surveys and appraisal tools developed on the basis of the Green Five taxonomy, as illustrated by a case presented by Biga, Dilchert, McCance, Gibby, & Doyle in Chapter 17.

In sum, organizations can benefit exceedingly from employee green behaviors by predicting, encouraging, and measuring them through human resource interventions. However, based on our field's understanding and knowledge of HR interventions, we expect that such efforts will not be equally effective. Of course, some might be more successful or immediate in increasing employee green behaviors. More importantly, not all HR interventions are likely to be equally effective in increasing all aspects of employee green behaviors. This once more emphasizes the importance of understanding this new criterion domain in detail, in order to most optimally tailor our interventions based on specific organizational environmental sustainability needs, goals, and missions.

Responding to Questions About Employee Green Behaviors and the Green Five Taxonomy

In this section, we respond to a series of questions that relate to the nature of employee green behaviors and the behavioral clusters that constitute it. Our hope is to further clarify the meaning of the constructs involved and illuminate their nomological network. We pay particular attention to distinguishing employee green behaviors from already well-examined behavioral domains in I-O psychology (for example, citizenship behaviors).

Should Greenwashing Be Part of the Green Five Taxonomy?

Greenwashing is a practice that is described in the marketing literature as manipulation of public opinion about the environmental sustainability or "greenness" associated with certain products (Laufer, 2003; Ramus & Montiel, 2005). In greenwashing, an organization's representations with regard to its products, processes, or services are managed by deception, including tactics of confusion, to manipulate public perception of said products, processes, or services as environmentally friendly, or "green." One question that we have been asked in presenting our work is whether greenwashing might be an employee green behavior.

Employees can use the tactic of greenwashing (Laufer, 2003) to portray environmentally unfriendly behaviors as good or environmentally neutral, overemphasize the environmental benefits of neutral behaviors, or highlight the benefits of environmentally friendly behaviors to the exclusion of other benefits. All of these strategies involve deception. Therefore, in the domain of employee green behaviors, greenwashing can be thought of as analogous to "faking" (cf. Dilchert, Ones, Viswesvaran, & Deller, 2006; Ones & Viswesvaran, 1998). Because the behavior of greenwashing itself does not contribute to environmental sustainability (regardless of the initial behavior that is being misrepresented), it does not fall in the domain of employee green behaviors.

Should Employee Green Behaviors Be Included as Part of the Organizational Citizenship Behaviors Domain?

A legitimate question is whether or not employee green behaviors can be subsumed under the rubric of organizational citizenship behaviors. Organizational citizenship behaviors (OCB) refer to discretionary, pro-social behaviors in work settings (Organ, 1988). They are not part of core task performance, but are nonetheless helpful to organizational functioning. Thus far, postulated facets of OCB have included altruism, courtesy, civic virtue, individual initiative, organizational loyalty, rule compliance, self-development, and sportsmanship (Podsakoff, MacKenzie, Paine, & Bachrach, 2000). There is empirical evidence that OCB can be grouped into two major categories, those that are directed to other individuals (interpersonal OCB) and those targeted at the organization (organizational OCB; see Hoffman & Dilchert, 2012).

The definition we have offered for employee green behaviors makes it clear that these behaviors are not necessarily extra-role. They can be either required or discretionary. For example, in the two critical incidents studies we conducted in the U.S. (Ones & Dilchert, 2010), we found that about 29 percent of the more than two thousand behaviors identified were required by the organization or employees' job duties. In our European data collection, we found that about 13 percent of the more than one thousand behaviors described were required by the organization or by job duties. In both cases, these required behaviors included both positive incidents of employee green behaviors and negative (harmful) behaviors. Thus, it is clear that employee green behaviors *can be*, but are not exclusively, discretionary.

Many of the behaviors identified as part of the Green Five and lower-order clusters were task performance behaviors that contributed to environmental sustainability (such as creating eco-friendly products and monitoring environmental impact). Particularly in green industries (renewable energy generation or green construction, for example; see Dierdorff, Norton, Drewes, Kroustalis, Ricvkin, & Lewis, 2009), one would expect employee green behaviors to constitute much of the task performance domain for most core jobs. Perhaps the same can be argued for green jobs (such as energy auditor or reclamation worker, for example): task performance in green jobs involves performing behaviors that *are linked with and contribute to environmental sustainability*. The Society for Human Resource Management, in a survey of 1,705 HR professionals, found that 40 percent of organizations were creating green jobs or adding green tasks and duties to existing positions; 5 percent were intending to do so (Schmit, 2011; see also Schmit, Fegley, Esen, Schramm, & Tomassetti, Chapter 4 in this volume).

In sum, employee green behaviors can fall into different job performance domains. They can be part of task performance, organizational citizenship behaviors, or even counterproductive work behaviors, as will be seen in the next section.

What Are the Links Between Environmentally Unfriendly Behaviors of Employees and Counterproductive Work Behaviors?

After reviewing influential conceptualizations and descriptions of counterproductive work behaviors (CWB) (for example, Sackett & DeVore, 2001; Spector & Fox, 2005), Ones and Dilchert (in press) defined CWB as "scalable actions and behaviors that employees engage in that detract from organizational goals or well-being. They include behaviors that bring about undesirable consequences for the organization or its stakeholders." Recall that our definition of employee green behaviors includes behaviors that detract from environmental sustainability. To the extent that organizational viability and sustainability are contingent upon environmental sustainability, employee un-green behaviors constitute a specific form of CWB. These behaviors can be characterized as irresponsible environmental behaviors among employees. Unfortunately, they are rarely (if ever) assessed as part of the CWB domain.

Environmentally irresponsible behaviors can be found in all behavioral domains of the Green Five. Across our two U.S.-based critical incidents studies, we found that about 25 percent of the behavioral examples provided were environmentally irresponsible (Dilchert, Ones, Wiernik, Hill, D'Mello, & Klein, 2010). For European data, about 18 percent of the critical incidents described were environmentally irresponsible behaviors. Expectedly, polluting, a behavior that directly harms ecosystems, was most frequently described and constituted more than 40 percent of behaviors in the Avoiding Harm/Harming meta-category. The Conserving category of the Green Five also contained a sizable proportion (over 30 percent) of environmentally irresponsible behaviors, mostly those relating to wastefulness. It also contributed most negative behaviors overall (about two-thirds of all environmentally unfriendly behaviors constitute wasteful use of resources or failures to recycle).

Among the Working Sustainably category, more than 10 percent of behaviors pertained to Working Unsustainably (the negative pole of the Working Sustainably domain that addresses irresponsible behaviors that could be replaced with more environmentally friendly ones). Of the behaviors in the Taking Initiative and Influencing Others meta-categories, only a few (between 1 and 3 percent) could be characterized as irresponsible and counterproductive, reflecting the proactive and social nature of many behaviors in these categories (that is, it is hard to find examples where employees purposefully use their influence or initiative to do direct or indirect harm to the environment).

Industrial and organizational psychologists and HR practitioners should not forget the dark side of employee green behaviors. We expect that organizational interventions can target a large proportion of employee "ungreen" behaviors by making responsible and green options more accessible and available. Employees' preferences may be altered by cognitively based interventions, including workplace training for sustainability. Environmentally unfriendly *habits* can be targeted by behavior change interventions. Our research suggests that the majority of un-green behaviors among employees is motivated by employees indifference or a simple lack of alternatives (Klein, D'Mello, Ones, Dilchert, Hill, & Wiernik, 2010). These will be fruitful areas for organizational interventions (sustainability awareness, job and workplace design). Personal traits and tendencies that are associated with CWB, including environmental irresponsibility, may be harder to address once employees are on the job (Ones, Viswesvaran, & Schmidt, 1993), and might instead call for better recruitment and employee selection.

What Is the Relationship Between Employee Green Behaviors and Pro-Environmental Behaviors?

Pro-environmental behaviors are defined as "individual behaviors contributing to environmental sustainability (for example, limiting energy consumption, avoiding waste, recycling, and environmental activism)" (Mesmer-Magnus, Viswesvaran, & Wiernik, Chapter 7 in this volume). These are volitional behaviors rooted in individuals' own initiative. They are not prescribed by the organization or by job demands (much like analogous, pro-social behaviors, for example). Typically, individual pro-environmental behaviors are undertaken as part of one's personal life (for example, purchasing an eco-friendly vehicle; using organic cleaners; reducing electricity use at home). They may be public (for example, taking a class in green home renovation, taking mass transportation) or private (not using home air conditioning on hot days; relying on natural lighting as much as possible; taking short showers).

At the construct level, positive employee green behaviors may be considered a specific form of pro-environmental behaviors. Their distinguishing feature is the setting in which they occur (the workplace) and a certain degree of organizational oversight involved. Operationalizations of pro-environmental behaviors have yet to include environmentally irresponsible behaviors as indicators of the negative pole of the construct—something we have explicitly accounted for in our conceptualization of employee green behaviors. Disengagement from pro-environmental behaviors is not the same as active irresponsible behaviors that harm the environment. More content-valid operationalizations of pro-environmental behaviors are needed. Lack of multidimensional models of pro-environmental behaviors is a hindrance to the scientific study of the pro-environmental behaviors domain (see Ones & Dilchert, in press). The tendency to focus on specific behavioral indicators of pro-environmental behavior (such as recycling) rather than construct valid, reliable scales (such as a comprehensive construct reflecting conservation) is also a major limitation.

Conclusions

A well-specified definition of what constitutes environmentally sustainable behaviors among employees is the first step in understanding, predicting, and modifying such behaviors in the workplace. This chapter offered a definition and carefully delineated the components of the behavioral domain of employee green behaviors. Similarities with and differences from other employee behavior domains were highlighted. The specifications for employee green behaviors can aid industrial and organizational psychologists in incorporating environmental sustainability into models of job performance.

The Green Five taxonomy described is based on empirical data that arose from work analytic approaches deeply rooted in industrial and organizational psychology (critical incidents methodology). It is not merely a theoretical model, but an empirically established taxonomy. At the same time, it is not based on atheoretical empiricism—psychological and functional considerations were incorporated in defining and refining the behavioral clusters. Each behavioral meta-category has a specific psychological core and serves a different function.

We hope that the Green Five taxonomy will be foundational in bringing coherence to the variability currently encountered in our field's understanding of environmental sustainability behaviors at the individual employee level. It attempts to provide a well-specified, clear, common terminology and classification system that can be utilized in greening work behaviors, jobs, and organizations in general. However, it will be important to be responsive to changes in the way work is organized and performed in organizations of the future. The content for each of the categories is likely to change as economies, technologies, resource availability, and the ways of organizing work evolve. A behavior that constitutes the eco-innovation of today might be tomorrow's outdated (and suboptimal) solution. But such changes are most likely to have an impact on the *behavioral indicators*, not necessarily the *categories* of employee green behaviors. In the face of constant change, taxonomies such as the one we have outlined in this chapter can offer stability for communicating scientific principles and shape applied practice in different settings and over time.

Our scholarly understanding of employee behaviors that promote environmentally conscious and ecologically sustainable organizations has lagged behind practice and societal demands. If organizations are to promote environmentally friendly workforces, there should be a clearer understanding of what constitutes "green" behaviors and how such behaviors are organized. The small amount of work on environmental sustainability has so far tended to focus on higher levels of analysis, such as characteristics associated with green jobs (Dierdorff, Norton, Drewes,

Kroustalis, Ricvkin, & Lewis, 2009), green organizations (Russo & Fouts, 1997), and even green nations (Emerson, Esty, Levy, Kim, Mara, de Sherbinin, et al., 2010). To be ecologically sustainable, we need to promote, influence, and change *employee behaviors* such that they are congruent with environmental sustainability goals of organizations. In order to thrive in a future green economy, industrial and organizational psychologists should understand the construct of employee green behaviors as they promote environmentally conscious and ecologically sustainable organizations.

References

Anderson, L., & Wilson, S. (1997). Critical incident technique. In D. L. Whetzel & G. R. Wheaton (Eds.), *Applied measurement methods in industrial psychology* (pp. 89–112). Palo Alto, CA: Davies-Black.

Campbell, J. P. (1990). Modeling the performance prediction problem in industrial and organizational psychology. In M. D. Dunnette & L. M. Hough (Eds.), *Handbook of industrial and organizational psychology* (Vol. 1, pp. 687–732). Palo Alto, CA: Consulting Psychologists Press.

Campbell, J. P., McCloy, R. A., Oppler, S. H., & Sager, C. E. (1993). A theory of performance. In N. Schmitt & W. C. Borman (Eds.), *Personnel selection in organizations* (pp. 35–70). San Francisco: Jossey-Bass.

De Young, R. (1993). Changing behavior and making it stick: The conceptualization and management of conservation behavior. *Environment and Behavior, 25,* 485–505.

Dierdorff, E. C., Norton, J. J., Drewes, D. W., Kroustalis, C. M., Ricvkin, D., & Lewis, P. (2009). *Greening of the world of work: Implications for O*NET®-SOC and new and emerging occupations.* Raleigh, NC: National Center for O*Net Development.

Dilchert, S., & Ones, D. S. (2011, April). Personality and its relationship to sustainable and unsustainable workplace behaviors. In S. Dilchert (Chair), *Focusing on employees to achieve environmentally sustainable organizations.* Symposium conducted at the annual conference of the Society for Industrial and Organizational Psychology, Chicago, Illinois.

Dilchert, S., Ones, D. S., Viswesvaran, C., & Deller, J. (2006). Response distortion in personality measurement: Born to deceive, yet capable of providing valid self-assessments? *Psychology Science, 48,* 209–225.

Dilchert, S., Ones, D. S., Wiernik, B. M., Hill, L., D'Mello, S., & Klein, R. M. (2010, April). Understanding environmentally unfriendly behaviors of employees. In A. Sanders & A. Huffman (Chairs), *Earth and I/O: Implications for a sustainable workforce.* Symposium conducted at the annual conference of the Society for Industrial and Organizational Psychology, Atlanta, Georgia.

Dunnette, M. D. (1963). A note on the criterion. *Journal of Applied Psychology, 47,* 251–254.

Elkington, J. (1998). *Cannibals with forks: The triple bottom line of 21st century business.* Gabriola Island, BC: New Society Publishers.

Emerson, J., Esty, D. C., Levy, M. A., Kim, C., Mara, V., de Sherbinin, A., et al. (2010). *2010 environmental performance index.* http://epi.yale.edu/file_columns/0000/0157/epi2010_report.pdf.

Frohman, A. L. (1999). Personal initiative sparks innovation. *Research-Technology Management, 42,* 32–38.

Highhouse, S., Hoffman, J. R., Greve, E. M., & Collins, A. E. (2002). Persuasive impact of organizational value statements in a recruitment context. *Journal of Applied Social Psychology, 32,* 1737–1755.

Hill, L., Ones, D. S., Dilchert, S., Wiernik, B. M., Klein, R. M., & D'Mello, S. (2011, April). Employee green behaviors in Europe: A cross-cultural taxonomic investigation. In S. Dilchert (Chair), *Focusing on employees to achieve environmentally sustainable organizations.* Symposium conducted at the annual conference of the Society for Industrial and Organizational Psychology, Chicago, Illinois.

Hoffman, B. J., & Dilchert, S. (2012). A review of citizenship and counterproductive behaviors in organizational decision-making. In N. Schmitt (Ed.), *The Oxford handbook of personnel assessment and selection* pp. 543–569. New York: Oxford University Press.

Hogan, J., & Holland, B. (2003). Using theory to evaluate personality and job-performance relations: A socioanalytic perspective. *Journal of Applied Psychology, 88,* 100–112.

Ilgen, D. R., & Hollenbeck, J. R. (1991). The structure of work: Job design and roles. In M. D. Dunnette & L. M. Hough (Eds.), *Handbook of industrial and organizational psychology* (2nd ed., Vol. 2, pp. 165–207). Palo Alto, CA: Consulting Psychologists Press.

Klein, R. M., D'Mello, S., Ones, D. S., Dilchert, S., Hill, L., & Wiernik, B. M. (2010, April). Green motives: Why employees engage in environmentally friendly behaviors. In D. S. Ones & S. Dilchert (Chairs), *Shades of green: Individual differences in environmentally responsible employee behaviors.* Symposium conducted at the annual conference of the Society for Industrial and Organizational Psychology, Atlanta, Georgia.

Klein, R. M., Ones, D. S., Dilchert, S., & Wiernik, B. M. (2011, April). *Development of the employee green motives scale.* Poster session presented at the annual conference of the Society for Industrial and Organizational Psychology, Chicago, Illinois.

Laufer, W. S. (2003). Social accountability and corporate greenwashing. *Journal of Business Ethics, 43,* 253–261.

Milano, C. (2009). It's getting easier to be green: Jobs in green science. *Science Careers.* http://sciencecareers.sciencemag.org/get -file.xqy?uri=/aaas/files/uploaded-files/pdf/f9f0fe20-44e4-4890 -820f-c99be43c73b7/science.opms.r0900069.pdf

Montgomery, D. B., & Ramus, C. A. (2007). Including corporate social responsibility, environmental sustainaibility, and ethics in calibrating MBA job preferences (Research Collection, Lee Kong Chian School of Business, Paper 939). Singapore.

National Academies of the G8+5. (2009). Joint statement on climate change and the transformation of energy technologies for a low carbon future. www.nationalacademies.org/includes/G8+5energy -climate09.pdf.

National Geographic and Globescan. (2008). *Greendex 2008: Consumer choice and the environment: A worldwide tracking survey.*

National Geographic and Globescan. (2009). *Greendex 2009: Consumer choice and the environment A worldwide tracking survey.*

Ones, D. S. (2011, April). A green workforce: Understanding and promoting green behaviors. In S. Dilchert (Chair), *Green HR: Environmentally sustainable organizations, jobs, and employees.* Symposium conducted at the Theme Track of the annual conference of the Society for Industrial and Organizational Psychology, Chicago, Illinois.

Ones, D. S., & Dilchert, S. (2009, August). Green behaviors of workers: A taxonomy for the green economy. In S. Dilchert & D. S. Ones (Chairs), *Environmentally friendly worker behaviors, senior leader wrongdoing, and national level outcomes.* Symposium conducted at the annual meeting of the Academy of Management, Chicago, Illinois.

Ones, D. S., & Dilchert, S. (2010, April). A taxonomy of green behaviors among employees. In D. S. Ones & S. Dilchert (Chairs), *Shades of green: Individual differences in environmentally responsible employee behaviors.* Symposium conducted at the annual conference of the Society for Industrial and Organizational Psychology, Atlanta, Georgia.

Ones, D. S., & Dilchert, S. (in press). Counterproductive work behaviors: Concepts, measurement, and nomological network. In N. R.

Kuncel (Ed.), *APA handbook of testing and assessment in psychology*. Washington, DC: American Psychological Association.

Ones, D. S., & Dilchert, S. (in press). Environmental sustainability at work: A call to action. *Industrial and Organizational Psychology: Perspectives on Research and Practice.*

Ones, D. S., Dilchert, S., & Viswesvaran, C. (in press). Cognitive abilities. In N. Schmitt (Ed.), *The Oxford handbook of personnel assessment and selection* pp. 179–224. New York: Oxford University Press.

Ones, D. S., Dilchert, S., Viswesvaran, C., & Judge, T. A. (2007). In support of personality assessment in organizational settings. *Personnel Psychology, 60,* 995–1027.

Ones, D. S., & Viswesvaran, C. (1998). The effects of social desirability and faking on personality and integrity assessment for personnel selection. *Human Performance, 11,* 245–269.

Ones, D. S., Viswesvaran, C., & Schmidt, F. L. (1993). Comprehensive meta-analysis of integrity test validities: Findings and implications for personnel selection and theories of job performance. *Journal of Applied Psychology, 78,* 679–703.

O'Rourke, M. (2010). To what extent do undergraduate business degree students find corporate social performance, and its elements, to be attractive in a potential employer? Unpublished master's thesis, Unitech Institute of Technology, Auckland, New Zealand.

Organ, D. W. (1988). *Organizational citizenship behavior: The good soldier syndrome.* Lexington, MA: D.C. Heath and Company.

Podsakoff, P. M., MacKenzie, S. B., Paine, J. B., & Bachrach, D. G. (2000). Organizational citizenship behaviors: A critical review of the theoretical and empirical literature and suggestions for future research. *Journal of Management, 26,* 513–563.

Ramus, C. A., & Montiel, I. (2005). When are corporate environmental policies a form of greenwashing? *Business and Society, 44,* 377–414.

Russo, M. V., & Fouts, P. A. (1997). A resource-based perspective on corporate environmental performance and profitability. *Academy of Management Journal, 40,* 534–559.

Sackett, P. R., & DeVore, C. J. (2001). Counterproductive behaviors at work. In N. Anderson, D. S. Ones, H. Sinangil Kepir, & C. Viswesvaran (Eds.), *Handbook of industrial, work and organizational psychology* (Vol. 1: Personnel psychology, pp. 145–164). London: Sage.

Schmit, M. J. (2011, April). Sustainability business practices in the workplace: Prevalence, methods, and outcomes. In S. Dilchert (Chair), *Green HR: Environmentally sustainable organizations, jobs, and employees.* Symposium conducted at the annual conference of the

Society for Industrial and Organizational Psychology, Chicago, Illinois.

Spector, P. E., & Fox, S. (2005). The stressor-emotion model of counterproductive work behavior. In S. Fox & P. E. Spector (Eds.), *Counterproductive work behavior: Investigations of actors and targets.* (pp. 151–174). Washington, DC: American Psychological Association.

Thorndike, R. L. (1960, September). Ten thousand careers and criteria. Paper presented at the annual conference of the American Psychological Association, Chicago, Illinois.

U.N. Department of Economic and Social Affairs. (2004). *World population to 2300.* New York: United Nations.

World Economic Forum. (2009). Business-expert task force on low-carbon economic prosperity: An open letter to G20 leaders. https://members.weforum.org/pdf/climate/G20 _ProsperityTaskForceLetter.pdf

CHAPTER SIX

Demographic Characteristics and Employee Sustainability

Rachael M. Klein,
Susan D'Mello,
and Brenton M. Wiernik

With many organizations competing to be more sustainable, companies can gain a competitive edge by calling upon the building blocks of the organization—the employees. The Society for Human Resource Management's (2010) survey of 1,705 human resource professionals found that 81 percent of organizations had added green duties to existing positions over the twelve-month period from June 2009 to June 2010. As these duties are added to employee jobs, it is important to understand the demographic characteristics of individuals who are most likely to be concerned and knowledgeable about the environment and willing to take action on its behalf. This chapter will help human resource managers and practitioners understand the demographics of environmental sustainability. Demographic variables are reviewed in terms of their contribution to workplace environmental sustainability efforts. Opportunities for training and support for greening efforts in organizations are identified, and possible organizational applications are presented and discussed.

This work was supported in part by the National Science Foundation through a Graduate Research Fellowship to Rachael Klein.

Importance of Understanding Demographic Differences in Environmental Sustainability

Previous examinations of demographic characteristics have proven useful in understanding how an employee's age, gender, education level, and income level may influence his or her workplace behavior. These examinations have focused on job performance (Kaufman, 1978; Ng & Feldman, 2008; Ng & Feldman, 2009), group performance (Wegge, Roth, Neubach, Schmidt, & Kanfer, 2008), productivity (Maglen, 1990; Wise, 1975), turnover (Colarelli, Dean, & Konstans, 1987; Healy, Lehman, & McDaniel, 1995; Lyness & Judiesch, 2001), integrity (Ones & Viswesvaran, 1998), organizational commitment (Colarelli, Dean, & Konstans, 1987), job preferences (Daymont & Andrisani, 1984), objective career success (operationalized as salary level and promotion; Ng, Eby, Sorensen, & Feldman, 2005), job and career satisfaction (Clark, Oswald, & Warr, 1996; Lyness & Thompson, 1997; Ng, Eby, Sorensen, & Feldman, 2005; Tait, Padgett, & Baldwin, 1989), and other important variables. Based on findings of demographic differences from these studies, researchers have been able to recommend ways in which organizations can best focus their time and effort with respect to supporting employees and improving their work performance. For instance, research examining the number of women advancing to management positions (Baron, Davis-Blake, & Bielby, 1986; Bowler, 1999; Morrison & von Glinow, 1990; Wolfers, 2006) and gender differences in compensation (Blau & Kahn, 2000; Glass Ceiling Commission, 1995) has helped organizations address the issues of glass ceilings and differential pay. Progress has been made in these areas over time, and researchers are able to monitor this progress and pinpoint areas in which work is still needed (Blau & Kahn, 2000; Lyness & Thompson, 1997).

In terms of recommendations based on age differences, Ng and Feldman (2008) suggested that organizations should spend more time providing older workers with supervisory and mentoring training instead of technical (that is, computer) training. The researchers reason that older workers are unlikely to compete effectively with younger employees in terms of technical training but, with proper supervisory and mentoring training, they can be effective in facilitating younger employees' performance. With respect to organizational action based on education, links between higher levels of education and desirable organizational outcomes such as productivity (Wise, 1975) are leading organizations to recognize the importance of education and to increasingly invest in training and development of their employees (Paradise, 2007). Such training and development efforts include organization-sponsored tuition reimbursement programs, which allow current employees to further their education, while still working for the organization (Hewitt Associates, 1999; Institute for Research on Higher Education, 1997).

Just as this past research has examined demographic corre-lates of work performance, we will review the literature on age, gender, education, and income differences in environmental sus-tainability variables and suggest ways that human resource manag-ers can utilize employees' environmental sustainability strengths and improve upon corresponding weaknesses. This chapter pro-vides a literature review of empirical work linking employee demographic characteristics of age, gender, education level, and income to environmental concern, knowledge, and behavior. We examine each of these demographic characteristics and the con-ceptual and theoretical bases for the differences that might exist. We will also provide suggestions for human resource managers seeking to tailor their environmental interventions and initiatives based on the demographic compositions of their workforces.

In the following sections, we first address findings related to gender differences[1] in environmental concern and behavior. We next examine whether younger workers are prone to youthful waste or whether their general tendencies to be open to change make them more likely to embrace innovative technologies and work practices, and thus more willing to change and work sustainably. Third, we discuss whether employees with higher levels of education are more likely to have higher levels of envi-ronmental knowledge, and are more or less likely to act with the

---

[1]Gender and sex are used synonymously in this chapter, based on convention in the industrial and organizational psychology literature (Cross, Copping, & Campbell, 2011; Judge & Livingston, 2008; Ostroff & Atwater, 2003; Ramaswami, Dreher, Bretz, & Wiethoff, 2010).

interest of the environment in mind. Last, employee income is examined in order to better understand whether green products and processes are a luxury only the rich can afford.

Until very recently, little research had been conducted examining environmental sustainability specifically in work settings. Fortunately, there is a broad literature on individuals' environmental behavior at home, and these environmental behaviors have been found to predict workplace sustainability quite well (Tudor, Barr, & Gilg, 2007). As such, findings from the household domain may generalize to the workplace in some circumstances and are included in our review. By understanding the demographic characteristics associated with environmentally friendly and savvy employees, human resource managers will be better equipped to support green workplace behaviors and to understand how different employees can best contribute to sustainability efforts.

Gender Differences

Gender differences in environmental concern and behavior may stem from broader psychological differences between the sexes. Gender socialization theory posits that women are raised to be nurturing, cooperative, and warm in order to take on roles as mothers, where they are typically in charge of child rearing, housework, and health-related issues. Men, on the other hand, learn to be competitive and independent and are expected to assume roles in the public domain to provide financially for their families (Gilligan, 1982). Social role theory contends that men and women will develop these different orientations as a result of observing and striving to fill different familial and occupational roles (Eagly & Wood, 1991). Men are more likely to have a "marketplace mentality," which may lead them to focus on economic growth without regard to the environmental costs of their actions. Conversely, Beutel and Marini (1995) found that female adolescents were more likely to value compassion, which encompasses concern and responsibility for others' well-being, and less likely than males to value materialism and competition. Although women in general rank the value of altruism higher than men did (Dietz, Kalof, & Stern, 2002), Andreoni and Vesterlund (2001) found that women were more altruistic when the monetary costs of helping were greater, whereas men were more altruistic when the costs were small. In terms of green behavior, men were found to cite cost-effectiveness and thrift as their motive for pro-environmental behavior at work more often than women did (Klein, D'Mello, Ones, Dilchert, Wiernik, & Hill, 2010). In sum, these value differences between men and women should result in differences in environmental behavior, especially when monetary issues are salient.

Men and women also view risk differently, which may be an important factor in determining one's level of concern about the environment and willingness to engage in green behaviors. Findings on gender differences and risk in general show that women are more concerned about risky actions or situations. A meta-analysis of literature on risk taking found women to be more risk averse than men for fourteen of sixteen types of risk (Byrnes, Miller, & Schafer, 1999). Women are also more likely to view the quality of the environment as connected to their personal well-being, the well-being of others, and the health of the planet (Stern, Dietz, & Kalof, 1993). Since women are more likely to focus on the health and welfare of the family (see above), environmental threats may be especially concerning to women. Women are likely to be particularly more concerned about environmental issues that directly threaten health and well-being, such as air pollution, ozone depletion, toxic waste, and acid rain.

Gender and Environmental Concern

Environmental concern is a set of beliefs about nature and one's relationship to it, including considerations of the seriousness and importance of environmental problems (Dunlap, Van Liere, Mertig, & Jones, 2000; Takács-Sánta, 2007). Consistent with findings that women are more risk-averse in general, women are also more likely to be concerned than men when asked about environmental issues associated with risk, such as toxic contamination (Bord & O'Connor, 1997; Davidson & Freudenburg, 1996; Slovic, 1992; Solomon, Tomaskovic-Devey, & Risman, 1989). For instance, women reported higher levels of concern than men about the effects of pollution on their health and well-being on the 1993

General Social Survey (Blocker & Eckberg, 1997). Davidson and Freudenburg (1996) also found that women were more concerned than men in eighteen of twenty studies examining gender differences in risk-related environmental issues.

Several researchers have noted a distinction between general environmental concern and more specific measures that gauge concern about particular issues such as toxic waste or pollution control (Davidson & Freudenburg, 1996; McStay & Dunlap, 1983; Mohai, 1992). Women tend to be more concerned about specific environmental issues, presumably because specific issues may pose a greater and more salient risk to health and safety than general environmental ones (Mohai, 1992). Results for general environmental concern are less consistent, and while some studies have found no relationship or that men are more concerned than women (Arcury, Scollay, & Johnson, 1987; Davidson & Freudenburg, 1996; McEvoy, 1972), the general trend when differences are observed is that women tend to be slightly more concerned than men (McStay & Dunlap, 1983; Stern, Dietz, & Kalof, 1993). Davidson and Freudenburg reviewed twenty-five studies that used general attitude surveys and found that women were more concerned in eleven of these studies, while a majority of the fourteen remaining studies found negligible differences in concern. McCright's (2010) analysis of 2001 through 2008 Gallup poll data showed that women were more likely to worry about climate change, which is consistent with previous findings (Brody, Zahran, Vedlitz, & Grover, 2008; O'Connor, Bord, & Fisher, 1999).

Only recently have studies been cumulated to examine the overall relationship between gender and environmental concern. A meta-analysis of six studies using the New Environmental Paradigm scale as a measure of general environmental concern found that women reported greater concern than men, although the relationship was quite small ($r = .07$; Zelezny, Chua, & Aldrich, 2000). These findings are robust across cultures, as a survey of undergraduates from fourteen countries from Europe, Latin America, and North America found that females reported higher environmental attitudes than men in ten of fourteen countries ($r = .04$). Across cultures, females were also more likely to believe that the environment should be preserved because of its intrinsic value ($r = .10$; Zelezny, Chua, & Aldrich, 2000). Findings from a meta-analysis of the literature examining the relationship between gender differences in environmental concern were consistent with previous findings indicating small gender differences in concern (Klein, Ones, & Dilchert, 2011). Women were consistently more concerned about the environment, especially with regard to specific issues, such as air pollution or acid rain.

Gender and Environmental Behavior

Given that women are slightly more concerned about environmental issues than men, it is not surprising that women are also generally more likely to engage in pro-environmental behaviors. Hines, Hungerford, and Tomera (1986–1987) cumulated four studies of gender and household environmental behaviors and found a small mean relationship between gender and environmental behavior, with women more likely to engage in green behaviors than men. A more recent meta-analysis based on thirteen studies found an average gender-household environmental behavior relationship of similar magnitude ($r = .10$; Zelezny, Chua, & Aldrich, 2000). The relationship between gender and pro-environmental behavior was also found to be robust across fourteen countries, with females reporting greater participation in pro-environmental behaviors than males in eleven of fourteen countries (Zelezny, Chua, & Aldrich, 2000).

Some researchers have made a distinction between "private" and "public" behaviors, to distinguish between different types of pro-environmental behavior, such as recycling at home (private) or protesting environmental issues with others (public). Several studies have found gender differences within these categories, with women more likely to participate in a greater number of private behaviors than men do, whereas men tend to perform public behaviors more often than women (McStay & Dunlap, 1983; Mohai, 1992). For example, women tend to be more likely to buy products because they believe them to be eco-friendly, recycle different types of materials (Mainieri, Barnett, Valdero, Unipan, & Oskamp, 1997), and reuse or mend things instead of discarding them (Ozanne, Humphrey, & Smith, 1999). Men, on the other hand, tend to be more likely to attend public meetings or hearings about the environment (Ozanne, Humphrey, &

Smith, 1999) and to vote for government policies addressing climate change (O'Connor, Bord, & Fisher, 1999). Other studies have reported no differences in the frequency of public behaviors (Tindall, Davies, & Mauboules, 2003). In a cross-national study, women were found to engage in more private green behaviors than men in all but three of twenty-two countries (Hunter, Hatch, & Johnson, 2004). In terms of public behavior, sizable differences existed for only six of the twenty-two countries; three of the six studies found that men engaged in more public green behaviors, while the other half found that women do so. Although women perform more green behaviors in private environments, men may be just as likely, if not more likely, to perform public pro-environmental behaviors. Given that the workplace is a public domain, there may be smaller differences in the relationship between gender and green behaviors at work.

In a meta-analysis of the literature on gender differences in household environmental behavior, Klein, Ones, and Dilchert (2011) found that women tend to perform most types of environmental behavior more often than men, although the magnitude of differences is small. Women tend to conserve more, make more responsible product choices, and take more initiative with respect to the environment. Men, however, are slightly more likely to encourage others to behave sustainably. All of these differences, however, vary by the setting and are influenced by situational contexts, so it may be difficult to generalize these trends to different settings such as workplaces.

Gender and Environmental Workplace Behavior

The gender-environmental behavior relationship within workplaces has only recently been examined. A meta-analysis of workplace studies conducted between 2008 and 2010 including 30,169 employees from seven of the world's ten GLOBE (cf. House, Hanges, Javidan, Dorfman, & Gupta, 2004) geographical clusters found that female *employees* engaged in more pro-environmental workplace behavior than men, although differences were very small (Klein, Ones, Dilchert, & Biga, 2011). The size of the relationship found within the workplace was in line with those previously found in household settings, although somewhat smaller, which could reflect either the differences in men's and women's tendencies to perform public behaviors or workplace constraints, such as company policies and procedures that limit the amount of control individuals have over their behavior at work.

D'Mello, Klein, Ones, Dilchert, Hill, Wiernik, and Biga (2010) used a sample of 2,316 employees to examine the differences within each behavioral facet from an empirically based taxonomy of employee green behaviors (Ones & Dilchert, 2010; see also Ones & Dilchert, Chapter 5 in this volume). This taxonomy consists of sixteen categories of sustainable work performance organized into five super-categories, the "Green Five": Avoiding Harm, Conserving, Working Sustainably, Influencing Others, and Taking Initiative. Women were more likely to engage in green behaviors related to reusing and repurposing (Conserving behaviors) and encouraging and supporting others (an aspect of Influencing Others). D'Mello, Klein, Ones, Dilchert, Hill, Wiernik, and Biga (2010) also interviewed 407 employees about green behaviors performed within the workplace. Men were more likely to engage in lobbying and activist behaviors, while women were found to be more likely to educate and train others for sustainability. It appears that women are easily able to perform what would be considered "private" behaviors, such as reusing and repurposing, within the workplace as well as incorporate their strengths in the area of cooperativeness and nurturance to encourage, support, educate, and train others.

Suggested Practices

As reviewed above, women are typically more concerned about the environment and are more likely to engage in most types of environmentally sustainable household behaviors than men are. These differences are relatively small, however. While evidence suggests that these trends continue in the workplace, it is important to be aware that women's higher engagement relating to pro-environmental causes may not currently reach its full potential within workplaces. Women are less likely to be in positions of power in the workplace; for instance, only 1.3 percent of publicly traded companies were led by female CEOs between 1992 and 2004 (Bowler, 1999; Wolfers, 2006). Thus, women are less likely to be involved in high-level strategic or operational decisions, including initiating programs and policies and making major purchasing decisions that could relate to environmental sustainability.

Organizations' environmental sustainability efforts can benefit from ensuring that women have a chance to fully contribute to the organization's environmental efforts by including them in environmental sustainability decision making. Women's potential could be harvested by incorporating their perspectives when determining job duties and designing training programs for sustainability. Men, on the other hand, are more likely to engage in behaviors involving influencing others, lobbying, and activism. Within the workplace, men are more likely to engage in behaviors related to advocating for green initiatives, as well as presenting the organization's initiatives to its stakeholders and the public. Given that men often focus on economic growth, they should be motivated to engage in green behaviors when they are made aware of cost benefits for the organization. Men may also be more motivated to perform green behaviors if green performance is tied to employee job performance. Being aware of gender differences in environmental concern and behavior helps in understanding how men and women can uniquely contribute to organizations' environmental efforts and how green interventions may be perceived differently by men and women.

Age Differences

As with gender, it is reasonable to expect that individuals of different ages may vary in their levels of environmental sustainability. It is likely that younger and older individuals have been subjected to dissimilar experiences, life responsibilities, and future prospects. Age differences have also been examined in relation to a variety of psychological construct domains, including personality and work values. All of these differences combine to create profiles of younger and older individuals, which suggest plausible patterns for age differences in environmental sustainability.

First, younger individuals are at different life stages than individuals from older generations (Savickas, Nota, Rossier, Dauwalder, Duarte, Guichard, Soresi, Van Esbroeck, & van Vianen, 2009). Because, on average, the remaining lifespan of younger individuals is longer than that of older individuals, younger individuals are more likely to encounter the consequences of their own environmental actions. We can thus expect younger individuals to be more concerned about environmental issues simply because they are more likely to suffer from negative consequences of unsustainable activity.

Beyond lifespan considerations, other age effects might lead younger individuals to hold more environmentally conscious concerns and attitudes. Dunlap and Van Liere (1978) suggest that power differentials lead younger individuals to be less engaged with the dominant social paradigm, which (in much of the industrialized world) emphasizes consumption and anthropocentric values. This separation might result in younger individuals being more open to adopting new and sustainable ideas and to display positive environmental values.

With regard to more stable individual differences, it has been demonstrated that many personality characteristics change notably as individuals age and mature (McCrae, Costa, De Lima, Simoes, Ostendorf, Angleitner, & Piedmont, 1999; Roberts, Walton, & Viechtbauer, 2006). Older individuals tend to display lower levels of social vitality–related facets of extraversion and are less neurotic on average, while younger individuals are more open to experience (Lucas & Donnellan, 2009; Roberts, Walton, & Viechtbauer, 2006). Many environmental sustainability efforts require openness to change, so it is likely that younger workers on average are more willing to consider new ideas and change relating to environmental sustainability. However, older individuals have been found to be more conscientious and agreeable (Lucas & Donnellan, 2009; Roberts, Walton, & Viechtbauer, 2006). These differences might lead older workers to display other types of positive environmental behavior, especially those that relate to diligence (for example, avoiding careless pollution).

Older and younger individuals also tend to differ in their work values (Cennamo & Gardner, 2008; Warr, 2008; Wong, Gardiner,

Lang, & Coulon, 2008). Older workers regard hard and persevering work as a moral imperative (Smola & Sutton, 2002), and they also tend to place more value on being frugal (Rhodes, 1983). Akin to differences in personality (especially conscientiousness), these value differences might result in older workers engaging in work behaviors that lead to conserving resources and following rules and regulations, thus positively impacting environmental sustainability in this manner.

These age differences allow us to describe broad archetypes of older and younger workers. It appears that younger workers may be more open to new ideas and change than older workers, and they are more likely to be in social positions that encourage them to be future-oriented in their thinking. This pattern of openness to change and consideration for the future suggests that younger workers should have greater environmental concern and more positive environmental attitudes than older individuals. Hence, younger workers might be more likely to engage in environmental behaviors at work, at least those that relate to promoting change or adopting new ideas. In contrast to younger workers, many older individuals tend to be resistant to new ideas and only change when a clear benefit is established or when there is great social pressure (Morris & Vankatesh, 2000). However, older workers tend to be more careful and frugal in their actions and value work that is done properly. This pattern suggests that older workers might be less concerned about the environment than younger individuals, but they should be more responsive to social cues and norms for environmental actions. Older workers may also be more likely to perform environmental actions that relate to frugal use, such as reducing the use of resources or recycling, as well as behaviors indicative of safe and proper work performance, such as preventing pollution or monitoring their own environmental impact. Next, we evaluate the veracity of these patterns of behavior as they relate to environmental sustainability in work settings.

Age and Environmental Concern

Many studies examining age and environmental concern have reported a small negative relationship; younger individuals were more concerned about the environment (Arcury & Christianson, 1993; Baldassare & Katz, 1992; Schultz, 2001). This difference is frequently attributed to younger people being less invested in social roles that emphasize industriousness and self-interest and more willing to consider new and different ways to approach problems (Van Liere & Dunlap, 1980). Additionally, it has been argued that younger workers are more likely to be exposed to media and advertisements that feature information about the environment, leading to greater concern than their older co-workers show (Fransson & Gärling, 1999).

The negative age effect with respect to environmental concern was consistently found throughout the 1980s and early 1990s, although some more recent studies have failed to replicate these findings. These studies often attribute the lack of a relationship between environmental concern and age in recent decades to growing environmental concern across entire populations (Fransson & Gärling, 1999). The contradictory findings could also be explained by investigations that confound the effects of age (individual maturation processes) with generational effects (resulting from the particular historical period during which individuals developed). Observed relationships between environmental concern and age are just as likely to be the result of maturational or generational effects. The reduction of age differences in recent studies could be the result of a generation effect whereby the cohort of young individuals growing up in the 1970s became more actively concerned about the environment as a result of the burgeoning environmental movement. As these highly concerned individuals have grown older, they have likely maintained their environmental beliefs and taught them to their children, attenuating any age differences in attitudes about the planet. Interestingly, age has been found to positively relate to environmental concern in nations without the strong environmental movement that led to this cohort effect. In China, Shen and Saijo (2008) found that older workers were slightly more concerned about specific environmental issues and the environment in general and were somewhat more likely to perform pro-environmental behaviors than their younger counterparts.

Despite these few contradictory findings, it does appear that younger individuals tend to have greater levels of environmental concern. Indeed, a recent meta-analysis confirmed that younger individuals had slightly greater commitment to the environment and slightly stronger pro-environmental attitudes across settings compared to older individuals (Wiernik, Ones, & Dilchert, 2011). The meta-analysis also confirmed that younger individuals tended to show moderately greater degrees of general environmental concern. However, this relationship was highly variable across studies, indicating that there might be moderating factors such as cultural influences. Overall, it appears that, in general, younger individuals have somewhat more favorable attitudes toward the environment and are moderately more concerned about environmental quality than older individuals.

Age and Environmental Knowledge and Awareness

Like environmental concern and attitudes, one might expect ecological knowledge and awareness of sustainability issues to vary across age groups. Unfortunately, very few studies have examined the relationship between environmental knowledge and age, and findings have been inconsistent across domains of environmental knowledge. For example, Arcury and Johnson (1987) found that younger workers were slightly more knowledgeable about energy production and the causes of pollution, but older workers were more likely to know more about local environmental conditions.

Inconsistent findings have also been reported for age and environmental awareness. Environmental awareness is the extent to which individuals are vigilant in noticing environmental problems and in drawing inferences about environmental conditions. In many studies, age has been negatively correlated with awareness. For example, Young (1980) found that older individuals were less likely to be aware of environmental issues. This is likely due to older individuals having less exposure to environmental issues through either formal education or social contact. Similarly, Bultena, Rogers, and Conner (1977) found that younger citizens of a regional community were more likely to be aware of local environmental projects and their possible impacts. However, other studies have found that older individuals were more aware of environmental issues (Gregory & Leo, 2003) or have found no relationship between age and environmental awareness (Ostman & Parker, 1987; Zeidner & Shechter, 1988).

Wiernik, Ones, and Dilchert (2011) conducted a meta-analysis of the disparate literature on the relationship between age and environmental awareness and knowledge. They found virtually no relationship between age and either environmental knowledge or environmental awareness. Neither younger nor older individuals were more aware of or knew more about environmental issues and solutions. While there are no meaningful age differences in terms of levels of environmental awareness or knowledge, we next examine whether there might be differences in terms of pro-environmental behavior performed by older and younger adults.

Age and Environmental Behavior

When it comes to research on actual environmental behaviors, the majority of recent research has examined household behaviors and other environmental actions outside of the workplace. In this domain, the relationship with age has been inconsistent. Some studies report that younger individuals engage in some pro-environmental behaviors slightly more often than older individuals do (Hines, Hungerford, & Tomera, 1986–1987). One potential explanation for these findings is that older people are less likely to compromise their personal comfort to be more sustainable. Many studies have found that, compared to younger individuals, older individuals tend to drive alone more often (Hunecke, Haustein, Böhler, & Grischkat, 2010; Samdahl & Robertson, 1989; Tanner, 1999; Whitmarsh & O'Neill, 2010) and use fewer alternative forms of transportation, such as carpooling, public transportation, biking, or walking, which tend to be less convenient (Thøgersen & Ölander, 2006). Young people also take fewer flights than older people, instead selecting slower, but more sustainable transportation options[2] (Whitmarsh & O'Neill, 2010).

---

[2]An alternative explanation for these findings is that younger individuals may drive and fly less because, on average, they have lower disposable income than older individuals. Thus, the cost of a car or air travel may be restrictive for younger individuals and financial considerations may influence their decision to use different modes of travel.

Additionally, younger individuals tend to use less energy in their households (Gatersleben, Steg, & Vlek, 2002) and are more willing to sacrifice comfort by reducing their heating, air conditioning (Samdahl & Robertson, 1989; Whitmarsh & O'Neill, 2010), and water usage (Whitmarsh & O'Neill, 2010) in order to preserve the environment.

Younger people also appear to be more willing to go out of their way and expend effort to be more environmentally sustainable. For example, some studies have found that younger people actively choose to buy more environmentally friendly products (Samdahl & Robertson, 1989) and shop at more environmentally responsible stores (Ogle, Hyllegard, & Dunbar, 2004). In addition, Saphores, Nixon, Ogunseitan, and Shapiro (2006) found that younger individuals were more willing to take electronic waste to recycling centers for disposal, rather than simply disposing of it in landfills. Zhang, Hussain, Deng, and Letson (2007) also found that younger people were more willing to volunteer time to support nature restoration efforts.

Despite these environmental areas in which younger people excel, older individuals tend to outperform their younger counterparts in some environmental domains. Many studies have found that older people tend to recycle more (Dolnicar & Grün, 2009; Gatersleben, Steg, & Vlek, 2002; Knussen & Yule, 2008; Li, 2003; Meneses & Palacio, 2005; Nixon, Saphores, Ogunseitan, & Shapiro, 2009). Also, older individuals are more likely to take actions to limit their use of resources by reducing consumption (Dolnicar & Grün, 2009; Olli, Grendstad, & Wollebaek, 2001; Whitmarsh & O'Neill, 2010), insulating their homes and installing energy efficient windows (Dolnicar & Grün, 2009), and driving in an environmentally responsible manner (Whitmarsh & O'Neill, 2010). Studies have also reported that older individuals make more environmentally friendly food choices (Gatersleben, Steg, & Vlek, 2002) and tend to base political decisions more on environmental reasons (Whitmarsh & O'Neill, 2010).

The meta-analysis of age and environmental behavior by Wiernik, Ones, and Dilchert (2011) has shown somewhat surprising results. Whereas older individuals were found to perform moderately more behaviors relating to conserving and avoiding environmental harm, other forms of behavior had negligible relationships with age. Younger individuals generally do not perform more behaviors related to sacrificing comfort or making responsible product choices. In conclusion, older people tend to limit their use, avoid environmental harm, and recycle more often in their daily private lives. These habits are consistent with their archetypical thriftiness and maturation during an era that emphasized the three Rs. However, neither younger nor older individuals tend to perform other forms of environmental behavior more often.

Age and Environmental Workplace Behavior

Recently, researchers have begun to directly examine sustainable behaviors in the workplace. Wiernik, Ones, Dilchert, and Biga (under review) examined age differences in sustainable work behaviors using the Ones and Dilchert (2010) taxonomy of employee green behaviors. Using a sample of 2,316 managers from eleven countries, the researchers examined the relationship between green work behaviors and age within countries and cross-nationally. A small, but generalizable, positive relationship between age and Conserving and Avoiding Harm behaviors was found. Across all eleven countries, older individuals performed more of these behaviors. Other forms of behavior did not show generalizable relationships with age. However, there were small to moderate positive relationships between age and other forms of employee green behavior (Working Sustainably, Taking Initiative, and Influencing Others) in Germany, Mexico, Singapore, and the United Kingdom. Thus, in some countries, there appears to be a pervasive tendency for older workers to perform slightly more green workplace behaviors.

Suggested Practices

Based on all of these research findings, how should organizations adapt environmental interventions to fit the age profiles of their workforces? Overall, differences between age groups tend to be small, so while some adaptation of interventions based on workforce age composition may be beneficial, the kinds of interventions that will appeal to older workers are likely to be similar to those that will be effective with younger workers. That being said, there are some areas in which small age differences do offer opportunities to tailor environmental interventions.

The first opportunity involves addressing the possibility that older workers are less concerned about environmental problems. If an organization's workforce is primarily composed of older workers, that organization may need to focus a great deal of effort on raising workers' environmental concern and improving workers' attitudes toward environmental issues. Compared to younger workers, older workers tend to be less open to change in their work habits and accept changes only if shown that these changes will have concrete benefits (Czaja, Charness, Fisk, Hertzog, Nair, Rogers, & Sharit, 2006). Hence, interventions should focus on showing older workers the benefits of environmental actions and encouraging them to embrace change for sustainability. Organizations may want to incorporate this information into programs that deal primarily with older workers, such as ongoing training programs and management seminars.

If an organization's workforce is primarily younger, however, organizations may want to instead focus interventions on encouraging workers to monitor their environmental impact and avoid waste. These organizations may need to help their younger workforce be more conscious of how they use resources and offer guidance on how to avoid being wasteful in their work. In the United States and other industrialized Western countries, younger employees likely were raised in societies that emphasized disposability and discarding old materials, and it may take a lot of encouragement from organizations for them to break these entrenched habits.

Additionally, organizations should encourage younger workers to pursue their environmental interests and turn their environmental concern into action. Despite higher levels of concern, younger individuals are not any more likely than older individuals to perform actual pro-environmental behaviors. Organizations may want to use programs that mostly attract younger employees, such as introductory training sessions and new employee orientations, to encourage young workers to start new environmental initiatives and offer ideas to improve organizational sustainability.

With these possible considerations in mind, organizations must remember that age differences in sustainability variables are small. Even though being aware of young people's slightly greater environmental concern and older workers' greater tendency to avoid waste may be helpful in tailoring training, organizations do not need to be too concerned about how age will affect environmental initiatives. This bodes well for organizational greening initiatives: old and young, all members of organizational workforces can contribute.

Education and Income Differences

In contrast to the previously examined demographic variables of gender and age, employee education and income levels are not necessarily fixed characteristics of individuals. Organizations may be able to provide employees with education or resources so that they can be better equipped to engage in pro-environmental behavior at work. First, however, it is important to understand the role education and income have on individuals' sustainable behavior. Are better-educated employees more environmentally sustainable? If so, greater sustainability is yet another positive societal outcome of general education (see Baum & Payea, 2004; Dee, 2004; Ingels, Curtin, Kaufman, Alt, & Chen, 2002; Kane & Rouse, 1995; Lleras-Muney, 2005; and Perna, 2003, for examples). Another question involves whether only individuals with relatively high incomes can afford to be environmentally friendly. Is environmental sustainability a luxury that only the wealthy can afford? If this is the case, individuals with higher incomes may have more experience with pro-environmental products and processes.

If education and income play a part in determining individuals' environmental concern and behavior, this may have implications for organizations, especially with regard to the education levels of their employees and organizational pay systems. We first discuss the literature on the relationship between education and environmental sustainability and suggest that differences are based on knowledge acquisition through formal education. Next, we discuss sustainability differences among income groups, proposing that differences depend on the financial costs associated with environmentally sustainable behaviors. Finally, we link both domains and discuss how this information can be used in practice.

Education and Environmental Knowledge and Concern

Through greater exposure to formal education, more highly educated individuals are likely to be exposed to a greater amount of information about environmental issues than those with lower education levels. Greater exposure may lead to greater levels of environmental knowledge, greater awareness of environmental issues (Althoff & Greig, 1977), and greater environmental concern (Hines, Hungerford, & Tomera, 1986–1987; Jaggi & Westacott, 1975).

Specifically focusing on environmental concern, Van Liere and Dunlap (1981) reported that, although a few studies found a negative or negligible relationship (for example, Kinnear, Taylor, & Ahmed, 1974), the majority of studies relating education to general environmental concern have found a moderate, positive relationship (Aaker & Bagozzi, 1982; Buttel & Flinn, 1978; Roberts, 1996). However, Fransson and Gärling (1999) suggested that this relationship has become smaller in recent years. This possible decrease in the strength of the relationship may be due to the digital revolution that has made access to information less reliant on formal education. For example, an increase in widespread use of the Internet allows for broader distribution of information, making it possible for people of all education levels to gain awareness of environmental issues. In an attempt to resolve the discrepancies in the relationship between education and environmental knowledge and concern, D'Mello, Wiernik, Ones, and Dilchert (2011) conducted a meta-analysis of the relevant literature ($N = 98,622$). The results indicated that education was moderately positively related to both environmental concern and environmental knowledge.

Education and Environmental Behavior

Knowledge and concern of employees are distal determinants of behavior and are less important to organizations than actual behavior. That is, what will really make a difference for organizations seeking to be more sustainable are the actual pro-environmental behaviors that employees perform on the job.

Environmental attitudes have been found to relate to self-reported environmental behavior, with some evidence that the relationship is stronger for certain attitudinal scales for more highly educated individuals (Tarrant & Cordell, 1997). Thus, the greater environmental knowledge and concern of better-educated individuals suggest that they should also perform more pro-environmental behaviors.

Indeed, the majority of the literature shows that more highly educated people do tend to engage in more environmentally responsible behaviors compared with those with less education, although a pioneering, small-scale meta-analysis conducted twenty-five years ago reported the relationship to be typically weak (Hines, Hungerford, & Tomera, 1986–1987). Nonetheless, it has repeatedly been found that the sociodemographic variable most strongly related to environmental volunteering is education level (Curtis, Grabb, & Baer, 1992; Edwards & White, 1980; Florin, Jones, & Wandersman, 1986). More-educated people also tend to engage in more recycling behaviors (Arbuthnot, 1977; Johnson, Bowker, & Cordell, 2004; Thøgersen & Ölander, 2006) and purchase more environmentally conscious products (Gatersleben, Steg, & Vlek, 2002; Thøgersen & Ölander, 2006). On the other hand, education level was found not to matter in regard to energy (Gatersleben, Steg, & Vlek, 2002) or car use (Hunecke, Haustein, Böhler, & Grischkat, 2010; Hunecke, Haustein, Grischkat, & Böhler, 2007; Thøgersen & Ölander, 2006). Also, with regard to very specific behavioral examples, less-educated people tend to purchase and use reusable bags more often than those with more advanced education (Lam & Chen, 2006).

In a contemporary meta-analysis of the education and environmental behavior literature, D'Mello, Wiernik, Ones, and Dilchert (2011) confirmed a general positive trend between education and sustainability. They reported that education level had small to moderate positive relationships with many environmental behaviors, particularly conserving behaviors, such as recycling, avoiding waste, and reusing materials. In contrast, education was largely unrelated to behaviors such as avoiding pollution or choosing responsible alternatives (such as using public transportation, buying green products).

Most of these findings can be explained by the greater levels of environmental knowledge individuals gain from more formal education; highly educated people know how to perform pro-environmental behaviors and why it would be beneficial to do so. For example, learning what can and cannot be recycled may be something that many people are exposed to on college campuses. The lack of differences for behaviors such as choosing responsible alternatives may reflect a preference for comfort and convenience, which is a frequently cited barrier to green behavior (Klein, D'Mello, Ones, Dilchert, Hill, & Wiernik, 2010). More-educated people may be aware of the harmfulness of driving, for example, but they may choose driving themselves over using public transportation because it is more convenient. Alternatively, less-educated individuals, who often have lower incomes (Morgan & David, 1963; Wise, 1975), may make these choices in order to reduce costs and save money (that is, owning a car is too expensive). In this vein, we next discuss the role of income in environmental sustainability.

Income Differences and Environmental Sustainability

Several possible explanations for a relationship between income and sustainability attitudes and behavior have been hypothesized. The social class hypothesis (Van Liere & Dunlap, 1980) predicts that a positive relationship would exist between social class and environmental concern. The rationale for this hypothesis was based on Maslow's (1970) needs hierarchy to posit that individuals with lower income would be too preoccupied with satisfying basic needs to exhibit concern for the environment, compared to members of the upper classes. Additionally, Morrison, Hornback, and Warner (1972) introduced the concept of relative deprivation, which suggests that the lower classes do not notice the extent of environmental degradation as much as upper classes because they tend to live and work in already crowded and polluted cities; thus, they may not be able to perceive environmental harm enough to be concerned or to take action. Given these hypotheses, it is reasonable to predict that higher-income individuals will display more concern for the environment and take more pro-environmental action.

Income and Environmental Concern and Knowledge

Results from the limited research on the relationship between income and environmental concern and knowledge have been highly variable. Van Liere and Dunlap's (1981) review of the literature on income and environmental concern found correlations ranging from strongly positive to strongly negative. Income has been found to be positively related to environmental concern by some researchers (Kinnear, Taylor, & Ahmed, 1974; McEvoy, 1972; Roper Organization, 1990), while others have reported a negative relationship (Roberts, 1996; Samdahl & Robertson, 1989). D'Mello, Wiernik, Ones, and Dilchert's (2011) meta-analysis was conducted with the hope of shedding light on these contradictory findings. They found that income was mostly unrelated to environmental concern, but that higher-income individuals were more knowledgeable about the environment (likely due to also being more highly educated) and, not surprisingly, more willing to pay to support the environment.

Income and Environmental Behavior

With regard to environmental behavior, studies of the relationship with income have been so few as to make drawing any conclusions very difficult. What research has been done suggests that the relationship with income appears to depend on the nature of the behavior. For instance, behaviors that involve reduction of use or reusing are performed more often by lower-income individuals, as they often involve saving money, whereas behaviors involving a greater monetary cost tend to be performed by higher-income groups. Lower energy use has been found to relate to lower household income[3] (Gatersleben, Steg, & Vlek, 2002); this is consistent with the findings for water usage, where higher-income individuals tend to use more (Corral-Verdugo, Bechtel, & Fraijo-Sing,

---

[3]Similar to driving and flying (see Footnote 2), younger individuals' tendencies to use less heating, air conditioning, and water might be confounded by income levels. It has been found that lower-income individuals tend to use less energy and water (Corral-Verdugo, Bechtel, & Fraijo-Sing, 2003; Gatersleben, Steg, & Vlek, 2002).

2003). Higher earners tend to purchase more reusable bags; however, there is no difference across income for the actual reuse of bags (Lam & Chen, 2006). Lower-income individuals have been found to recycle less than higher earners; however, this difference appears to be the result of a lack of opportunity to recycle for low-income individuals, as these income differences in recycling nearly disappear if everyone has access to recycling facilities (Berger, 1997). D'Mello, Wiernik, Ones, and Dilchert's (2011) meta-analytic findings confirm that income is positively related to behaving sustainably only when the behavior is more readily available to high-income individuals (for example, household recycling). However, income tends to be negatively related to environmental behavior when the behaviors help save money (for example, reducing energy use, saving electricity). Other environmental behaviors are unrelated to income.

Suggested Practices

Many of the disparities in environmental knowledge, concern, and behavior across education and income levels could be due to lack of financial resources and opportunity for lower-income and less-educated individuals. Income and education level are not permanent characteristics of an individual, and the same individuals might behave differently if they had the money to do so or were better informed.

Individuals who are better educated and have higher incomes tend to be more knowledgeable and concerned about the environment, and they tend to engage in more behaviors that are differentially available to high-income individuals, such as household recycling. These findings can offer organizations guidance on how they might adapt their sustainability initiatives. For instance, employees with lower incomes and less education may need more training on green products and processes used within the organization, since they may have had less exposure or access to these products outside of the workplace, especially when costly technologies or specific environmental or procedural knowledge is involved.

The issue of income levels is a bit thornier. Depending on the desired pro-environmental behaviors, organizations can build components into their compensation systems to encourage and motivate, and even enable, sustainability behaviors. Lower-income employees may be motivated by having contests for being green or by coming up with new ways to be sustainable at work, with monetary or highly valued awards as extrinsic motivation to elicit sustainable behavior. Additionally, organizations may need to ensure that opportunities for sustainable behaviors are readily available to employees without obstacles or high costs. If great effort or financial expense is required to work sustainably, individuals low in education and income are not likely to be able to afford to do so.

Morrison, Hornback, and Warner's (1972) concept of relative deprivation also suggests some potential areas for intervention for lower-income individuals. The workplace is a potential avenue for encouraging individuals to take pride in their environment and recognize how their contributions can maintain and improve it. By working in clean and environmentally friendly work settings, individuals from economically depressed areas may start to notice and care about environmental degradation. Organizations could emphasize each employee's role in maintaining an environmentally friendly working environment and support this with training or programs underscoring how individual employees can make an impact on the environment. Examples of such programs include employee-sponsored environmental service activities (like cleaning up parks), which are already in place in some organizations. These may be particularly valuable for lower-income employees, who can contribute to helping the environment and witness first-hand the beneficial effects of their actions.

The overall education level of organizational workforces may be important to take into account when considering environmental sustainability initiatives. For organizations with less-educated workforces, the road to sustainability may be more difficult. Such employees are less likely to be knowledgeable about environmental issues or concerned about solving them. Interventions may need to target information and knowledge gaps. In industries and occupations that require high levels of education and typically yield high salaries, organizations are likely to face fewer challenges regarding educating their employees and raising environmental concern. In these settings, organizations might be better served by focusing effort on motivating employees to put their environmental concerns into action, perhaps by encouraging employees to start new green initiatives or to consider environmental issues when making business decisions. These employees are likely to actually engage in pro-environmental behaviors if they are actively encouraged to do so in their workplaces.

Conclusions

This chapter summarized the literature examining demographic and background variables of gender, age, education, and income in relation to environmental attitudes, knowledge, and behavior. Several themes emerged in our examination of these relationships. When taking a closer look at gender differences, we found that women tend to show slightly more concern for the environment (Klein, Ones, & Dilchert, 2011). Furthermore, women are more likely to engage in more private green behaviors such as reusing and repurposing, whereas men tend to engage in more public behaviors such as lobbying and activism (Hunter, Hatch, & Johnson, 2004; McStay & Dunlap, 1983; Mohai, 1992). When the gender and environmental behavior relationship is examined specifically in the workplace, the same general behavioral findings are revealed, with men engaging in more public behaviors (D'Mello, Klein, Ones, Dilchert, Hill, Wiernik, & Biga, 2010). Women engage in more private behaviors at work than men; however, they also display more interpersonal behaviors such as training and educating others about sustainability and encouraging others to behave in a more environmentally friendly manner (D'Mello, Klein, Ones, Dilchert, Hill, Wiernik, & Biga, 2010).

When looking at age differences, younger people are more concerned and knowledgeable about the environment; however, this knowledge and concern often do not appear to translate into more pro-environmental behavior (Wiernik, Ones, & Dilchert, 2011). Younger people tend to be more willing to go out of their way to be green, whereas older people seem to be less willing to sacrifice comfort to be sustainable. However, older individuals still tend to perform more green behaviors, especially in terms of recycling and conservation. Similar results have been found in workplace settings, with older employees recycling and conserving more often and younger employees sometimes taking greater initiative and changing the ways in which they complete tasks (Wiernik, Hill, Ones, Dilchert, D'Mello, & Klein, 2010).

Finally, we reviewed educational and income level differences. More highly educated individuals tend to be more aware of environmental issues and more concerned about the environment (D'Mello, Wiernik, Ones, & Dilchert, 2011). These differences are likely the result of different levels of knowledge acquisition regarding the environment through formal education. In terms of income level, individuals with lower incomes tend to engage in behaviors relating to lowering costs such as saving energy (Gatersleben, Steg, & Vlek, 2002). Higher-income individuals tend to recycle more; however, when there is equal access to recycling facilities, the difference disappears (Berger, 1997). Whether it is money or access to facilities, most income level differences seem to result from a lack of resources and opportunity among low-income individuals. It is likely that individuals of all income levels can equally contribute to organizational goals if environmentally sustainable resources are made accessible to all employees within the workplace.

As organizations are comprised of many types of individuals, it is vital to understand how each employee can make a meaningful contribution to the organization's sustainability efforts. In this chapter, we offered several suggestions to human resource managers for dealing with various sociodemographic variables. Educational interventions should be implemented in organizations in order to equalize the level of knowledge regarding severity of issues, possible solutions, and costs and benefits of the various environmental sustainability solutions. In this way, individuals with less environmental knowledge, such as older and less-educated workers, may be better informed about the ways to behave sustainably. Different industries may be targeted by looking at the average employee education and income level and determining where their development needs are, so that interventions may be designed accordingly. In addition, groups that traditionally hold less power in organizations, such as women and younger employees, should be given greater decision-making power in sustainability-related decisions, allowing greater diversity in values and ideas to be translated into more innovative environmental initiatives. Finally, individuals who show great potential for taking charge, such as younger, more educated employees, should be encouraged to take leadership roles on the implementation of new sustainability initiatives. This will foster skill development in green leadership, which is a valuable asset to organizations.

In today's marketplace, organizations have no choice but to embrace sustainability initiatives to remain competitive. The above review and suggestions outline the optimal ways to develop workplace sustainability behaviors for employees of various sociodemographic backgrounds. Given proper training and interventions, all employees can help organizations reach their environmental sustainability goals.

References

Aaker, D., & Bagozzi, R. (1982). Attitudes toward public policy alternatives to reduce air pollution. *Journal of Marketing & Public Policy, 1,* 85–94.

Althoff, P., & Greig, W. (1977). Environmental pollution control. *Environment and Behavior, 9,* 441–456.

Andreoni, J., & Vesterlund, L. (2001). Which is the fair sex? Gender differences in altruism. *Quarterly Journal of Economics, 116,* 293–312.

Arbuthnot, J. (1977). The roles of attitudinal and personality variables in the prediction of environmental behavior and knowledge. *Environment and Behavior, 9,* 217–232.

Arcury, T., & Christianson, E. (1993). Rural-urban differences in environmental knowledge and actions. *The Journal of Environmental Education, 25,* 19–25.

Arcury, T., & Johnson, T. (1987). Public environmental knowledge: A statewide survey. *Journal of Environmental Education, 18,* 31–37.

Arcury, T., Scollay, S., & Johnson, T. (1987). Sex differences in environmental concern and knowledge: The case of acid rain. *Sex Roles, 16,* 463–472.

Baldassare, M., & Katz, C. (1992). The personal threat of environmental problems as predictor of environmental practices. *Environment and Behavior, 24,* 602–616.

Baron, J. N., Davis-Blake, A., & Bielby, W. T. (1986). The structure of opportunity: How promotion ladders vary within and among organizations. *Administrative Science Quarterly, 31,* 248–273.

Baum, G., & Payea, K. (2004). *Education pays 2004: The benefits of higher education for individuals and society.* Washington, DC: College Board.

Berger, I. (1997). The demographics of recycling and the structure of environmental behavior. *Environment and Behavior, 29,* 515–531.

Beutel, A., & Marini, M. (1995). Gender and values. *American Sociological Review, 60,* 436–448.

Blau, F. D., & Kahn, L. M. (2000). Gender differences in pay. *Journal of Economic Perspectives, 14,* 75–99.

Blocker, T., & Eckberg, D. (1997). Gender and environmentalism: Results from the 1993 General Social Survey. *Social Science Quarterly, 78,* 841–858.

Bord, R., & O'Connor, R. (1997). The gender gap in environmental attitudes: The case of perceived vulnerability to risk. *Social Science Quarterly, 78,* 830–840.

Bowler, M. (1999). Women's earnings: An overview. *Monthly Labor Review, 122,* 13–21.

Brody, S., Zahran, S., Vedlitz, A., & Grover, H. (2008). Examining the relationship between physical vulnerability and public perceptions of global climate change in the United States. *Environment and Behavior, 40,* 72–95.

Bultena, E. M., Rogers, D. L., & Conner, K. A. (1977). Toward explaining citizens' knowledge about a proposed reservoir. *Journal of Environmental Education, 9,* 24–36.

Buttel, F., & Flinn, W. (1978). Social class and mass environmental beliefs. *Environment and Behavior, 10,* 433–450.

Byrnes, J., Miller, D., & Schafer, W. (1999). Gender differences in risk taking: A meta-analysis. *Psychological Bulletin, 125,* 367–383.

Cennamo, L., & Gardner, D. (2008). Generational differences in work values, outcomes and person-organization values fit. *Journal of Managerial Psychology, 23,* 891–906.

Clark, A. Oswald, A., & Warr, P. (1996). Is job satisfaction U-shaped in age? *Journal of Occupational and Organizational Psychology, 69,* 57–81.

Colarelli, S. M., Dean, R. A., & Konstans, C. (1987). Comparative effects of personal and situational influences on job outcomes of new professionals. *Journal of Applied Psychology, 72,* 558–566.

Corral-Verdugo, V., Bechtel, R., & Fraijo-Sing, B. (2003). Environmental beliefs and water conservation: An empirical study. *Journal of Environmental Psychology, 23,* 247–257.

Cross, C. P., Copping, L. T., & Campbell, A. (2011). Sex differences in impulsivity: A meta-analysis. *Psychological Bulletin, 137,* 97–130.

Curtis, J., Grabb, E., & Baer, D. (1992). Voluntary association membership in fifteen countries: A comparative analysis. *American Sociological Review, 57,* 139–152.

Czaja, S. J., Charness, N., Fisk, A. D., Hertzog, C., Nair, S. N., Rogers, W. A., & Sharit, J. (2006). Factors predicting the use of technology: Findings from the center for research and education on aging and technology enhancement (CREATE). *Psychology and Aging, 21,* 333–352.

Daymont, T. N., & Andrisani, P. J. (1984). Job preferences, college major, and the gender gap in earnings. *The Journal of Human Resources, 19,* 408–428.

Davidson, D., & Freudenburg, W. (1996). Gender and environmental risk concerns. *Environment and Behavior, 28,* 302–339.

Dee, T. S. (2004). Are their civic returns to education? *Journal of Public Economics, 88,* 1697–1720.

Dietz, T., Kalof, L., & Stern, P. C. (2002). Gender, values, and environmentalism. *Social Science Quarterly, 83,* 353–364.

D'Mello, S., Klein, R., Ones, D. S., Dilchert, S., Hill, L., Wiernik, B., & Biga, A. (2010, April). An examination of sex differences and green behaviors at work. In D. S. Ones and S. Dilchert (Chairs), *Shades of green: Individual differences in environmentally responsible employee behaviors.* Symposium conducted at the annual conference of the Society for Industrial and Organizational Psychology, Atlanta, Georgia.

D'Mello, S., Wiernik, B., Ones, D. S., & Dilchert, S. (2011, April). The relationship between education level, income, and environmentalism: A meta-analysis. In S. Dilchert (Chair), *Focusing on employees to achieve environmentally sustainable organizations.* Symposium conducted at the annual conference of the Society for Industrial and Organizational Psychology, Chicago, Illinois.

Dolnicar, S., & Grün, B. (2009). Environmentally friendly behavior: Can heterogeneity among individuals and contexts/environments be harvested for improved sustainable management? *Environment and Behavior, 41,* 693–714.

Dunlap, R. E., & Van Liere, K. D. (1978). The "new environmental paradigm": A proposed measuring instrument and preliminary results. *Journal of Environmental Education, 9,* 10–19.

Dunlap, R. E., Van Liere, K. D., Mertig, A. G., & Jones, R. E. (2000). New trends in measuring environmental attitudes: Measuring endorsement of the new ecological paradigm: A revised NEP scale. *Journal of Social Issues, 56,* 425–442.

Eagly, A., & Wood, W. (1991). Explaining sex differences in social behavior: A meta-analytic perspective. *Personality and Social Psychology Bulletin, 17,* 306–315.

Edwards, J., & White, R. (1980). Predictors of social participation: Apparent or real? *Nonprofit and Voluntary Sector Quarterly, 9,* 60–73.

Florin, P., Jones, E., & Wandersman, A. (1986). Black participation in voluntary associations. *Nonprofit and Voluntary Sector Quarterly, 15,* 65–86.

Fransson, N., & Gärling, T. (1999). Environmental concern: Conceptual definitions, measurement methods, and research findings. *Journal of Environmental Psychology, 19,* 369–382.

Gatersleben, B., Steg, L., & Vlek, C. (2002). Measurement and determinants of environmentally significant consumer behavior. *Environment and Behavior, 34,* 335–362.

Gilligan, C. (1982). *In a different voice: Psychological theory and women's development.* Cambridge, MA: Harvard University Press.

Glass Ceiling Commission. (1995). *Good for business: Making full use of the nation's human capital.* Washington, DC: Glass Ceiling Commission.

Gregory, G. D., & Leo, M. D. (2003). Repeated behavior and environmental psychology: The role of personal involvement and habit formation in explaining water consumption. *Journal of Applied Social Psychology, 33,* 1261–1296.

Healy, M. C., Lehman, M., & McDaniel, M. A. (1995). Age and voluntary turnover. *Personnel Psychology, 48,* 335–345.

Hewitt Associates. (1999). *Survey findings: Design and administration of educational reimbursement plans.* Lincolnshire, IL: Hewitt Associates.

Hines, J., Hungerford, H., & Tomera, A. (1986–87). Analysis and synthesis of research on responsible environmental behavior: A meta-analysis. *Journal of Environmental Education, 18,* 1–8.

House, R. J., Hanges, P. M., Javidan, M., Dorfman, P., & Gupta, V. (2004). *Culture, leadership, and organizations: The GLOBE study of 62 societies.* Thousand Oaks, CA: Sage.

Hunecke, M., Haustein, S., Böhler, S., & Grischkat, S. (2010). Attitude-based target groups to reduce the ecological impact of daily mobility behavior. *Environment and Behavior, 42,* 3–43.

Hunecke, M., Haustein, S., Grischkat, S., & Böhler, S. (2007). Psychological, sociodemographic, and infrastructural factors as determinants of ecological impact caused by mobility behavior. *Journal of Environmental Psychology, 27,* 277–292.

Hunter, L., Hatch, A., & Johnson, A. (2004). Cross-national gender variation in environmental behaviors. *Social Science Quarterly, 85,* 677–694.

Ingels, S. J., Curtin, T. R., Kaufman, P., Alt, M. N., & Chen, X. (2002). *Coming of age in the 1990s: The eighth-grade class of 1988 12 years later*

(NCES Publication Number 2002321). Washington, DC: Office of Educational Research and Improvement.

Institute for Research on Higher Education (IRHE). (1997). Where the dollars are: The market for employer-paid continuing education. *Change: The Magazine of Higher Learning, 29,* 39–42.

Jaggi, B., & Westacott, G. (1975). Third-world managers' attitudes toward pollution. *Journal of Applied Psychology, 60,* 392–394.

Johnson, C., Bowker, J., & Cordell, H. (2004). Ethnic variation in environmental belief and behavior: An examination of the new ecological paradigm in a social psychological context. *Environment and Behavior, 36,* 157–186.

Judge, T. A., & Livingston, B. A. (2008). Is the gap more than gender? A longitudinal analysis of gender, gender role orientation, and earnings. *Journal of Applied Psychology, 93,* 994–1012.

Kane, T. J., & Rouse, C. E. (1995). Labor market returns to two and four-year college. *American Economic Review, 85,* 600–614.

Kaufman, H. G. (1978). Continuing education and job performance: A longitudinal study. *Journal of Applied Psychology, 63,* 248–251.

Kinnear, T., Taylor, J., & Ahmed, S. (1974). Ecologically concerned consumers: Who are they? *The Journal of Marketing, 38,* 20–24.

Klein, R., D'Mello, S., Ones, D. S., Dilchert, S., Hill, L., & Wiernik, B. (2010, April). Green motives: Why employees engage in environmentally friendly behaviors. In D. S. Ones and S. Dilchert (Chairs), *Shades of green: Individual differences in environmentally responsible employee behaviors.* Symposium conducted at the annual conference of the Society for Industrial and Organizational Psychology, Atlanta, Georgia.

Klein, R., D'Mello, S., Ones, D. S., Dilchert, S., Wiernik, B., & Hill, L. (2010, April). Gender differences in motivations behind environmental behaviors. In S. Dilchert (Chair), *Organizational and group differences in environmentally responsible employee behaviors.* Symposium conducted at the annual conference of the Society for Industrial and Organizational Psychology, Atlanta, Georgia.

Klein, R., Ones, D. S., & Dilchert, S. (2011, April). Meta-analysis of gender differences in environmental knowledge, concern, and behavior. In S. Dilchert (Chair), *Focusing on employees to achieve environmentally sustainable organizations.* Symposium conducted at the annual conference of the Society for Industrial and Organizational Psychology, Chicago, Illinois.

Klein, R., Ones, D. S., Dilchert S., & Biga, A. (2011, April). *Meta-analysis of gender differences in green workplace behaviors across cultural regions.*

Poster session presented at the annual conference of the Society for Industrial and Organizational Psychology, Chicago, Illinois.

Knussen, C., & Yule, F. (2008). "I'm not in the habit of recycling": The role of habitual behavior in the disposal of household waste. *Environment and Behavior, 40,* 683–702.

Lam, S., & Chen, J. (2006). What makes customers bring their bags or buy bags from the shop? A survey of customers at a Taiwan hypermarket. *Environment and Behavior, 38,* 318–332.

Li, S. (2003). Recycling behavior under China's social and economic transition: The case of metropolitan Wuhan. *Environment and Behavior, 35,* 784–801.

Lleras-Muney, A. (2005). The relationship between education and adult mortality in the United States. *Review of Economic Studies, 72,* 189–221.

Lucas, R. E., & Donnellan, M. B. (2009). Age differences in personality: Evidence from a nationally representative Australian sample. *Developmental Psychology, 45,* 1353–1363.

Lyness, K. S., & Judiesch, M. K. (2001). Are female managers quitters? The relationships of gender, promotions, and family leaves of absence to voluntary turnover. *Journal of Applied Psychology, 86,* 1167–1178.

Lyness, K. S., & Thompson, D. E. (1997). Above the glass ceiling? A comparison of matched samples of female and male executives. *Journal of Applied Psychology, 82,* 359–375.

Maglen, L. R. (1990). Challenging the human capital orthodoxy: The education-productivity link re-examined. *The Economic Record, 66,* 281–294.

Mainieri, T., Barnett, E., Valdero, T., Unipan, J., & Oskamp, S. (1997). Green buying: The influence of environmental concern on consumer behavior. *The Journal of Social Psychology, 137,* 189–204.

Maslow, A. H. (1970). *Motivation and personality.* New York: Harper and Row.

McCrae, R. R., Costa P. T., Jr., de Lima, M. P., Simões, A., Ostendorf, F., Angleitner, A., & Piedmont, R. L. (1999). Age differences in personality across the adult life span: Parallels in five cultures. *Developmental Psychology, 35,* 466–477.

McCright, A. (2010). The effects of gender on climate change knowledge and concern in the American public. *Population and Environment, 32,* 66–87.

McEvoy, J. I. (1972). The American concern with the environment. In W. R. Burch, Jr., N. H. Cheek, Jr., & L. Taylor (Eds.), *Social behavior, natural resources and the environment* (pp. 214–236). New York: Harper and Row.

McStay, J., & Dunlap, R. (1983). Male-female differences in concern for environmental quality. *International Journal of Women's Studies, 6,* 291–301.

Meneses, G., & Palacio, A. (2005). Recycling behavior: A multidimensional approach. *Environment and Behavior, 37,* 837–860.

Mohai, P. (1992). Men, women, and the environment: An examination of the gender gap in environmental concern and activism. *Society & Natural Resources, 5,* 1–19.

Morgan, J., & David, M. (1963). Education and income. *The Quarterly Journal of Economics, 77,* 423–437.

Morris, M. G., & Vankatesh, V. (2000). Age differences in technology adoption decisions: Implications for a changing work force. *Personnel Psychology, 53,* 375–403.

Morrison, A. M., & von Glinow, M. A. (1990). Women and minorities in management. *American Psychologist, 45,* 200–208.

Morrison, D., Hornback, K., & Warner, W. (1972). The environmental movement: Some preliminary observations and predictions. In W. R. Burch, Jr., N. H. Cheek, Jr., & L. Taylor (Eds.), *Social behavior, natural resources, and the environment* (pp. 259–279). New York: Harper and Row.

Ng, T. W. H., Eby, L. T., Sorensen, K. L., & Feldman, D. C. (2005). Predictors of objective and subjective career success: A meta-analysis. *Personnel Psychology, 58,* 367–408.

Ng, T. W. H., & Feldman, D. C. (2008). The relationship of age to ten dimensions of job performance. *Journal of Applied Psychology, 93,* 392–423.

Ng, T. W. H., & Feldman, D. C. (2009). How broadly does education contribute to job performance? *Personnel Psychology, 62,* 89–134.

Nixon, H., Saphores, J., Ogunseitan, O., & Shapiro, A. (2009). Understanding preferences for recycling electronic waste in California: The influence of environmental attitudes and beliefs on willingness to pay. *Environment and Behavior, 41,* 101–124.

O'Connor, R., Bord, R., & Fisher, A. (1999). Risk perceptions, general environmental beliefs, and willingness to address climate change. *Risk Analysis, 19,* 461–471.

Ogle, J., Hyllegard, K., & Dunbar, B. (2004). Predicting patronage behaviors in a sustainable retail environment: Adding retail characteristics and consumer lifestyle orientation to the belief-attitude-behavior intention model. *Environment and Behavior, 36,* 717–741.

Olli, E., Grendstad, G., & Wollebaek, D. (2001). Correlates of environmental behaviors: Bringing back social context. *Environment and Behavior, 33,* 181–208.

Ones, D. S., & Dilchert, S. (2010, April). A taxonomy of green behaviors among employees. In D. S. Ones & S. Dilchert (Chairs), *Shades of green: Individual differences in environmentally responsible employee behaviors.* Symposium conducted at the annual conference of the Society for Industrial and Organizational Psychology, Atlanta, Georgia.

Ones, D., & Viswesvaran, C. (1998). Gender, age, and race differences on overt integrity tests: Results across four large-scale job applicant data sets. *Journal of Applied Psychology, 83,* 35–42.

Ostman, R. E., & Parker, J. L. (1987). Impact of education, age, newspapers, and television on environmental knowledge, concerns, and behaviors. *Journal of Environmental Education, 19,* 3–9.

Ostroff, C., & Atwater, L. E. (2003). Does whom you work with matter? Effects of referent group gender and age composition on managers' compensation. *Journal of Applied Psychology, 88,* 725–740.

Ozanne, L., Humphrey, C., & Smith, P. M. (1999). Gender, environmentalism, and interest in forest certification: Mohai's paradox revisited. *Society & Natural Resources, 12,* 613–622.

Paradise, A. (2007). *State of the industry: ASTD's annual review of trends in workplace learning and performance.* Alexandria, VA: ASTD.

Perna, L. W. (2003). The private benefits of higher education: An examination of the earnings premium. *Research in Higher Education, 44,* 451–472.

Ramaswami, A., Dreher, G. F., Bretz, R., & Wiethoff, C. (2010). Gender, mentoring, and career success: The importance of organizational context. *Personnel Psychology, 63,* 385–405.

Rhodes, S. R. (1983). Age-related differences in work attitudes and behavior: A review and conceptual analysis. *Psychological Bulletin, 93,* 328–367.

Roberts, B. W., Walton, K. E., & Viechtbauer, W. (2006). Patterns of mean-level change in personality traits across the life course: A meta-analysis of longitudinal studies. *Psychological Bulletin, 132,* 1–25.

Roberts, J. (1996). Green consumers in the 1990s: Profile and implications for advertising. *Journal of Business Research, 36,* 217–231.

Roper Organization. (1990). *The environment: Public attitudes and individual behavior.* New York: Roper Organization.

Samdahl, D., & Robertson, R. (1989). Social determinants of environmental concern: Specification and test of the model. *Environment and Behavior, 21*, 57–81.

Saphores, J., Nixon, H., Ogunseitan, O., & Shapiro, A. (2006). Household willingness to recycle electronic waste: An application to California. *Environment and Behavior, 38*, 183–208.

Savickas, M. L., Nota, L., Rossier, J., Dauwalder, J. P., Duarte, M. E., Guichard, J., Soresi, S., Van Esbroeck, R., & van Vianen, A. E. M. (2009). Life designing: A paradigm for career construction in the 21st century. *Journal of vocational behavior, 75*, 239–250.

Shen, J., & Saijo, T. (2008). Reexamining the relations between sociodemographic characteristics and individual environmental concern: Evidence from Shanghai data. *Journal of Environmental Psychology, 28*, 42–50.

Schultz, W. (2001). The structure of environmental concern: Concern for self, other people, and the biosphere. *Journal of Environmental Psychology, 21*, 327–339.

Slovic, P. (1992). Perceptions of risk: Reflections on the psychometric paradigm. In D. Golding & S. Krimsky (Eds.), *Theories of risk* (pp. 117–152). New York: Praeger.

Smola, K. W., & Sutton, C. D. (2002). Generational differences: Revisiting generational work values for the new millennium. *Journal of Organizational Behavior, 23*, 363–382.

Society for Human Resource Management. (2010). Green jobs—Are they here yet? SHRM poll. Retrieved from www.shrm.org/Research/SurveyFindings/Articles/Pages/GreenJobsAreTheyHereYet.aspx

Solomon, L., Tomaskovic-Devey, D., & Risman, B. (1989). The gender gap and nuclear power: Attitudes in a politicized environment. *Sex Roles, 21*, 401–414.

Stern, P. C., Dietz, T., & Kalof, L. (1993). Value orientations, gender, and environmental concern. *Environment and Behavior, 25*, 322.

Tait, M., Padgett, M. Y., & Baldwin, T. T. (1989). Job and life satisfaction: A reevaluation of the strength of the relationship and gender effects as a function of the date of the study. *Journal of Applied Psychology, 74*, 502–507.

Takács-Sánta, A. (2007). Barriers to environmental concern. *Human Ecology Review, 14*, 26–38.

Tanner, C. (1999). Constraints on environmental behaviour. *Journal of Environmental Psychology, 19*, 145–157.

Tarrant, M., & Cordell, H. (1997). The effect of respondent characteristics on general environmental attitude-behavior correspondence. *Environment and Behavior, 29*, 618–637.

Thøgersen, J., & Ölander, F. (2006). To what degree are environmentally beneficial choices reflective of a general conservation stance? *Environment and Behavior, 38,* 550–569.

Tindall, D., Davies, S., & Mauboules, C. (2003). Activism and conservation behavior in an environmental movement: The contradictory effects of gender. *Society & Natural Resources, 16,* 909–932.

Tudor, T., Barr, S., & Gilg, A. (2007). A tale of two locational settings: Is there a link between pro-environmental behaviour at work and at home? *Local Environment, 12,* 409–421.

Van Liere, K. D., & Dunlap, R. E. (1980). The social bases of environmental concern: A review of hypotheses, explanations and empirical evidence. *Public Opinion Quarterly, 44,* 181–197.

Van Liere, K. D., & Dunlap, R. E. (1981). Environmental concern: Does it make a difference how it's measured? *Environment and Behavior, 13,* 651–676.

Warr, P. (2008). Work values: Some demographic and cultural correlates. *Journal of Occupational and Organizational Psychology, 81,* 751–775.

Wegge, J., Roth, C., Neubach, B., Schmidt, K., & Kanfer, R. (2008). Age and gender diversity as determinants of performance and health in a public organization: The role of task complexity and group size. *Journal of Applied Psychology, 93,* 1301–1313.

Whitmarsh, L., & O'Neill, S. (2010). Green identity, green living? The role of pro-environmental self-identity in determining consistency across diverse pro-environmental behaviours. *Journal of Environmental Psychology, 30,* 305–314.

Wiernik, B., Hill, L., Ones, D. S., Dilchert, S., D'Mello, S., & Klein, R. (2010, April). Youthful waste versus older inflexibility? Age differences in green behavior. In S. Dilchert (Chair), *Organizational and group differences in environmentally responsible employee behaviors.* Symposium conducted at the annual conference of the Society for Industrial and Organizational Psychology, Atlanta, Georgia.

Wiernik, B., Ones, D. S., & Dilchert, S. (2011, April). *The relationship between individual age and sustainability: A meta-analysis.* Poster session presented at the annual conference of the Society for Industrial and Organizational Psychology, Chicago, Illinois.

Wiernik, B., Ones, D. S., Dilchert, S., & Biga, A. (under review). Age differences in green work behaviors across 11 countries. Manuscript submitted for publication.

Wise, D. (1975). Academic achievement and job performance. *The American Economic Review, 65,* 350–366.

Wolfers, J. (2006). Diagnosing discrimination: Stock returns and CEO gender. *Journal of the European Economic Association, 4,* 531–541.

Wong, M., Gardiner, E., Lang, W., & Coulon, L. (2008). Generational differences in personality and motivation: Do they exist and what are the implications for the workplace? *Journal of Managerial Psychology, 23*, 878–890.

Young, R. (1980). The relationship between information levels and environmental approval: The wilderness issue. *The Journal of Environmental Education, 11*, 25–30.

Zeidner, M., & Shechter, M. (1988). Psychological responses to air pollution: Some personality and demographic correlates. *Journal of Environmental Psychology, 8*, 191–208.

Zelezny, L., Chua, P., & Aldrich, C. (2000). New ways of thinking about environmentalism: Elaborating on gender differences in environmentalism. *Journal of Social Issues, 56*, 443–457.

Zhang, Y., Hussain, A., Deng, J., & Letson, N. (2007). Public attitudes toward urban trees and supporting urban tree programs. *Environment and Behavior, 39*, 797–814.

CHAPTER SEVEN

The Role of Commitment in Bridging the Gap Between Organizational Sustainability and Environmental Sustainability

Jessica Mesmer-Magnus,
Chockalingam Viswesvaran,
and Brenton M. Wiernik

Environmental sustainability refers to meeting the "the needs of the present without compromising the ability of future generations to meet their own needs" (Brundtland, 1987). The objective of organizations involves generating value for their stakeholders. Humanity at large is a stakeholder in all organizations. Thus, organizational sustainability—the ability of an organization to compete and remain viable over time—depends on the success of organizations in positively impacting environmental sustainability. However, currently, there is an often-lamented gap between organizational sustainability and environmental sustainability. On

---

The authors would like to thank Megan Wiernik for her valuable assistance in preparing the graphic figure for this chapter.

one hand, environmental sustainability is threatened. Our planet is under stress from human activities, and the resources to sustain life are being irreversibly taxed. Resources that have traditionally fueled economic development are being depleted, with potentially disastrous consequences (Viswesvaran & Ones, 2010). On the other hand, organizations face stiff competition for viability fueled by increased globalization and rapid, dynamic changes in the technology of production. As Stern (2000) has pointed out, organizations are responsible for much of the economic activity that creates environmental calamities and consumes resources in excess of the carrying capacity of our planet. The purpose of this chapter is to suggest one major way that this gap between organizational sustainability and environmental sustainability can be bridged. Our suggestion relies on human resources of organizations and a key variable: commitment.

A Vital and Renewable Resource of Organizations: Employees

Organizations today face multiple challenges and are tirelessly pursuing economic goals, including increasing productivity in the face of depleting resources. Yet, in all this, all organizations, for profit and non-profit, private and public, large and small, local and international, struggle to maintain a competitive advantage over their peers. Competitive advantage refers to the ability of an organization to operate in ways that allow it to perform at consistently higher levels than other companies in the industry and is built on two principles: perceived customer value and uniqueness (Porter, 1998). Perceived customer value and uniqueness can be attained through multiple means, including acquiring unique financial or economic capability (that is, producing goods cheaper), developing outstanding product capability, and attaining unique organizational capability (for example, superior human resources). Of the different sources available for organizations to build a competitive advantage, the source most difficult for competitors to replicate is organizational capability (Pfeffer, 1994). All other advantages are too often easily replicated by competitors. Organizational capability is the only reliable source of sustainable advantage to organizations.

Given that our planet's resources are limited and strained, environmentally sustainable strategies may be the most pertinent source of competitive advantage for organizations to pursue. In this chapter, we discuss and review research and practices with the aim of providing an understanding of the ways in which organizational sustainability and environmental sustainability can be concurrently achieved when employees and organizations are both committed. We distinguish among three forms of commitment: (1) employee commitment to the organization, (2) individual commitment to the environment, and (3) organizational commitment to environmental sustainability. When all three forms of commitment are present and aligned, a variety of behaviors and outcomes can be expected to ensue such that organizational sustainability and environmental sustainability become complementary rather than competing objectives. Thus, in this analysis, the three Cs of commitment are conceptualized as the three pillars of human resources for sustainable organizations and a sustainable planet.

Table 7.1 provides a complete summary of important constructs and their definitions covered in this chapter. We also provide examples of antecedents and consequences for each variable to highlight processes leading to the emergence of each variable, as well as to outcomes that can be affected. In the following sections, we first review the literature on employee commitment to organizations. We discuss the definitions, the different forms and dimensions of employee commitment, and the benefits organizations can derive from committed employees. Second, we discuss how individual environmental commitment is related to individual environmental behaviors, both generally and in the workplace. Third, we review the literature on organizational commitment to environmental sustainability, exploring how commitment leads to sustainability initiatives and the integration of sustainability into broader organizational goals. Finally, we discuss how these three forms of commitment may combine to lead to both organizational and environmental sustainability.

Table 7.1. Key Variables for Bridging the Gap Between Organizational and Environmental Sustainability: Their Definitions, Example of Antecedents, and Consequences

Variable	Definition	Examples of Proposed/ Demonstrated Antecedents	Examples of Proposed/ Demonstrated Consequences
Environmental Sustainability	Meeting "the needs of the present without compromising the ability of future generations to meet their own needs" (Brundtland, 1987) "Improving the quality of human life while living within the carrying capacity of supporting eco-systems" (IUCN, UNEP, WWF, 1991)	• Sum of all human activity, past and present, that affects earth's ecological systems (includes activities of individuals, organizations, entire economies) • Human-environment interactions	• Sustainability of the world's ecosystems • Sustainability of species • Sustainability of humanity on earth • Economic sustainability • Organizational sustainability
Organizational Sustainability	Capability of an organization to compete and remain viable over time	• Economic conditions • Legal conditions • Ecological conditions • Socio-political systems • Resource availability • Technological availability • Management • Strategy, including environmental strategy • Environmental management	• Continued contributions to stakeholder interests and well-being

Employee Commitment (to the Organization)	Reflects the extent to which he/she is bonded to and/or linked with an organization	• Demographic variables (such as age, organizational tenure) • Job satisfaction • Personality • Organizational support • Transformational leadership • Role clarity/ambiguity • Role conflict • Organizational justice	• Intent to turnover • Turnover • Absenteeism • Overall job performance • Organizational citizenship behavior
Individual Environmental Commitment	Extent to which an individual is dedicated to environmental sustainability and is willing to engage in pro-environmental behaviors	• Environmental knowledge • Environmental awareness • Environmental attitudes • Perceived behavioral control • Social norms • Moral norms • Personality (for example, altruism, openness) • Interests • Demographic variables (age/generation, gender) • National cultural background	• Intent to engage in pro-environmental behavior • Intent to perform employee green behaviors • Pro-environmental behavior • Employee green behavior

Continued

Table 7.1. Continued

Variable	Definition	Examples of Proposed/ Demonstrated Antecedents	Examples of Proposed/ Demonstrated Consequences
Organizational Commitment to Environmental Sustainability	Extent to which an organization is dedicated to environmental sustainability and is willing to engage in and incorporate environmental sustainability considerations into its operations, to support organizational initiatives aimed at environmental sustainability	• Top management and leadership support • Corporate culture • Culture and societal values • Economic conditions • Stakeholder pressures	• Environmental sustainability initiatives • Environmental sustainability • Organizational sustainability • Employee green behaviors • Pro-environmental behavior • For environmentally committed employees: employee commitment
Pro-Environmental Behaviors	Individual behaviors contributing to environmental sustainability (such as limiting energy consumption, avoiding waste, recycling, environmental activism). A distinguishing feature of these behaviors is that they are (1) intentional and (2) freely selected (that is, not under organizational control)	• Environmental knowledge • Environmental awareness • Environmental attitudes • Perceived behavioral control • Social norms • Moral norms • Personality (for example, altruism, openness) • Interests • Demographic variables (age/ generation, gender) • National cultural background	• Intent to engage in pro-environmental behavior • Intent to perform employee green behaviors • Pro-environmental behavior • For organizations committed to environmental sustainability: employee green behaviors

Term	Definition		
Employee Green Behaviors	Scalable actions and behaviors that employees engage in that are linked with and contribute to or detract from environmental sustainability (Ones & Dilchert, Chapter 5 in this volume)	• Environmental knowledge • Environmental awareness • Environmental attitudes • Environmental commitment • Personality • Motives/motivation • Values • Demographic variables (age/generation, gender) • Perceived and actual organizational control, including job requirements • Organizational support • For organizations committed to environmental sustainability: employee commitment	• For organizations committed to environmental sustainability: improved productivity • Environmental sustainability • Organizational sustainability
Environmental Sustainability Initiatives	Organizationally sponsored programs and interventions aiming to enhance environmental sustainability and thus organizational sustainability	• Organizational commitment to environmental sustainability • Societal expectations • Legal requirements • Stakeholder pressures	• Environmental sustainability • Organizational sustainability • Employee green behaviors • Pro-environmental behavior • For environmentally committed employees: employee commitment

Employee Commitment to the Organization, Employee Behaviors, and Organizational Sustainability

Theoretical Underpinnings and Measurement of Employee Commitment

An employee's organizational commitment reflects the extent to which he or she is bonded to and linked with an organization (Mathieu & Zajac, 1990). Regardless of operationalization, definitions of organizational commitment regard it as "a psychological state that (a) characterizes the employee's relationship with the organization and (b) has implications for the decision to continue or discontinue membership in the organization" (Meyer, Allen, & Smith, 1993, p. 539). Several aspects and dimensions of commitment have been studied over the years (Cooper-Hakim & Viswesvaran, 2005). These have included attitudinal, calculative, normative, affective, and continuance commitment.

Attitudinal commitment has been defined as "the relative strength of an individual's identification with and involvement in a particular organization . . . characterized by . . . (a) a strong belief in and acceptance of the organization's goals and values, (b) a willingness to exert considerable effort on behalf of the organization, and (c) a strong desire to maintain membership in the organization" (Mowday, Steers, & Porter, 1979, p. 226). Calculative commitment is defined as "a structural phenomenon which occurs as a result of individual-organizational transactions and alterations in side-bets or investments over time" (Hrebiniak & Alutto, 1972, p. 556). Normative commitment refers to the process whereby the combination of individual predispositions (i.e., tendency toward organizational loyalty, duty attitudes, perceived individual-organizational value congruence) and organizational decisions/actions/practices (selection, promotion, compensation, development, etc.) result in the development of commitment to the organization (Mathieu & Zajac, 1990; Wiener, 1982).

Parallel to the classification of commitment dimensions as attitudinal, calculative, and normative commitments, Allen and Meyer (1990, 1996) proposed that the various organizational commitment constructs might logically be organized into a three-dimensional commitment construct, reflecting the three key ways in which employees may feel attached to their organization: (1) *affective* (which denotes an "emotional attachment to, identification with, and involvement in the organization"), (2) *normative* (which denotes "a perceived obligation to remain in the organization"), and (3) *continuance* commitment (which denotes "the perceived costs associated with leaving the organization" (Meyer, Stanley, Herscovitch, & Topolnytsky, 2002, p. 21). The majority of organizational commitment work in the past decade has conceptualized it according to this three-dimensional framework. Although all three components of organizational commitment are likely to be negatively associated with employees' turnover intentions, logically, there may be a different pattern of relationships with other correlates, owing to the differences in the nature of employee attachment to the organization across the three dimensions of commitment (Fishbein, 1967; Fishbein & Ajzen, 1975; Meyer & Allen, 1991).

Beyond these three dimensions of commitment, other forms of organizational commitment have been identified, although these have subsequently either been included within one of the dimensions of Meyer and Allen's (1991, 1997) Three-Component Model of Commitment or differentiated from the commitment construct altogether. For example, organizational identification (Hall, Schneider, & Nygren, 1970) constitutes one of the sub-dimensions of attitudinal commitment defined by Mowday, Steers, and Porter (1979) and is included within the affective commitment sub-dimension defined by Meyer and Allen. However, Riketta (2005) and Riketta and Van Dick (2005) meta-analytically compared the organizational commitment and organizational identification constructs and found differences in their pattern of relationships with some correlates/outcomes. They proposed this could be explained (a) by the likelihood that organizational identification is one of the precursors to organizational attachment rather than a form of commitment or (b) as a function of the various ways in which each construct has been operationalized in the extant literature. Cooper-Hakim and Viswesvaran (2005) identified more than twenty-five different commitment constructs and assessed their intercorrelations by meta-analytically cumulating results across 997 studies. A key finding in Cooper-Hakim and

Viswesvaran's study is the positive manifold of correlations across the different commitment constructs, suggesting an underlying overall psychological construct of "employee commitment" to the organization.

In all its manifestations, we view employee commitment as a key ingredient of employee psychological engagement (cf. Macey & Schneider, 2008). Although employee psychological engagement includes several attitudinal variables such as job satisfaction, involvement, and commitment, we believe that in understanding and explaining employee behaviors, employee commitment is less ambiguous than the other two. Both job satisfaction and involvement have potential liabilities when they are considered on their own. For example, job satisfaction can be conceptualized as a dispositional construct (Judge & Larsen, 2001) or as a construct arising from contextual variables (e.g., salary, co-workers, supervisor; Acker, 2004). Similarly, involvement can be conceptualized as a task- or work-based variable or an organizationally based variable. Conceptually, only the construct of commitment embeds the employee in a specific organizational milieu and gives a relatively uncontaminated evaluation of an employee's dedication to an organization and the strength of his or her bond.

Employee Commitment and Employee Behaviors

A significant amount of research, including several large-scale meta-analyses (cf. Cooper-Hakim & Viswesvaran, 2005; Mathieu & Zajac, 1990; Meyer, Stanley, Herscovitch, & Topolnytsky, 2002; Riketta & Van Dick, 2005), has been undertaken to explore and document the role of commitment in the workplace. The nomological network of employee commitment is well understood. Seven categories of antecedent/correlate variables have been explored in relation to organizational commitment: (1) personal characteristics (age, education, tenure, ability, job level, etc.; Mathieu & Zajac, 1990; Meyer, Stanley, Herscovitch, & Topolnytsky, 2002), (2) role states (e.g., role conflict, ambiguity, overload; Mathieu & Zajac, 1990; Meyer, Stanley, Herscovitch, & Topolnytsky, 2002), (3) job characteristics (skill variety, autonomy, challenge; Mathieu & Zajac, 1990), (4) group/leader relations (cohesiveness, leader communication, leader consideration, task interdependence, etc.; Mathieu & Zajac, 1990; Meyer, Stanley, Herscovitch, & Topolnytsky, 2002), (5) organizational characteristics (size, centralization, etc.; Mathieu & Zajac, 1990), (6) motivation (job involvement, stress, occupational commitment, etc.; Mathieu & Zajac, 1990; Meyer, Stanley, Herscovitch, & Topolnytsky, 2002), and (7) job satisfaction (overall job satisfaction, workgroup satisfaction, supervisor satisfaction, etc.; Mathieu & Zajac, 1990; Meyer, Stanley, Herscovitch, & Topolnytsky, 2002).

In addition, employee commitment to the organization is associated with a number of outcomes that have the potential to significantly affect an organization's ability to sustain itself over time. For example, an important predictor of organizational sustainability is low turnover among its employees, and organizational commitment has consistently been found to be negatively correlated with employee withdrawal behaviors, intent to look for a new job, intent to leave the organization, and actual turnover (Cooper-Hakim & Viswesvaran, 2005; Mathieu & Zajac, 1990; Riketta & Van Dick, 2005). Having a consistent, committed workforce enables an organization to maintain its culture and organizational memory, which are paramount to organizational effectiveness and viability (Goodman, Zammuto, & Gifford, 2001; Gregory, Harris, Armenakis, & Shook, 2009; Ostroff, Shin, & Kinicki, 2005). Additionally, with low turnover, large influxes of new employees do not have to be trained and socialized, and those individuals that are hired are likely to be socialized into the organization by members who are highly committed to the organization and its values, thus more easily preserving the organization's culture and competitiveness (Saks, Uggerslev, & Fassina, 2007) and, we suggest, long-term sustainability. Low levels of recruitment and selection activities are also likely to lead to cost savings, another potential advantage for organizational sustainability. Beyond these direct savings, research suggests that recruiters and organizational recruitment practices can have a significant effect on an organization's culture, effectiveness, and sustainability (Braddy, Meade, Michael, & Fleenor, 2009; Stone, Stone-Romero, & Lukaszewski, 2007); with low turnover, the potential for negative effects associated with organizational recruitment practices on culture can be minimized.

Beyond reduced turnover, individuals who are committed to their organization display job performance that is superior to that of individuals who have lower organizational commitment (Cooper-Hakim & Viswesvaran, 2005; Mathieu & Zajac, 1990). These employees are also likely to be more involved in their jobs, which contributes to effective performance (Cooper-Hakim & Viswesvaran, 2005). Research also suggests committed employees are more likely to engage in the types of organizational citizenship and extra-role behaviors that benefit organizational bottom-line performance (Meyer, Stanley, Herscovitch, & Topolnytsky, 2002; Riketta & Van Dick, 2005). Riketta and Van Dick (2005) reported sizable meta-analytically obtained correlations between organizational commitment and organizational extra-role behavior (ρ = .36), general extra-role behavior (ρ = .35), and turnover intentions (ρ = −.48). Other large-scale meta-analyses have also reported significant correlations between organizational commitment and incidence of workplace violence (Hershcovis & Barling, 2010), workplace harassment (Willness, Steel, & Lee, 2007), organizational citizenship behaviors (Chiaburu & Harrison, 2008; Nielsen, Hrivnak, & Shaw, 2009), and counterproductive work behavior (Dalal, 2005). Effective employee job performance and incidence of extra-role behaviors are crucial for organizational sustainability by way of enhanced competitiveness and viability (Harter, Schmidt, & Hayes, 2002), so improving organizational commitment to encourage these behaviors is essential.

Beyond individual behavior, Mathieu and Zajac (1990) noted that, although group cohesiveness and team member relations may promote organizational commitment, the process is likely reciprocal, such that high levels of organizational commitment promote aspects of effective group functioning, including enhanced cohesiveness, efficient team process, effective team member relations, team commitment, and team member commitment to group goals. Effective group functioning promotes high levels of individual and team performance (Marks & Panzer, 2004), both of which have positive implications for organizational sustainability (Harter, Schmidt, & Hayes, 2002). Further, given that organizational commitment reduces work withdrawal and turnover, the synergy (with regard to process, production, etc.) as well as the elaborate group cognition that develops within these teams will be sustainable over time, further reinforcing individual, team, and organizational performance (DeChurch & Mesmer-Magnus, 2010; Marks, DeChurch, Mathieu, Panzer, & Alonso, 2005).

The overarching conclusion from this voluminous research is that employee commitment is substantially correlated with several important workplace behaviors and outcomes that contribute to organizational sustainability. These results reinforce the notion that low levels of organizational commitment among employees can have significantly deleterious effects on an organization's competitiveness, viability, and bottom-line performance.

Employee Commitment to Organizational Sustainability Initiatives

As researchers have consistently found a positive manifold surrounding the various types of employee commitment (organizational commitment, work commitment, team commitment, union commitment, career commitment, etc.; Allen & Meyer, 1990; Cooper-Hakim & Viswesvaran, 2005; Mathieu & Zajac, 1990; Meyer, Stanley, Herscovitch, & Topolnytsky, 2002), it is logical that employee commitment to organizational sustainability initiatives would also be positively associated with organizational commitment. After all, an important aspect of affective organizational commitment is identification with an organization's values and principles (Mowday, Steers, & Porter, 1979). Employees highly (affectively) committed to their organization are likely to adopt and act in accordance with organizational sustainability initiatives (green management practices, corporate social responsibility initiatives, environmental sustainability programs, etc.).

Although there is currently no research that directly tests this assumption, theory and research in the corporate social responsibility (CSR) literature does provide support for this proposition. For example, Collier and Esteban (2007) argue that the crucial predictor of viable corporate social responsibility practices is an organizational workforce that is motivated and committed to the effective delivery of such practices. The single best predictor of this employee motivation/commitment, according to these authors, is high employee commitment to and identification with the organization. Similarly, Harter, Schmidt, and Hayes (2002) found significant positive relationships among employee satisfaction, organizational commitment, engagement, and business-unit outcomes (many of which can be linked to socially responsible business practices). Riketta and Van Dick (2005) reported moderate positive correlations between organizational commitment and a variety of employee-enacted extra-role behaviors, reinforcing the idea that committed employees would be inclined to act in ways which would support a number of organizational initiatives, particularly those which are seen to be an extension of organizational values. Indeed, Ligeti and Oravecz (2009) argue that organizations are most successful in gaining employee support for CSR initiatives when their employees see these programs as logical extensions of the organizational ethical values and core business practices.

Rettab, Brik, and Mellahi (2009) explored the relationships among corporate social responsibility, organizational competitiveness, corporate reputation, and employee organizational commitment using an international sample. They report evidence that the link between corporate social responsibility practices and employee organizational commitment may be reciprocal in that CSR practices enhance organizational reputation and performance, which in turn enhance employee organizational commitment. Committed employees are then more likely to enact behaviors which support the maintenance of CSR initiatives. Similarly, Nielsen and Thomsen (2009) found employees high in organizational commitment were likely to engage in informal and word-of-mouth communications with co-workers as well as external stakeholders that supported the implementation of CSR programs.

Thus, this body of research on CSR shows that, in addition to increased bottom-line performance, organizations can expect employee organizational commitment to also lead to greater support for and success of corporate social responsibility initiatives, including organizational environmental sustainability initiatives.

Individual Environmental Commitment: Pro-Environmental Behaviors and Employee Green Behaviors

People can improve environmental sustainability through their actions and behaviors. Pro-environmental behaviors encompass all individual behaviors that contribute to environmental sustainability. Such behaviors are volitional, intentional, and entirely under the control of individuals. Thus, the research literature on pro-environmental behaviors has tended to focus on behaviors in non-work settings (Ones & Dilchert, 2009). Although behaviors such as reducing use, avoiding waste, recycling, and preventing pollution (see Ones & Dilchert, Chapter 5 in this volume) can be performed at work or in personal lives, the latter affords a degree of individual control over behavior that may not be possible in organizational settings.

Employee green behaviors refer to those actions and behaviors "employees engage in that are linked with and contribute to or detract from environmental sustainability" (Ones & Dilchert, Chapter 5). Employee actions directed to environmental sustainability can be manifestations of both individual and organizational choices. As such, employee green behaviors are related to pro-environmental behaviors but are distinguishable based on a number of key features (for example, job/work context, diminished degree of personal control).

In this section, we review and extend influential models aimed at understanding pro-environmental behaviors and employee green behaviors, highlighting key findings about the role of environmental attitudes. We propose that commitment to the environment (that is, individual environmental commitment) is a key ingredient for individual environmental behaviors in or outside of work settings.

Individual Environmental Commitment and Pro-Environmental Behaviors

Environmental attitudes play a pivotal role in explaining the processes involved in pro-environmental behaviors. Attitudes can be defined as psychological tendencies that are "expressed by evaluating a particular entity with some degree of favor or disfavor" (Eagly & Chaiken, 1993, p. 1). Accordingly, environmental attitudes reflect favorability with which individuals view the environment in general or specific ecological issues in particular. Early models of pro-environmental behaviors recognized that environmental knowledge by itself was insufficient to bring about pro-environmental actions and that knowledge would have to act through attitudes to affect behavior (Kollmuss & Agyeman, 2002). Subsequent models involving environmental behaviors tended to rely on the "theory of reasoned action" (TRA) (Fishbein & Ajzen, 1975) and its extended version "theory of planned behavior" (TPB) (Ajzen, 1988, 1991). Vast research summarized in meta-analyses supports the general tenets of the theory that attitudes lead to behavioral intentions and intentions are the more proximal determinant of behavior.

The most influential meta-analysis of TPB (Armitage & Conner, 2001, cited 1,864 times in the research literature) found that attitudes correlated .49 with behavior ($k = 115$) and behavioral intention correlated .47 with behavior ($k = 48$). Within the environmental literature, echoing findings from an earlier smaller scale meta-analysis, Bamberg and Möser's (2007) meta-analysis reported an unreliability corrected mean correlation of .42 ($k = 17$) between environmental attitudes and pro-environmental behavior. Overall, then, it is clear that attitudes are important determinants of behavior in general and that environmental attitudes, in particular, are potent predictors of pro-environmental behaviors.

Despite the predictive value of environmental attitudes, it is important to distinguish them from environmental commitment. Environmental commitment can be defined as the extent to which an individual is dedicated to environmental sustainability and is willing to engage in pro-environmental behaviors. Environmental commitment characterizes the employee's relationship with environmental sustainability and has implications for individual intentions and behaviors. In our view, environmental commitment drives intentions and behaviors. For individuals to behave in environmentally sustainable ways, they should be committed to the environment and express intent to behave pro-environmentally. Past research in environmental psychology has confounded environmental commitment either with behavioral intention (Smythe & Brook, 1980) or attitudes (Cottrell, 2003). Environmental attitudes describe favorability of opinion; commitment describes dedication to environmental sustainability and willingness to behave pro-environmentally. Intentions describe reasoned and *communicated* plans to engage in behavior. The purpose of the foregoing discussion is not to suggest that other determinants are irrelevant to environmentally responsible behavior, but rather to suggest incorporating environmental commitment into models of pro-environmental behaviors. Of course, other proximal determinants such as moral norms and perceived behavioral control, as well as distal determinants such as social norms, feelings of guilt, awareness of problems, and internal attributions, all have a role to play as well (Bamberg & Möser, 2007; Hines, Hungerford, & Tomera, 1986/87).

Individual Environmental Commitment and Employee Green Behaviors

To date, very little research has been conducted in work settings examining the relationship between individual environmental commitment and employee green behaviors. As we have already noted, research has demonstrated that environmental behaviors at work are subject to more organizational control than non-work environmental behaviors. Based on over two thousand critical incidents gathered from U.S.-based organizations, Ones and Dilchert (2010) reported that about 30 percent of pro-environmental behaviors at work were required by organizations. Similarly, 25 percent of environmentally unfriendly behaviors were required by employers. Parallel findings were reported by Hill, Dilchert, Wiernik, Klein, and D'Mello (2011) using data from fourteen European countries. Eleven percent of pro-environmental behaviors and 25 percent of eco-unfriendly behaviors were required. Thus, it is important to consider the effect that the organizational context can have on the relationship between individual environmental commitment and employee green behaviors.

Institutional, structural, and social barriers in work settings are likely to have a significant influence on employee green behaviors. Organizational control over activities taking place in the workplace can moderate the link between environmental commitment and employee green behaviors. When organizational control is weak, employees can express their environmental commitment freely. Thus, the link between environmental commitment and employee green behaviors should be strong. When organizational control is strong, employee green behaviors can be expected to vary less as a function of employees' environmental commitment. Interestingly, in this case, employee commitment to the organization can play a role. In organizations in which environmental sustainability is an explicit goal, the link between employee commitment (to the organization) and employee green behaviors ought to be strong. In support of this hypothesis, in an organization that places a high premium on environmental sustainability, McCance, Biga, Gibby, and Massman (under review) found that employee engagement (including an organizational commitment scale, alpha = .88) correlated in the .25 to .31 range with employee green behaviors (unreliability corrected correlations in the .29 to .35 range; Ns = 8,094 – 8,348 employees).

However, we suspect that in organizations that can be characterized as "eco-unfriendly," employee commitment to the organization can be negatively related to employee green behaviors. This leads us to the third C or "commitment" variable in bridging the gap between organizational sustainability and environmental sustainability—organizational commitment to the environment.

Organizational Commitment to the Environment: Environmental Sustainability Initiatives and Integration of Environmental Sustainability Considerations into Operations and Functions

Organizations vary in their degree of eco-friendliness and environmental responsibility (D'Mello, Klein, Ones, Dilchert, Wiernik, & Hill, 2010; D'Mello, Ones, Klein, Wiernik, & Dilchert, 2011; McWilliams & Siegel, 2001). The degree of organizational eco-friendliness/responsibility can be inferred from two major categories of indicators: (1) environmental sustainability initiatives and

(2) integration of environmental sustainability goals and considerations into organizational missions, operations, and functions.

Organizations that undertake a greater number of environmental initiatives are more eco-friendly. In this vein, D'Mello, Klein, Ones, Dilchert, Wiernik, and Hill (2010) demonstrated that organizations could be scaled in terms of the environmental initiatives reported on company websites. If nothing else, environmental sustainability initiatives raise environmental awareness among stakeholders and contribute to organizational reputations as valuing environmental sustainability (Bohdanowicz, 2006; Hasseldine, Salama, & Toms, 2005).

Organizations can also embed sustainability into their missions, operations, and functions. Embedding sustainability into the mission involves an explicit recognition that the organizational raison d'être encompasses economic, social, and ecological goals (that is, the triple bottom line; Elkington, 2004). Operational greening of organizations involves transition to or use of eco-friendly options in all aspects of organizational operations (for example, production, logistics). Finally, embedding environmental sustainability into organizational functions refers to the greening of various functional areas (for example, marketing, human resources).

Why do organizations vary in environmental sustainability initiatives? Why do some organizations more readily embed environmental sustainability considerations into their operations or functional areas, whereas others do not? Several antecedents can be proposed: corporate culture valuing environmental sustainability, national culture and societal values, and economic conditions are some obvious choices. A variable with significant impact is top management and leadership support. Rodgers, Hunter, and Rogers (1993) conducted a meta-analysis to examine the influence of top management support on success of organizational initiatives and found an effect size of about one-third of a standard deviation unit difference between cases where there was support versus where there was none. We suspect the impact to be as strong, if not stronger, for environmental sustainability efforts and initiatives in organizations.

We propose organizational environmental commitment to be the variable that mediates the impact of economic variables, corporate culture, and top management support on organizational sustainability embeddedness and environmental initiatives. In other words, organizations committed to environmental sustainability will behave in more environmentally sustainable ways.

Bridge Between Organizational Sustainability and Environmental Sustainability: The Three Cs

Figure 7.1 provides a visual depiction of how the gap between organizational sustainability and environmental sustainability is bridged using the three commitment-based pillars: employee commitment to the organization, organizational commitment to environmental sustainability, and individual environmental commitment. No pillar is sufficient for the task by itself.

As noted above, environmental commitment among individuals (employees and other stakeholders) leads to pro-environmental behaviors. However, employee green behaviors can only successfully take place in organizations committed to environmental sustainability. Individuals who are environmentally committed to the environment are not likely to be attracted to, selected by, or remain with organizations which are relatively low in their environmental commitment. In the event that they end up working for organizations with low commitment to the environment, they would manifest their pro-environmental behavior in their personal lives only.

Organizational commitment to environmental sustainability leads to environmental sustainability initiatives and operational integration of environmental sustainability. However, without environmental commitment from employees, our model suggests that environmental sustainability goals cannot be reached. Organizational environmental initiatives are transformed into environmental sustainability achievements through employee green behaviors (Dilchert & Ones, Chapter 8 in this volume).

Employee commitment to the organization is the third pillar in linking organizational and environmental sustainability. Above, we reviewed literature making the links between employee commitment and organizational sustainability clear. We also suggested that, in eco-friendly organizations, employee commitment can

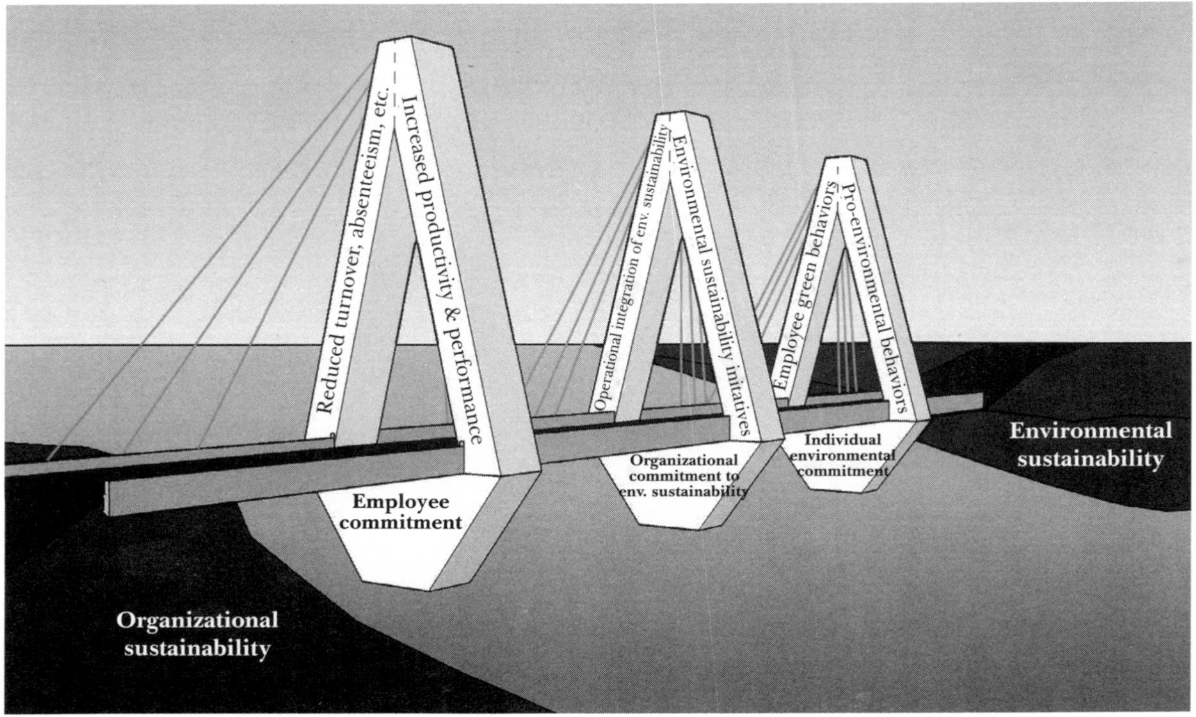

Figure 7.1. Three Cs in Bridging the Gap Between Organizational and Environmental Sustainability

lead to employee green behaviors. Here, we further clarify the potential linkages. Based on the review of the nomological network presented here, we will sketch some process mechanisms that could potentially explain the link between employee commitment and environmental sustainability. At this stage, the mechanisms we present are some plausible mechanisms; their veracity awaits future empirical research.

Specifically, we present four pathways to explain why employee commitment can result in environmentally sustainable behaviors. We first argue that employee commitment can increase job performance, productivity, et cetera, that result in greater organizational slack in resources, leaving more resources available for sustainability initiatives and to sustain programs to train and reward environmentally sustainable behaviors. Second, employee commitment results in lower turnover rates, which allow organizations to formulate stable policies and work procedures to promote environmentally sustainable behaviors. Third, when tasks and jobs are green, greater employee commitment results in greater involvement (in jobs, teams, organizations, occupations), resulting in stronger engagement with the sustainable behaviors required for the job. Finally, our last potential mechanism is the mediating effects of organizational citizenship behaviors, which create an organizational culture of ethicality and citizenship that supports sustainability initiatives when they are introduced. We briefly elaborate on the four mechanisms below.

Employee Commitment → Job Performance → Organizational Performance → Organizational Slack → Environmental Sustainability: The Weakest Link

Employee commitment has been linked to individual job performance and productivity in multiple meta-analyses. Mathieu and Zajac (1990) reported a significant but small meta-analytically derived correlation between organizational commitment and job performance ($\rho = .14$). These results did not differ substantially fifteen years later when Cooper-Hakim and Viswesvaran (2005) reported their updated meta-analysis on the commitment construct ($\rho = .17$) between organizational commitment and job performance based on a sample of 185 studies and 42,354 respondents. Organizational performance can be modeled as a function of individual employees contributing to it (Pritchard, Harrell, DiazGranados, & Guzman, 2008); that is, organizational success is built upon the individual performance of employees. Organizations performing well are likely to develop a slack of organizational resources, giving them the financial capability to initiate and sustain environmental initiatives. Thus, organizations with committed employees are likely to be the ones that are able to afford supporting sustainability initiatives, thus contributing to environmental sustainability. Note, however, that this link is quite tenuous; other connections between commitment and sustainability may be much clearer.

Employee Commitment → Reduced Turnover → Employee Green Behaviors: A Surprising Link

As summarized in our review of the correlates of employee commitment, employee commitment is negatively related to turnover, intentions to turnover, and related constructs (cf. Cooper-Hakim & Viswesvaran, 2005; Mathieu & Zajac, 1990; Meyer, Stanley, Herscovitch, & Topolnytsky, 2002; Riketta & Van Dick, 2005). Meta-analyses have also established sizable positive correlations between employee commitment and organizational cultural factors, such as perceived organizational support (Ng & Sorensen, 2008; Riggle, Edmondson, & Hansen, 2009), workgroup climate (Chiaburu & Harrison, 2008), effective organizational socialization practices (Bauer, Bodner, Erdogan, Truxillo, & Tucker, 2007; Saks, Uggerslev, & Fassina, 2007), and career commitment (Cooper-Hakim & Viswesvaran, 2005). Essentially, these meta-analyses indicate that increased employee commitment to organizations leads to more stable and enduring workforces and organizational cultures.

Low levels of organizational withdrawal generate workforce continuity. This continuity makes it easier for organizations to successfully implement employee sustainability interventions, as employees are likely to remain with the organization long enough for the intervention to have an effect. In addition, the enduring organizational culture which can be produced through a stable workforce leads to more effective newcomer socialization, extending the benefits of interventions supporting employee green behaviors to new hires. Finally, stability of top management allows for long-term orientation in strategy formulations. When managers remain with an organization for an extended period, they are able to incorporate long-term goals, such as environmental sustainability, into their operational strategies. Thus, when management turnover is low, environmental sustainability will be more likely to be effectively introduced and supported in the organization.

In support of these linkages, Ones, Dilchert, and Biga (2010) presented data from twenty-two samples from eleven countries, which showed that perceived organizational support correlated moderately with employee green behaviors (correlations in the .20s). These relationships were stronger among employees with longer tenure. Data from a single multinational organization (N > 12,000) were consistent with these findings (Biga, Ones, Dilchert, & Gibby, 2010b). Employees with the lowest levels of withdrawal (that is, longest tenure) performed the most employee green behaviors in this organization, which was committed to environmental sustainability. Thus, the continuous organizational culture that results from employee commitment, reduced withdrawal, and organizational support leads to increased employee green behavior and employee sustainability.

Employee Commitment + Job Involvement → Employee Green Behaviors: Strong When Tasks and Jobs Are Green

Empirical research has shown that employee commitment is positively associated with job involvement. Cooper-Hakim and Viswesvaran (2005) reported a meta-analytically derived mean correlation between organizational commitment and job involvement of .52 (corrected for unreliability) based on 142 studies and 47,856 respondents. Employees with high job involvement are heavily engaged with and passionate about their jobs. When employees work in green jobs or in jobs containing green tasks (for example, pollution cleanup), this task engagement associated with high job involvement will lead employees to perform more employee green behaviors as part of their normal job performance and will lead them to perform these green tasks with more engagement and vigor. When high job involvement is combined with high employee commitment to the organization, involvement and affective commitment can be complementary (Blau & Boal, 1987). When employees are both committed to the organization and passionate about their jobs, they are likely to give exceptional effort to succeed in their work. Thus, when employees' jobs have significant tasks that relate to environmental sustainability, the combined effect of job involvement and employee commitment on employee green behaviors can be expected to be quite strong.

Employee Commitment → OCB → Organizational Climates of Citizenship and Ethicality → Employee Green Behaviors

Higher levels of employee commitment have been linked to group cohesion and organizational citizenship behaviors, such as helping co-workers and supporting organizational initiatives (Cooper-Hakim & Viswesvaran, 2005). When many employees consistently perform these citizenship behaviors over time, organizational norms develop to support and maintain these behaviors (Ehrhart & Naumann, 2004), creating a culture of citizenship and ethicality. When environmental sustainability initiatives are introduced in a workplace, employees in organizations with these norms of citizenship behaviors, mutual helping, ethical climates, and social responsibility values are likely to embrace and support such initiatives. Thus, by encouraging employees to support sustainability initiatives, climates of citizenship and ethicality can promote employee green behaviors. Biga, Ones, Dilchert, and Gibby (2010a) supported this link and reported moderate positive correlations between ethical climate perceptions and employee sustainability behaviors (two samples, $N = 12,626$). Environmental commitment can lead to employee green behaviors by creating and maintaining an organizational culture supporting citizenship and sustainability.

Conclusions and Need for Additional Research

There is a dearth of research examining the mechanisms and processes that can bridge the gap between organizational sustainability and environmental sustainability. The above four pathways are merely four of the multiple paths, process mechanisms, and linkages that may exist. Continued research will need to replicate and explore some of the propositions detailed above, and new hypotheses will need to be proposed and examined. Given that employee commitment is a source of sustainable competitive advantage and that organizations are likely to find environmentally sustainable strategies essential for survival in the future, it is incumbent on organizational researchers to cumulate more empirical studies exploring the links between the three commitment variables and both organizational and environmental sustainability.

Employee commitment to the organization has broad-reaching implications for organizational competitiveness, viability, and sustainability. When organizations are successful in promoting organizational commitment among employees, they benefit from enhanced job performance and involvement, greater prevalence of organizational citizenship and extra-role behaviors, improved team and department processes and productivity, and reduced incidence of work withdrawal behaviors (including absenteeism, turnover intentions, and turnover). Further, these organizations may benefit from employees who are committed to supporting the creation and implementation of organizational sustainability and related corporate social responsibility initiatives. This is all the more important as such initiatives have become essential to an organization's ability to compete in a global marketplace. In addition, organizational commitment to the environment is the key determinant of environmental sustainability initiatives and embedding environmental sustainability into organizations. Finally, individual environmental commitment is essential for both pro-environmental behaviors and employee green behaviors. Aligning and connecting these three pillars is the only way to bridge the gap between organizational sustainability and environmental sustainability. Doing so will require the full spectrum of skills that industrial and organizational psychologists have to offer to organizations.

References

Acker, G. M. (2004). The effect of organizational conditions (role conflict, role ambiguity, opportunities for professional development, and social support) on job satisfaction and intention to leave among social workers in mental health care. *Community Mental Health Journal, 40,* 65–73.

Ajzen, I. (1988). *Attitudes, personality, and behavior.* Chicago, IL: Dorsey Press.

Ajzen, I. (1991). The theory of planned behavior. *Organizational Behavior and Human Decision Processes, 50,* 179–211.

Allen, N. J., & Meyer, J. P. (1990). The measurement and antecedents of affective, continuance, and normative commitment to the organization. *Journal of Occupational Psychology, 63,* 1–18.

Allen, N. J., & Meyer, J. P. (1996). Affective, continuance, and normative commitment to the organization: An examination of construct validity. *Journal of Vocational Behavior, 49,* 252–276.

Armitage, C. J., & Conner, M. (2001). Efficacy of the theory of planned behaviour: A meta-analytic review. *British Journal of Social Psychology, 40,* 471–499.

Bamberg, S., & Möser, G. (2007). Twenty years after Hines, Hungerford, and Tomera: A new meta-analysis of psycho-social determinants of pro-environmental behaviour. *Journal of Environmental Psychology, 27,* 14–25.

Bauer, T. N., Bodner, T., Erdogan, B., Truxillo, D. M., & Tucker, J. S. (2007). Newcomer adjustment during organizational socialization: A meta-analytic review of antecedents, outcomes, and methods. *Journal of Applied Psychology, 92,* 707–721.

Biga, A., Ones, D. S., Dilchert, S., & Gibby, R. E. (2010a, April). Ethical climate perceptions and sustainability: An individual level analysis. In S. Dilchert (Chair), *Organizational and group differences in environmentally responsible employee behaviors.* Symposium conducted at the annual conference of the Society for Industrial and Organizational Psychology, Atlanta, Georgia.

Biga, A., Ones, D. S., Dilchert, S., & Gibby, R. E. (2010b, April). Perceptions of organizational support and employee sustainability. In D. S. Ones & S. Dilchert (Chairs), *Shades of green: Individual differences in environmentally responsible employee behaviors.* Symposium conducted at the annual conference of the Society for Industrial and Organizational Psychology, Atlanta, Georgia.

Blau, G., & Boal, K. (1987). Using job involvement and organizational commitment interactively to predict turnover. *Journal of Management, 15,* 115–127.

Bohdanowicz, P. (2006). Environmental awareness and initiatives in the Swedish and Polish hotel industries—survey results. *International Journal of Hospitality Management, 25,* 662–682.

Braddy, P. W., Meade, A. W., Michael, J. J., & Fleenor, J. W. (2009). Internet recruiting: Effects of website content features on viewers' perceptions of organizational culture. *International Journal of Selection and Assessment, 17*, 19–34.

Brundtland, G. (1987). *Our common future: The World Commission on Environment and Development.* Oxford: Oxford University Press. Retrieved from www.un-documents.net/wced-ocf.htm.

Chiaburu, D. S., & Harrison, D. A. (2008). Do peers make the place? Conceptual synthesis and meta-analysis of coworker effects on perceptions, attitudes, OCBs, and performance. *Journal of Applied Psychology, 93*, 1082–1103.

Collier, J., & Esteban, R. (2007). Corporate social responsibility and employee commitment. *Business Ethics: A European Review, 16*, 19–33.

Cooper-Hakim, A., & Viswesvaran, C. (2005). The construct of work commitment: Testing an integrative framework. *Psychological Bulletin, 131*, 241–259.

Cottrell, S. P. (2003). Influence of sociodemographics and environmental attitudes on general responsible environmental behavior among recreational boaters. *Environment and Behavior, 35*, 347–375.

Dalal, R. S. (2005). A meta-analysis of the relationship between organizational citizenship behavior and counterproductive work behavior. *Journal of Applied Psychology, 90*, 1241–1255.

DeChurch, L. A., & Mesmer-Magnus, J. R. (2010). The cognitive underpinnings of effective teamwork: A meta-analysis. *Journal of Applied Psychology, 95*, 32–53.

D'Mello, S., Klein, R., Ones, D. S., Dilchert, S., Wiernik, B., & Hill, L. (2010, April). Organizations go green: A behaviorally informed taxonomy of organizational sustainability. In S. Dilchert (Chair), *Organizational and group differences in environmentally responsible employee behaviors.* Symposium conducted at the annual conference of the Society for Industrial and Organizational Psychology, Atlanta, Georgia.

D'Mello, S., Ones, D. S., Klein, R. M., Wiernik, B. M., & Dilchert, S. (2011, April). *Green company rankings and reporting of pre-environmental efforts in organizations.* Poster session presented at the annual conference of the Society for Industrial and Organizational Psychology, Chicago, Illinois.

Eagly, A. H., & Chaiken, S. (1993). *The psychology of attitudes.* Orlando, FL: Harcourt Brace Jovanovich.

Elkington, J. (2004). Enter the triple bottom line. In A. Henriques & J. Richardson (Eds.), *The triple bottom line: Does it all add up?*

Assessing the sustainability of business and CSR (pp. 1–16). London: Earthscan.

Ehrhart, M. G., & Naumann, S. E. (2004). Organizational citizenship behavior in work groups: A group norms approach. *Journal of Applied Psychology, 89*, 960–974.

Fishbein, M. (1967). Attitude and the prediction of behavior. In M. Fishbein (Ed.), *Readings in attitude theory and measurement* (pp. 477–492). Hoboken, NJ: John Wiley & Sons.

Fishbein, M., & Ajzen, I. (1975). *Belief, attitude, intention, and behavior.* Reading, MA: Addison-Wesley.

Goodman, E. A., Zammuto, R. F., & Gifford, B. D. (2001). The competing values framework: Understanding the impact of organizational culture on the quality of work life. *Organization Development Journal, 19*, 58–68.

Gregory, B. T., Harris, S. G., Armenakis, A. A., & Shook, C. L. (2009). Organizational culture and effectiveness: A study of values, attitudes, and organizational outcomes. *Journal of Business Research, 62*, 673–679.

Hall, D. T., Schneider, B., & Nygren, H. T. (1970). Personal factors in organizational identification. *Administrative Science Quarterly, 17*, 555–573.

Harter, J. K., Schmidt, F. L., & Hayes, T. L. (2002). Business-unit-level relationship between employee satisfaction, employee engagement, and business outcomes: A meta-analysis. *Journal of Applied Psychology, 87*, 268–279.

Hasseldine, J., Salama, A. I., & Toms, J. S. (2005). Quantity versus quality: The impact of environmental disclosures on the reputations of UK PLCs. *The British Accounting Review, 37*, 231–248.

Hershcovis, S. M., & Barling, J. (2010). Towards a multi-foci approach to workplace aggression: A meta-analytic review of outcomes from different perpetrators. *Journal of Organizational Behavior, 31*, 24–44.

Hill, L., Ones, D. S., Dilchert, S., Wiernik, B. M., Klein, R. M., & D'Mello, S. (2011, April). Employee green behaviors in Europe: A cross-cultural taxonomic investigation. In S. Dilchert (Chair), *Focusing on employees to achieve environmentally sustainable organizations.* Symposium conducted at the annual conference of the Society for Industrial and Organizational Psychology, Chicago, Illinois.

Hines, J. M., Hungerford, H. R., & Tomera, A. N. (1986/87). Analysis and synthesis of research on responsible environmental behaviour: A meta-analysis. *Journal of Environmental Education, 18*, 1–8.

Hrebiniak, L. G., & Alutto, J. A. (1972). Personal and role-related factors in the development of organizational commitment. *Administrative Science Quarterly, 17*, 555–573.

IUCN, UNEP, & WWF. (1991). *Caring for the Earth: A strategy for sustainable living.* Gland, Switzerland.

Judge, T. A., & Larsen, R. J. (2001). Dispositional affect and job satisfaction: A review and theoretical extension. *Organizational Behavior and Human Decision Processes, 86*, 67–98.

Kollmuss, A., & Agyeman, J. (2002). Mind the gap: Why do people act environmentally and what are the barriers to pro-environmental behavior? *Environmental Education Research, 8*, 239–260.

Ligeti, G., & Oravecz, A. (2009). CSR communication of corporate enterprises in Hungary. *Journal of Business Ethics, 84*, 137–149.

Macey, W. H., & Schneider, B. (2008). The meaning of employee engagement. *Industrial and Organizational Psychology, 1*, 3–30.

Marks, M. A., DeChurch, L. A., Mathieu, J. E., Panzer, F. J., & Alonso, A. (2005). Teamwork in multiteam systems. *Journal of Applied Psychology, 90*, 964–971.

Marks, M. A., & Panzer, F. J. (2004). The influence of team monitoring on team processes and performance. *Human Performance, 17*, 25–41.

Mathieu, J. E., & Zajac, D. M. (1990). A review and meta-analysis of the antecedents, correlates and consequences of organizational commitment. *Psychological Bulletin, 108*, 171–194.

McCance, A. S., Biga, A., Gibby, R. E., & Massman, A. (under review). Environmental sustainability from the employees' perspective: Organization sensing at P&G. In S. Dilchert (Chair), *Human resources and its role in environmental sustainability: Case studies.* Symposium submitted for review for the annual conference of the Society for Industrial and Organizational Psychology, San Diego, California.

McWilliams, A., & Siegel, D. (2001). Corporate social responsibility: A theory of the firm perspective. *Academy of Management Review, 25*, 117–127.

Meyer, J. P., & Allen, N. J. (1991). A three-component conceptualization of organizational commitment. *Human Resource Management Review, 1*, 61–89.

Meyer, J. P., & Allen, N. J. (1997). *Commitment in the workplace: Theory, research, and application.* Thousand Oaks, CA: Sage.

Meyer, J. P., Allen, N. J., & Smith, C. A. (1993). Commitment to organizations and occupations: Extension and test of a three-component model. *Journal of Applied Psychology, 78*, 538–551.

Meyer, J. P., Stanley, D. J., Herscovitch, L, & Topolnytsky, L. (2002). Affective, continuance, and normative commitment to the organization: A meta-analysis of antecedents, correlates, and consequences. *Journal of Vocational Behavior, 61,* 20–52.

Mowday, R. T., Steers, R. M., & Porter, L. W. (1979). The measurement of organizational commitment. *Journal of Vocational Behavior, 14,* 224–247.

Ng, T. W. H., & Sorensen, K. L. (2008). Toward a further understanding of the relationships between perceptions of support and work attitudes: A meta-analysis. *Group and Organization Management, 33,* 243–268.

Nielsen, T. M., Hrivnak, G. A., & Shaw, M. (2009). Organizational citizenship behavior and performance: A meta-analysis of group-level research. *Small Group Research, 40,* 555–577.

Nielsen, A. E., & Thomsen, C. (2009). CSR communication in small and medium-sized enterprises: A study of the attitudes and beliefs of middle managers. *Corporate Communications: An International Journal, 14,* 176–189.

Ones, D. S., & Dilchert, S. (2009, August). Green behaviors of workers: A taxonomy for the green economy. In S. Dilchert & D. S. Ones (Chairs), *Environmentally friendly worker behaviors, senior leader wrongdoing, and national level outcomes.* Symposium conducted at the annual meeting of the Academy of Management, Chicago, Illinois.

Ones, D. S., & Dilchert, S. (2010, April). A taxonomy of green behaviors among employees. In D. S. Ones and S. Dilchert (Chairs), *Shades of green: Individual differences in environmentally responsible employee behaviors.* Symposium conducted at the annual conference of the Society for Industrial and Organizational Psychology, Atlanta, Georgia.

Ones, D. S., Dilchert, S., & Biga, A. (2010, November). *Perceptions of organizational support and employee sustainability.* Paper presented at the annual international conference on business and sustainability, Portland, Oregon.

Ostroff, C., Shin, Y., & Kinicki, A. J. (2005). Multiple perspectives of congruence: Relationships between value congruence and employee attitudes. *Journal of Organizational Behavior, 26,* 591–623.

Pfeffer, J. (1994). *Competitive advantage through people.* Boston, MA: Harvard Business School Press.

Porter, M. E. (1998). *Competitive advantage: Creating and sustaining superior performance: With a new introduction.* New York: The Free Press.

Pritchard, R. D., Harrell, M. M., DiazGranados, D., & Guzman, M. J. (2008). The productivity measurement and enhancement system: A meta-analysis. *Journal of Applied Psychology, 93,* 540–567.

Rettab, B., Brik, A. B., & Mellahi, K. (2009). A study of management perceptions of the impact of corporate social responsibility on organizational performance in emerging economics: The case of Dubai. *Journal of Business Ethics, 89,* 371–390.

Riggle, R. J., Edmondson, D. R., & Hansen, J. D. (2009). A meta-analysis of the relationship between perceived organizational support and job outcomes: 20 years of research. *Journal of Business Research, 62,* 1027–1030.

Riketta, M. (2005). Organizational identification: A meta-analysis. *Journal of Vocational Behavior, 66,* 358–384.

Riketta, M., & Van Dick, R. (2005). Foci of attachment in organizations: A meta-analytic comparison of the strength and correlates of work-group versus organizational identification and commitment. *Journal of Vocational Behavior, 67,* 490–510.

Rodgers, R., Hunter, J. E., & Rogers, D. L. (1993). Influence of top management commitment on management program success. *Journal of Applied Psychology, 78,* 151–155.

Saks, A. M., Uggerslev, K. L., & Fassina, N. E. (2007). Socialization tactics and newcomer adjustment: A meta-analytic review and test of a model. *Journal of Vocational Behavior, 70,* 413–446.

Smythe, P. C., & Brook, R. C. (1980). Environmental concerns and actions: A social-psychological investigation. *Canadian Journal of Behavioural Science, 12,* 175–186.

Stern, P. C. (2000). Psychology and the science of human-environment interactions. *American Psychologist, 55,* 523.

Stone, D. L., Stone-Romero, E. F., & Lukaszewski, K. M. (2007). The impact of cultural values on the acceptance and effectiveness of human resource management policies and practices. *Human Resource Management Review, 17,* 152–165.

Viswesvaran, C., & Ones, D. S. (2010). Employee selection in times of change. In G. P. Hodgkinson & J. K. Ford (Eds.), *International Review of I/O Psychology, Volume 25* (pp. 169–225). London: John Wiley & Sons.

Wiener, Y. (1982). Commitment in organizations: A normative view. *Academy of Management Review, 7,* 418–428.

Willness, C. R., Steel, P., & Lee, K. (2007). A meta-analysis of the antecedents and consequences of workplace sexual harassment. *Personnel Psychology, 60,* 127–162.

CHAPTER EIGHT

Measuring and Improving Environmental Sustainability

Stephan Dilchert
and Deniz S. Ones

There is no doubt that human activity is at the root of global environmental problems (Stern, 2000a; United Nations Environment Programme, 2008). Our economic activity degrades the natural environment and threatens the sustainability of the planet. Environmental degradation has many causes, among them the consumption of non-renewable resources and harmful emissions. Managing economic, social (that is, human), and environmental resources responsibly in organizational settings will be critical to contribute to long-term sustainability.

A thorough understanding of how organizational activities can be managed in environmentally sustainable ways requires input from organizational and behavioral scholars and practitioners and needs to be based on individual and organizational level measurement. At the individual level, the degree to which employees contribute to or detract from environmental sustainability can be observed, measured, and influenced. At the organizational level, corporate environmental performance can be conceptualized and measured to help manage the triple bottom line (Elkington, 1998; Savitz & Weber, 2006). The goal of this chapter is to highlight some of the ways that environmental sustainability has been conceptualized and measured at both levels, review approaches to positively impact environmental sustainability at the individual level, and summarize important variables that relate to it at the organizational level. It is hoped that this review will increase the knowledge base on and understanding of those issues, and that it will aid industrial and organizational psychologists in their efforts to improve environmental sustainability in organizations and their workforces.

Environmental Sustainability at the Individual Level

In economic terms, individual employee behaviors are a vital input for organizations, and the degree to which they contribute to or detract from environmental sustainability can and should be assessed like other aspects of an organization's operations (including as part of life cycle analysis). Unfortunately, so far little research examining organizational environmental impact has focused on employees or the individual level of analysis (Klein, D'Mello, & Wiernik, Chapter 6 in this volume; Mesmer-Magnus, Viswesvaran, & Wiernik, Chapter 7; Ones & Dilchert, Chapter 5). Here, we first review the broader literature on pro-environmental behaviors, describe variables that have been established as their determinants, and discuss how this research from environmental psychology can inform HR practice in organizations.

Conceptualizing and Measuring Pro-Environmental Behaviors

As psychologists, our strength lies in measuring, understanding, and managing individual behaviors that have an impact on the environment. Almost forty years ago, Maloney and Ward stated that "the ecological crisis is a crisis of maladaptive behavior. Thus, the problem falls squarely in the domain of psychology. Ultimately, the solution lies with the sciences that deal with changing human behavior. Indeed, ecology is uniquely psychology's problem. In this regard, psychology's task is to articulate the problem in terms of individual behavior and thus to develop guidelines for ameliorative programs" (Maloney & Ward, 1973, p. 583). Our field can define, describe, and measure individual pro-environmental behaviors so that they can be predicted, explained, and changed.

The environmental and ecological psychology literature contains numerous labels that have been used to describe the behavioral criterion domain of interest. Table 8.1 lists various *general* behavioral categories and notes example papers that utilize each label. The proliferation of labels used to describe the construct domain of interest, for the most part, appears to be unintentional. The construct labels listed in the table have in common the set of specific behaviors they encompass (for example, recycling, reducing resource/energy use, activism), hypothesized determinants (for example, values, knowledge), and theories used to explain them (for example, Theory of Planned Action/Behavior; Value-Belief-Norm Theory).

Some definitions for pro-environmental behaviors that have been offered refer to "behaviors engaged in that are environmentally protective" (Scott & Willits, 1994, p. 239), "actions which contribute towards environmental preservation and/or conservation" (Axelrod & Lehman, 1993, p. 153), and "behavior that harms the environment as little as possible, or even benefits the environment" (Steg & Vlek, 2009, p. 309). The many specific forms of behaviors that have been investigated under this umbrella include pollution reduction (Cordano & Irene Hanson, 2000), waste management (Swami, Chamorro-Premuzic, Snelgar, & Furnham, 2011), energy conservation (Costanzo, Archer, Aronson, & Pettigrew, 1986), household energy use (Poortinga, Steg, & Vlek, 2004), recycling (Schultz & Oskamp, 1996), travel mode choice behavior (Hunecke, Blöbaum, Matthies, & Höger, 2001), eco-driving (Barkenbus, 2010), environmental activism (Séguin, Pelletier, & Hunsley, 1998), environmental policy support (Rauwald & Moore, 2002), antipollution behavior (Hamid & Cheng, 1995), and eco-innovation (Dilchert & Ones, 2011; Jansson, 2011). Although many of these behavioral constructs have been assessed using multiple items measures, at the extreme end of specific behavior measurement, researchers have relied on single item measures to index the domain (McGuinness, Jones, & Cole, 1977; Van Liere & Dunlap, 1978; Vining & Ebreo, 1992).

Some pro-environmental behavior measures distinguish between sub-domains of behavior. For example, Sia and

Table 8.1. Environmental Sustainability Behaviors at the Individual Level

Construct Label	Papers Defining, Describing, or Measuring the Construct
Ecological behavior(s)	Kaiser (1998); Kaiser, Wolfing, & Fuhrer (1999)
Environmental behavior(s)	Diekmann & Preisendorfer (1992); Scott & Willits (1994);
Environmental action(s)	Axelrod & Lehman (1993); Corraliza & Berenguer (2000)
Responsible environmental behavior	Barr (2003); McKenzie-Mohr, Nemiroff, Beers et al. (1995)
Ecologically responsible behavior	Brown & Kasser (2005)
Conservation behavior	Cook & Berrenberg (1981); De Young (1993); Granzin & Olsen (1991); Schultz, Gouveia, Cameron et al. (2005)
Environmentally responsible behavior	Borden & Schettino (1979); De Young (2000); Kaplan (2000); Iwata (2002)
Environmentally significant behavior	Gatersleben, Steg, & Vlek (2002); Stern (2000a,b)
Pro-environmental behavior	Lindenberg & Steg (2007); Siegfried, Tedeschi, & Cann (1982)
Pro-ecological behaviors	Ellen (1994)
Environmentally conscious behaviors	Ellen, Wiener, & Cobb-Walgren (1991); Lee & Holden (1999)
Environmentally friendly behavior	Dolnicar & Grün (2009)
Sustainable behavior	McKenzie-Mohr (2000)
Eco-friendly behavior	Ohtomo & Hirose (2007)
Green behavior	Lin & Ho (2010)

colleagues' measure contains the following scales: eco-management, persuasion, consumerism, political action, and legal action. Kaiser's (1998) measure (adapted from Fejer, 1989) includes pro-social behavior, ecological garbage removal, water and power conservation, ecologically aware consumer behavior, garbage inhibition, volunteering in nature protection activities, and ecological automobile use. Berger's (1997) structural analyses revealed that "environmental behaviors are structured around specific environmental issues such as water, energy, or waste disposal and suggest that recycling may operate as a first step toward the adoption of other behaviors" (p. 515). However, there appears to be little consistency in the sub-domains uncovered and measured in the pro-environmental behavior literature (see Stern, 2000b, for a contrary perspective).

Although some authors have assumed that pro-environmental behaviors are uncorrelated or too heterogeneous to form a single construct domain (Schahn & Holzer, 1990; Siegfried, Tedeschi, & Cann, 1982; Weigel, Vernon, & Tognacci, 1974), others have proposed and successfully measured general (composite) pro-environmental behaviors with psychometric rigor (for example, Fejer & Stroschein, 1991; Kaiser, 1998; Maloney, Ward, & Braucht, 1975; Schahn, Damian, Schurig, & Füchsle, 1999; Sia, Hungerford, & Tomera, 1985; Smith-Sebasto & Fortner, 1994). There appears to be a psychological construct core to pro-environmental behaviors, contradicting earlier arguments that "behaviors which are not commonly related cannot easily be brought under the same normative denominator" (Midden & Ritsema, 1983, p. 40). What the multitude of specific actions and behaviors described here have in common is that they can be described as "environmentally significant" (Stern, 2000a); they can be scaled in terms of their impact on the environment. Stern offers the following definition and examples:

> "Environmentally significant behavior can reasonably be defined by its impact: the extent to which it changes the availability of materials or energy from the environment or alters the structure and dynamics of ecosystems or the biosphere itself (see Stern, 1997). Some behavior, such as clearing forest or disposing of household waste, directly or proximally causes environmental change (Stern, Young, & Druckman, 1992). Other behavior is

environmentally significant indirectly, by shaping the context
in which choices are made that directly cause environmental
change (e.g., Rosa & Dietz, 1998; Vayda, 1988). For example,
behaviors that affect international development policies,
commodity prices on world markets, and national environmental
and tax policies can have greater environmental impact indirectly
than behaviors that directly change the environment."
[Stern, 2000b, p. 408]

In measuring pro-environmental behaviors, the following features of the behaviors may be important. First, there is a distinction between public versus private behaviors. Behaviors directed
at affecting change (public behaviors) need to be distinguished
from personal choices and behaviors (private behaviors). The
former includes both environmental activism (McAdam, McCarthy, & Zald, 1988) and non-activist behaviors that are nonetheless
in the public arena (for example, contributing to environmental
organizations, supporting and accepting environmental regulation, higher taxes for environmental protection). Second, a
distinction between efficiency (eco-innovations to reduce environmental impact) and curtailment behaviors (for example, conservation behaviors) may be important (Stern & Gardner, 1981a,
1981b). Third, environmentally friendly options are not equally
available to individuals, based on where they live (country, region
of the world, rural/urban area) and where they work (industry,
specific organization) (Kaiser, 1998). This has consequences for
the degree to which individuals can engage in pro-environmental
behaviors. Fourth, specific pro-environmental behaviors are not
equally easy or difficult. In other words, base rates of pro-
environmental behaviors can be expected to co-vary with the
difficulty to perform them. Fifth, specific pro-environmental
behaviors have differential impact on or value for the environment. As Stern (2000b) notes, "some types of choice, such as
infrequent decisions to purchase automobiles and major household appliances, tend to have much greater environmental impact
than others, such as changes in the level of use of the same equipment" (p. 410). One important implication this literature has
for our field is the value of collaborating with environmental
scientists in determining priorities among pro-environmental
behaviors that are to be targeted with workplace initiatives.

Enhancing Pro-Environmental Behaviors

Determinants of Pro-Environmental Behaviors

Individuals, and by extension employees, can help attain long-term environmental sustainability by behaving in environmentally responsible ways. Determinants of pro-environmental behaviors must be identified in order to understand, predict, and modify individual behaviors that contribute to or detract from environmental sustainability. Here, we briefly review research that has identified such determinants. We focus on three categories of variables with the relatively large literatures surrounding them: environmental awareness and knowledge, attitudinal variables, and contextual variables. In our review, we rely on meta-analytic findings because meta-analyses minimize and control for artifactual cross-study variability due to sampling error and unreliability in measurement, among others (Hunter & Schmidt, 2004). The results of meta-analytic investigations in this domain are summarized in Table 8.2. Where meta-analytic syntheses are lacking, we reference influential qualitative reviews and large sample studies.

Environmental awareness and knowledge. Awareness of environmental problems and consequences of individual behaviors is a pre-condition for pro-environmental action, and lack of awareness is a major barrier (Hansla, Gamble, Juliusson, & Gärling, 2008). In a meta-analysis documenting the influence of psycho-social variables on pro-environmental behavior, Bamberg and Möser (2007) reported an unreliability corrected correlation of .19 between awareness and pro-environmental behavior ($N = 8{,}276$; $k = 18$). Combining structural equation modeling and meta-analytic techniques (see Viswesvaran & Ones, 1995), Bamberg and Möser also showed that problem awareness had an indirect effect on pro-environmental behavior. Problem awareness appeared to lead to feelings of guilt and formation and utilization of moral norms, which in turn predicted pro-environmental behavior.

Environmental *knowledge* has a similar effect in that knowledge about environmental problems is a possible pre-condition for developing moral norms. Knowledge in this case has been used to refer to both declarative knowledge about environmental problems and procedural knowledge (for example, "how to take action on a particular environmental problem"; Hines, Hungerford,

Table 8.2. Determinants of Individual Pre-Environmental Behaviors

Variable	N	k	ρ	Source
Environmental problem awareness	8,276	18	.19	Bamberg & Möser (2007)
Environmental knowledge	not reported	17	.30	Hines, Hungerford, & Tomera (1986/1987)
Educational level	not reported	11	.19	Hines, Hungerford, & Tomera (1986/1987)
Personal responsibility	not reported	6	.33	Hines, Hungerford, & Tomera (1986/1987)
Moral norms	6,840	11	.39	Bamberg & Möser (2007)
Causal attributions	1,866	6	.24	Bamberg & Möser (2007)
Guilt feelings	3,203	5	.30	Bamberg & Möser (2007)
Locus of control (including efficacy perceptions)	not reported	14	.37	Hines, Hungerford, & Tomera (1986/1987)
Perceived behavioral control	8,029	18	.30	Bamberg & Möser (2007)
Social norms	7,325	18	.31	Bamberg & Möser (2007)
Attitudes	not reported	51	.35	Hines, Hungerford, & Tomera (1986/1987)
Attitudes	6,751	17	.42	Bamberg & Möser (2007)
Verbal commitment	not reported	6	.49	Hines, Hungerford, & Tomera (1986/1987)
Environmental behavior intentions	5,654	15	.52	Bamberg & Möser (2007)

Note: N = total sample size. k = number of studies. ρ = corrected correlation.

& Tomera, 1986/1987). In a meta-analysis pooling data from seventeen studies, Hines, Hungerford, and Tomera reported an unreliability corrected correlation of .30 between environmental declarative/procedural knowledge and pro-environmental behavior. The larger magnitude of this relationship, compared with the effect for environmental awareness, underscores the role of environmental know-how for pro-environmental actions. Similarly, *educational level* is related to pro-environmental behaviors, but to a lesser degree; the corrected correlation with pro-environmental behaviors is .19 (Hines, Hungerford, & Tomera, 1986/1987; $k = 11$). A high-level education and awareness of environmental problems and consequences of behaviors have some limited value, but play less of a role than environmental knowledge. To enable environmental performance, it is important to know that something needs to be done, but it is even more important to know what and how to do it. Environmental knowledge will help individuals prioritize behaviors in terms of their effectiveness and environmental value.

Attitudinal variables. Attitudinal variables form the basis of theories that focus on the processes involved in motivating pro-environmental behavior. For example, the Norm Activation Model (NAM) views pro-environmental behavior as pro-socially motivated (Blamey, 1998). Value-Belief-Norm (VBN) theory of environmentalism is a domain-specific theory that also focuses on norms, but specifically models the interplay among values, norms, and beliefs as key antecedents of pro-environmental behavior (Stern, Dietz, Abel, Guagnano, & Kalof, 1999). In contrast to these theories, the Theory of Planned Behavior suggests a rational choice model (Ajzen, 1991).

According to NAM, moral norms are the key to understanding pro-environmental behaviors. If individuals feel personally responsible and morally obligated to behave in environmentally responsible ways, pro-environmental behaviors are likely to follow (Schwartz, 1977). The meta-analyses of Hines, Hungerford, and Tomera (1986/1987) and Bamberg and Möser (2007) have reported corrected correlations of .33 and .39 for *personal responsibility* and *moral norms*, respectively (ks = 6 and 11). VBN theory of environmentalism (Stern, 2000b) also postulates that personal moral norms are direct, proximal determinants of pro-environmental behavior. However, the theory goes on to specify that values form the basis of beliefs, which in turn result in moral norms. Thus, VBN theory conceptualizes beliefs to be the chief mediating mechanism between values and moral norms. Although no meta-analysis has reported the relationships among VBN theory variables and pro-environmental behaviors, the theory as a whole has received support in several studies (Bratt, 1999; Stern, Dietz, Abel, Guagnano, & Kalof, 1999; Stern, Dietz, & Guagnano, 1995; Wiidegren, 1998).

Causal attributions describe cognitive processes in forms of perceptions of individuals regarding the origin of the problems they encounter. It is assumed that if individuals recognize that their own behaviors contribute to environmental problems (internal attributions), *feelings of guilt* ensue and cause ameliorative pro-environmental behaviors as a result (Bamberg & Möser, 2007; Baumeister, Stillwell, & Heatherton, 1994). Thus, causal attributions are more distal, and feelings of guilt are more proximal determinants of pro-environmental behavior. Meta-analytic findings are consistent with this conceptualization. Corrected correlations with pro-environmental behavior have been reported as .24 ($N = 1,866$, $k = 6$) for causal attributions and .30 ($N = 3,203$, $k = 5$) for guilt feelings.

In a recent review of the literature, Steg and Vlek (2009) noted that both NAM and VBN are useful for explaining low-cost pro-environmental behaviors. They note, however, that these theories "have far less explanatory power in situations characterized by high behavioral costs or strong constraints on behavior" (p. 311). The theory that appears to have greater utility given behaviors with higher costs and under stronger constraints is the Theory of Planned Behavior (TPB) (Bamberg & Schmidt, 2003). Applied to pro-environmental behaviors, this theory links social norms, perceived behavioral control, attitudes, and behavioral intentions with actual behavior. Behavioral intentions are the most proximal antecedents of pro-environmental behavior. Perceived behavioral control and attitudes are mediating variables through which social norms exert their influence. Consistent with this theory, *perceived behavioral control, social norms*, and *attitudes* correlate in the .30 to .42 range with pro-environmental behaviors (unreliability corrected correlations; $Ns = 6,751 - 8,029$, $ks = 14 - 18$, Bamberg & Möser, 2007). Indicators of behavioral intentions, namely *verbal commitment* and *environmental behavioral intentions*, are more closely related to pro-environmental variables. The meta-analytic, corrected mean correlations are .49 ($k = 6$; Hines, Hungerford, & Tomera, 1986/1987) and .52 ($N = 5,654$, $k = 15$; Bamberg & Möser, 2007), respectively.

As detailed above, attitudinal variables have been shown to be related to pro-environmental behaviors. Yet, caution may be in order. Stern (2000b) noted that it is possible that "the more important a behavior is in terms of its environmental impact, the less it depends on attitudinal variables, including environmental concern" (p. 416). Black, Stern, and Elworth (1985) reported that, in conserving energy, as cost and effort associated with the behaviors increased, the variance explained by social-psychological variables declined. Attitudinal variables may be less important for truly environmentally significant behaviors. Additional studies are needed to examine this hypothesis.

Contextual variables. Contextual variables have not been well specified or uniformly conceptualized in studies examining pro-environmental behaviors at the individual level. Given that most individual-level studies do not sample the entire range of contexts and do not sample from the full spectrum of context variables, the magnitudes of contextual variables' effects on pro-environmental behaviors is unclear at best. Individual studies have focused on some specific contextual variables. These have included social influences (for example, community norms and expectations, behavioral modeling), incentives (rewards) and costs of pro-environmental behaviors, as well as legal requirements and governmental regulations (Ölander & Thøgersen, 1995; Stern, 1999; Thøgersen, 2005). Several studies have noted the importance of the availability of environmentally friendly alternatives and pricing as contextual determinants (van Diepen & Voogd, 2001; Vining & Ebreo, 1992). Constraints and capabilities related to institutions and organizations (such as jobs, industry, policies), built environment (such as buildings), and available technology may also be important, and different economic and political systems also play a role. However, an understanding of each factor's relative influence requires sampling of a multitude of contexts (that is, different institutions, organizations, economic systems where community norms and expectations, costs, rewards, and legal requirements differ). Moreover, contextual variables can play a variety of roles in the prediction of pro-environmental behavior—they can be direct, proximal, or distal determinants and moderate or mediate relationships between other variables. One should note that individual pro-environmental behaviors can actively shape contextual variables as well. Individuals create and utilize technologies, construct physical and social structures, and lobby for changes in economic and political systems. Person-environment interaction will be a fruitful field for future research on environmental sustainability, possibly more so than for other areas of psychology.

Interventions for Pro-Environmental Behaviors

We have thus far focused on the variables that serve to explain variability in pro-environmental behaviors. Research on behavioral interventions examines the effectiveness of approaches to enhance pro-environmental behavior (that is, a mean increase among those targeted by the intervention). Several papers have reviewed the behavioral interventions directed at environmental behavior change (Dwyer, Leeming, Cobern, Porter, & Jackson, 1993). In their early meta-analysis, Hines and colleagues (1986/1987) summarized results of experimental studies examining the effectiveness of incentives, appeals, information, and feedback. Most recently, Osbaldiston and Schott (2011) presented an updated meta-analysis that examined the effectiveness of a far greater number of behavioral interventions. Table 8.3 summarizes the findings from both Hines, Hungerford, and Tomera and Osbaldiston and Schott.[1]

---

[1]Across all categories, we note that the effect sizes reported by Hines, Hungerford, and Tomera (1986/1987) are typically much larger than those reported by Osbaldiston and Schott (2011). There are three potential reasons for this. First, Osbaldiston and Schott's meta-analysis focused on objective changes in behavior and only observed, non-self-reported behavioral outcomes were used in the computation of effect sizes. Hines and colleagues did not report the measurement method of the behaviors in the studies included, but inclusion of both self-reported behaviors and objective behavioral change is likely. Second, Hines and colleagues reported corrected correlations between interventions and behavior. We converted these values to standardized effect sizes (d values). It is possible that Hines et al.'s table reporting the correlations accidently mislabeled the standardized effect sizes (mean differences between experimental groups or conditions) as correlations, which could also explain the extremely large values from their study. Third, Osbaldiston and Schott's values are much

Table 8.3. Effect of Interventions on Individual Pro-Environmental Behaviors

Focus of Intervention	Behavioral Intervention	k	δ	Pro-Environmental Behavior Measurement method	Source
Convenience/salience	Increasing ease	19	0.49	objective; non-self-report	Osbaldiston & Schott (2011)
Convenience/salience	Prompts	44	0.62	objective; non-self-report	Osbaldiston & Schott (2011)
Convenience/salience	Appeals	16	2.00[a]	self-report and objective	Hines et al. (1986/1987)
Information	Justifications	44	0.43	objective; non-self-report	Osbaldiston & Schott (2011)
Information	Instructions	50	0.31	objective; non-self-report	Osbaldiston & Schott (2011)
Information	Information	8	1.07[a]	self-report and objective	Hines et al. (1986/1987)
Monitoring/feedback	Feedback	60	0.31	objective; non-self-report	Osbaldiston & Schott (2011)
Monitoring/feedback	Feedback	13	0.58[a]	self-report and objective	Hines et al. (1986/1987)
Monitoring/feedback	Rewards	36	0.46	objective; non-self-report	Osbaldiston & Schott (2011)
Monitoring/feedback	Incentives	47	1.91[a]	self-report and objective	Hines et al. (1986/1987)
Psycho-social processes	Social modeling	26	0.63	objective; non-self-report	Osbaldiston & Schott (2011)
Psycho-social processes	Cognitive dissonance	13	0.94	objective; non-self-report	Osbaldiston & Schott (2011)
Psycho-social processes	Commitment	32	0.40	objective; non-self-report	Osbaldiston & Schott (2011)
Psycho-social processes	Goal setting	15	0.64	objective; non-self-report	Osbaldiston & Schott (2011)

Note: k = number of studies. δ = meta-analytic, standardized mean difference (Cohen's d value and Hedge's g). [a] = Obtained by converting corrected correlations reported by Hines, Hungerford, and Tomera (1986/1987) into d values.

Behavioral interventions can be organized around four major focal themes: (1) convenience/salience interventions, (2) informational interventions, (3) monitoring/feedback interventions, and (4) psycho-social process interventions. *Convenience and salience* interventions aim to make pro-environmental behaviors easier or a more regular occurrence for individuals targeted by the intervention. This includes providing prompts and appeals to participants to engage in the desired behaviors. These types of interventions appear to produce standardized effect sizes in the .50 to .60 range. *Informational* interventions can provide either justifications or instructions to participants, and target knowledge and skills. Meta-analytic standardized effect size for these approaches are slightly weaker at .43 and .31, respectively. *Monitoring and feedback* interventions can provide feedback or incentives and rewards for engaging in pro-environmental behaviors. The meta-analytically obtained effect sizes for these approaches are .31 and .46, respectively.

A variety of *psycho-social processes* have also been investigated with regard to pro-environmental behavior. In this context, social modeling is conceptualized as "any kind of passing of information via demonstration or discussion in which the initiators indicate that they personally engage in the behavior" (Osbaldiston & Schott, 2011, p. 16). Cognitive dissonance interventions highlight intra-individual misalignment between preexisting beliefs or attitudes and new information and use this dissonance to motivate participants to behave in ways that will resolve it. Commitment was operationalized as "verbal or written commitment to engage in a behavior, most frequently by signing a pledge card" (Osbaldiston & Schott, 2011, p. 17). Goal setting asked participants to aim for a "predetermined goal" in improving their environmentally relevant behaviors. The effect sizes for social modeling, commit-

---

more conservative because of the methodological choices made. The authors substituted 0.00 where statistically nonsignificant effects were reported without accompanying effect sizes (instead of excluding those studies), and they also reduced the influence of outliers at the high end. Finally, their mean effect sizes (Hedge's *g*) were not corrected for attenuation due to unreliability. Nonetheless, given uncertainty about the Hines, Hungerford, and Tomera meta-analysis, here we focus on the findings from the Osbaldiston and Schott meta-analysis.

ment, and goal setting were in the .40 to .64 range. The effect for cognitive dissonance interventions was larger at .94 standard deviation units.

Osbaldiston and Schott (2011) also examined the effectiveness of behavioral interventions for specific pro-environmental behaviors. Interventions directed at public recycling were most effective (standardized mean d value = 1.05). By contrast, home energy conservation was least influenced by interventions (standardized mean d = .26). The number of studies contributing to these analyses was not large enough to provide robust examinations of different intervention types for specific behavior categories, although the results are reported in their Table 4. Overall, most behavioral interventions targeting pro-environmental behaviors appear to produce sizable effects. The average standardized d value across 253 estimates was .45 (Osbaldiston & Schott, 2011).

Implications for Human Resource Management

Although there is voluminous literature in environmental psychology devoted to describing, predicting, understanding, and influencing environmentally significant behavior at the individual level, there is a dearth of studies that have been conducted in work settings. Several frequently studied categories of pro-environmental behaviors assessed in general ecological behavior measures do not apply in work settings (for example, consumerism, political action, ecologically aware consumer behavior, household energy conservation). Recently, we developed a scale for measuring employee green behaviors based on a taxonomy from the domain of work (Ones & Dilchert, 2009, 2010, and Chapter 5 in this volume). Current research is in the process of exploring the nomological network for this scale by examining relationships with personality variables (Dilchert & Ones, 2011), motives (Klein, Ones, Dilchert, & Wiernik, 2011), and demographic variables such as age (Wiernik, Ones, Dilchert, & Biga, under review).

We expect declarative knowledge, procedural knowledge, and motivation (see Campbell, Gasser, & Oswald, 1996)—including personality characteristics associated with motivation, motives, values, attitudes, effort, and so forth—to be the most direct determinants of individual behaviors that impact the environment in work settings. We also expect contextual influences to be sizable. In work settings, a few relevant contextual factors have recently been documented as well. Ones, Dilchert, and Biga (2010) reported that organizational support variables were associated in the .20s with environmentally friendly behaviors at work across thirty thousand employees in eighty countries, and that relationships were stronger (in the .30s) for employees with very long organizational tenure. Biga, Ones, Dilchert, and Gibby (2010) found that employee green behaviors correlated significantly with perceptions of ethical climates that workers operated in. Finally, there appear to be notable differences between managerial and non-managerial jobs in terms of green behaviors undertaken. Surprisingly, managers appear to engage in more eco-friendly behaviors than non-managers, and the effect is even stronger for top-level managers (Ones, Dilchert, Biga, & Gibby, 2010). This bodes well for organizational efforts aiming to implement environmental management systems. When environmental responsibility is not a strong part of organizational culture, top management must act as champion of pro-environmental change (Daily & Huang, 2001). As Hardcastle, Wilms, and Zell (1994) noted, "People will follow management's direction. Whatever management does, and in what direction they push, and how hard they push dictates where this company eventually goes" (p. 108). Rodgers, Hunter, and Rogers (1993) concluded, "Effective program installations depend on the level of top management commitment: the stronger the commitment, the greater the potential for program success" (p. 151).

Environmental Sustainability at the Organizational Level

Environmental degradation in general, and pollution in particular, is caused by human behavior, which is one of the reasons why we have argued for a shift in emphasis from the organizational to the employee level in trying to understand environmental sustainability at work (Ones & Dilchert, Chapter 5 in this volume). However, even if individuals are at the root of companies' environmental decisions (positive and negative), there is clearly a need for assessing environmental performance on the organizational level as well. Although organizations themselves would not exist, operate, and thus pollute without the members that operate within them, the majority of negative environmental impact is observed on the organizational level (Stern, 2000a). In this section of our chapter, we provide an overview of conceptualization and measurement of organizational environmental performance and describe some of its most important correlates.

Conceptualizing and Measuring Organizational Environmental Performance

The first question that needs to be addressed is a definitional one. What is organizational environmental performance? Many organizations and scholars have answered this question by describing a list of firm-level metrics believed to reflect organizational environmental performance. Indeed, the term "metrics" is sometimes used synonymously with environmental performance indicators (see, for example, Global Environmental Management Initiative [GEMI], 1998). Examples of metrics commonly used to indicate organizational environmental performance include the amount of waste generated, raw material and water used, number of environmental safety violations received, amount of air emissions released or fossil fuels consumed, and—on the positive side— proportion of materials recycled or amount of waste avoided. In this section, we will make a distinction between such metrics and more complex indicators and indices of environmental performance and will argue that measurement needs to go beyond a detached tally of *environmental outcomes* to also consider organizations' active environmental efforts in reducing their future environmental footprint.

Metrics and Indicators

A *metric* is a single quantitative measure that, by itself, often does not hold meaning to those interpreting it. For example, the amount of greenhouse gas emissions for certain manufacturing facilities might be measured in terms of metric tons of CO_2 released into the atmosphere (or methane, nitrous oxide, etc.). Such metrics can be easily compared across facilities and organizations, but are difficult to interpret with regard to their relative environmental impact. An *indicator*, on the contrary, uses several metrics to describe the state or quality of a system. In the above case, an indicator might be the amount of greenhouse gases emitted by a given facility for each unit produced. An even better indicator could take into account emissions released as a result of sourcing, production, and activities related to the sales and distribution process.

The advantage of simple metrics is the ease with which they can be obtained, as they usually require making fewer assumptions and are expressed on simple scales. Gathering suitable indicators, however, can facilitate comparisons of environmental performance across locations, organizations, and even industries. Good indicators must be based on accurate metrics, create meaning by considering the correct metrics in combination, and provide useful data based on appropriate norms.

Many large organizations now publicly report their environmental performance, but the variety of performance indicators employed is great. The appropriate measures will depend on many factors, such as organizational size or industry, but measurement quality needs to take precedence over convenience. The purpose of tracking and reporting environmental performance indicators ought to be developmental—to provide a benchmark for future improvement. Unfortunately, the choice of specific metrics employed is often influenced by other considerations. In 1995, the National Association for Environmental Management conducted a survey that showed that the top two reasons for tracking environmental metrics were cost control and government regulation. Employee and community considerations were two of the least mentioned motivations. Recent years have brought about an increase in environmental concern and more comprehensive reporting among some leading companies. Nonetheless, there is much room for improvement.

In order for organizations to dramatically improve their environmental performance, measurement decisions should take into account a more comprehensive conceptualization of environmental sustainability. Availability of data and ease of data collection are important, but should not be the guiding considerations. For example, the Global Environmental Management Initiative (GEMI), a non-profit group of for-profit companies with a joint interest in environmental sustainability, suggests using metrics that are already being collected for other business purposes (GEMI, 1998). It specifically referred to "data that are routinely tracked and reported . . . that are required by regulatory agencies" (p. 24). Although such an approach will lead to cost savings and efficiency in reporting environmental performance metrics and indicators, the majority of environmental performance indicators gathered in this way will be lagging (that is, express past metrics) rather than leading (estimating and projecting future results). Moreover, such an approach will forego the opportunity to be proactive about making a positive environmental impact, as it focuses on what is sufficient and required, rather than needed and desired.

Environmental Performance Indices

An environmental performance index (EPI) aggregates several indicators to provide a comprehensive evaluation of environmental performance for a company's operations. This typically includes an overall (numerical) score, but can also include facet-level scores that assess environmental sustainability in different key domains (such as emissions, waste management, environmental policy). An EPI can be developed for a single company (see examples in GEMI, 1998) or span organizations and industries. In the former case, the EPI is typically benchmarked against a base year. In the latter case, EPIs employ normalized indicators to enable comparisons of relative environmental performance across business and sectors.

Environmental performance indices provide several advantages over single metrics and indicators: They paint a more inclusive portrait of environmental performance because they can cover different domains. At the same time, they preserve the simplicity of individual measures by aggregating indicators into a single score while also offering the advantage of increased reliability (akin to scales composed of multiple items compared with single item measures). Such output is easily compared across organizations and over time, increasing understanding and use of environmental performance data among stakeholders. Finally, combining multiple indicators into an EPI provides the opportunity to differentially weight indicators based on their relative importance or contribution to the "green bottom line." Of course, there are several issues associated with the use of EPIs as well. Scale properties of scores or rankings generated by EPIs are often inadequate. Weighting the individual indicators can be difficult and most often involves subjective judgments that can skew results in favor of some organizations or industries. The lack of transparency in weighting indicators reduces acceptance of EPIs in many cases. Moreover, it can also be argued that some aspects of environmental performance are not compensatory, and that aggregate indices sometimes mask poor performance in crucial domains (Singh, Murty, Gupta, & Dikshit, 2007). Finally, to the degree that EPIs are based on lagging indicators that express past environmental performance (which is most often the case), they are not ideally suited for stimulating corrective action.

From a psychometric point of view, basic principles of measurement and scale design (dimensionality, reliability) need to be considered with regard to EPIs, but are often neglected, especially in indices that were developed outside the academic context. Some of these problems are apparent when considering the most popular measure of organizational environmental performance—the environmental ratings provided by Kinder, Lydenberg, Domini Research & Analytics (KLD). The KLD ratings were originally developed in the financial sector to guide investment decisions based on corporate social responsibility criteria; its data aggregation methods are proprietary. They are now generally acknowledged as the largest available database of its kind (Deckop, Merriman, & Gupta, 2006) and as the most widely used measure of organizational environmental performance for research purposes (Waddock, 2003). The KLD ratings reflect both past environmental performance (using seven environmental "concerns" categories: hazardous waste, regulatory problems, ozone depleting chemicals, substantial emissions, agricultural chemicals, climate change, and other concerns) and potential future environmental performance based on current practices (seven environmental "strengths" categories: beneficial products and services; pollution prevention; recycling; clean energy; communications; property, plant and equipment; and other strengths). Detailed definitions of the environmental strengths and concerns subscores are available in Chatterji, Levine, and Toffel (2009).

Despite their importance for socially responsible investing and their ubiquitousness in academic research, as a measure of organizational environmental performance the KLD ratings are not without controversy. First, even though there is a richness of data available in public databases such as the U.S. Environmental Protection Agency's (EPA) Toxic Release Inventory (TRI) and from increasingly detailed sustainability reports disclosed by companies themselves, the KDL uses only a dichotomous scoring system on its fourteen environmental subscores (continuous scoring would be desirable; Chatterji, Levine, & Toffel, 2009). In addition, it is now well known that the convergent correlations among the seven subscores for environmental strengths and weaknesses vary widely, and that many are negatively correlated (range −.64 to .41 and −.60 to .65; mean $r = .01$ and .17 for environmental strengths and environmental concerns, respectively; see Walls, Phan, & Berrone, 2011). As a result, both display relatively low internal consistency reliability (Cronbach's alpha = .24 and .65 for strengths and concerns subscales, respectively). The two subscores are correlated—albeit positively—indicating that organizations that exhibit more environmental strengths also exhibit more concerns (Chatterji, Levine, & Toffel, 2009; Delmas & Blass, 2010). Even though such a pattern of intercorrelations does not speak to the usefulness of the individual subscores (which have been shown to relate to other, objective indicators, such as toxic emissions), it speaks against combining them into an overall score, which is the point if the KDL is used as an environmental performance index.

In addition to measurement issues, there are conceptual problems with the current measurement of organizational environmental performance using EPIs. Walls, Phan, and Berrone (2011) criticized many of the available indices (including the KDL) on the grounds that none of them are based in theory. Walls and colleagues' work focused on environmental strategy (which they posit is often erroneously equated to organizational environmental performance), using a content analytic approach to construct a theory-based measure that they subjected to convergent and discriminant validation. Their framework consists of six organizational capabilities, one of which is human resources (for example, having environmental training programs, participating in reporting systems). Our field needs to develop similar aggregate indices for environmental performance (versus strategy), which would allow comprehensive assessments of proactive and reactive organizational practices based on both objective, quantifiable indicators and sound theoretical models of environmental performance. To provide useful frameworks for improving organizational environmental performance, a hallmark of such models ought to be a focus on leading indicators and proactive environmental practices, rather than a simple aggregate of pollution metrics.

Environmental outcomes versus efforts. Our field can provide a unique perspective on the measurement of organizational environmental performance. First, many of the issues regarding scale construction raised in regard to EPIs (dimensionality, reliability, convergent and discriminant validity) are core areas of expertise for I-O psychologists. Second, our field can contribute by further clarifying the distinction between effort and its outcomes and how this distinction relates to performance measurement.

Environmental performance metrics quantify the environmental consequences of business operations, but they don't necessarily reflect their environmental value in light of possible alternatives. Ideally, our measurement of organizational environmental performance would take into account whether an organization operates responsibly, both by normative standards and in light of its own capabilities. In doing so, one needs to distinguish between organizational environmental efforts and their outcomes. For example, one could imagine an organization that does not pollute, but that also does nothing to improve the sustainability of its operations. Conversely, there might be examples of businesses that report adverse environmental events, despite having engaged in all possible efforts to avoid them and mitigate their effects. An outcome-focused system of metrics will not properly represent organizational environmental performance.

Environmental events or outcomes are an interaction between a company's way of doing business and the economic, legal, and regulatory environment an organization is operating in. Hence, they are also subject to influence outside of the organization's control. We believe that measures of organizational environmental performance should reflect organizational initiatives (as well as their success), because these express performance more directly, in addition to the outcomes reflected in many of the indicators discussed so far. The distinction between organizational effort and environmental outcome is similar to that which exists between employee behaviors that contribute to job performance versus distal outcomes of such behaviors, which are often a poor measure of an employee's performance (see Campbell, 1990). Such a distinction will result in more nuanced measurement and greater comparability across organizations of different size and industries. At the same time, it will provide an opportunity to hold businesses accountable for missed opportunities to prevent or repair environmental degradation, even in the absence of evidence of pollution. Efforts such as the International Chamber of Commerce's Business Charter for Sustainable Development or the ISO 14001 are good steps in this direction. Their focus is on assessing which of the elements of important environmental management practices are in place. If paired with a theory-based, content-analytic approach (see Walls, Phan, & Berrone, 2011), one can evaluate organizational environmental efforts (and hence performance) against a comprehensive set of standards or principles that indicate good environmental business practices *and* objective performance. This also reflects recommendations by the Global Environmental Management Initiative (2007), which distinguished outcome and process metrics, with the latter representing leading metrics that focus on causes of an organization's environmental impact. Just one such example relevant for the field of HR might be comprehensive reporting of environmental education and training efforts among an organization's workforce. What systems are in place to educate new hires on the relevant environmental safety regulations? What proportion of the current workforce has been trained, and what is the frequency with which acquired environmentally relevant knowledge and skills are refreshed, tested, and certified? Often, such process-focused indicators can be more informative than information about negative environmental events or organizational safety records reflecting only lagging outcomes.

Correlates of Organizational Environmental Performance

For some time, organizational scholars have searched for correlates and causes of organizational environmental performance, often alongside or in the context of corporate social performance. Here, we briefly summarize selected variables of import that have been investigated at the organizational level.

Corporate Financial Performance
Strategic management has long focused on the link between environmental and financial performance, testing the assumption

that socio-environmental responsibility provides a competitive advantage by "weighing and addressing the claims of various constituents in a fair, rational manner" (Orlitzky, Schmidt, & Rynes, 2003, p. 405). "Instrumental stakeholder" and "good management theory" predict that environmentally responsible organizations do better financially because they attract similarly responsible consumers, have better reputations, and are subjected to fewer activist protests and less governmental regulation (see Chatterji, Levine, & Toffel, 2009). Conversely, "slack resources theory" postulates a reverse relationship, whereby financially successful companies can afford to engage in environmentally responsible efforts that are supposed to be associated with (at least initial) increases in cost or reduced profit margins. Orlitzky, Schmidt, and Rynes' (2003) seminal meta-analytic study on corporate social, environmental, and financial performance showed that there is indeed a modest but nontrivial positive relationship between organizational environmental and financial performance. The mean true score correlation was .12 ($k = 139$). Orlitzky and colleagues were able to show that the relationship is bidirectional (and of equal strength)—providing support for both the good management and slack resources theories. Unfortunately, their analysis of causality utilized combined environmental and social performance measures, which might not be highly correlated (see Orlitzky, 1998). Nonetheless, the available evidence suggests that environmental programs do have a business value, but at the same time, good business enables companies to intensify their environmental efforts in a "virtuous cycle" (Waddock & Graves, 1997, p. 307).

Firm Size

In addition to financial performance, organizational environmental performance can also be linked to firm size. Evidence suggests that larger firms are at least perceived as more socially responsible (Fombrun & Shanley, 1990). Stanwick and Stanwick (1998) hypothesized that larger organizations might be under increased societal scrutiny, encouraging higher social and environmental performance. They investigated a subset of Fortune 500 companies for which objective pollution data (air emissions from the EPA's TRI) were available. Indeed, across six consecutive years (1987 to 1992), firm size (operationalized as total sales) was negatively associated with this measure of pollution (average sample size weighted $r = -.15$, mean $N = 116$ organizations). In a study of over eight hundred firms in New Zealand, Collins, Lawrence, Pavlovich, and Ryan (2007) showed that firm size (operationalized as number of employees) related positively to adoption of pro-environmental strategies and identified customers and government as the most significant external pressures, which were, however, exceeded in importance by management's personal values and pressure from employees as explanatory factors. A review and UK survey study by Bowen (2000, 2002) suggest that organizational size becomes irrelevant once company visibility and slack resources are controlled for.

Etzion (2007) summarized additional hypotheses leading to a potential relationship between firm size and environmental performance: Smaller firms might possess less environmental know-how and might be more concerned with matters of economic survival, but at the same time face fewer constraining factors stifling environmental initiatives. The few attempts at clarifying the causal nature of the relationship between organizational size and environmental performance have so far been mostly limited to specific industries (for example, Sharma & Henriques, 2005).

Industry

Much of the organizational-level research on environmental sustainability is at the market level (conducted across industries), exemplified by studies that investigate Fortune 500 data, employ ranking databases of environmental sustainability (such as *Newsweek*'s Green 500 and KDL), or databases of objective environmental metrics (for example, TRI), some of which have been reviewed here. Different industries have, of course, different environmental footprints, and being aware of industry-specific effects is important when conducting cross-industry research on organizational environmental performance (Etzion, 2007). Even though consumers might perceive organizations in some industries as less environmentally friendly due to the nature of the products or services they offer (for example, energy and fossil fuels, petrochemical), industry membership can have the opposite effect on environmental efforts and policy. For example, Henriques and Sadorsky (1996) showed that organizations were more likely to institute environmental sustainability plans in the natural resources and manufacturing than in the service sector. Banerjee, Easwar, and Kashyap (2003) showed that motivation for engaging in environmentalism (internal and external orientation as well as strategy) differed by industry type. In sectors with general high environmental impact, public concern (and, to a lesser extent, regulation) had the highest impact, while gaining a competitive advantage through environmental leadership was more important for organizations in a medium-impact sector. In both cases, top management commitment played a mediating role. Management-related factors (commitment as well as cognitive processes; see Delmas & Toffel, 2004, regarding the latter) might be the reason why industry-specific stakeholder pressures and regulations nonetheless do not result in uniform organizational responses and environmental performance within particular industries (see Milstein, Hart, & Ilinitch, 2002).

Interestingly, even when structural features of organizations are considered, human resources can make a difference. For example, organizational leader characteristics appear to be related to corporate social performance. Female CEOs as well as CEOs with degrees in the humanities appear to have a positive impact (Manner, 2010).

Conclusion

In this chapter we reviewed the conceptualization and measurement of environmental sustainability at both individual and organizational levels of analysis; we also discussed key variables influencing it at the individual level and its correlates at the organizational level. Certainly, there are unique findings and useful conclusions to be drawn from the literature focusing on each respective level. However, in reviewing research for this chapter, we were struck by how, for the most part, neither individual-level nor organizational-level research has considered the role of employees and human resource management in improving environmental sustainability of organizations.

Individual-level analyses appear to have mostly focused on behaviors that take place outside of work contexts. Individuals and organizations are considered unlinked entities in this literature (for example, Stern, 2000a). In contrast, organizational-level analyses have focused on organizational outcomes, obscuring the role of individual actions and behaviors for organizational environmental sustainability. Human resources are key for all organizational systems and processes. Industrial-organizational psychologists must integrate knowledge from both levels of analysis to ensure success of the organizational transformations that are necessary to sustain this planet.

Ultimately, organizations can and must evolve and improve in their interactions with the natural environment. This is only possible with the aid of their human resources. We hope that the research and findings reviewed in this chapter can provide ideas to industrial and organizational psychologists and HR practitioners about how jobs, work behaviors, and organizations can be transformed to meet humanity's biggest challenge—environmental sustainability.

References

Ajzen, I. (1991). The Theory of Planned Behavior. *Organizational Behavior and Human Decision Processes, 50,* 179–211.

Axelrod, L. J., & Lehman, D. R. (1993). Responding to environmental concerns: What factors guide individual action? *Journal of Environmental Psychology, 13,* 149–159.

Bamberg, S., & Möser, G. (2007). Twenty years after Hines, Hungerford, and Tomera: A new meta-analysis of psycho-social determinants of pro-environmental behaviour. *Journal of Environmental Psychology, 27,* 14–25.

Bamberg, S., & Schmidt, P. (2003). Incentives, morality, or habit? Predicting students' car use for university routes with the models of Ajzen, Schwartz, and Triandis. *Environment and Behavior, 35,* 264–285.

Banerjee, S. B., Easwar, S. I., & Kashyap, R. K. (2003). Corporate environmentalism: Antecedents and influence of industry type. *The Journal of Marketing, 67,* 106–122.

Barkenbus, J. N. (2010). Eco-driving: An overlooked climate change initiative. *Energy Policy, 38,* 762–769.

Barr, S. (2003). Strategies for sustainability: Citizens and responsible environmental behaviour. *Area, 35,* 227–240.

Baumeister, R. F., Stillwell, A. M., & Heatherton, T. F. (1994). Guilt: An interpersonal approach. *Psychological Bulletin, 115,* 243–267.

Berger, I. E. (1997). The demographics of recycling and the structure of environmental behavior. *Environment and Behavior, 29,* 515–531.

Biga, A., Ones, D. S., Dilchert, S., & Gibby, R. E. (2010, April). Ethical climate perceptions and sustainability: An individual level analysis.

In S. Dilchert (Chair), *Organizational and group differences in environmentally responsible employee behaviors.* Symposium conducted at the annual conference of the Society for Industrial and Organizational Psychology, Atlanta, Georgia.

Black, J. S., Stern, P. C., & Elworth, J. T. (1985). Personal and contextual influences on househould energy adaptations. *Journal of Applied Psychology, 70,* 3–21.

Blamey, R. (1998). The activation of environmental norms: Extending Schwartz's model. *Environment and Behavior, 30,* 676–708.

Borden, R. J., & Schettino, A. P. (1979). Determinants of environmentally responsible behavior. *The Journal of Environmental Education, 10,* 35–39.

Bowen, F. E. (2000). Environmental visibility: A trigger of green organizational response? *Business Strategy and the Environment, 9,* 92–107.

Bowen, F. E. (2002). Does size matter? Organizational slack and visibility as alternative explanations for environmental responsiveness. *Business & Society, 41,* 118–124.

Bratt, C. (1999). The impact of norms and assumed consequences on recycling behavior. *Environment and Behavior, 31,* 630–656.

Brown, K. W., & Kasser, T. (2005). Are psychological and ecological well-being compatible? The role of values, mindfulness, and lifestyle. *Social Indicators Research, 74,* 349–368.

Campbell, J. P. (1990). Modeling the performance prediction problem in industrial and organizational psychology. In M. D. Dunnette & L. M. Hough (Eds.), *Handbook of industrial and organizational psychology* (Vol. 1, pp. 687–732). Palo Alto, CA: Consulting Psychologists Press.

Campbell, J. P., Gasser, M. B., & Oswald, F. L. (1996). The substantive nature of job performance variability. In K. R. Murphy (Ed.), *Individual differences and behavior in organizations* (pp. 258–299). San Francisco: Jossey-Bass.

Chatterji, A. K., Levine, D. I., & Toffel, M. W. (2009). How well do social ratings actually measure corporate social responsibility? *Journal of Economics and Management Strategy, 18,* 125–169.

Collins, E., Lawrence, S., Pavlovich, K., & Ryan, C. (2007). Business networks and the uptake of sustainability practices: The case of New Zealand. *Journal of Cleaner Production, 15,* 729–740.

Cook, S. W., & Berrenberg, J. L. (1981). Approaches to encouraging conservation behavior: A review and conceptual framework. *Journal of Social Issues, 37,* 73–107.

Cordano, M., & Irene Hanson, F. (2000). Pollution reduction preferences of U.S. environmental managers: Applying Ajzen's theory of planned behavior. *Academy of Management Journal, 43,* 627–641.

Corraliza, J. A., & Berenguer, J. (2000). Environmental values, beliefs and actions. *Environment and Behavior, 32*, 832–848.

Costanzo, M., Archer, D., Aronson, E., & Pettigrew, T. (1986). Energy conservation behavior: The difficult path from information to action. *American Psychologist, 41*, 521–528.

Daily, B. F., & Huang, S.-C. (2001). Achieving sustainability through attention to human resource factors in environmental management. *International Journal of Operations and Production Management, 21*, 1539–1552.

De Young, R. (1993). Changing behavior and making it stick. The conceptualization and management of conservation behavior. *Environment and Behavior, 25*, 485–505.

De Young, R. (2000). Expanding and evaluating motives for environmentally responsible behavior. *Journal of Social Issues, 56*, 509–526.

Deckop, J. R., Merriman, K. K., & Gupta, S. (2006). The effects of CEO pay structure on corporate social performance. *Journal of Management, 32*, 329–342.

Delmas, M., & Blass, V. D. (2010). Measuring corporate environmental performance: The trade-offs of sustainability ratings. *Business Strategy and the Environment, 19*, 245–260.

Delmas, M., & Toffel, M. W. (2004). Stakeholders and environmental management practices: An institutional framework. *Business Strategy and the Environment, 13*, 209–222.

Diekmann, A., & Preisendörfer, P. (1992). Persönliches Umweltverhalten: Diskrepanzen zwischen Anspruch und Wirklichkeit. *Kölner Zeitschrift für Soziologie und Sozialpsychologie, 44*, 226–251.

Dilchert, S., & Ones, D. S. (2011, April). Personality and its relationship to sustainable and unsustainable workplace behaviors. In S. Dilchert (Chair), *Focusing on employees to achieve environmentally sustainable organizations.* Symposium conducted at the annual conference of the Society for Industrial and Organizational Psychology, Chicago, Illinois.

Dolnicar, S., & Grün, B. (2009). Environmentally Friendly Behavior. *Environment and Behavior, 41*, 693–714.

Dwyer, W. O., Leeming, F. C., Cobern, M. K., Porter, B. E., & Jackson, J. M. (1993). Critical review of behavioral interventions to preserve the environment. *Environment and Behavior, 25*, 275–321.

Elkington, J. (1998). *Cannibals with forks: The triple bottom line of 21st century business.* Gabriola Island, BC: New Society Publishers.

Ellen, P. S. (1994). Do we know what we need to know? Objective and subjective knowledge effects on pro-ecological behaviors. *Journal of Business Research, 30*, 43–52.

Ellen, P. S., Wiener, J. L., & Cobb-Walgren, C. (1991). The role of perceived consumer effectiveness in motivating environmentally conscious behaviors. *Journal of Public Policy and Marketing, 10,* 102–117.

Etzion, D. (2007). Research on organizations and the natural environment, 1992–present: A review. *Journal of Management, 33,* 637–664.

Fejer, S. (1989). Aspekte zur Änderbarkeit von Verbraucherverhalten durch Social-Marketing–eine empirische Analyse eines konkreten Beispiels. Unpublished master's thesis, University of Duisburg, Duisburg, Germany.

Fejer, S., & Stroschein, F. R. (1991). Die Ableitung einer Guttman-Skala für sozial—und ökologiebewußtes Verhalten. *Planung und Analyse, 18,* 5–12.

Fombrun, C., & Shanley, M. (1990). What's in a name? Reputation building and corporate strategy. *Academy of Management Journal, 33,* 233–258.

Gatersleben, B., Steg, L., & Vlek, C. (2002). Measurement and determinants of environmentally significant consumer behaviour. *Environment and Behavior, 34,* 335–362.

Global Environmental Management Initiative. (1998). *Measuring environmental performance: A primer and survey of metrics in use.* Washington, DC: Author.

Global Environmental Management Initiative (GEMI). (2007). *The metrics navigator.* Washington, DC: Author.

Granzin, K. L., & Olsen, J. E. (1991). Characterizing participants in activities protecting the environment: A focus on donating, recycling, and conservation behaviors. *Journal of Public Policy and Marketing, 10,* 127.

Hamid, P. N., & Cheng, S.-T. (1995). Predicting antipollution behavior. *Environment and Behavior, 27,* 679–698.

Hansla, A., Gamble, A., Juliusson, A., & Gärling, T. (2008). The relationships between awareness of consequences, environmental concern, and value orientations. *Journal of Environmental Psychology, 28,* 1–9.

Hardcastle, A. J., Wilms, W. W., & Zell, D. M. (1994). Cultural transformation at NUMMI. *Sloan Management Review, 36,* 99–113.

Henriques, I., & Sadorsky, P. (1996). The determinants of an environmentally responsive firm: An empirical approach. *Journal of Environmental Economics and Management, 30,* 381–395.

Hines, J. M., Hungerford, H. R., & Tomera, A. N. (1986/1987). Analysis and synthesis of research on responsible environmental behavior: A meta-analysis. *The Journal of Environmental Education, 18,* 1–8.

Hunecke, M., Blöbaum, A., Matthies, E., & Höger, R. (2001). Responsibility and environment. *Environment and Behavior, 33,* 830–852.

Hunter, J. E., & Schmidt, F. L. (2004). *Methods of meta-analysis.* Thousand Oaks, CA: Sage.

Iwata, O. (2001). Attitudinal determinants of environmentally responsible behavior. *Social Behavior and Personality: An International Journal, 29,* 183–190.

Iwata, O. (2002). Coping style and three psychological measures associated with environmentally responsible behavior. *Social Behavior and Personality: An international journal, 30,* 661–669.

Jansson, J. (2011). Consumer eco-innovation adoption: Assessing attitudinal factors and perceived product characteristics. *Business Strategy and the Environment, 20,* 192–210.

Kaiser, F. G. (1998). A general measure of ecological behavior. *Journal of Applied Social Psychology, 28,* 395–422.

Kaiser, F. G., Wolfing, S., & Fuhrer, U. (1999). Environmental attitude and ecological behaviour. *Journal of Environmental Psychology, 19,* 1–19.

Kaplan, S. (2000). Human nature and environmentally responsible behavior. *Journal of Social Issues, 56,* 491–508.

Karp, D. G. (1996). Values and their effect on pro-environmental behavior. *Environment and Behavior, 28,* 111–133.

Klein, R. M., Ones, D. S., Dilchert, S., & Wiernik, B. M. (2011, April). *Development of the employee green motives scale.* Poster session presented at the annual conference of the Society for Industrial and Organizational Psychology, Chicago, Illinois.

Lee, J. A., & Holden, S.J.S. (1999). Understanding the determinants of environmentally conscious behavior. *Psychology and Marketing, 16,* 373–392.

Lin, C.-Y., & Ho, Y.-H. (2010). The influences of environmental uncertainty on corporate green behavior: An empirical study with small and medium-size enterprises. *Social Behavior and Personality: An International Journal, 38,* 691–696.

Lindenberg, S., & Steg, L. (2007). Normative, gain and hedonic goal-frames guiding environmental behavior. *Journal of Social Issues, 63,* 117–137.

Maloney, M. P., & Ward, M. P. (1973). Ecology: Let's hear from the people. An objective scale for the measurement of ecological attitudes and knowledge. *American Psychologist, 28,* 583–586.

Maloney, M. P., Ward, M. P., & Braucht, G. N. (1975). A revised scale for the measurement of ecological attitudes and knowledge. *American Psychologist, 30,* 787–790.

Manner, M. (2010). The impact of CEO characteristics on corporate social performance. *Journal of Business Ethics, 93,* 53–72.

McAdam, D., McCarthy, J. D., & Zald, M. N. (1988). Social movements. In N. J. Smelser (Ed.), *Handbook of sociology* (pp. 695–737). Sage: Thousand Oaks, CA.

McGuinness, J., Jones, A. P., & Cole, S. G. (1977). Attitudinal correlates of recycling behavior. *Journal of Applied Psychology, 62,* 376–384.

McKenzie-Mohr, D. (2000). Promoting sustainable behavior: An introduction to community-based social marketing. *Journal of Social Issues, 56,* 543–554.

McKenzie-Mohr, D., Nemiroff, L. S., Beers, L., & Desmarais, S. (1995). Determinants of responsible environmental behavior. *Journal of Social Issues, 51,* 139–156.

Midden, C. J., & Ritsema, B. S. (1983). The meaning of normative processes for energy conservation. *Journal of Economic Psychology, 4,* 37–55.

Milstein, M. B., Hart, S. L., & Ilinitch, A. (2002). Coercion breeds variation: The differential impact of isomorphic pressures on environmental strategies. In A. J. Hoffman & M. J. Ventresca (Eds.), *Organizations, policy and the natural environment: Institutional and strategic perspectives* (pp. 151–172). Palo Alto, CA: Stanford University Press.

National Association for Environmental Management. (1995). *Performance measurement of EHS Management Programs Survey.*

Ohtomo, S., & Hirose, Y. (2007). The dual-process of reactive and intentional decision-making involved in eco-friendly behavior. *Journal of Environmental Psychology, 27,* 117–125.

Ölander, F., & Thøgersen, J. (1995). Understanding of consumer behaviour as a prerequisite for environmental protection. *Journal of Consumer Policy, 18,* 345–385.

Ones, D. S., & Dilchert, S. (2009, August). Green behaviors of workers: A taxonomy for the green economy. In S. Dilchert & D. S. Ones (Chairs), *Environmentally friendly worker behaviors, senior leader wrongdoing, and national level outcomes.* Symposium conducted at the annual meeting of the Academy of Management, Chicago, Illinois.

Ones, D. S., & Dilchert, S. (2010, April). A taxonomy of green behaviors among employees. In D. S. Ones & S. Dilchert (Chairs), *Shades of green: Individual differences in environmentally responsible employee behaviors.* Symposium conducted at the annual conference of the Society for Industrial and Organizational Psychology, Atlanta, Georgia.

Ones, D. S., Dilchert, S., & Biga, A. (2010, November). Perceptions of organizational support and employee sustainability. Paper presented at the annual international conference on business and sustainability, Portland, Oregon.

Ones, D. S., Dilchert, S., Biga, A., & Gibby, R. E. (2010). Managerial level differences in eco-friendly employee behaviors. In S. Dilchert (Chair), *Organizational and group differences in environmentally responsible employee behaviors.* Symposium conducted at the annual conference of the Society for Industrial and Organizational Psychology, Atlanta, Georgia.

Orlitzky, M. (1998). A meta-analysis of the relationship between corporate social performance and firm financial performance. Unpublished doctoral dissertation, University of Iowa, Iowa City, Iowa.

Orlitzky, M., Schmidt, F. L., & Rynes, S. L. (2003). Corporate social and financial performance: A meta-analysis. *Organization Studies, 24,* 403–441.

Osbaldiston, R., & Schott, J. P. (2011). Environmental sustainability and behavioral science: Meta-analysis of proenvironmental behavior experiments. *Environment and Behavior, X,* 1–43.

Poortinga, W., Steg, L., & Vlek, C. (2004). Values, environmental concern, and environmental behavior. *Environment and Behavior, 36,* 70–93.

Rauwald, K. S., & Moore, C. F. (2002). Environmental attitudes as predictors of policy support across three countries. *Environment and Behavior, 34,* 709–739.

Rosa, E. A., & Dietz, T. (1998). Climate change and society: Speculation, construction and scientific investigation. *International Sociology, 13,* 421–425.

Rodgers, R., Hunter, J. E., & Rogers, D. L. (1993). Influence of top management commitment on management program success. *Journal of Applied Psychology, 78,* 151–155.

Savitz, A. W., & Weber, K. (2006). *The triple bottom line: How today's best-run companies are achieving economic, social, and environmental success-and how you can too.* San Francisco: Jossey-Bass.

Schahn, J., Damian, M., Schurig, U., & Füchsle, C. (1999). *Konstruktion und Evaluation der dritten Version des Skalensystems zur Erfassung des Umweltbewußtseins (SEU-3) (Diskussionspapier Nr. 84).* Heidelberg, Germany: University of Heidelberg.

Schahn, J., & Holzer, E. (1990). Studies of individual environmental concern. *Environment and Behavior, 22,* 767–786.

Schultz, P. W., Gouveia, V. V., Cameron, L. D., Tankha, G., Schmuck, P., & Franěk, M. (2005). Values and their relationship to environmental concern and conservation behavior. *Journal of Cross-Cultural Psychology, 36,* 457–475.

Schultz, P. W., & Oskamp, S. (1996). Effort as a moderator of the attitude-behavior relationship: General environmental concern and recycling. *Social Psychology Quarterly, 59,* 375–383.

Schwartz, S. H. (1977). Normative influences on altruism. In L. Berkowitz (Ed.), *Advaces in experimental social psychology* (Vol. 10, pp. 221–279). New York: Academic Press.

Scott, D., & Willits, F. K. (1994). Environmental attitudes and behavior: A Pennsylvania survey. *Environment and Behavior, 26,* 239–260.

Séguin, C., Pelletier, L. G., & Hunsley, J. (1998). Toward a model of environmental activism. *Environment and Behavior, 30,* 628–652.

Sharma, S., & Henriques, I. (2005). Stakeholder influences on sustainability practices in the Canadian forest products industry. *Strategic Management Journal, 26,* 159–180.

Sia, A. P., Hungerford, H. R., & Tomera, A. N. (1985). Selected predictors of responsible environmental behavior: An analysis. *Journal of Environmental Education, 17,* 31–40.

Siegfried, W. D., Tedeschi, R. G., & Cann, A. (1982). The generalizability of attitudinal correlates of proenvironmental behavior. *Journal of Social Psychology, 118,* 287–288.

Singh, R. K., Murty, H. R., Gupta, S. K., & Dikshit, A. K. (2007). Development of composite sustainability performance index for steel industry. *Ecological Indicators, 7,* 565–588.

Smith-Sebasto, N. J., & Fortner, R. W. (1994). The environmental action internal control index. *Journal of Environmental Education, 25,* 23–29.

Stanwick, P. A., & Stanwick, S. D. (1998). The relationship between corporate social performance, and organizational size, financial performance, and environmental performance: An empirical examination. *Journal of Business Ethics, 17,* 195–204.

Steg, L., & Vlek, C. (2009). Encouraging pro-environmental behaviour: An integrative review and research agenda. *Journal of Environmental Psychology, 29,* 309–317.

Stern, P. C. (1999). Information, incentives, and proenvironmental consumer behavior. *Journal of Consumer Policy, 22,* 461–478.

Stern, P. C. (2000a). Psychology and the science of human-environment interactions. *American Psychologist, 55,* 523–530.

Stern, P. C. (2000b). Toward a coherent theory of environmentally significant behavior. *Journal of Social Issues, 56,* 407–424.

Stern, P. C., Dietz, T., Abel, T., Guagnano, G. A., & Kalof, L. (1999). A value-belief-norm theory of support for social movements: The case of environmentalism. *Research in Human Ecology, 6,* 81–97.

Stern, P. C., Dietz, T., & Guagnano, G. A. (1995). The new ecological paradigm in social-psychological context. *Environment and Behavior, 27,* 723–743.

Stern, P. C., & Gardner, G. T. (1981a). Habits, hardware, and energy conservation. *American Psychologist, 36,* 426–428.

Stern, P. C., & Gardner, G. T. (1981b). Psychological research and energy policy. *American Psychologist, 36,* 329–342.

Stern, P. C., Young, O. R., & Druckman, D. (Eds.). (1992). *Global environmental change: Understanding the human dimensions.* Washington, DC: National Academy Press.

Swami, V., Chamorro-Premuzic, T., Snelgar, R., & Furnham, A. (2011). Personality, individual differences, and demographic antecedents of self-reported household waste management behaviours. *Journal of Environmental Psychology*, *31*, 21–26.

Thøgersen, J. (2005). How may consumer policy empower consumers for sustainable lifestyles? *Journal of Consumer Policy*, *28*, 143–177.

United Nations Environment Programme. (2008). *Green jobs: Towards decent work in a sustainable, low carbon world.* Retrieved from www .unep.org/labour_environment/features/greenjobs.asp.

van Diepen, A., & Voogd, H. (2001). Sustainability and planning: Does urban form matter? *International Journal of Sustainable Development*, *4*, 59–74.

Van Liere, K. D., & Dunlap, R. E. (1978). Moral norms and environmental behavior: An application of Schwartz's norm-activation model to yard burning. *Journal of Applied Social Psychology*, *8*, 174–188.

Rosa, E. A., & Dietz, T. (1998). Climate change and society: Speculation, construction and scientific investigation. *International Sociology*, *13*, 421–425.

Vining, J., & Ebreo, A. (1992). Predicting recycling behavior from global and specific environmental attitudes and changes in recycling opportunities. *Journal of Applied Social Psychology*, *22*, 1580–1607.

Viswesvaran, C., & Ones, D. S. (1995). Theory testing: Combining psychometric meta-analysis and structural equations modeling. *Personnel Psychology*, *48*, 865–885.

Waddock, S. A. (2003). Myths and realities of social investing. *Organization and Environment*, *16*, 369–380.

Waddock, S. A., & Graves, S. B. (1997). The corporate social performance-financial performance link. *Strategic Management Journal*, *18*, 303–319.

Walls, J. L., Phan, P. H., & Berrone, P. (2011). Measuring environmental strategy: Construct development, reliability, and validity. *Business and Society*, *50*, 71–115.

Weigel, R. H., Vernon, D. T., & Tognacci, L. N. (1974). Specificity of the attitude as a determinant of attitude-behavior congruence. *Journal of Personality and Social Psychology*, *30*, 724–728.

Wiernik, B. M., Ones, D. S., Dilchert, S., & Biga, A. (under review). Age differences in green work behaviors across 11 countries.

Wiidegren, Ö. (1998). The New Environmental Paradigm and personal norms. *Environment and Behavior*, *30*, 75–100.

Wohler, K. (1996). Preferences and predictors for ecologically responsible behavior of vacationers. *Gruppendynamik: Zeitschrift für Angewandte Sozialpsychologie*, *27*, 21–32.

CHAPTER NINE

Creating and Maintaining Environmentally Sustainable Organizations
Recruitment and On-Boarding

Talya N. Bauer,
Berrin Erdogan,
and Sully Taylor

Recent changes in the global environment have led companies to realize that by solely focusing on maximization of shareholder financial returns, the long-term economic viability of their firms is threatened by inattention to "use of resources, waste management, pollution, climate change and biodiversity" (Grayson, Jin, Lemon, Rodriguez, Slaughter, & Tay, 2008, p. 2). Climate change has the potential to create vast desert lands in many countries. A recent report indicates that due to the rise in global temperatures, it is possible that the Horn of Africa will lose between 80 and 94 percent of its agriculture activity (Oxfam, 2009). There is a growing realization that economic sustainability of the firm is intertwined with environmental sustainable development.

We gratefully acknowledge the support of the Loacker Sustainability Research Fellowship in our work in the area of employee environmental engagement. We would like to thank Caroline Lewis and Layla Mansfield for their help with our preparation of this article.

The World Commission on Economic Development defines sustainable development as "development that meets the needs of the present without compromising the ability of future generations to meet their own needs" (WorldWatch, 2009). Most companies, however, define sustainability as "the triple bottom line," which is conceptualized as pursuing economic, environmental, and social goals simultaneously (Bansal, 2002; Hart & Milstein, 2003). Within this, the environmental bottom line is based on the assumption that "ecosystems have limited regenerative capability and that the earth's land, air, water, and biodiversity will be compromised by irresponsible actions" (Bansal, 2002, p. 23), and sustainable firms will be those that preserve that regenerative capability while achieving economic and social goals (Osland, Drake, & Feldman, 1999).

In this chapter, we focus primarily on the environmental aspects of sustainability. Specifically, we will discuss how organizations may build a culture emphasizing sustainability using HR practices. HR practices that may create and maintain a sustainable culture include recruitment and selection, on-boarding and training, performance appraisals, and management of reward systems. By hiring and selecting employees who share a passion for environmental issues, by educating employees in environmental matters, and by incorporating environmental issues into the assessment and rewarding of performance, organizations may gain a competitive advantage and increase the sustainability of their business operations.

Recruitment and Selection for Environmental Sustainability

The first section of this chapter will address work that has been done in the area of recruitment for environmental sustainability. In order for sustainably focused firms to obtain the needed skills, attitudes, and behaviors, the first step is to attract and recruit the right potential employees. At the same time, an organization having a sustainable organizational culture and reputation can be a strategic tool for an organization's ability to attract high quality job candidates. This overview will include examples of research in this area as well as examples of recruitment practices. Finally, we will review potential individual differences in attitudes of potential recruits and their implications for practice.

Research on Recruitment for Environmental Sustainability

Conceptual writing and empirical research on the links between environmentally sustainable firms and employee attraction have grown in the last decade. Research shows that individuals are attracted to organizations with good reputations (Turban & Cable, 2003). They are also attracted to firms with values consistent to their own (Highhouse, Hoffman, Greve, & Collins, 2002). And finally, they tend to be attracted to organizations which they perceive as having a strong person-job and person-organization fit with themselves (Chapman, Uggerslev, Carroll, Piasentin, & Jones, 2005). Fernandez, Junquera, and Ordiz (2003) have argued that companies that have a reputation for having a culture emphasizing sustainability will attract the most skilled employees.

The link between a sustainable culture and organizational attractiveness has been found in surveys. For example, Chong (2009) reports on illuminating findings such as a survey conducted by Cone Inc. in 2002, in which 80 percent of respondents in the United States mentioned that they would refuse to work in a company that is known as a "bad citizen." Similarly, in 2007 NetImpact surveyed more than two thousand MBA students, and more than half of them indicated that they would be willing to accept a lower salary to work for a socially responsible organization. In addition, more than 80 percent of those individuals interviewed for the *Edelman 2008 Annual Trust Barometer* said that a company's environmental record is important for whether they trust the company or not. These findings suggest that, by developing a reputation emphasizing sustainable development and ecological sensitivity, organizations can increase their attractiveness to potential candidates, increasing the ability of the organization to access a wider and higher quality candidate pool. In other words, companies that have built a reputation for environmental sustainability should have little difficulty attracting highly qualified candidates because they will be regarded as more trustworthy and better places to work.

More formal studies also support this contention. For example, Wei-Chi and Wen-Fen Yang (2010) examined the relationship between company image and organizational attractiveness. They proposed that social identity and signaling theories explain the relationship. According to social identity theory, employees will derive their own images from the image of the organization, and negative images will threaten those individual images, may bring unfavorable comments from friends and family, and may depress the employees. Signaling theory suggests that candidates tend to infer what type of an organization they are interacting with during recruitment from the image they hold of the company. Wei-Chi and Wen-Fen Yang's studies with a total of more than eight hundred students showed that citizenship image was positively related to organizational attractiveness. The values associated with caring for and acting to help preserve the physical environment can be an important factor for individuals considering to which organizations to apply for jobs. While the research is limited in quantity, researchers have established that potential recruits are more attracted to organizations with positive ecological stances than to those that do not have positive ecological stances (Aiman-Smith, Bauer, & Cable, 2001; Bauer & Aiman-Smith, 1996; Strand, Levine, & Montgomery, 1981). For example, Bauer and Aiman-Smith (1996) used an experimental design to find that students were more highly attracted to an organization that professed caring for the environment. In their follow-up study, Aiman-Smith, Bauer, and Cable (2001) found that an organization's environmental stance was related to the attractiveness of the organization above pay and layoff potential. Similarly, Behrend, Baker, and Thompson (2009) found that a fictitious firm's positive environmental message on its website could influence applicant attraction, regardless of the environmental stance of the individuals viewing the information.

Examples of Recruitment Practices for Environmental Sustainability

While a reputation for environmental sustainability will be useful in general in an organization's recruitment efforts, it is also critical for these organizations to attract candidates whose values align with the core mission revolving around environmental sustainability. This is particularly important for the maintenance of the organization's culture supporting environmental sensitivity. For this reason, we see that organizations that have a reputation for being environmentally conscious actively seek candidates who are concerned about environmental matters. Aveda, which is renowned in the cosmetics industry for its leadership in sustainable innovation and for its packaging efforts maximizing post-consumer recycled content of plastics, emphasizes these values in their recruitment efforts. For example, in their online job application system, the first message potential job applicants come across is that the company is looking for candidates who are personally committed to environmental sustainability (Aveda, 2011; see also Johnson & Miller, Chapter 14 in this volume). Patagonia, the outdoor clothing company that is famous for its clothing made of recycled materials such as soda bottles, goes one step further and asks job applicants to be environmentally responsible in the preparation of their application materials (Patagonia, 2011).

Individual Differences in Attitude Toward Environmental Sustainability

In practice, however, it should be pointed out that not all applicants are likely to be equally attracted due to different attitudes toward the environment. For example, Rodrigo and Arenas (2008) conducted a qualitative study in the construction industry in Chile. They identified three types of employees regarding their corporate social responsibility (CSR) attitudes. CSR refers to perceptions of how much care an organization takes toward "doing the right thing," which includes toward the environment. Using their typology of employees, they found that *committed employees* are very concerned and enthusiastic about CSR issues. *Indifferent employees* primarily care about their own work and careers. *Dissident employees* are frustrated that money spent on environmental issues is not being spent on salaries or other employee initiatives. They have a sense of justice, but it is focused on themselves.

In another typology, Soyez, Hoffmann, Wunschmann, and Gelbrich (2009) noted that employee ecological orientation has four dimensions. *Egocentric individuals* are those who are dedicated to sustainability because they enjoy nature. *Ecocentric individuals* care about the environment for its own sake. *Anthropocentric individuals* believe that nature serves humans and therefore needs to be protected. *Environmentally apathetic* individuals tend to believe that environmental concerns have been exaggerated. Obviously, firms focused on environmental goals must take these varying attitudes into account during recruitment. The ability of an organization with a reputation for environmental sustainability to attract job candidates will to some extent depend on the ecological value orientations of employees, and it is probable that such a reputation will be more powerful in attracting job applicants in the case of egocentric, ecocentric, and anthropocentric individuals.

On-Boarding Employees for Sustainability

Our next section focuses on the on-boarding of new employees. Once applicants find an organization attractive enough to join, the process of new employee on-boarding begins (Bauer, Bodner, Erdogan, Truxillo, & Tucker, 2007). In this section we review the on-boarding process and how environmentally friendly attitudes and behaviors can be developed and retained over time, as well as share examples of on-boarding practices.

On-boarding opens a rich avenue for fostering environmentally friendly job attitudes and behaviors. In particular, once hired into the firm, the inculcation of the firm's sustainability values and goals should be a well-thought-out processes. It has been found that what happens in the first few months of a new manager's joining into the hiring firm—the on-boarding process—can have enormous implications for the newcomer's success in his or her job (Bauer, 2010). Employees are likely to form their beliefs about the depth of the company's commitment to social and environmental goals in the first months on the job based on the norms encountered, anecdotes told, and mentoring they receive. Organizations need to be aware of how to socialize new employees to foster environmentally friendly behaviors.

A key component for companies to communicate the depth of their commitment to environmental goals is through the creation of a corporate culture that reinforces this commitment. In practice, this can be done in several ways. For example, Nike created the position of "vice president of sustainable business and innovation." By having such a position, Nike is signaling to new and established employees that they value sustainability and the environment. As Hannah Jones, who currently holds this position at Nike, notes, "I didn't expect to go into business." She says she joined Nike's sustainability team in order to see whether it was "more effective to shout from the outside or work from the inside" (*FastCompany*, 2010). She decided she could get more traction and positive outcomes for the environment from inside a large manufacturing organization than from outside of it.

Research on On-Boarding for Environmental Sustainability

In addition, several studies have examined the link between environmentally friendly corporate cultures and employee socialization. Many of them emphasize key HRM policies that are characteristic of sustainable cultures. For example, del Brio, Fernandez, and Junquera (2007) note that communication of environmental objectives by top management, as well as allocation of resources, help build a sustainable culture, while Ferrell, LeClair, and Ferrell (1997) found in their study of fast food restaurant managers that perceived organizational environmental efforts were related to the perception that the organization was socially responsible. In a study of European companies that are environmentally proactive, Ramus and Steger (2000) found that "employees who perceived strong signals of organizational and supervisory encouragement were more likely to develop and implement creative ideas that positively affected the natural environment than employees who did not perceive such signals" (p. 622), further illustrating the power of supervisory as well as organizational actions in nurturing sustainability oriented cultures.

Examples of On-Boarding Practices for Environmental Sustainability

The attention to training and development, through such actions as company-organized seminars, can also help create a sustainable culture (del Brio, Fernandez, & Junquera, 2007; Haugh & Talwar,

2010). For example, at PricewaterhouseCoopers, field assignments in developing countries are part of their global leadership development program. In their "Ulysses Project," teams of high potential managers work in cross-sector partnerships with NGOs to develop greater understanding of global sustainable development (Pless, Maak, & Stahl, 2011). Finally, participating in environmental activities can also increase new employee awareness of ecological efforts of the organization (Hunton-Clarke, Wehrmeyer, McKeown, Clift, & King, 2002). As an example, Patagonia employees may leave their jobs to join an environmental initiative, while continuing to receive their salaries and benefits through the company's internship programs that are open to current employees.

In other words, part of the new employee socialization process is to make employees aware of the organization's efforts toward sustainability, through company orientation and training programs, formal communication by upper management, and involvement of new employees in corporate environmental efforts. Simple exposure to the efforts of an organization and being a part of these efforts will increase new employee awareness and commitment to environmental efforts of the organization. For example, imagine the situation of a new employee asked to bring cups to the company get-together. When the employee arrives at the social gathering with Styrofoam cups in hand, if he is gently told to think of greener alternatives next time, he will be given a powerful form of feedback. Such peer pressure will be as effective as any written reward system whereby employees are assessed for their environmental initiatives and performance.

In another example of making this process personal, Wal-Mart developed the "Personal Sustainability Project" through which each participant picks some part of his or her life that is not sustainable and sets a goal to make it more sustainable. While this is a voluntary program, those who embrace it have seen great success. This success seems to stem from the personal nature of the goals.

Benefits of Effective On-Boarding

Employees who are on-boarded effectively through an interactive process of socialization into an organization will perform better in sustainable firms. Effective socialization also helps with retention as well as job attitudes and innovative behavior. Several studies have established a link between corporate environmental activities and job attitudes of employees. For example, in a study of a multinational organization in the UK, researchers found that perceived corporate commitment to sustainability was significantly related to organizational commitment and trust in management (Andersson, Shivarajan, & Blau, 2005). In a study of more than one thousand employees in Turkey, Elci and Alpkan (2009) found that when employees perceived their organization as environmentally responsible, they reported higher work satisfaction.

Post-On-Boarding Performance Management Practices for Environmental Sustainability

This section provides an overview of post-on-boarding practices, such as performance management for environmental sustainability. It includes an overview of research that has been done in this area and examples of practice in this area.

New employees will get their cues about how important an ecological mindset is from many sources, including company leadership, rewards and incentive systems, and written performance assessment of employees. Therefore, ensuring that these HR systems incorporate desired employee behaviors targeting the environment would increase the likelihood of successful on-boarding of new employees in a corporate culture emphasizing sustainability. Besides communicating with new employees in the area of environmental sustainability, performance management and rewards systems may be utilized to indoctrinate employees in the environmental values of the organization. Assessing employee environmental initiatives as part of a performance appraisal system, providing employees recognition for their environmental initiatives and efforts, and providing rewards and other incentives for employee efforts in this area have been observed as critical in fully engaging employees in the organizational efforts toward ecological sustainability (del Brio, Fernandez, & Junquera, 2007; Nord & Fuller, 2009). The structure of the performance and pay system can also matter. In a study of the pay structure of CEOs of high-polluting companies, for example, it was found that more pollution prevention occurred in firms using long-term company results as a basis for rewards (Berrone & Gomez-Mejia, 2009).

Examples of Post-On-Boarding Performance Management for Environmental Sustainability

When Wal-Mart embarked on their sustainability initiative, they brought in former Sierra Club champion Adam Werbach to help them run a key environmental initiative designed to teach 1.3 million employees about sustainability. One of the things that struck Werbach about Wal-Mart was their clear strategy to integrate evaluations and bonuses to sustainability performance. This is a key goal of Andy Ruben, Wal-Mart's vice president of sustainability (Sacks, 2007). Similarly, since 2008, Intel utilizes the company's environmental performance in its calculation of all employee bonuses. At Westpac, an Australian bank group, all new employees have "a corporate responsibility component to their scorecard" and each executive team member has an emissions-reduction target for the year in his or her personal performance scorecard (Cohen, 2010, p. 127).

Recommendations for Practice

The final section of this chapter includes specific recommendations for practice. While the growing research evidence suggests that organizational HR activities may benefit organizational actions toward sustainability, more research is needed. However, there is still much that we do know that can be implemented in practice today, which will be described in the following section. In addition, a best practices checklist is included for both recruitment and on-boarding.

Recommendation for Practice: Use the Recruitment Best Practices Checklist

Best practices in terms of recruitment for environmental sustainability are shown in Table 9.1. Organizations should consider how each best practice for recruitment can be conducted to

Table 9.1. Best Practices for Recruitment with an Emphasis on Environmental Sustainability

Recruiting Best Practices	Recommendations for Developing Environmental Sustainability During Recruiting
Evaluate your current recruitment practices.	Update anything that isn't working and be sure that you are including environmental sustainability content as part of the program.
Have recruitment material that sends consistent messages regarding your organization during recruitment.	Get buy-in at all levels of your green initiatives, goals, and values.
Be honest and avoid greenwashing.	Communicate the difference between your current status as well as goals and aspirations for the future regarding the environment.
Use technology to facilitate the process.	This is an easy way to cut down on paper and model sustainable practices.
Lead by example.	Engage in green recruitment practices such as virtual interviews to save on carbon emissions and paperless options during the recruitment process.
Ensure that the program is monitored over time.	Follow up with new employees to be sure that environmental sustainability isn't being lost during their recruitment process.

emphasize environmental issues for both current employees who run recruitment programs and potential recruits. For example, a recruitment best practice is to include information about what the organization is really like. Therefore, information about an organization's goals and initiatives around the environment can be integrated into this process by including environmental sustainability content as part of the program.

Recommendation for Practice: Use the On-Boarding Best Practices Checklist

Best practices in terms of on-boarding for environmental sustainability are shown in Table 9.2. Organizations should consider how each best practice for on-boarding can be conducted to emphasize environmental issues for both current and new employees. For example, an on-boarding best practice is to include a formal orientation program. However, environmental sustainability can be integrated into this process by including environmental sustainability content as part of the program.

Recommendation for Practice: Reinforce Recruitment and On-Boarding with Other HRM Practices

We have focused in this chapter on the individual practices within recruitment, on-boarding, and post-on-boarding performance management that are effective in promoting environmental sustainability. At the same time, it is clear that, unless there is an integrated approach to the design and implementation of these practices within a company, the intended positive impacts will not be forthcoming. Thus, the HR practices for sustainability described in this chapter should be embedded in, and reinforced by, the larger strategic HRM system of the company. What would this look like in a firm pursuing environmental sustainability?

HRM scholars have generally found that, in order for individual HR practices to have their full positive effect on achieving strategic outcomes, it is necessary to adopt a strategic HRM focus that matches the company's organizational goals with the appropriate set of HRM practices that are also consistent with each other (Ambec & Lanoie, 2008; Delery, 1998; Jackson, Renwick, Jabbour & Müller-Camen, 2011; Schuler & Jackson, 1987). There are several practical implications of this research for the HR function in firms pursuing environmental sustainability. First, it is important to select that set of HRM policies and practices that most closely aligns with the particular environmental sustainability outcomes desired by the company. If the firm is seeking to mitigate environmental risk or cost (Hart & Milstein, 2003), for example, then desired employee behaviors will be focused on

Table 9.2. Best Practices for On-Boarding Adapted from Bauer (2010) with an Emphasis on Environmental Sustainability

On-Boarding Best Practices	Recommendations for Developing Environmental Sustainability During On-Boarding
Implement the basics prior to the first day on the job.	Include environmental sustainability expectations as part of that process.
Use formal orientation programs.	Include environmental sustainability content as part of the program.
Develop a written on-boarding plan.	Include specific environmental sustainability goals in the written on-boarding plan.
Make on-boarding participatory.	Consider programs such as Wal-Mart's Personal Sustainability Project, where employees are involved in choosing goals.
Ensure that the program is monitored over time.	Follow up with new employees to be sure that environmental sustainability isn't being lost during their on-boarding process.
Use technology to facilitate the process.	This is an easy way to cut down on paper and model sustainable practices.
Use milestones, such as 30, 60, 90, and 120 days on the job—and up to one year post-organizational entry—to check employee progress.	While environmental sustainability is important, new employees need to focus on learning the basics right away. Following up at key milestones is important for reinforcing and maintaining a focus on sustainability.
Engage stakeholders in planning and include key stakeholder meetings as part of the program.	New employees with managers and co-workers who do not show commitment to environmental sustainability will not do as well as those who do. Having meetings with key stakeholders can help new employees see support for this.
Be clear with new employees in terms of objectives, timelines, roles, and responsibilities	As with any other type of goals, being clear in terms of these factors will help with environmental sustainability.

following standard safety routines, or careful scrutiny of present production processes to find ways to decrease the level of inputs or the use of environmentally detrimental materials. On the other hand, within companies seeking to replace present products or services with more environmentally friendly ones, employees will be asked to contribute innovative ideas and focus on eco-innovations (Hart & Milstein, 2003). The HRM system must also encourage alignment horizontally, across the different parts of the company. Dan Henkle, senior vice president for global responsibility at the GAP, emphasizes how crucial this alignment was in his company's sustainability journey: "It was really important to collectively align with a single philosophy. . . . Was there one message from the Global Responsibility and Global Sourcing teams?" (SHRM, 2011, p. 26).

Second, a strategic HRM system must encourage the ability to work with outside stakeholders, such as suppliers, in order to achieve environmental goals. This can sometimes include greater cohesion between the internal company HRM system and that of crucial suppliers. For example, when inter-organizational HR practices are in conflict between important partners, quality problems can result (Koulikoff-Souviron & Harrison, 2007). For HR managers, identifying the multiple stakeholders (for example, suppliers, employees, communities at home and abroad) that need to be involved in order to successfully achieve environmental goals, and designing strategic HRM systems that encompass that recognition, has become crucial.

Finally, the overall impact of the HRM system on employees' well-being and on their communities may be important to examine, as this can be tied to negative outcomes for the environment when people are not healthy or have decreased social capital from their employment situation (Pfeffer, 2010). A truly strategic HRM system for environmental sustainability recognizes that, for the company to achieve its environmental goals, the health, stability, and welfare of the people affected by the set of HRM policies it adopts must be given high priority in its design. Employees who force themselves to come to work when they are sick because of fear of losing their jobs will give scant attention or commitment to ensuring plant safety or material waste reduction on the shop floor.

Recommendation for Practice: Engage All Relevant Stakeholders

Organizations can be more effective in attracting and retaining key individuals if they have established themselves as leaders in the community. Building an image as a trustworthy and fair organization would necessitate the organization to treat each stakeholder with respect. In other words, while treating the environment and future generations as stakeholders, the organization should not neglect its responsibility toward its current employees and their families. In this regard, the Northwest U.S. fast food company Burgerville has gained distinction in its industry for offering full health benefits to all its employees. "Burgerville's decision in 2005 to provide *affordable* healthcare coverage to all employees working over twenty hours a week for at least six months was truly unique within the quick service restaurant industry: for $20/month individuals receive full medical, dental, and vision coverage with no deductible, a worker and spouse pay $30 monthly, and family plans cost just $90. Health benefits are frequently cited as by far the most appreciated benefit available to employees. As one employee stated, 'I'm treated differently because I have an insurance card'" (Burgerville Case, 2011). This action underscores for employees that Burgerville's environmental initiatives, such as working to utilize 100 percent renewable energy in all of its operations, are not greenwashing but part of an integrated sustainability strategy.

Recommendation for Practice: Consider Partnering on Environmental HRM Research

It seems that, while organizational sustainability has been linked to job attitudes of employees, we currently know little about how it affects actual work behaviors of employees as well as employee retention. Do organizations that have a reputation for sustainability engender safer employee behaviors, higher job performance, and lower turnover? To the degree that organizational values around ecological sustainability engender higher levels of trust in organization and management, positive organizational and individual outcomes are expected. Understanding how sustainability affects retention of employees and actual performance is critical for making a strong case for initiatives supporting environmental sustainability. Therefore, we would recommend that practitioners and academics collaborate on answering this question. Any data that is revealed linking environmental sustainability to employee outcomes would both add to the literature and create an additional incentive for other organizations on the fence about whether to commit fully to an environmentally sensitive agenda.

Conclusion

In this chapter we have summarized the limited work that has been done on sustainability in the workplace and recruitment and new employee on-boarding. We reviewed the work done to date and generated potential future research directions. Our hope is that this chapter will help to stimulate research and practice for recruitment and on-boarding that leads to more environmentally sustainable outcomes.

References

Aiman-Smith, L., Bauer, T., & Cable, D. M. (2001). Are you attracted? Do you intend to pursue? A recruiting policy-capturing study. *Journal of Business and Psychology, 16,* 219–237.

Ambec, S., & Lanoie, P. (2008). Does it pay to be green? A systematic overview. *Academy of Management Perspectives, 22,* 45–62.

Andersson, L., Shivarajan, S., & Blau, G. (2005). Enacting ecological sustainability in the MNC: A test of an adapted value-belief-norm framework. *Journal of Business Ethics, 59,* 295–305.

Aveda. (2011). www.aveda.com/about/employment/default.tmpl.

Bansal, P. (2002). The corporate challenges of sustainable development. *Academy of Management Executive, 16,* 122–131.

Bauer, T. N. (2010). *New employee onboarding: A guide to understanding and effectively managing onboarding.* SHRM Foundation's Effective Practice Guideline Series. Arlington, VA: SHRM. Available at www.shrm.org/about/foundation/products/Pages/OnboardingEPG.aspx.

Bauer, T. N., & Aiman-Smith, L. (1996). Green career choices: The influence of ecological stance on recruiting. *Journal of Business and Psychology, 10*, 445–458.

Bauer, T. N., Bodner, T., Erdogan, B., Truxillo, D. M., & Tucker, J. S. (2007). Newcomer adjustment during organizational socialization: A meta-analytic review of antecedents, outcomes, and methods. *Journal of Applied Psychology, 92*, 707–721.

Behrend, T. S., Baker, B., & Thompson, L. F. (2009). Effects of proenvironmental recruiting messages: The role of organizational reputation. *Journal of Business & Psychology, 24*, 341–350.

Berrone, P., & Gomez-Mejia, L. (2009). Environmental performance and executive compensation: An integrated agency-institutional perspective. *Academy of Management Journal, 52*, 103–126.

Burgerville Case: Building a sustainability culture. www.sba.pdx.edu/cgls/research.php.

Chapman, D. S., Uggerslev, K., Carroll, S., Piasentin, K., & Jones, D. A. (2005). Applicant attraction to organizations and job choice: A meta-analytic review of the correlates of recruiting outcomes. *Journal of Applied Psychology, 90*, 928–944.

Chong, M. (2009). Employee participation in CSR and corporate identity: Insights from a disaster-response program in Asia-Pacific. *Corporate Reputation Review, 12*, 106–119.

Cohen, E. (2010). *CSR for HR*. Sheffield, UK: Greenleaf Publishing.

del Brio, J. A., Fernandez, E., & Junquera, B. (2007). Management and employee involvement in achieving an enironmental and competitive advantage: An emperical study. *The International Journal of Human Resource Management, 18*, 491–522.

Delery, J. E. (1998). Issues of fit in strategic human resource management: Implications for research. *Human Resource Management Review, 8*, 289–309.

Edelman. (2008). *Edelman 2008 trust barometer: The ninth global opinion leaders study.* www.edelman.com/trust/2008/TrustBarometer08 _FINAL.pdf.

Elci, M., & Alpkan, L. (2009). The impact of perceived organizational ethical climate on work satisfaction. *Journal of Business Ethics, 84*, 297–311.

Fernandez, E., Junquera, B., & Ordiz, M. (2003). Organizational culture and human resources in the environmental issue: A review of the literature. *International Journal of Human Resource Management, 14*, 634–656.

FastCompany. (2010). #8 Hannah Jones. The 100 most creative people. www.fastcompany.com/100/node/467.

Ferrell, O. C., LeClair, D. T., & Ferrell, L. (1997). Environmental activities related to social responsibility and ethical climate. *Journal of Marketing Management, 7,* 1–13.

Grayson, D., Jin, Z., Lemon, M., Rodriguez, M., Slaughter, S., & Tay, S. (2008). A new mindset for corporate responsibility. White paper sponsored by BT and Cisco: British Telecommunications plc and Cisco Systems.

Hart, S. L., & Milstein, M. B. (2003). Creating sustainable value. *Academy of Management Executive, 17,* 56–67.

Haugh, H., & Talwar, A. (2010). How do corporations embed sustainability across the organization? *Academy of Management Learning & Education, 9,* 384–396.

Highhouse, S., Hoffman, J. R., Greve, E. M., & Collins, A. E. (2002). Persuasive impact of organizational value statements in a recruitment context. *Journal of Applied Social Psychology, 32,* 1737–1755.

Hunton-Clarke, L., Wehrmeyer, W., McKeown, P., Clift, R., & King, H. (2002). Employee participation in environmental initiatives. *Greener Management International, 40,* 45–56.

Jackson, S.E., Renwick, D.W.S., Jabbour, C.J.C., & Müller-Camen, M. (2011). State-of-the-art and future directions for green human resource management: Introduction to the special issue. *German Journal of Research in Human Resource Management, 25,* 99–116.

Koulikoff-Souviron, M., & Harrison, A. (2007). The pervasive human resource picture in interdependent supply relationships. *International Journal of Operations & Production Management, 27,* 8–27.

NetImpact. (2007, May). New leaders, new perspectives: A NetImpact survey of MBA student opinions on the relationship between business and social/environmental issues. www.netimpact.org/associations/4342/files/MBA%20Perspectives.pdf.

Nord, W., & Fuller, S. (2009). Increasing corporate social responsibility through an employee-centered approach. *Employee Responsibilities and Rights Journal, 21,* 279–290.

Osland, J., Drake, B., & Feldman, H. (1999). The stewardship of natural and human resources. In C. Dempsey & R. Butkus (Eds.), *All creation is growing* (pp. 168–192). New Berlin, WI: Liturgical Publications.

Oxfam. (2009, July 6). Oxfam briefing paper. www.oxfam.org.uk/resources/policy/climate_change/downloads/bp130_suffering_science.pdf.

Patagonia. (2011). www.patagonia.com/us/patagonia.go?assetid=4491&ln=33.

Pfeffer, J. (2010). Building sustainable organizations: The human factor. *Academy of Management Perspectives, 24,* 34–45.

Pless, N., Maak, T., & Stahl, G. (2011). Developing globally responsible leaders through international service learning programs: The Ulysses experience. *Academy of Management Learning and Education, 10.*

Ramus, C. A., & Steger, U. (2000). The roles of supervisory support behaviors and environmental policy in employee "ecoinitiatives" at leading-edge European companies. *Academy of Management Journal, 43,* 605–626.

Rodrigo, P., & Arenas, D. (2008). Do employees care about CSR programs? A typology of employees according to their attitudes. *Journal of Business Ethics, 83,* 265–283.

Sacks, D. (2007). Working with the enemy. FastCompany.com. www.fastcompany.com/node/60374/print.

Society for Human Resource Management (SHRM). (2011). Advancing sustainability: HR's role.
www.shrm.org/Research/SurveyFindings/Articles/Pages/
AdvancingSustainabilityHR%E2%80%99sRole.aspx.

Schuler, R. S., & Jackson, S. E. (1987). Linking competitive strategies with human resource management practices. *Academy of Management Executive, 1,* 207–219.

Soyez, K., Hoffmann, S., Wunschmann, S., & Gelbrich, K. (2009). Pro-environmental value orientation across cultures. Development of a German and Russian scale. *Social Psychology, 40,* 222–233.

Strand, R., Levine, R., & Montgomery, D. (1981). Organizational entry preferences based upon social and personnel policies: An informational integration perspective. *Organizational Behavior and Human Decision Process, 27,* 50–68.

Turban, D. B., & Cable, D. M. (2003). Firm reputation and applicant pool characteristics. *Journal of Organizational Behavior, 24,* 733–751.

Wal-Mart (2009). Wal-Mart sustainability report: Associates' personal sustainability projects.
http://walmartstores.com/sites/sustainabilityreport/2009/s_ao
_psp.html.

Wei-Chi, T., & Wen-Fen Yang, I. (2010). Does image matter to different job applicants? The influences of corporate image and applicant individual differences on organizational attractiveness. *International Journal of Selection & Assessment, 18,* 48–63.

WorldWatch, I. (2009). *Report on progress toward a sustainble society.* New York, London: W.W. Norton & Company.

CHAPTER TEN

Leadership and Environmental Sustainability

Ellen Van Velsor
and Laura Quinn

People everywhere are revisiting the role of business in society, particularly as it relates to climate change and environmental degradation and protection. Government regulation and education both have a role to play in creating a sustainable world, yet business is the institution that has the global reach and influence to impact significant change. Early on, organizations trying to focus more on the environment were concerned about the costs of sustainable operations and avoiding environmental disasters. However, companies increasingly recognize that a focus on protecting and improving the environment brings with it cost savings, stakeholder respect, and opportunities for much needed innovation and employee engagement. Yet even today, government and business organizations that have managed to redefine their purpose as one that includes environmental protection and enhancement are still in the minority. One lesson these few have learned is that leadership is critical to successful action over time.

When people talk about leadership, they are often referring to the actions of individuals in positions of authority. That is certainly the main way leadership is enacted and understood in most sectors (for example, business, government, education) and around the world. However, people also look to organizations to lead, be those government organizations, corporate entities, or business schools. In other words, we look to collective leadership to grapple with the challenges we face when it comes to the environmental sustainability (ES) of our world, recognizing that individuals do not solve these problems alone.

In our work, we see collective leadership as grounded in interdependence—of individuals, groups, organizations, and social systems. So to positively affect the future of societies worldwide, we focus on building organizational leadership cultures that create and support environmental sustainability through their strategies, their operations, and the development, delivery, and disposal of their products and services.

This chapter focuses on the role of individual and collective beliefs and leadership practices in creating and sustaining environmentally responsible organizations. We see individual and collective beliefs and leadership practices as vital and interlinked elements of organizational culture and as key to creating the organizational direction, alignment, and commitment to sustainability that are needed if our world is to prosper over time. The chapter summarizes and integrates recent conceptual frameworks and empirical research results on leadership as those relate to environmental sustainability and aims to foster a better understanding of what it takes to focus organizational cultures on sustainability through their operations, products, and services.

The Role of Leadership in Creating Environmentally Responsible Organizations

We begin from the idea that leadership involves three tasks: setting direction, creating alignment, and building commitment (DAC) toward the longer range outcome of environmental sustainability(Drath, McCauley, Palus, Van Velsor, O'Connor, & McGuire, 2008). We see the DAC framework as a useful one for understanding leadership because it does not limit us to seeing leadership as originating only in the actions of people with formal authority, even though those people are important sources of leadership in organizations. Rather, seeing leadership as DAC allows us to understand that leadership results from the work of teams, the collective practices in organizations, and the systems operating at the societal level. Individual leaders work to create direction, alignment, and commitment within their organizations; and organizational cultures are built around certain beliefs about how direction, alignment, and commitment are created and recognized. These organizational level belief systems support certain sets of practices generally seen as leadership (for example, individuals leading by virtue of position power, teams creating leadership in a self-managed way, everyone expected to contribute to DAC); and the specific patterns of beliefs and practices and their interaction can be seen as the collective leadership culture of an organization (Drath, McCauley, Palus, Van Velsor, O'Connor, & McGuire, 2008). More specifically, we argue that an environmentally responsible organizational leadership culture plays a central role in driving movement of the organization's strategies, policies, and operations toward increased environmental sustainability, both in terms of what individual leaders do and how the collective culture adapts. Until recently, we knew little about the beliefs and practices that make up this kind of culture and thereby support environmentally responsible action in and by organizations.

How ES Leadership Is Different

Certainly, much has been written, researched, and applied in the field of leadership. The reader might reasonably ask, "What differentiates leadership for ES from traditional leadership?" Our view is that building a leadership culture that supports ES means producing leadership (DAC) in a context of significant novelty and complexity characterized by new and expanded value propositions, multi-faceted standards of success, shifting social contracts, a wide and diverse array of stakeholders with often competing interests, and multi-sector collaborations that go outside traditional industry relationships. Enacting leadership for sustainability means encountering complexity beyond the scope of any one organization, requiring effective boundary spanning across organizational lines, and the creation of synergies across an entire system/society—challenges typically not dealt with in traditional organizational leadership frameworks. ES leadership requires individual and collective leadership *in* the organization, leadership *of* the organization, and leadership *beyond* the organization (Osborn & Hunt, 2002).

A Critique of the Competency Approach to Leadership

To date, research has focused primarily on identifying individual leader competencies required to lead organizations in their change efforts towards sustainability (Ferdig, 2007; Hind, Wilson, & Lenssen, 2009; McGaw, 2005). In this research stream, a whole array of individual-level competencies has been suggested, which partially overlap, but so far, have not been integrated. However, competencies (skills or behaviors people/organizations are capable of) and practices (what people/organizations actually do) are very different domains of leadership (Carroll, Levy, & Richmond, 2008; D'Amato, Eckert, Ireland, Quinn, & Van Velsor, 2010). Reliance on competency frameworks in the study of leadership tends to leave us with the idea that individuals act in isolation and separate from context. They imply that people *will* do what they are capable of doing and that the same generic skills or behaviors are relevant to all situations or groups (Carroll, Levy, & Richmond, 2007). For example, while an organization may be full of leaders who are capable of reflection, boundary spanning, or strategic thinking, the organizational culture may not support these behaviors in practice, and leaders at all levels who may "have" these competencies may not feel empowered or motivated to enact them.

While the competencies approach is doubtless very useful in terms of thinking about what qualities we should develop in individuals, the focus on leadership competencies can be criticized on at least two fronts. The first is methodological. Much of the current research on sustainability leadership is based on asking managers or HR professionals what they believe are important leadership skills and abilities, rather than focusing on what individuals or organizations actually do when they are successful in developing and executing strategies focused on sustainability. Thus, the competencies gathered from such research are not validated by actual, practical actions—they are merely probable predecessors to such action.

Table 10.1. Two Key Issues in Approaches to Sustainability Leadership

	Competencies	*Practices*
Individual	*Potential* Individual Actions or Capability to Act	*Actual* Individual Actions or Behaviors
Collective	*Potential* Organizational Action or Capability to Act	*Actual* Organizational Actions or Behaviors

The second critique is theoretical. Competencies are typically conceptualized on an individual level only. Thus, competency-based leadership models are prone to a limited view of leadership, that is, one residing entirely within the individual leader (Carroll, Levy, & Richmond, 2007; Meindl, Ehrlich, & Dukerich, 1985). Not only will successes be attributed to individual leaders rather than the organizational collective, but the search for the most important competencies also abets the conclusion that, once leaders with such competencies have been identified and put in place, the organization will have the ability to implement and sustain globally responsible business operations and action will follow suit. However, competencies, per se, are no guarantee for individual or organizational action, or for successful organizational outcomes. Table 10.1 presents a simple illustration of this idea.

Stage Models of Organizational Sustainability

Several scholars have begun to frame the development of organizations in terms of stage models of sustainability, or of closely related concepts like corporate citizenship or global responsibility (Mirvis & Googins, 2006; Nidumolu, Prahalad, & Rangaswami, 2009; van Marrewijk & Werre, 2003; Wartick & Cochran, 1985). These attempts are typically grounded in the idea that individuals and groups develop beliefs, values, and practices in order to deal with ongoing and emerging challenges (Drath, McCauley, Palus, Van Velsor, O'Connor, & McGuire, 2008). When current beliefs and practices are ineffective, new perspectives and approaches are tried until more adequate systems and organizational cultures emerge. This process is often seen as resulting in a sequence of development stages (van Marrewijk & Werre, 2003). To account for the different levels of sustainability commitment across organizations, these stage development frameworks typically are conceptualized as a continuum, characterizing an organization's approach to socially and environmentally responsible activities on differing levels, from the completely absent to the radically transformative.

What these frameworks have in common is the idea that organizations develop increasingly complex and flexible cultures and systems in response to:

- Increasing demands for social, environmental, and fiscal responsibility,
- Enhanced opportunities for partnership,
- Changed economic, social, and environmental realities,
- A changed sense of the relationship of the organization to its increasingly complex environment, and
- A host of other challenges and conditions they may face (see Campbell, 2007).

And they share an assumption that individuals and collectives develop together; that is, collective or culture development drives the development of individuals who are part of that system, and the individual development of members of the collective (especially of people in key leadership roles) can drive collective or culture development.

For all these reasons, we believe it is important to improve our understanding of leadership practices—the observable shared individual and collective behaviors that shape and ultimately define the leadership culture (Pasmore, Lafferty, & Spencer, 2009). Looking at actual leadership practices is a relatively novel approach, and it is important to identify and codify these (plus the beliefs/cultures that support those practices) in order to both help organizations move forward and also to build sound theoretical models of leadership and sustainability.

A Note About Our Research

Our initial study was comprised of fifty-four semi-structured interviews with senior managers in five multi-national organizations. We also conducted two focus groups at each site, with each group comprised of a cross-section of employees having no formal responsibility for sustainability initiatives. In these interviews and focus groups our focus was broader than leadership beliefs and practices for environmental sustainability. We were interested, more generally, in globally responsible leadership—a term we used to encompass both environmental sustainability and social or financial responsibility issues. Most of these companies took a "triple bottom line" approach to global responsibility, focusing on achieving balance among three priorities: people (social), planet (environmental), and profit (financial). Two of the five organizations had a primary focus on the environment, given their lines of business (global shipping and manufacturing). Yet we did not see significant differences in the practices described by organizations focused on ES and other organizations with a more balanced focus or a priority focus on social issues (for example, eliminating hunger/malnutrition, providing affordable medicines).

In terms of methodology, we followed a comparative case-study approach (Eisenhardt & Graebner, 2007), employing perspective awareness, double coding, and inter-coder consensus (see D'Amato, Eckert, Ireland, Quinn, & Van Velsor, 2010, for a full explanation). We are currently in the second phase of this research, using a survey developed from these interviews to collect additional data on the relationship among leadership beliefs and practices (measured as both frequency of practices and mastery of practices at a collective level).

Challenges of Leadership with Respect to Environmental Sustainability

Our initial research has borne out what earlier scholars have argued, namely that ES leadership beliefs and practices arise in response to the challenges faced by individuals and organizations in a world increasingly questioning the current state of sustainability. To take on an ES agenda—setting the direction, creating the alignment, and maintaining the commitment to sustainability and other social issues—most business organizations must transform themselves from organizations that prioritize short-term financial goals and shareholder returns into ones that balance the need for financially robust operations with care for the environment and for the interests of a wide variety of stakeholders. Although many organizations may start with individual leader development or assume that the problem to be solved is a lack of individual leader competencies, developing individual leaders is neither sufficient nor necessarily the best starting place for creating the organizational-level transformation needed for sustainability. What is needed is an organizational culture transformation that will legitimize and support new individual and group behaviors.

More specifically, we have come to understand this culture transformation as having three broad areas of challenge and change for organizations. These are (1) creating and communicating an organizational direction that makes sense at all levels of the business and both internally and externally, (2) creating alignment by operationalizing an environmentally sustainable business vision and strategy throughout the organization worldwide, and (3) building and maintaining commitment to sustainability among all of an organization's stakeholders. We begin by describing the leadership practices identified by managers in our study and grouping these under the three leadership tasks as described. *Direction* results from the development of a sustainability vision, strategies, and policies, as well as the frequent communication of that vision and actions related to it. *Alignment* comes about as a result of attention to operationalizing or embedding those strategies into the day-to-day work of all functions, lines of business, and regions. It also results from the individual and organizational practice of engaging across boundaries and from efforts to put in place organization-wide systems for performance accountability with respect to ES. Finally, building and maintaining *commitment* is something that must happen at all levels and is characterized by visible top management support for ES, a focus on developing employees who feel empowered to drive sustainable business practice, and a clear emphasis on ethical action throughout the organization. Following this discussion of ES leadership practices that work, we will turn to a shorter discussion of some of the beliefs and values that lie at the foundation of the organizations in our study.

Leadership Practices That Work

The following eight leadership practices are both organizational (processes, policies, systems, and collective behaviors) and individual (things leaders and/or employees actually do). Some are described by other scholars and researchers using different frameworks (Maak, 2007; Mirvis & Googins, 2006; Pless, 2007; Starik & Rands, 1995; van Marrewijk & Werre, 2003). And consistent with the thinking of other scholars (such as Starik & Rands, 1995), we have not found there to be one formula for success. Instead, these practices represent a compilation of those seen by leaders themselves as working to help their organizations move closer to sustainability, with many paths potentially leading to that same outcome.

ES Leadership: Setting Direction

Setting direction includes both creating and communicating vision, strategy, and policy around environmental sustainability. It is often, but not always, one of the early tasks in an organization intending to become more socially responsible in its work. We say often, but not always, because we learned in our research that organizations adopting environmentally sustainable policies early (before much was known or discussed in the literature or media about companies' role in ES), were often somewhat surprised to learn that terms like "CSR" provide a framework for what they had already been doing for years, without having incorporated that into a formal statement of vision or a formal strategy. Yet, regardless of when organizations began to formalize their ES stance, all agreed that the development and frequent communication about a sustainability vision, strategy, and policies were key practices leading to their success. They also reported that the practices that go into setting an ES direction are not ones that are done once and for all. Direction must be set and reset, and reset again, based on changing stakeholder issues, unexpected events, changing markets, and increased understanding of context. With a resetting of direction, alignment needs to be reexamined and commitment rebuilt. So it is important to remember that the DAC process is a challenging one, with each of the elements in dynamic tension with the others.

Developing vision, strategy, and policies. Although articulating a vision along with supporting strategy and policies is not always a first step in a firm's journey toward sustainability, these statements create a foundation from which communications can be consolidated and activities already underway can be seen as important and as having executive and organizational support (D'Amato, Eckert, Ireland, Quinn, & Van Velsor, 2010; Starik & Rands, 1995). As such, developing vision, strategy, and policies in support of sustainability is a key element of success. Having a clear vision for sustainability (the "why"), developing a clear sustainability strategy (the "how"), and developing long-term sustainability goals that can be further specified in the shorter-term goals of divisions and units (the "what") paves the way for smooth integration of sustainable practices.

Particularly with regard to environmental action and employee relations, in best practice companies, goals and strategies set from the top of the organization typically go above and beyond compliance or what is required by law. These can include the development of specific strategies such as pollution prevention strategies, product stewardship strategies, and sustainable development strategies (Fowler & Hope, 2007; Hart, 1995). While one may infer from stage models that strategies like these might be developed and operationalized in sequence, that may not be the case. In an interesting case study of Patagonia, authors Fowler and Hope (2007) show that these three strategies can be effectively embedded and pursued simultaneously, rather than being approached sequentially with success at one stage (like product stewardship) being dependent on achieving another (such as pollution prevention). In our research, we see organizations usually implementing these strategies via small steps toward major goals, making efforts that are consistent and frequent.

Communicating about ES strategy and actions. Communication is a major contributor to the success of sustainability efforts in all of the best practice organizations with whom we have worked. The focus on communication in these companies is both internal and external and often both top-down and bottom-up. Processes are in place for frequent senior management communication about the importance of environmental responsibility, current related activities, and progress on sustainability goals. Communication about such goals and initiatives crosses all organizational levels and is incorporated into the regular orientation processes for new employees.

The ways in which messages about sustainability are framed and delivered is key to sustainability taking root within these organizations. Our studies point to a recipe for good communication as threefold: (1) a positive and compelling delivery, (2) relating sustainability to the language of business, and (3) relating the message to employee interest in meaningful work. Many managers view the way in which the message is delivered as critical, feeling it is important to use vivid examples, emotion, and creativity to communicate.

Communications that motivate people to use environmentally sustainable practices in their work are those that appeal to their motivation to do the right thing and to feel good about their work. Managers in best practice companies emphasize the importance of avoiding the "doom and gloom" scenarios typical in many discussions of sustainability and focusing instead on the opportunities and positive outcomes sustainability offers. Managers also see that global responsibility must be addressed using business language, rather than sustainability language. For example, reducing waste in all phases of the business is not just "earth friendly"; it reduces costs and provides support for job retention, especially in tough economic times. Finally, in all the organizations we see as successful, multiple channels of communication are used to carry these messages (webinars, newsletters, company meetings, etc.).

Externally, senior managers in these organizations take a visible stand by making speeches and conference presentations on what the company is doing and the importance of ES to solve major issues such as climate change. In addition, stakeholder dialogue is an ongoing process, involving key community leaders in areas where the companies have operations, NGOs having agendas related to company operations, and representatives of government and industry regulatory groups and suppliers. The content of these dialogues often focuses on the needs and expectations of various stakeholder groups, how these can be best met in partnership with business, and increasing awareness of the organization's current efforts, as well as its longer-term sustainability vision. Overall, there is a focus on continuous communication between organization and stakeholder groups that encourages mutual understanding of issues, as well as both sharing of information and dialogue about implementation challenges.

ES Leadership: Creating Alignment

Alignment pertains to the embedding of strategy into day-to-day business operations and the organization of work. When alignment is good, all employees know how their own jobs, their functions, or their lines of business impact the planet and what practices and policies are in place in their day-to-day contexts to enable the organization to focus on sustainability. Under this leadership task, we say more about three practices mentioned by managers in our study: operationalizing sustainability, engaging across boundaries, and putting in place performance accountability for ES.

Operationalizing sustainability. In operationalizing sustainability, organizations incorporate sustainability principles into the day-to-day development and production of goods and services, the ways resources and waste are handled, how stakeholders are engaged, and the ways employees think about their day-to-day jobs and the work of their teams, divisions, or functions.

Leadership practices that work to further integrate ES into the business include specifying actions or setting specific direction at a local level (rather than dictating a detailed plan from headquarters), so that socially or environmentally sensitive business plans and policies make sense and have the greatest possible impact. It is critical to use processes for the discovery of local stakeholder needs and to take those needs into account in planning and implementation of sustainability efforts and operations.

In addition to the local focus, it is a best practice to be sure that materials related to sustainability policies, strategies, and goals are translated into the languages appropriate for specific locations, facilitating easy understanding and application. Another example of good operationalization is the integration of sustainability-related goals with specific employee job roles and descriptions, thus providing a clear connection between abstract vision and strategy and the job tasks of mid- and lower-level managers and other employees. This effort enables employees at all levels of the organization to make sense of the organization's focus on sustainability as it applies to their own day-to-day work and to see the part they play in the organization's success.

Engaging across boundaries. As the concept of sustainability requires an organization to focus on impacts beyond the traditional "walls" of the organization, we find that the practice of engaging across a variety of boundaries is important in many ways. External to the organization, engagement includes partnerships and regular meaningful involvement (beyond simple communication) with a variety of external stakeholders on ES issues and initiatives. External stakeholders include NGOs, government bodies (local and national), community agencies doing work on which the company depends (for example, local schools and colleges), and the media. Many effective companies are active participants in networks focused on social and environmental responsibility, such as the Globally Responsible Leadership Initiative (www.grli.org) or the United Nations' Global Compact (www.unglobalcompact.org). These networks provide organizations with potential partnership opportunities, opportunities to engage in or fund research to further their ES goals, and a group of like-minded colleagues with whom to problem solve and from whom to learn. Internally, engagement across boundaries often takes the form of teamwork on special social or environmental projects or cross-functional collaboration on sustainability-related innovation.

Performance accountability. In organizations successfully implementing sustainability strategy, there are goals, formal measures, audits, certifications, and reporting in place and active at the organizational level. Business units are required to have clearly stated, sustainable working procedures and standards incorporated into unit goals and based on high standards set by senior management. The balanced scorecard is a tool we often see used toward this end (Crawford & Scaletta, 2005).

In addition to setting goals, units and unit managers are provided ample feedback with regard to their performance in implementing sustainable practices and business operations (practices/operations based on consideration of people, planet, and profit), and managers receive periodic reports on their own progress, as well as company progress overall.

In many organizations, the attitude of performance development also extends to stakeholders. In one company we worked with, managers are taught that relations with suppliers have to be respectful. That is, they are not expected to "squeeze" suppliers to get the best price, but rather they are expected to "develop" suppliers, specifically in terms of what it means to conduct environmentally responsible business.

Another example of accountability is an organization's formal reporting of its sustainability efforts. Many organizations create annual reports and use the standards developed by organizations like the Global Reporting Initiative (www.globalreporting.org). These standards require that corporate responsibility reports address the materiality, transparency, reliability, context, and completeness of the information reported.

Environmental Sustainability Leadership: Building and Maintaining Commitment

Building and maintaining commitment to sustainability is about ensuring engagement at all levels of the organization. It encompasses the process of building initial commitment to a company's ES vision and strategy, as well as maintaining motivation and engagement in the face of economic or other challenges that inevitably occur over time. Consistent and visible top management support is clearly a key element. While it is typically the senior management group that creates a strategy, their visible personal commitment to that strategy, in good times and bad, is essential to it success. Secondly, developing employees who feel empowered to enact ES strategies and policies was also seen as important in the organizations we studied. Training employees to make decisions in their own jobs that push toward the ES vision, and then supporting and celebrating them when they do, is critical. And finally, visible ethical actions on the part of people in positions of authority was seen by these managers as valuable role modeling and as a visible demonstration of the commitment of senior leadership to sustainability.

Visible top management support of ES. Of course, putting in place strategies, goals, and objectives is one way organizational members know there is top management support for sustainability. Yet more is needed; and we see additional leadership practices being used in organizations that are approaching what Starik & Rands (1995) call "environmentally sustainable organizations" (ESOs).

In the most sustainability-oriented companies, the CEO plays a central and active role, with the top management team, in making the sustainability strategy and goals visible, raising awareness about global responsibility, and exhibiting personal commitment to this agenda. Some of the specific practices we see employed by those CEOs, COOs, and other top leaders include introducing various internal written and spoken communication channels (discussed further in the communication section below) to demonstrate their commitment and raise employee awareness, providing special or targeted resources (money, staff time, expertise) to projects that create social and environmental good either locally or nationwide (more about this below), and creating/ approving a formal sustainability (or corporate social responsibility) leadership position or group to spearhead or consolidate work in this area and to keep focus on these goals high. The creation of this position is often seen as a mark of the organization's commitment to sustainability and as an indicator of the seriousness with which that is being pursued. In these cases, the position itself, as well as the person occupying it, is seen as a key driver of sustainability efforts. However, creating a position and/or group may foster the impression that sustainability responsibility is "walled off," that the organization's sustainability goals belong to that unit, and may create a set of boundaries that inhibit communication and diminish personal responsibility among those not in the designated group (Starik & Rands, 1995). This potential issue makes frequent and clear communication from the top about leadership intent and process even more important.

Developing ES-empowered employees. Employee empower-ment is either an explicitly stated core value or implicit in the culture, systems, and leadership practices of best-practice ES orga-nizations. In either case, it is a value that is put into practice in decision making at the local level and within teams, as well as in the idea generation necessary for facing many of the challenges to implementing sustainability. At one organization we studied, empowerment is one of five core organizational values; but beyond that, employees are expected to participate with knowledge, ideas, and opportunities, and the company is committed to the idea that attention will be given to their contributions.

Empowerment is also an active focus for employee develop-ment in these organizations. In best practice companies, men-toring, coaching, and training activities contribute to the responsibility efforts by providing not only the basic understand-ing necessary for empowered decision making, but also technical training for specific areas of operation and help and advice when obstacles are encountered or energy for the work begins to fade. Concepts of sustainability or responsibility are included in the on-boarding processes, as well as in regular management develop-ment training. In addition to the formal and informal devel-opment on sustainability, employees are asked to contribute ideas for sustainability projects and processes and are allowed the authority to make decisions with respect to how to (not *whether* to) implement sustainability policies into their regular work. Senior managers in these companies often see their role as weigh-ing in on the side of social and/or environmental responsibility when a younger manager is struggling with a decision with sustain-ability implications, particularly when those are competing with a focus on short-term financial gain.

Acting ethically. The final area of leadership practice involves supporting ethical action in an organization. This set of practices is often understood by organizational members as a display of authenticity—seeing individual and organizational behavior that is in line with the company's sustainability vision, values, strategy, and stated goals. Many leaders in these organizations exhibit environmentally responsible behaviors at work and at home (recy-cling, doing more with less, etc.) and are seen at work as being consistent in their words and in their own decisions and deeds.

As an organizational practice, supporting ethical action can take the form of using participative processes for decision making. While not necessarily ethical in themselves, participative processes are a tangible demonstration of the valuing of employee empowerment to promote environmental sustainability. The process also provides access to the widest set of views, particularly important when operating far from a company's home base. In addition to participative processes, in some of these companies there is an explicitly stated triple bottom line criteria (people, planet, and profit) to which employees and managers can refer in making almost any operational decision. This works to ensure that the principles of ES are kept front and center so as to best support ethical, globally responsible decisions when priorities may become unclear or a situation is complex.

Finally, the organizations most effective at globally responsible and environmentally sustainable practices demonstrate their ethics by engaging in full transparency in reporting, not only their financial status, but the status of progress on their environmental and social goals. Most organizations state they avoid "greenwashing," that is, saying that they will do something "sustainable" and not following up with the corresponding actions, or making it appear that they are doing more "good" than they are actually doing.

Next, we briefly describe the beliefs, mindsets, and values most evident in these companies—organizations well on their way to creating cultures that can both sustain our environment and help the companies prosper in the coming years. We see these mindsets and values as just a subset of those providing the foundation for the leadership practices needed to create and sustain an ES culture.

Beliefs and Values That Support Sustainability

Some of the mindsets that we have seen operating in companies with a strong focus on sustainability are listed and described in Table 10.2 (Quinn & Van Velsor, 2010). While it is probably the case that changes in practice are most often preceded by changes in beliefs (or the introduction of organizational members with new beliefs), one should remember that beliefs and practices are

Table 10.2. Beliefs That Support Sustainable Leadership Practice

An ethic of "perform, don't advertise"—if you are standing for what's right and true, it will sell itself; engage in responsible leadership with respect to social and environmental issues because it is the right thing to do and not primarily for the reputational benefits it provides.

Seeing sustainability leadership as a powerful idea and an opportunity—to reduce costs, create a more ethical climate in the organization, and to form the basis for further, more focused action and innovation.

Sustainability as an ongoing process requiring a long-term perspective—when faced with deciding between quarterly profits and the "right" thing to do, organizations taking a longer-term view seem more able to use practices that reflect a "both/and" versus an "either/or" option.

Jumping in is the best way to get started—everyone will never be absolutely ready, so it is counterproductive to wait until everyone is on board or until the organization is forced to attend to ES.

Everyone has a role to play in bringing the organization along—an attitude toward openness and employee involvement to sustainability that is key to building commitment to the organizational change and alignment work that must be done.

Care for one's own environmental footprint should be a part of one's "home" life, as much as it is part of one's work environment.

Awareness that business operations have a huge contribution to make by changing their practices with respect to environmental damage and social responsibility and belief that organizations should use their influence to create positive change.

mutually reinforcing. Practices that are dictated or required can sometimes produce new beliefs and change in views as to what is possible or will be rewarded. And existing beliefs about the best ways to do the organization's work will, in turn, open or close the door to the individual behaviors and organizational practices described earlier.

Implications and New Directions for Research

While we have attempted to convey not only the results of our own research, but the connection of that work to the work of other scholars focusing on leadership and sustainability, there is clearly still a lot of unexplored territory in this field and much to do in terms of developing practical leadership development tools and approaches that can help create leadership cultures that support sustainable business operations. We see future research and practical needs as closely intertwined.

First, we have only begun to understand what organizations actually do when they successfully transform themselves from a primary focus on a financial bottom line to more of a focus on environmentally sustainable operations. More research is needed to fully elaborate models of leadership practices and beliefs that support and enhance the sustainability of our world. In turn, that knowledge needs to be turned into both individual and organizational assessments, as well as other tools to help companies better understand their current cultures and competencies and what areas for improvement may be the highest priority for development. Those of us in the leadership development field also need to make available interventions and services for culture transformation with the specific goal of creating direction, alignment, and commitment to sustainability in organizations.

We need to know more about the relationship between existing development stage models of environmental citizenship or sustainability leadership and the practices and beliefs that characterize each stage. Having those relationships more fully articulated would allow us to better help organizations see where they are in their own development at present and the beliefs and practices that need to be cultivated to pull them to the next stage of this journey.

We also know little about what represents best practice in developing leadership for sustainability, both at the individual level (leader competencies) and the organizational level (culture transformation). Drath, Palus, and McGuire (2010) suggest strategic work in cross-boundary teams, intentional use of dialogue, support for intersystemic decision making, and the use of action learning teams (among other ideas) as ways to move a leadership culture to greater interdependence—a state that seems characteristic of organizations achieving a higher stage of corporate citizenship or sustainability leadership. Yet, we don't know how well any of these approaches work. As leadership development that is specifically targeted to sustainability grows in popularity, we will have more opportunities to assess the impact of various approaches and methods and will begin to develop a sense of what works and what does not. We sense the demand for leadership development toward these ends is growing, although perhaps not fast enough. Research oriented to identifying and quantifying the benefits of this kind of culture and business model change can help drive interest in creating more wide-spread change in organizations around the world.

Bibliography

Beck, D., & Cowan, C. (1996). *Spiral dynamics*. Malden, MA: Blackwell.

Campbell, J. L. (2007). Why would corporations behave in socially responsible ways? An institutional theory of corporate social responsibility. *Academy of Management Review, 32*, 946–967.

Carroll, A. (1979). A three-dimensional conceptual model of corporate performance. *Academy of Management Review, 4*(4), 497–505.

Carroll, B., Levy, L., & Richmond, D. (2008). Leadership as practice: Challenging the competency paradigm. *Leadership, 4*(4), 363–379.

Crawford, D., & Scaletta, T. (2005, October). The balanced scorecard and corporate social responsibility: Aligning values for profit. *CMA Management*, pp. 20–27.

D'Amato, A., Eckert, R., Ireland, J., Quinn, L., & Van Velsor, E. (2010). Beyond competencies: Leadership practices for corporate global responsibility. *Journal of Global Responsibility, 1*, 225–249.

Drath, W., McCauley, C., Palus, C., Van Velsor, E., O'Connor, P., & McGuire, J. (2008). Direction, alignment, commitment: Toward a more integrative ontology of leadership. *Leadership Quarterly, 19*, 635–653.

Drath, W., Palus, C., & McGuire, J. (2010). Developing interdependent leadership. In E. Van Velsor, C. McCauley, & M. Ruderman (Eds.), *The Center for Creative Leadership handbook of leadership development* (3rd ed.) (pp. 405–428). San Francisco: Jossey-Bass.

Eisenhardt, K. M., & Graebner, M. E. (2007). Theory building from cases: Opportunities and challenges. *Academy of Management Journal, 50*, 25–32.

Ferdig, M. A. (2007). Sustainability leadership: Co-creating a sustainable future. *Journal of Change Management, 7*, 25–35.

Fowler, S., & Hope, C. (2007). Incorporating sustainable business practices into company strategy. *Business Strategy and the Environment,* *16,* 26–38.

Hart, S. L. (1995). The natural resource-based view of the firm. *Academy of Management Review, 20*(4), 986–1014.

Hind, P., Wilson, A., & Lenssen, G. (2009). Developing leaders for sustainable business. *Corporate Governance, 9,* 7–20.

Maak, T. (2007). Responsible leadership, stakeholder engagement, and the emergence of social capital. *Journal of Business Ethics, 74,* 329–343.

McGaw, N. (2005). Developing leaders for a sustainable global society. *Strategic Human Resource Review, 4,* 32–35.

Meindl, J., Ehrlich, S., & Dukerich, J. (1985). The romance of leadership. *Administrative Science Quarterly, 30,* 78–102.

Mirvis, P., & Googins, B. (2006). *Stages of corporate citizenship.* Boston: Boston College Center for Corporate Citizenship.

Nidumolu, R., Prahalad, C., & Rangaswami, M. (2009, September). Why sustainability is now the key driver of innovation. *Harvard Business Review,* pp. 57–64.

Osborn, R., & Hunt, J. (2002). Toward a contextual theory of leadership. *Leadership Quarterly, 13,* 797–837.

Pasmore, B., Lafferty, K., & Spencer, S. (2009). *Developing a leadership strategy: A critical ingredient for organizational success.* Greensboro, NC: Center for Creative Leadership.

Pless, N. M. (2007). Understanding responsible leadership: Role identity and motivational drivers. *Journal of Business Ethics, 74,* 437–456.

Quinn, L., & Van Velsor, E. (2010). Developing globally responsible leadership. In E. Van Velsor, C. McCauley, & M. Ruderman (Eds.), *Center for Creative Leadership handbook of leadership development* (3rd ed.) (pp. 345–374). San Francisco: Jossey-Bass.

Starik, M., & Rands, G. (1995). Weaving an integrated web: Multilevel and multisystem perspectives of ecologically sustainable organizations. *Academy of Management Review, 20,* 908–935.

Van Marrewijk, M., & Werre, M. (2003). Multiple levels of sustainability. *Journal of Business Ethics, 44,* 107–119.

Wartick, S., & Cochran, P. (1985). The evolution of the corporate social performance model. *Academy of Management Review, 10,* 758–769.

Part Three

Case Studies Illustrating the Implementation of Environmental Initiatives

Part Three of this volume describes some of the challenges and successes experienced by human resource and organization development professionals in several organizations that are actively engaged in pursuing environmental sustainability. After reading these case studies, academics and practitioners alike will have greater appreciation for the human resource complexities associated with creating environmentally sustainable organizations.

Chapter 11, "Environmental Sustainability and Employee Engagement at 3M," by Karen Paul and Kevin Nilan, describes the HR strategies that have connected employee engagement with sustainability at 3M. The authors provide a historical overview of 3M's flagship initiative "Pollution Prevention Pays" (3P) and the company's pioneering global corporate environmental policy, which predated governmental environmental regulations in many countries. Through their 3P program, 3M takes a very pragmatic approach to encourage the prevention of pollution, and Paul and Nilan provide examples of engagement initiatives focused on education, assessment, and recognition to foster environmental sustainability.

Chapter 12, "EcoVision at Sherwin-Williams," by Cathy DuBois, reports on a leadership-driven implementation of sustainability strategy at Sherwin-Williams. The company provides a good example for how strong leadership vision and employee initiatives can shape corporate sustainability strategy. DuBois describes how Sherwin-Williams modified traditional HR practices to reflect its focus on sustainability, starting with the recruiting process, which highlights the sustainability vision and requisite competencies.

Chapter 13, "HR and Sustainability at Daimler AG," by Jürgen Deller, Theresa Schnieders, and Angela Titzrath, provides an example for technology- and product-driven environmental sustainability. This case describes Daimler's efforts toward incorporating the HR function into sustainability activities. Particular attention is paid to the organizational structures established by Daimler to support sustainability in company-wide operations. Challenges in implementing current programs internationally are highlighted.

Chapter 14, "HR Initiatives for Environmental Mission Alignment at Aveda Corporation," by Holly Johnson and Kristin Miller, discusses Aveda Corporation's effort of mission-aligned hiring. As a company that was built on the premise of environmental responsibility, Aveda relies on employees who are dedicated to the company's mission. The organization redesigned its employee selection process to select employees who will behave in an environmentally responsible way at work.

Chapter 15, "Environmental Sustainability Initiatives in Ugandan Light Industry," by Daniel Manitsky and Patrice Murphy, describes several projects in Uganda that illustrate how change management principles can be used to improve the ability of organizations with minimal resources to adopt environmentally sustainable practices while also improving economic and social performance. Working with OD professionals skilled in the Rapid Results Approach to creating change, the focal organizations engaged employees in focused change efforts designed to quickly achieve ambitious results for the organizations while also promoting learning for the organization and its staff.

Chapter 16, "Human Resource Development Initiatives for Managing Environmental Concerns at McDonald's UK," by Julie Haddock-Millar, Michael Müller-Camen, and Derek Miles, describes two human resource development initiatives carried out at McDonald's in the United Kingdom. The initiatives involved establishing voluntary "environmental champions" and compulsory environmental education. Extensive qualitative data reveal that these initiatives raised employee awareness of environmental concerns and also resulted in changes in the operational practices of McDonald's restaurants, which in turn changed employee behaviors and improved the company's environmental reporting statistics.

Chapter 17, "Environmental Sustainability and Organizational Sensing at Procter & Gamble," by Andrew Biga, Stephan Dilchert, Silke McCance, Robert Gibby, and Anne Doyle Oudersluys, details the role of organization sensing in tying Procter & Gamble's sustainability goals to employees' work behaviors and outcomes. For Procter & Gamble, a key question in their employee opinion survey is the effect that corporate sustainability initiatives have on whether the company remains an employer of choice. However, rather than focusing only on the corporate sustainability efforts, the company has recently started to assess individual employee behaviors linked to environmental sustainability as well. This enables Procter & Gamble to tie a variety of organization-level variables to employees' environmentally responsible behaviors on the job.

Chapter 18, "Sustainability in Coffee Sourcing and Implications for Employee Engagement at Caribou Coffee," by John Muros, Kevin Impelman, and Lewis Hollweg, presents results of Caribou Coffee's employee survey and shows that employees' perceptions of corporate sustainability programs are linked to satisfaction and employee retention. Muros and colleagues describe a training-based intervention and internal communication initiatives to increase employee engagement. The insights they gained will be of interest to everyone working in an organization that has recently begun to pursue environmental sustainability initiatives.

CHAPTER ELEVEN

Environmental Sustainability and Employee Engagement at 3M

Karen B. Paul
and Kevin J. Nilan

Long before the concept of sustainability came to the forefront of corporate consciousness, 3M served as a leader in environmental management. Starting in the 1960s, the company sought to reduce its impact on the environment while conserving resources. The flagship initiative was called the Pollution Prevention Pays (3P) program. What began as a pioneering concept more than thirty-five years ago thrives today due to the excellence of its design as well as the innovation and engagement of 3M employees worldwide. Since inception, the 3M 3P program has prevented more than three billion pounds of pollutants and saved the company nearly $1.4 billion in costs. Over the next few years, 3M will continue to build on its world-leading progress by driving further progress toward its sustainability goals to reduce volatile air emissions, improving energy efficiency, and reducing waste. In addition, 3M will continue to address global climate change and greenhouse gas emissions on top of its 77 percent reduction since 1990.

This case study describes the "Green HR" strategies that have connected and promoted employee engagement with sustainability at 3M. We review the history of 3M's environmental sustainability program and key factors leading to its success over the years. Specifically, we address the following questions: How does 3M's 3P program actively engage employees in fostering sustainable growth? How does 3M integrate sustainability into all of its products and processes? What are the key determinants for successfully building broad-based employee engagement for sustainability? The case concludes by discussing how employee education, assessment, and recognition all contribute to the organizational sustainability mission.

Dr. Joseph Ling, 3Mer, and the Father of Pollution Prevention

The year was 1971, the Beatles were breaking up, the World Trade Center had just been completed, and the floppy disc invented when Dr. Joseph Ling, a 3Mer, was advocating a holistic approach to environmental sustainability in his testimony before the U.S. Congress regarding the creation of new drinking water quality regulations. Dr. Ling argued the proposed legislation would generate significant air pollution and waste because it relied heavily upon pollution controls. In its place, Dr. Ling suggested pollution prevention as a more prudent approach.

Joseph Ling, who retired in 1984, was a pioneer in the field of environmental and air quality management and is recognized worldwide as the father of pollution prevention. Throughout Dr. Ling's distinguished career, he revolutionized the way 3M and society as a whole understand and manage their environmental impact. He was one of the first to articulate and embrace a holistic approach to environmental management that considers the environmental impacts to all media (air, water, and land) when evaluating policy and program decisions.

At 3M, Dr. Ling integrated his novel ideas into the company's business processes. In 1975, the year Microsoft was founded and catalytic convertors were first introduced into cars, Dr. Ling launched 3M's innovative Pollution Prevention Pays (3P) program. The 3P program is based on the premise that pollution *prevention* is more environmentally effective, technically sound, and economical than conventional pollution *controls*. 3P seeks to eliminate pollution at the source through product reformulation, process modification, equipment redesign, and the recycling and reuse of waste materials. 3M elevated its commitment to the environment in 1975 when the board of directors adopted the 3M Environmental Policy. This global corporate environmental policy, believed to be the first policy with measurable results from a major manufacturing company, is a comprehensive statement of 3M's environmental commitment with special emphasis on preventing the creation of pollution.

While Dr. Ling's impact on 3M's operations and air emissions was vast, his greatest impact comes from his efforts to spread these ideas globally. In 1976, Dr. Ling first presented his ideas at the Non-Waste Technology and Production Conference sponsored by the United Nations (UN) Economic Commission for Europe. Shortly after, countries such as the United Kingdom, France, Germany, and Sweden adopted pollution prevention as a formal part of their environmental policies. At this time, Dr. Ling was approached by the director of the UN Environmental Program to develop a booklet explaining pollution prevention theories for distribution to UN member countries. In addition, Dr. Ling further spread his ideas by serving as an advisor to three sitting U.S. presidents, the United Nations, and the U.S. Environmental Protection Agency (EPA); serving as a delegate to the U.S.–U.S.S.R environmental treaty in 1979; speaking at conferences throughout the United States, Europe, and Asia; and serving on numerous boards and associations.

Until his death in 2005, Dr. Ling continued to advocate a holistic pollution prevention approach and donate his time to advancing proactive, science-based environmental decision making. Dr. Ling believed employees were the key to organizational sustainability because of their insights into where improvement in products and processes could be made.

The 3P Program and Its Impact Today

3P was initiated as a framework, built around a simple and very pragmatic approach to both encourage and recognize employees for preventing pollution. Since its inception, 3P has inspired more than 8,100 projects worldwide, all of them proposed by employees. Through product reformulation, process modification, equipment redesign, and the recycling and reuse of waste materials, the generation of three billion pounds of pollution has been prevented and 3M has saved $1.4 billion in raw material and pollution control costs—all in the first year of implementation of the projects. Today, 3P is more important than ever. It continues to help 3M reduce its environmental footprint and does so in a way that is most sustainable: through prevention rather than control.

3P succeeds because it actively engages employees in fostering sustainable growth. It encourages employees to use their first-hand knowledge of products, materials, processes, equipment, and waste. The basic steps of the program can be described as follows. When an employee generates an idea for preventing pollution, he or she first forms a team to scope out the problem and develop a potential solution. The costs and savings (from a pollution and monetary perspective) are identified. If the team members decide to move forward, they prepare a proposal and submit it to their management for approval and funding. Not surprisingly, managers are frequently eager to fund these projects for the potential cost savings alone. Once a local project is underway, the team may submit it to a 3P Coordinating Committee for recognition as a corporate 3P project. The committee considers how effective the project has been at reducing pollution, as well as costs saved and the level of technical innovation involved. 3P designation brings no financial rewards, but is considered an honor within the corporation, providing intrinsic motivation to employees.

By 2010, thirty-five years after the 3P program launch, 3P ideas and initiatives from employees provide much of the philosophical basis for 3M's environmental, health, and safety programs. The prevention approach, along with extensive employee involvement, are core to 3M's culture. Here, we provide only a few illustrative examples of the many, many employee-driven projects.

Examples of 3P Projects

3M's Prairie du Chien, Wisconsin, facility reduced volatile organic compound (VOC) emissions and other air pollutant emissions to a point where it was no longer necessary to operate the facility's energy-intensive pollution control system. Coating reformulations and equipment modifications over time resulted in a reduction of approximately 90 percent of VOC and other air emissions. After achieving these reductions, the project team worked with the Wisconsin Department of Natural Resources to gain regulatory approval for shutting down the facility's pollution control system, saving 550 tons of greenhouse gas emissions annually from reduced electricity use and fuel combustion. By preventing pollution at the source, the team both reduced environmental impact and generated significant cost savings for the company.

A team from 3M Brazil's Sumaré facility was awarded an Environmental, Health, and Safety Achievement Award for their project to reduce water use by nearly sixteen million gallons a year. Access to clean water is a major issue for the Sumaré facility. The underground geology of the region makes well water both scarce and expensive. The facility was previously using water from a nearby lake, but the high water demand in the region has led to significant reductions in the lake's water level, making it an unsustainable resource. A reverse osmosis system, along with changes to the facility's boiler water treatment regime, allows the plant to reuse approximately 5,000 cubic meters of its waste water each month, reducing its water use and saving nearly $200,000 annually.

3M's Yamagata, Japan, facility has eliminated all of their landfill waste. The facility began by attempting to eliminate as much waste as possible through pollution prevention. After maximizing waste prevention activities, the remaining waste was separated into the four waste management categories of reuse, recycling, waste to energy, and incineration. Yamagata placed the greatest emphasis on finding ways to reuse the waste internally or finding ways to sell the waste to external markets. Waste was sent to an outside incinerator only when reuse, recycling, or waste to energy was not possible. 3M Yamgata's efforts have led to an 83 percent reduction in total waste since their zero landfill activities began.

Values, Leadership, and Engagement for Environmental Sustainability

In this section, we outline some of the key determinants of success for environmental sustainability programs. 3M has won many accolades for its own environmental sustainability initiatives. The 3P program alone received two presidential awards (President George H. W. Bush's Environment and Resource Conservation Challenge Citation in 1992 and President Clinton's Sustainable Development Award in 1996). 3M has also been cited as the only industrial company recognized seven years in a row by the U.S. Environmental Protection Agency and the U.S. Department of Energy with the Energy Star for Sustained Excellence Award for Energy Management. In addition, 3M has been included in the 2010/11 Dow Jones Sustainability Index with "Gold Class" distinction and has been part of the Index since its inception. Further, Interbrand's Best Global Green Brands for 2011 ranks 3M as number two on its list of "greenest" brands. Interbrand's methodology considers both public perception of a brand's environmental performance and the brand's actual performance based on publicly available information.

These sustainability accomplishments make the company unique among highly complex and diverse industrial organizations. Here, we describe how 3M builds broad-based employee engagement for environmental sustainability into its organizational culture, thereby strengthening its long tradition of environmental sustainability.

3M consists of approximately thirty-five product divisions grouped into six large market-leading businesses. 3M has subsidiaries in sixty-eight countries. Additionally, a corporate staff exists in key functional areas (Legal, HR, etc.) to facilitate the company's business. The interplay between the line businesses and corporate staff helps reinforce key initiatives and messages. Both play important albeit different roles in employee engagement. In the case of environmental sustainability, there are three interdependent systems operating simultaneously that fuel 3M's mission. First, executive management devises and implements global policies. Second, corporate staff groups develop messages and materials from the policies, which help build understanding of the policy's thrust. Third, the businesses identify and put into action strategies to promote those policies, messages, and materials in the products and services provided to their customers.

Values

Underlying everything at 3M are the company's values. Early in 3M's history, 3Mers recognized that doing business in new, smarter ways would not only create a more viable company, but it could also help the company meet its social responsibilities and reduce its impact on the environment. Both of these two objectives are integral to ethical business conduct at 3M. Sustainability is viewed as a natural extension of the 3M values, which include:

- Act with uncompromising honesty and integrity in everything we do.
- Satisfy our customers with innovative technology and superior quality, value, and service.
- Provide our investors an attractive return through sustainable, global growth.
- Respect our social and physical environment around the world.
- Value and develop our employees' diverse talents, initiative, and leadership.
- Earn the admiration of all those associated with 3M worldwide.

At 3M, the corporate culture—with its concern for the social and physical environment and its encouragement of employee initiative—lends itself to the promotion of sustainability. Still, there are two additional factors which perhaps are even more critical for building and maintaining broad-based employee commitment to sustainability: leadership and employee engagement.

Leadership

For sustainability values to take hold among employees, management must set the company's environmental goals and communicate them effectively to employees. At 3M, this communication must include more than a passive announcement.

Rather, management must specifically ask for employee help and define the necessary tasks. Leadership demonstrates the importance of sustainability by showing how it fits with other corporate strategies. In 3M's experience, most employees want to be environmentally responsible of their own accord. If they believe management is truly supportive and if they receive adequate direction, employees are easily motivated to pursue environmental sustainability goals. This section introduces some of the key leadership characters that were instrumental in formulating 3M's environmental sustainability strategy over the years.

3M has a history of strong leaders. One such prominent leader was William L. McKnight, company president (1929 to 1949) and 3M's first chairman of the board (1949 to 1966). Among McKnight's contributions over his sixty-year career were his pioneering vision and emphasis on corporate values. Under CEO McKnight, 3M emphasized the business, the employees, and the social and physical environment. Later, Dr. Ling added to McKnight's pioneering view of environmentalism by enumerating exactly how 3M could approach its business while at the same time proactively protect all of the earth's resources.

3M Company Chairman and Chief Executive Officer L.D. DeSimone (1991 to 2001) took both a very public and a very strong view toward corporate environmentalism. Trained as a chemical engineer, DeSimone helped establish 3M's aggressive environmental goals in 1990. Then, in partnership with Frank Popoff, chairman of Dow Chemical Company, DeSimone co-authored the book *Eco-Efficiency,* published in 1997. In the book, the authors marry the concept of value creation and environmental concerns and discuss eco-efficiency as a management philosophy. Like Ling, DeSimone leveraged his role and became the chair of the World Business Council for Sustainable Development, articulating the essence of 3M's philosophy on sustainable development.

This long legacy of leadership action toward environmental sustainability goals was furthered in 2008, under the direction of 3M's current CEO, Dr. George Buckley. 3M launched three strategic principles to further elaborate and reinforce the company's position on sustainability.

- *Economic Success:* Build lasting customer relationships by developing differentiated, practical, and ingenious solutions to their sustainability challenges.
- *Environmental Protection:* Provide practical and effective solutions and products to address environmental challenges for ourselves and our customers.
- *Social Responsibility:* Engage key stakeholders in dialogue and take action to improve 3M's sustainability performance.

These principles were developed to provide 3M businesses and corporate staff groups with a flexible and meaningful framework to engage customers and key stakeholders around sustainability. Included in Buckley's vision was for 3Mers to actively partner with customers to address environmental challenges using 3M products and technologies. To 3M, these principles mean meeting the needs of today's society, while respecting the ability of future generations to meet their own.

Engagement

To successfully drive the sustainability principles throughout this large multi-national corporation, employee engagement became critical. To be successful, sustainability requires a multi-level, multidisciplinary approach. Employees at all levels must be actively engaged or the objectives of developing new products and reviewing existing products and processes to help customers will fall short of expectations. As part of a much larger employee engagement initiative, human resources took a proactive approach of closely tying sustainability to both the employee engagement and employment brand initiatives.

At 3M, employee engagement is defined worldwide as "an individual's sense of purpose and focused energy, evident to others in the display of personal initiative, effort, and persistence directed toward *organizational goals.*" Sustainability is part of 3M's organizational goals. Sustainability provides a way for many employees to become energized by connecting to the world around them and by using innovative approaches to solve customer problems within a sustainable development framework.

Sustainability helps 3M employees connect their own work to society at large.

3M was well positioned to leverage its workforce toward sustainability with the philosophical stage set by McKnight, Ling, DeSimone, and Buckley. The company has always relied heavily upon employee engagement. Innovation, arguably 3M's most treasured asset, rests upon and is fueled by employee engagement. New employees at 3M quickly learn of the expectations around involvement and taking action. Thus, it was natural for 3M to treat sustainability as it treats innovation—something powered by concerned employees working to solve customer challenges.

"Green HR" Strategies That Promote Employee Engagement with Sustainability

This section takes a more detailed look at three HR strategies that support environmental sustainability at 3M: employee education, assessment, and recognition. These HR strategies, in combination with the corporate values and leadership outlined above, support employee engagement with sustainability in the organization. 3M's "Green HR" strategies are articulated by Angela S. Lalor, senior vice president of human resources: "Our approach to sustainability is reached through and by our employees. Human resources as a function can support the businesses in this corporate endeavor through the education, assessment, and recognition of these efforts."

Education

One very prominent component of 3M's support for environmental sustainability is education. 3M deploys learning modules delivered in traditional classroom settings and also leverages the Internet. 3M has an external website (www.mmm.com/sustainability) and internal website called the Sustainability Center. The internal website is accessible to 3M employees worldwide and exists to educate employees about sustainability. Employees can access volumes of historical information about such things as 3P contributions, air emissions, water stewardship, waste management, and biodiversity. The site provides customer-facing employees with facts and figures about corporate, business, and product data possibly of use when responding to customer queries or creating local marketing materials. Employees can also download videos and presentations for business purposes.

As part of its education strategy, 3M also chose to focus employee attention on key facts about sustainability. In this case, 3M sought to improve the overall fluency and comfort of its workforce in discussing 3M's approach to sustainability. Taking a cue from nightly TV, a cross-functional team of corporate staffers created a video titled "10 Things Every Employee Should Know About Sustainability at 3M." The video was filmed as part of an ongoing employee engagement series and featured the CEO and many of his direct reports, each highlighting one of the ten items with stories and facts. The list of ten items serves as a framework for messaging to employees and is being communicated globally through local meetings, online home pages, in-house newspaper articles, and bulletin board postings.

Other venues 3M is using to educate employees include a Sustainability Speaker Series and social media. In fact, 3M has used social media extensively (DIY video for a YouTube-like internal video posting, blogs, wikis, and the internal social networking site). A recent employee engagement video contest helped to unleash the creative energies of employees and provided tools and techniques for creating new patterns of communication. The purpose of the video contest was to encourage the use of social media within the company as well as provide video footage that could be used for elaborating on key messages such as sustainability for 3M. Several winning entries can be seen currently on 3M Careers Facebook page on the topics of sustainability and employee engagement. 3M has found that sustainability is a key topic of interest among many new recruits, and the video contest provided an engaging method of providing information and allowing applicants an insider's view of the issue.

Another example of an educational event occurred during the United Nations–sponsored World Environment Day, held June 5, 2009. 3M hosted an employee-oriented web event focused on sustainability and innovation. The day's UN theme was "Your Planet Needs You—Unite to Combat Climate Change." 3M's live web event built upon the UN theme and involved 3M's global workforce. Through its linked-program design, 3M drew attention to and reinforced the priority of environmentalism. 3M also communicated to its global workforce that environmentally sensitive design was part of everyone's job description. Similar to the UN event, 3M's web event brought together employees and leaders to discuss climate change and environmentalism in the context of customer priorities. Unique to the 3M event was a desire to *listen* to employee input on solutions for how best to integrate those priorities when responding to needs in future markets. Again, the idea was to find different levers to help increase awareness of sustainability and be engaging to employees.

3M has also created a series of environmental solutions catalogs. Each catalog showcases 3M products that can help customers address their own environmental and energy challenges. The catalogs were developed to assist 3M's marketing and sales community when responding to customer and consumer interest regarding the environmental profile of 3M products. The catalogs include a wide range of products and claims, including claims concerning a product's performance (reduce energy use for the consumer) and manufacturing footprint. These catalogs have proven extremely useful in educating employees about many of the things 3M has done to foster environmental sustainability.

A "sustainable" product is one that is produced, used, and disposed of without depleting the earth's resources or damaging the environment. Attributes of sustainable products include use of renewable resources in manufacturing, the responsible use of non-renewable resources, minimizing transportation to conserve fossil fuel, responsible manufacturing to reduce pollution, and recyclability of the product. For example, while many people are familiar with 3M's famous Post-it® Notes, many are unaware that these are not only recyclable but are made from a minimum of 30 percent post-consumer content. The product is also made with paper from well-managed forests where trees are replanted. Examples of many more environmentally sustainable 3M products are featured in these catalogs.

Table 11.1. 2009 Survey Results

Opinions on Sustainability	Percent Favorable
3M makes business choices that support the environment, such as waste reduction and disposal, energy conservation, and vendor selection.	85 percent
3M's sustainability efforts have increased my overall satisfaction with working here.	61 percent
I can confidently talk with my friends and neighbors about how 3M supports the sustainability of our customers and company.	72 percent

Assessment

Measurement is part of any strong strategy. Earlier in this chapter we shared a number of 3M's key metrics for environmental sustainability. As part of the Green HR strategy, there was also a desire to check on leadership's views of sustainability. Human resources choose to obtain data by leveraging the 3M Leadership Survey for this purpose. The 3M Leadership Survey is a biennial survey of 3M's global leadership. The survey examines results by function, business, and region. The survey encourages leaders to provide candid input and highlights areas of strength and opportunity on key strategic topics from the view of the corporation. Table 11.1 presents selected results on some relevant items. Results indicate that the majority of 3M leaders recognize the efforts 3M is taking toward sustainability.

Recognition

Employee recognition can range from a supervisor's pat on the back to more formalized awards, and communicates the importance of employee initiative to a company's environmental sustainability progress. Below, we highlight two of several annual awards that recognize the most outstanding contributions by individuals and teams towards 3M's sustainability goals. In giving these awards, 3M seeks to establish the context in which they are presented in proportion to the significance of the respective contribution.

- *Pollution Prevention Pays (3P) Awards* salute employees and teams that apply innovative thinking to projects that significantly reduce waste, prevent pollution, and provide a positive economic benefit. These efforts are generally the result of employees who view pollution prevention as a personal responsibility rather than a job requirement.
- *Environment, Health, and Safety Achievement Awards* are open to every 3M employee or employee team worldwide that demonstrates innovation and leadership to enhance environmental, health, and safety performance, reduce costs, and drive growth via new products and processes. Categories for this award are for individual lifetime achievement and team awards.

Summary

3M's environmental sustainability efforts thrive today inside this large, global manufacturing giant because sustainability defines the way 3M wants to do business. 3M's sustainability design is simple and straightforward and it works well because each employee understands and buys into the inherent "goodness," "appropriateness," or "correctness" of the mission itself. Employees' values and those of the company are well aligned. Employees easily embrace 3M's holistic, preventative philosophy. They also embrace leveraging their unique expertise in the design, re-design, manufacture, tooling, and re-tooling of processes to "out-think" pollution. What began as a pioneering concept years ago thrives today due to the multi-level, multidisciplinary approach used to develop broad-based employee engagement and commitment to sustainable growth at 3M.

Consistent with 3M's mission and values, sustainability represents the only viable path for the company to co-exist with the global environment. 3M's global sustainability initiative facilitates, encourages, rewards, and celebrates employee excellence in preventing pollution. The efficacy of the 3P initiative is principally in the hands of employees, who leverage their knowledge of 3M products, 3M processes, and 3M technologies.

CHAPTER TWELVE

EcoVision at Sherwin-Williams

Leadership at All Levels

Cathy L. Z. DuBois

Founded in 1866, the Sherwin-Williams Company is a global leader in the development, manufacture, distribution, and sale of coatings and related products to professional, industrial, commercial, and retail customers. Sherwin-Williams is a values-driven organization that places high priority on corporate social responsibility (CSR). Their environmental sustainability (ES) program, EcoVision, comprises one aspect of their CSR program. EcoVision's success rests upon a constellation of factors, from which four themes emerge: (1) the business rationale underlying EcoVision, (2) the presence of the human resource (HR) function as a true strategic player in the organization and as an EcoVision leader, (3) the use of HR systems to support pushing the boundaries of ES goals and actions, and (4) the variety of HR actions that facilitate pervasive engagement in EcoVision across all levels of employees. Sherwin-Williams' experience exemplifies the value of approaching ES from a whole systems perspective. This case study demonstrates how HR leadership plays a critical role in embedding ES thinking and action throughout the organization.

The Tipping Point: Why Environmental Sustainability and Why Now?

Environmental sustainability efforts increasingly impact an organization's capacity to create competitive advantage, particularly in the light of changing business conditions. Three key contextual factors are currently driving sustainability strategies: declining natural resources, escalating stakeholder demands for "green" products and processes, and radical transparency of organizational information to other organizations and to the public (Laszlo & Zhexembayeva, 2011). In fact, the very purpose of corporations is being redefined, shifting from a sole focus on profit to a focus on creating shared value for firms and the social and environmental systems within which they operate (Porter & Kramer 2011). Fortune 1000 companies have widely adopted sustainability strategies (Gibbs & Soell, 2011), and 80 percent of Fortune Global 250 companies now disclose their sustainability performance (Apotheker, 2010).

The Sherwin-Williams Company adopted a sustainability strategy in 2006, inspired by the vision of CEO Christopher Connor, who clearly perceived how stakeholder preferences were creating a sustainability imperative for the firm. In 2006, Connor included a screening of Al Gore's *An Inconvenient Truth* in the agenda for the senior strategy retreat. Despite the presence of occasional disagreements vocalized throughout the film, the senior executive team recognized the significance of its message. The film made it clear that the environment had emerged as a compelling issue for the public and was now part of the cultural context not only in the U.S. but worldwide. Sherwin-Williams' executive team was well aware of the legal challenges, costs, and negative press associated with the organization's past experiences with lead-based products. These product-related challenges had clarified for companies throughout the coatings industries that environmental issues are directly tied to business issues. The discussion among Sherwin-Williams senior executives that followed screening of the film set in motion a series of ES-related actions at the company. These initiatives became formally articulated in their 2009 corporate social responsibility report, *Caring in Full Color* (Sherwin-Williams, 2010). This report articulates the company's ES initiative in the context of their three-dimensional corporate identity, which is detailed below.

Sherwin-Williams the Employer

Headquartered in Cleveland, Ohio, Sherwin-Williams employs 30,000 people in its one hundred manufacturing and distribution centers and more than 3,500 company-operated paint stores. Its facilities are located in twenty countries, and its products are sold in over seventy countries. Sherwin-Williams is a mature company (founded 145 years ago) and highly successful within its industry (it is the largest producer of paints and coatings in the U.S. and among the largest worldwide). As such, Sherwin-Williams had clearly established that it could successfully make and sell its products. In fact, company executives had long possessed the capability and the willingness to expand the boundaries of their thinking to consider what more the company could do to create value beyond what their products offered. This enabled the senior executive team to respond at the cultural "tipping point" (Gladwell, 2000) at which ES entered the mainstream public conversation. Increasing societal concern for the environment was consistent with the Sherwin-Williams culture of caring, for the notion of acting responsibly had been engrained in the company's corporate culture since its inception.

Sherwin-Williams the Citizen

The history of Sherwin-Williams as a values-based company was reflected in the Code of Principles articulated in 1906 by Walter Cottingham, who became the company's second CEO. The principles promote "loyalty to the company and to each other," fostering "good fellowship among ourselves," and being "considerate, polite, and courteous in all out dealings with and without the company." Such consideration was reflected in the employee safety programs instituted in the first factories, which expanded through the years and spilled over to the community in subsequent years.

As the organization evolved, leaders articulated seven values that guide their business practices: innovation, integrity, growth, people, performance, quality, and service. These values underlie how employees are treated and Sherwin-Williams' commitment to its products and consumers. In 1964, the Sherwin-Williams Foundation was created to support a wide range of community projects in the United States and around the world. The company's demonstrated record of actions reflective of caring provided an ideal context for their ES program.

Sherwin-Williams the Steward

Sherwin-Williams' past experience with products that were formerly lead-based inspired the senior executives to ask themselves during their 2006 retreat, "In fifty years down the road, what will our employees wish we had done?" The executives felt strongly that their response should be void of a political stance; thereby they did not align their ES initiatives with concern for global warming, which was a politicized topic at the time (see Dunlap, 2008; Maron & Rahim, 2010). Instead, they framed their ES initiatives as a proactive response to long-term concerns for the environment and the organization. As Tom Hopkins, senior vice president of human resources, noted in conversation with the author, "Who can argue against clean air, clean water, and cost savings?"

Sherwin-Williams' EcoVision program is described as the "company-wide commitment to look for and implement ways that reduce our impact on the environment" (Sherwin-Williams, 2010). The EcoVision mission statement reflects the theme of caring in the context of environmental stewardship, with a goal to be "a recognized leader in the development of sustainable processes, products, and activities that preserve natural resources, protect the environment, and contribute to social improvement" (Sherwin-Williams, 2010). Thus, EcoVision is aligned with the company's values-based approach to business and their commitment to playing a leadership role in their industry. Such a substantively founded initiative makes sense to both employees and customers and is responsible to employees, shareholders, and communities in which the company operates.

Human Resources as a Strategic Leader

To effect consistent and clear organizational change throughout a large, internationally operating organization requires a strong leadership team. As noted earlier, the CEO had brought the issue of environmental sustainability to his senior executive team and highlighted the link to business results for Sherwin-Williams. Thus, the most important point of buy-in was explicit from the start. Once the business rationale for the initiative was clear, senior executives were convinced of its importance. They concluded that a team effort was required to cascade the initiative throughout the organization. Such an approach was facilitated by the fact that every member of Sherwin-Williams' senior executive team was viewed as an equal partner, including HR. In fact, the HR function had long been a key strategic player at Sherwin-Williams; HR executives offered the same kind of business-relevant solutions to support organizational needs as did executives in other functional areas.

The two senior executives who stepped into the lead as architects of ES-related change management included Tom Hopkins, senior vice president of HR, and Tom Seitz, senior vice president of strategic excellence initiatives. Both men have enjoyed lengthy careers at Sherwin-Williams; they know the company well and have worked together in a variety of capacities for many years. Hopkins joined Sherwin-Williams in 1981 as an intern in the training function; he worked his way into his first VP of HR position in 1986 for the South Central Division, followed in 1990 by VP of HR for the Paint Stores Group, and finally the senior VP of HR in 1997. Seitz signed on in 1970 as a formulator, held a variety of positions in technical, engineering, manufacturing, and logistics, followed by a variety of management roles, including president of the Consumer Group, after which he became the senior VP of strategic excellence initiatives in 2007. They eagerly talked to the author about ES at Sherwin-Williams and were clearly proud of the substantive and impactful ES initiatives underway. They reported that their leadership efforts capitalized on the strong support they knew they could rely on from the senior executive team. Although HR serves as the architect of organizational change management at Sherwin-Williams, all senior executives understand their respective change management responsibilities and take them very seriously.

The emergence of Hopkins and Seitz as leaders was the natural result of prior activities they had initiated at the company. Environmental sustainability issues had emerged from a 1998 operations excellence initiative they had jointly led, which emphasized customer service, cost, safety, quality, and people. Formerly the president of Sherwin-Williams' Consumer Division, Seitz joined the senior executive team when an organizational focus on strategic and operations excellence solidified during the period of 2004 to 2007. This focus was driven by the fact that Sherwin-Williams had factories all over the world, each with a given footprint of technological capability; the goal was to maximize what each plant could produce.

Through their in-depth knowledge of the company and their joint leadership of organizational excellence initiatives, these executives became highly familiar with how employees did their work and how operations functioned. They also encountered employees scattered throughout the organization who were passionate about ES, and who had therefore implemented individual actions to reduce environmental impact within the scope of their own jobs. Hence, the pivotal senior executive strategy retreat that initiated the company-wide EcoVision initiative also marked the convergence of ES-related concerns among executives with grassroots ES efforts that had emerged among employees.

Environmental Sustainability Task Force

Following the senior executive retreat, Hopkins and Seitz convened an initial core group of environmentally passionate employees into a task force. The ES Task Force is a steering committee that includes a select group of representatives from a range of areas across the organization: HR, health and safety, technical, regulatory, marketing, operations, and sales, to name a few. It is notable that the group does not have formal reporting relationships within the organization. Members are tasked with a focus on longer-range ideas. Hopkins and Seitz initiated this group by seeding it with "true believers"—employees who were personally committed to the cause of ES. Thus, it was hoped that members were inherently motivated and sufficiently aware of relevant external developments to competently address long-term considerations.

The goal of the ES Task Force, led by Hopkins and Seitz, was to determine how to leverage the emergent efforts that were located in a variety of facilities and departments throughout the world into an organization-wide initiative. The diversity of group members' jobs and expertise supported a rich exchange of ideas on how to build employee acceptance. From the start, the ES Task Force made a conscious effort to avoid hype and "greenwashing"; Sherwin-Williams' approach to ES would be one of substance and integrity.

The task force created a clear distinction between environmentally responsible processes and products, and also between use of the terms "sustainability" and "green." Sherwin-Williams associated the term *sustainability* with processes; it would be used to create and reflect operational efforts to lower consumption of resources and the organization's carbon footprint. The term *green* was associated with the company's products; this would provide a clear signal for consumers who seek environmentally friendly products. The goal was to create operations-, marketing-, and innovations excellence that not only met standards, but pushed to set new ones. Sherwin-Williams' goal was to offer products to consumers that were not only the best within their categories, but were created using the best technology and responsible processes.

To capture employee attention about ES and to engage employees in a manner that offered clear feedback, the ES Task Force initiated an energy savings contest, the "Kick-Off Challenge," among the company's three largest facilities in Cleveland, Ohio. This contest communicated to employees that ES had become a significant and important issue to the company, raised employee awareness about what they could do to support ES, documented who was taking action (as well as the nature of that action), and created excitement that motivated employees broadly to embrace the new ES goals. The initial competition set in motion a series of contests that covered energy use, recycling, and waste and spread through production and distribution facilities worldwide. The benefit of these competitions was two-fold: First, they brought about significant financial savings and a reduction of the company's carbon footprint reductions, in line with the senior executives' team initial goals. Second, the contests generated waves of enthusiasm and participation from Sherwin-Williams employees that would provide the basis for the EcoVision initiative.

Implementation of EcoVision: Realizing the Gains

The initial campaign described here generated sufficient employee engagement to create significant reductions in costs and carbon emissions. On the basis of this success and the conviction that ES could provide competitive advantage for the organization, in 2008 Sherwin-Williams launched the EcoVision initiative. EcoVision is grounded in five articulated principles: Conservation, Accountability, Responsibility, Innovation, and Respect. The EcoVision mission statement reflects the full people-planet-profit perspective:

> "Sherwin-Williams is committed to being a recognized leader in the development of sustainable processes, products and activities that are profitable, preserve natural resources and contribute to social improvement." (Sherwin-Williams, 2010, p. 12)

That same year the company demonstrated further commitment to ES by joining the Environmental Protection Agency's (EPA) Climate Leaders program. Alignment with this voluntary government-industry partnership would allow the company to work with the EPA to set goals for reduction of greenhouse gas emissions and develop approved methods to track performance toward their goals. This relationship would provide visibility for Sherwin-Williams' ES commitment and hold the organization publicly accountable for meeting stated goals.

ES Task Force members recognized that an enduring and powerful impact would require the creation of systems that would embed ES deeply into the fabric of the organization. Such systems could remove variability in employee performance while allowing for creativity; they could institutionalize a sweeping set of sustainable actions across the entire workforce. One of the most powerful systems they put in place is the EcoMet Database. EcoMet houses a host of metrics that reflect progress toward articulated ES goals. EcoMet is updated monthly by employees at plants, distribution centers, and other large Sherwin-Williams facilities around the world. Any facility can enter its metrics into this database.

The system provides a tool for locations to track their own energy usage, waste generation, and recycling rates, as well as a means to access how other locations are doing. As such, it provides an opportunity to communicate successes throughout the organization and a sense of urgency to exceed targeted metrics to stay ahead of other locations.

The "best practices" database located on the Sherwin-Williams operations excellence website provides a second system that supports sustainability-related employee activity. Employees access this database to record details about the sustainability-related actions they take and exchange questions with other locations. When employees at any location have mastered a set of ES actions/goals, they consult this database to glean ideas for new programs and new perspectives on established ones. Together, these two systems store information that provides a virtual means to shape best practice the world over. They play an essential role in creating self-sustaining, employee-driven, and organization-wide monitored progress toward ES goals at Sherwin-Williams.

Employee Engagement Initiatives

Members of the ES Task Force realized the importance of actively engaging employees throughout the organization in EcoVision. Toward this end they created three initiatives: hands-on "dumpster dives," ES forum groups, and an ES suggestion website. Each initiative will be briefly described here.

Dumpster Dives

Dumpster dives allow employees to experience the proportion of recyclable material that they throw into trash receptacles at work. To ensure safety, employees don protective suits and masks before they embark upon emptying a full trash dumpster. As each item is removed, it is sorted into its appropriate pile: one pile for each category of recyclables (paper, metal, plastic, cardboard), and one pile for trash that cannot be recycled and must go to a landfill. The process is highly engaging and creates clear visual images for employees. They experience how the cumulative actions of a small group of individuals have a tangible impact, and by extension the magnitude of difference this can create if employees throughout the company adopt better recycling behaviors. Dumpster dives across Sherwin-Williams locations were described as having generated a level of camaraderie behind this ES initiative that no amount of employee training could have created.

Forum Groups

Environmental sustainability forum groups were also established. In contrast to the long-term vision orientation of the ES Task Force, the goal of ES forum groups is to engage employees in resolving specific problems with a short-term focus. Each functional area (marketing, innovation excellence, operations excellence, et cetera) has a forum group that meets quarterly, with active subcommittees that meet monthly. Like the ES Task Force, ES forums lack a formal reporting structure and thereby function as flexible, informal centers of excellence. To support success, an in-house organization development specialist allocates about 30 percent of his or her time to build and maintain these groups.

Environmental sustainability forum members can either be assigned a specific issue to be resolved or they can generate one of their own choosing. Because each forum develops its own excellence initiatives through peer review of ideas, employees bring their ideas to the group and share them openly. Plans evolve over time as ideas are exchanged, both within the group and between groups through the "best practices" database noted above, and best practices are duplicated and leveraged for further improvement. For example, collective employee innovation drove modifications to the process and equipment used to fill cans with product, reducing the amount of product remaining in the equipment when filling was complete from ninety-nine gallons to one gallon. This dramatically reduced the amount of water and chemicals used to clear the equipment for the next product, as well as significantly decreased product waste; these results reflect mutual wins for the planet as well as for company profits.

Suggestion Website

The ES suggestion website offers a means for all employees throughout the company to submit ideas for how work processes can be designed more sustainably. Once submitted, these suggestions are directed in a timely manner to a key person in the respective area that the suggestion addresses. For example, if an employee's suggestion was to set up recycling at company events, the suggestion would be directed to the head of building management; if the suggestion addressed energy efficiency at a particular facility, it would be directed to the head of engineering. Employees can choose whether to submit suggestions anonymously or include their names and receive a direct reply. It is worth noting that, although the suggestion website is an actively used employee resource, most employees choose to communicate their ideas directly to their supervisors or even directly to the CEO or COO. It seems that with regard to environmental sustainability, the company's employees are confident about sharing their ideas, and they do so frequently.

Role of the HR Function

The HR function actively participates in the ES employee engagement exchanges and supportively monitors communications to ensure that they remain clear and productive. For example, they might facilitate sessions or connect employees with others who have needed information. In general, the HR function is tasked with finding ways to remove organizational roadblocks that might arise when employees take steps to instigate change for the purpose of increasing ES.

Performance Management

To increase employee accountability for ES, HR has aligned performance assessment and incentives with ES goals. Environmental sustainability-related incentive goals were initially limited to senior executives; subsequently they spread to successive levels within the management team. Now that EcoVision is well established and embedded in the organization's business practices, ES-related goals are broadly considered in annual performance planning for managerial and nonmanagerial employees alike.

The high priority given to effective performance management at Sherwin-Williams is a key element underlying the success of these HR-related ES initiatives. All executives are held responsible for employee engagement, and they hold the managers who report to them accountable for managing employees in ways that facilitate success and engagement. In fact, managers are evaluated on a regular basis for their sites' performance using metrics from the EcoMet database. These managers have clearly specified sustainability goals that are directly linked to sustainability performance, as well as to the financial incentives they receive.

The performance management process includes joint goal setting by managers and employees, with signoff by the manager's supervisor. This performance management process ensures that employees and managers share similar expectations regarding work priorities, process, and system utilization, as well as identification of performance metrics and how goal success is evaluated. Each facility has employees' environmental responsibilities formally specified in their job descriptions, such as tracking, reporting, training, permitting, generating public communiqués, and site assessments/investigation/remediation. Employees who work in environmental, health, engineering, marketing, technical, HR, and supply chain are most likely to have specific ES-related performance and/or incentive goals. All operating employees have safety responsibility as part of their personal goals. Sales employees benefit from increased customer demand for green products, which is often associated with ES-related goals that are increasingly required by project specifications. Sherwin-Williams' employees have come to "own" the sustainability aspects of their jobs; they expect that they will create sustainability processes and "green" products; this is now part and parcel of their work. The fact that ES goals now share importance with sales, profit, and production goals reflects the significant success of the ES change management process.

Seitz also identified the OP-16 schedule as a powerful tool. This schedule is part of every Sherwin-Williams business's annual operating plan. The document outlines each team's continuous improvement goals for the coming year, with specified metrics designed to drive improvement in the company's sustainability profile; this list is maintained and regularly reviewed. While nearly all continuous improvement projects have some sustainability component, those projects that are most related to sustainability are called out. The OP-16 schedule is part of a rigorous annual review by the senior management team (up to and including the CEO) with each of the operating teams. Results are tracked monthly and reported quarterly in the senior management book that is reviewed at the CEO's staff meeting with all of the division presidents and controllers.

Employee Recognition

HR also facilitates the celebration of ES-related successes to motivate and energize employees. They offer company-wide recognition through corporate awards, as well as department- and division-level recognition that tends to be more informal, more personal, and therefore often powerful. One of Sherwin-Williams' four standard corporate awards (cost reduction, technical achievement, quality, and corporate marketing) was awarded in 2007 to the cross-functional team that developed the energy efficiency lighting retrofit project, which was implemented throughout all plants and distribution centers. This recognition was awarded to highlight the synergistic juxtaposition of cost reduction with ES goal attainment. Further, because the new lighting mimics natural sunlight, it allowed employees to see their work more clearly, which enhanced the environment as well as improved safety. Similarly, a division award for environmental sustainability impact was extended to employees who developed a roof coating (sold in Sherwin-Williams Brazil) that reflects sunlight and lowers the overall cooling costs on commercial buildings.

Recruiting and Organizational Commitment

The perspective of the Sherwin-Williams management team is that workers get attracted to the organization for rational reasons, but they stay because of their affective commitment. Thus, from an organizational culture point of view, the focus is on creating an environment that nurtures success by facilitating employee performance.

EcoVision has engaged employees on the level of their emotions, and managers report that the notion of ES resonates with their workforce. EcoVision and the company's green product line are featured on the company website and in employee recruiting because they attract talented employees. The company hires a large number of young employees every year, who are generally well educated and aware of the range and scope of current environmental challenges. For example, from 2007 to 2010 Sherwin-Williams continued to hire about seven hundred college graduates annually, despite the difficult recession in the building products segments; in 2011 over 950 graduates were hired. These new hires are skilled with the latest technology and motivated to apply it in innovative ways to address environmental challenges.

On the whole, employees in this values-based organization view the need to reverse the environmental damage that manufacturing organizations have caused to date as an essential element of their role and responsibility in the social milieu. They demand clean air, water, and natural landscapes fifty years from now, and EcoVision has been an effective means to harness their passion for environmental sustainability at work. Thus, EcoVision is an employee value proposition; the employees hold the organization to a high standard, and the organization is willing to commit and follow through with serious actions, as the organizational gains far exceed the monetary costs.

The Metrics: Measuring the Impact of EcoVision

From the initial "kick-off challenge," measuring the impact of employee ES actions has been a priority for Sherwin-Williams. Seitz noted, "We are strong believers in the saying, 'What gets measured gets improved.'" The five major categories of measurements include production, energy, natural resources, waste, and recycling; within each of these broad categories are subcategories, such as electrical use, water use, and diesel consumption. There are about 106 sustainability metrics tracked on the EcoMet database at all operations around the world.

The first six months of contests resulted in energy consumption reductions of 1.2 million kilowatt hours and a 25 percent increase in recycling, which translated into a $90,000 energy savings and a 1,088-ton reduction in carbon emissions (Sherwin-Williams, 2010). Subsequent measures have included annual decreases in electricity and natural gas consumption, solid and liquid waste generation by manufacturing, distribution, retail, and administration sectors, increase in solid and liquid waste recycling by sector, and diesel fuel consumption by the distribution sector. These figures are translated into savings per year in terms of dollars, energy, methane, nitrogen oxide, and carbon dioxide and communicated to employees and shareholders. The numbers are impressive, and these metrics provide clear feedback to employees on the magnitude of tangible impact created by their participation in EcoVision. This feedback is a key component of a self-generating cycle of goal setting and continuous improvement for fostering environmental sustainability in the workplace. ES metrics are routinely published and updated on the Sherwin-Williams website and are also found in company sustainability reports and annual reports.

The Bottom Line: Leaders Who Choose to Lead

Organizational operations at Sherwin-Williams reflect the conviction that to act responsibly is not only the right thing to do, but that it can be the basis of a more effective organization. As a values-based organization, Sherwin-Williams seeks a balance between being an effective, sustainable business enterprise and being a responsible corporate citizen. As noted earlier, the strength of the company's ES initiatives is grounded in their business-focused, win-win principles of attending to people, profit, and planet in a manner that addresses the needs of all stakeholders.

Membership in the elite group of EPA Climate Leaders reflects their position as an organizational leader in environmental sustainability.

Sherwin-Williams is proud to be ahead of the mark and setting standards for others to follow, and as a result has no concerns about potential future changes in the regulatory market. Their current ES goal is zero waste, which requires reduction, reuse, and recycling to the extent that no waste ends up in landfills. This requires an ambitious commitment to ES that is both espoused and enacted throughout the entire workforce, from the CEO to the factory floor. Christopher Connor, CEO of Sherwin-Williams, relies on his workforce to achieve the company's ambitious ES goals: "As a corporate citizen, we call on the vibrancy of our people to truly change the face of our world for the better. And they deliver, time and again" (Sherwin-Williams, 2010, p. 2).

This review has also highlighted the leadership of Tom Hopkins, senior VP of HR, and Tom Seitz, senior VP of strategic excellence initiatives, who together with the ES Task Force they created, set in motion a cascading series of events that culminated in EcoVision. The success of these combined efforts rests with the bottom line: executives recognized how ES could positively impact the organization's success and subsequently weaved ES into the very fabric of the organization's mission and culture to empower employees at all levels to take leadership in effecting change. Even though employee ES efforts were present before the first environmental sustainability contest and forum, their impact was limited because they were scattered throughout different parts of the organization and not systematized in a manner that connected them to the core business. The current efforts that support EcoVision have inspired employees across the organization and culminated in organizational results that are clearly measured and communicated to employees and external stakeholders. The coherent program of EcoVision and its support systems is successful because it has given employees knowledge, engaged them at the level of their emotions and actions, rewarded their progress, and celebrated their positive impact on the environment and the business.

References

Apotheker, L. (2010, January 29). Davos: Sustainability is the new mantra. *Bloomberg Businessweek.* www.businessweek.com/globalbiz/content/jan2010/gb20100129_909498.htm.

Dunlap, R. E. (2008, May 29). Partisan gap on global warming grows. www.gallup.com/poll/107593/partisan-gap-global-warming-grows.aspx.

Gibbs & Soell. (2011). Sense & sustainability study: Perspectives on corporate sustainability among consumers and Fortune 1000 executives. www.gibbs-soell.com/home/pulse-check/2011-gibbs-soell-sense-sustainability-study/

Gladwell, M. (2000). *The tipping point: How little things can make a big difference.* New York: Little Brown.

Kearney, A. T. (2009, February). Companies with a commitment to sustainability tend to outperform their peers during the financial crisis. www.atkearney.com/index.php/News-media/companies-with-a-commitment-to-sustainability-tend-to-outperform-their-peers-during-the-financial-crisis.html.

Kell, G., & Lacy, P. (2010, June 25). Study: Sustainability a priority for CEOs. *Bloomberg Businessweek.* www.businessweek.com/managing/content/jun2010/ca20100624_678038.htm.

Laszlo, C., & Zhexembayeva, N. (2011). *Embedded sustainability: The next big competitive advantage.* Sheffield, UK: Greenleaf Publishing.

Maron, D. F., & Rahim, S. (2010, November 3). House goes republican; enviros brace for climate change. *New York Times.* www.nytimes.com/cwire/2010/11/03/03climatewire-house-goes-republican-enviros-brace-for-clim-93751.html.

Porter, M. E., & Kramer, M. R. (2011). The big idea: Creating shared value. *Harvard Business Review, 89*(1/2), 62–77.

Sherwin-Williams. (2010). Caring in full color. www.sherwin-williams.com/pdf/about/csr/CorporateSustainability_English.pdf.

CHAPTER THIRTEEN

HR and Sustainability at Daimler AG

Jürgen Deller,
Theresa Schnieders,
and Angela Titzrath

The Company

Daimler AG is a leading global automotive company and a pioneer in safe and emission-free mobility. Its roots go back to 1886 when Gottlieb Daimler and Carl Benz independently invented the automobile. Daimler-Benz (now Daimler) AG was founded in 1926, and the activities of the company have since been marked by many innovations. As a world leader in the field of active and passive safety, the company developed the innovative concept of a "passenger safety cell" with impact crumple zones as early as 1951. Equally innovative, Daimler developed the anti-lock braking system, airbag, and electronic stability control for passenger cars. In addition to these safety innovations, for many years Daimler has been highly active in the field of emission-free mobility. The company invented the first hydrogen-powered test vehicles as early as 1975. The first hybrid bus (with combined diesel/battery drive) followed in 1979. For many years, Daimler has also been engaged in the development of battery-electric vehicles. The company developed the first electric-powered passenger car test vehicle in 1982. Today, Daimler provides four different types of electric vehicles (from city car to van) with batteries and fuel-cells.

At present, Daimler AG's business units, Mercedes-Benz Cars, Mercedes-Benz Vans, Daimler Trucks, Daimler Buses, and Daimler Financial Services, offer an industry-unique product range of quality cars, trucks, vans, and buses, as well as a full range of automotive financial services, including financing, leasing, insurance, and fleet management. The company sells its vehicles and services in nearly every country in the world and has production facilities on five continents, with a total workforce of 260,100 employees, including 164,000 in Germany. In this case study, we outline the organizational structures that support environmental sustainability at this large multi-national corporation. We then provide a working definition of environmental sustainability in the human resource management context, before focusing on selected HR initiatives and international management development that support environmental sustainability at Daimler AG.

Sustainability at Daimler AG

Sustainability has a long tradition at Daimler, but the origin of the concept lies in the area of research and development. Much of Daimler's sustainability activities were initially focused on optimization of vehicle technology; only later was the concept of sustainability broadened to also include aspects beyond the ecological dimension. The ideas that originated with regard to reducing the environmental impact of Daimler's products were later advanced to inform the entire group's concept of sustainability. This development is interesting in that it is in contrast to current industry trends. Environmental sustainability has always been the first and primary focus of sustainability at Daimler, and it did not develop out of a program of corporate *social* responsibility. Today, Daimler's sustainability approach is multi-faceted and the group's activities have been closely interlinked with general developments in society, culminating in the creation of a group-wide sustainability effort in the year 2000. Daimler's conceptualization of sustainability today reflects the triple bottom line concept: ecology, economy, and social issues.

Stakeholder Inclusiveness

Daimler's current sustainability program spans the years 2010 to 2020 and covers five fields of action: sustainability management, product responsibility, industrial environmental protection, employees, and the social environment. As part of this effort, Daimler has been publishing an annual sustainability report since 2008, which details the company's progress in each field. The most recent report (Daimler AG, 2011), provides an interesting analysis that yields insights into the focus of this sustainability program and the relative importance of environmental issues.[1] In order to evaluate internal and external expectations concerning the company's efforts and to appropriately prioritize among them, Daimler conducted a multi-stage "materiality analysis." One goal of the analysis is to achieve stakeholder inclusiveness in defining the company's sustainability goals. This process involves both employees and customers, as well as representatives of governments, environmental-, and human rights organizations (Weber, 2011). Based on overall corporate strategy and starting with a broad list of possible initiatives, the materiality analysis used surveys, benchmarking, and communication with stakeholder groups to narrow down and prioritize goals and activities for the company's sustainability strategy. "The aim of this dialogue is to find out what expectations people have of [the company] as a globally operating automaker, and what [the company has] to strive to achieve in order to have sustained success. . . . Because these various perspectives do not always match, [Daimler] conduct[s] a multi-stage materiality analysis in order to determine the intersection between them and prioritize results" (Daimler, 2011, p. 10).

Figure 13.1 presents results for the most recent effort. Several observations can be made that are of relevance to the topic at

---

[1] It is interesting to note that a focus on environmental sustainability also reflects current stakeholder preference, as determined by a survey of readers who studied Daimler's 2010 sustainability report. In responding to the question of what topic Daimler should report on more in the future, respondents ($N = 116$) attributed a higher priority to "environmental protection in the product life cycle" (48.3 percent) than to either "social commitment" (44.8 percent) or "responsible corporate governance" (35.3 percent) (see Daimler, 2011, p. 9).

Figure 13.1. Materiality Matrix

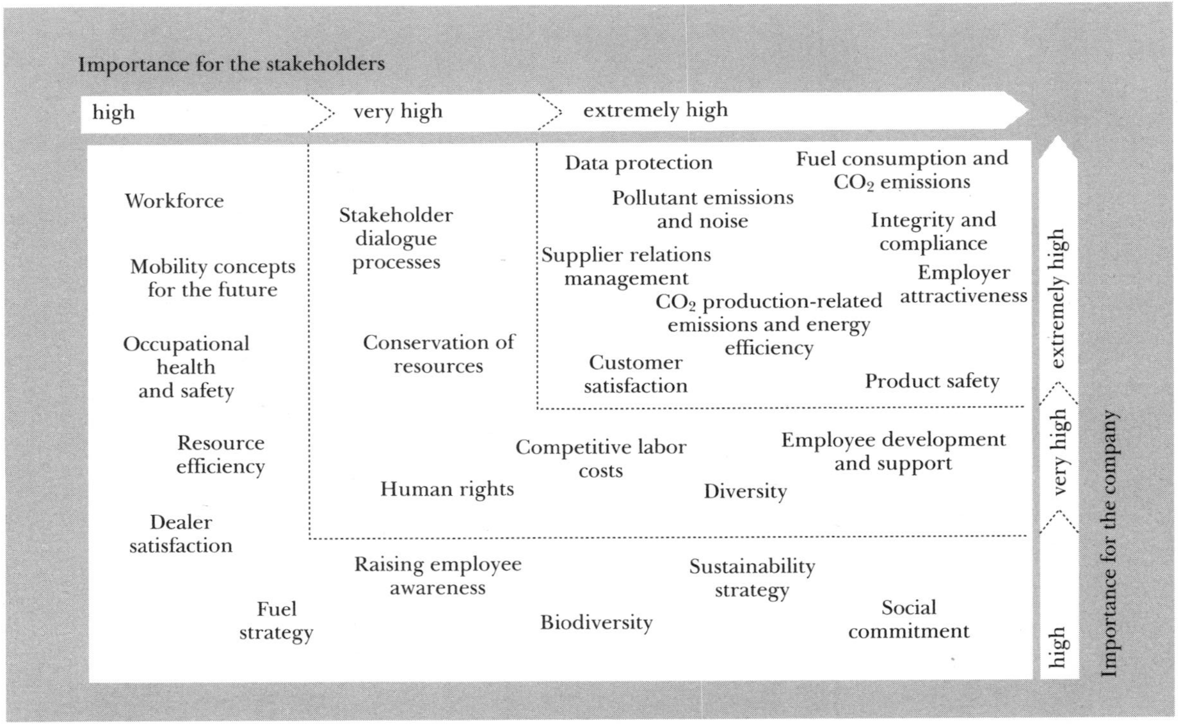

Source: Daimler AG, 2011.

301

hand: First, both the company's and stakeholders' priorities overlap, mostly in product-based areas of emissions and safety, which are reflective of Daimler's initial sustainability focus. However, the company also places a high emphasis on workforce issues, which are lower on the list of some stakeholder groups. As part of this case, we briefly outline several such initiatives currently underway at Daimler. In the years that follow implementation of these relatively new initiatives (such as training and employee awareness programs), it will be interesting to observe whether the overlap of external stakeholder and company priorities will shift in this direction.

Leadership Structures and Human Resource Management for Sustainability

Progress toward sustainability goals at Daimler is managed by the Sustainability Board, which was established by a board of management resolution in 2008. The Sustainability Board groups together the company's existing management functions to coordinate sustainability initiatives throughout the group and provide implementation support for the operative units. The board supplements the already existing management structures within the group, for example, in corporate environmental protection, in the business practices office within the legal and compliance department, or the global diversity office within the human resources function. It consists of representatives from personnel and labor policies, group purchasing, public affairs, communications, e-drive and future mobility, and environmental protection, as well as group research and Mercedes-Benz car development.

Under the direction of Daimler board of management member Dr. Thomas Weber, the committee meets four times annually and coordinates significant company-wide sustainability initiatives. As committee chairman, Weber set the goal for Daimler to be among the most sustainable auto manufacturers worldwide. To this end, the board assesses and analyzes the company's sustainability performance and prepares decision-making documents for the board of management and company CEO Dr. Dieter Zetsche. Other areas of responsibility are oversight of activities targeted at climate protection (CO_2 reduction), sustainability in procurement, staff responsibilities, compliance, stakeholder dialogue, and community relations. The Sustainability Board also coordinates the annual sustainability dialogue, a group-wide forum to discuss sustainability issues with internal and external experts (see below).

The Sustainability Board is supported by the sustainability office, which meets eight times a year. It coordinates corporate departments and established bodies involved in sustainability activities, such as the group compliance board, corporate environmental protection, and the HR sustainability committee, as well as the donations and sponsorship committee. In doing so, it integrated the sustainability relevant functions throughout the group and across divisions.

Because of Daimler's strong history and focus on environmental sustainability with regard to product technology, sustainability-related concepts were first introduced in core functions of the organization (research and development). Human resource management has lagged behind this development for a long time and needs to answer a host of questions, such as: What is the function's contribution to the organization's sustainability concept? What do sustainable recruiting, selection, training, or performance management mean?

First, human resource management provides the company with a competitive workforce to develop and manufacture environmentally sensitive products. But the contribution of human resource management goes beyond that, since it not only bears the responsibility to recruit individuals with appropriate skills but also to support their personal and individual development. Daimler's global human resources strategy is based on five pillars: "profitability, a competitive workforce, future-oriented managerial expertise, a high level of attractiveness as an employer, and a professional organization that focuses on principles of sustainability" (Daimler, 2011, p. 34). For human resource management, supporting sustainability efforts means having the right people (matching potential and placement needs) in the right place (cross-functional and business unit experiences on a global level) at the right time (supporting individual development).

As a result, the concept of sustainability has been sharpened considerably within the HR context in recent years. Although there is still no final definition, the following understanding has been developed: "Sustainability means for HR to ensure the future of Daimler AG with a competitive workforce. HR is charged to support flexible solutions aligned with current and future organizational needs. Therefore, we use goal-oriented methods, processes, and tools to make a contribution to corporate social responsibility towards our employees and society."

People-focused sustainability activities are coordinated by the Human Resources Sustainability Committee, which brings together the relevant HR functions at Daimler. The goal is *holistic* implementation, controlling, and reporting of relevant metrics that relate the group's activities to sustainability. The committee is headed by the head of human resources and labor policy, who is also a member of the Corporate Sustainability Board.

Examples of People-Focused Sustainability Efforts

Sustainability dialogue. Daimler's annual sustainability dialogue is a central component of the group's sustainability effort because it plays an important role in determining sustainability strategy and goals. It is the umbrella event for the group's institutionalized sustainability efforts. The forum brings together representatives from politics, societal associations, and community groups, scientific bodies, and non-profit organizations with Daimler AG executives. Its goal is to facilitate communication with interest groups of critical importance to sustainability efforts in order to generate joint solutions with practical application. The sustainability dialogue contributes to the materiality analysis for the group's sustainability strategy (see above), which outlines and prioritizes sustainability goals.

The sustainability dialogue currently takes place annually in Germany, and plans for its future include establishing similar forums internationally. First efforts in this direction began when Daimler staged the "Daimler Sustainability Forum" at the UN Pavilion at the 2010 World Expo in Shanghai. As stakeholder inclusiveness with regard to the group's sustainability efforts is broadened internationally in the future, it will be crucial to observe whether sustainability goals established by this dialogue will change as well. One challenge for Daimler will be to maintain a unified sustainability strategy that nonetheless allows for local idiosyncrasies and goals based on regional sustainability needs.

Green recruiting. The supply of sustainability-minded talent is critical to Daimler if the group wants to maintain and further strengthen its history of eco-friendly product development. Supplying such talent starts with recruiting. Daimler has recognized that two strategic future-oriented issues are of great import for increasing employer attractiveness: environmental sustainability and presence in emerging markets. Hence, both have been declared priorities for HR marketing, in order to strengthen the group's position globally. The ten-year sustainability plan (2010 to 2020) provides a target year of 2012 for implementation of these efforts (see Daimler, 2011, p. 14). Employer branding and recruiting are examples of people-focused sustainability initiatives that are entirely HR driven.

Environmental education. Talent supply via external recruiting is only one way in which HR supports realization of corporate sustainability goals. Another way is through development of internal talent through training activities that increase sustainability-related knowledge and skills. At Daimler, these programs are targeted at employees and managers. The focus is two-fold; environmental education focuses on environmental responsibility in general and on practical application of environmental protection at the company in particular. In addition to training managers and employees, Daimler trains auditors who monitor environmental sustainability management systems of facilities as well as auditors of suppliers (see below). Internal sustainability awareness training initiatives have a current implementation target date of 2012 (Daimler, 2011).

Supplier sustainability training. Another example of a people-focused initiative is the sustainability pilot training program Daimler offered in Turkey in May 2010. This pilot program is noteworthy in that it had an external focus and was targeted at training suppliers to the company and because it was conducted in cooperation with other auto manufacturers (Ford, General Motors, Renault, and Toyota). The cooperative nature of the program was not only efficient but reinforced for external stakeholders the importance that automakers attribute to the issue of sustainability. The training addressed issues of working conditions and environmental standards, as well as the demands they place on management systems. In 2010, about 140 suppliers participated, and anecdotal reports are evidence of high interest and uniformly positive reactions to this initiative. As a result, Daimler again cooperated with other automakers to implement a similar program in Brazil. Plans for 2012 and beyond include running similar training programs specifically designed for suppliers in high-risk countries. The company sees these programs as a way to ensure sustainability vertically, especially where the supply chain includes smaller companies that otherwise might not have the resources or incentives to conduct such training efforts themselves.

Leadership evaluation and development. Management development at Daimler AG is based on a uniform and internationally consistent system. Through the "Leadership Evaluation and Development" (LEAD) process, all managers are subject to regular performance management and career development. This process ensures comprehensive leadership evaluation and development as part of human resource management. LEAD results provide a holistic picture of current performance and potential of management at the Daimler group.

With adoption of the ten-year sustainability strategy, sustainability was incorporated into the Daimler target system (Weber, 2011), and individual managers are held accountable for progress toward sustainability goals. LEAD enables Daimler to track awareness and implementation of these goals, as well as required management skills and their development on an individual level. In addition, LEAD tracks managers' understanding of trends and innovation capacity with regard to products and processes, communication skills, as well as aspects of global corporate responsibility to develop managers as responsible parts of global society. Sustainability has developed to be a decisive competitive advantage for Daimler and is thus integrated in executive management development.

LEAD offers a good example of an HR process that is comparable across global divisions and not compromised by national or regional peculiarities. LEAD is effective in supporting Daimler's strategic goals (including sustainability goals), because it is used consistently internationally. In this way, a distinct "Daimler way" is defined and nurtured.

Challenges for the Future

The need to ensure environmental sustainability will only increase in the future, both across industries, for automakers in general, and for Daimler AG in particular. The company has strategically defined the topic of energy and propulsion technologies as major issues. In addition to the technological aspect, the company has identified issues such as human rights, diversity and the aging workforce, health management, and employee retention as main challenges for the future. In human resource management, an evolution of the concept of sustainability is underway and needs to move beyond the simple supply of competent personnel to meet the company's obligations in this regard.

Given Daimler's world-wide presence, one current goal is to increase its sustainability efforts internationally. In the future, vocational training, for instance, will be more standardized internationally and the annual sustainability dialogue will be widened in international reach. Furthermore, development initiatives will be broadened. The LEAD program will be applied to experts and administrators, ensuring a full understanding of a wider range of employees' performance and potential, including sustainability-related skills. The international implementation is viewed as a core challenge for the HR function. It is Daimler's express goal not to create regionally specific systems of staff development. However, to what extent a uniform approach is feasible and to which degree regional factors have an impact on sustainability concepts and implementation remains to be seen.

Another challenge for Daimler AG will be the further development and definition of the sustainability concept itself, as a broadly accepted definition is required to increase awareness among the workforce. The aim is to achieve a clear understanding of the concept and to promote acceptance and implementation across the group. This requires recognizing that sustainability cannot be achieved in each area or division independently. To sharpen the understanding of a shared conceptualization is a key future challenge for Daimler AG.

Daimler AG is a good example for the development of sustainability in a company driven by technology. Sustainability-related concepts have first been introduced in core functions of the organization. While HR (particularly in Germany, where Daimler is headquartered) does have substantial experience in terms of corporate social responsibility, its role in supporting corporate environmental goals is still being defined. However, Daimler is unique in that the company started its pursuit of the triple bottom line with environmental sustainability. The biggest task ahead, which is reflected in the multipronged approach of the current ten-year sustainability strategy, is to branch out environmental initiatives and permeate all functions of the group.

References

Daimler AG. (2011). Daimler—360 facts on sustainability. www.daimler.com/Projects/c2c/channel/documents/2003966 _Daimler_Sustainability_Report_2011.pdf.

Weber, T. (2011). Interview: Sustainability as part of Daimler's target system. www.daimler.com/dccom/0-5-1380308-1-1399327-1-0-0-0-0 -0-16696-0-0-0-0-0-0-0-0.html.

CHAPTER FOURTEEN

HR Initiatives for Environmental Mission Alignment at Aveda Corporation

Holly Johnson
and Kristin Miller

The Company

Aveda was founded in 1978 as a manufacturer of flower- and plant-based beauty products, with the goal of providing industry professionals with high performance products that would be better for the planet. The organization is deeply rooted in its mission and has a long history of environmental leadership and responsibility. In 1989, Aveda was the first company to endorse and sign the CERES Principles, a code of conduct that encourages higher standards of corporate environmental performance and disclosure (see Coalition for Environmentally Responsible Economies, 2010). The principles mandate annual, public reporting on environmental management structures and results. Aveda's most recent Earth and Community Care Report (Aveda, 2010) builds on this twenty-year history of environmental and social reporting and provides much detail on the company's sustainability initiatives.

Aveda's commitment to environmental sustainability is founded in a culture of product-based innovation and people-focused initiatives that reinforce responsibility throughout its operations and also include vendors and the company's customers. As one of the world's foremost manufacturers of premium hair color, hair care, skin care, aroma, makeup, and lifestyle products made with pure plant and flower essences, the company also has a wide reach through its network of affiliated salons and educational institutes and academies. In 1989, Aveda opened the first free-standing Environmental Lifestyle store in New York City. In 1992, Aveda initiated the first Earth Day events with its salon network to broaden the reach of its sustainability efforts beyond its products. The event was the precursor to the company's highly successful Earth Month Campaign, which began in 1999 when $300,000 was raised. In 2011, the campaign raised $4.2 million; total funds raised by the Earth Month Campaign have exceeded $22 million.

At the same time, Aveda continues to lead in terms of environmentally sustainable sourcing and production. To maintain a supply of high-quality and sustainable naturally derived ingredients, Aveda has maintained partnerships with several indigenous peoples beginning in the early 1990s (for example, the Yawanawa in the Brazilian rainforest, a cooperative of women and families in the Maranhao region in Brazil, and Mardu Peoples of Kuktabubba, Australia). In 1996, Aveda launched the first 100 percent organic beauty product (Aveda All-Sensitive Body Oil) and in 1997 the first air-propelled hair spray. The company also pioneered the first 100 percent post-consumer recycled PET product package (in 2002) and the first refillable lipstick case (in 2004). Aveda was the first beauty company to manufacture its products with 100 percent renewable wind energy at its primary manufacturing facility in Blaine, Minnesota, in 2006; and beginning in 2008, its wind energy purchases offset 100 percent of the energy used by the primary manufacturing facility in Minnesota, the company headquarters, and the Aveda Institute Minneapolis. Aveda purchases wind energy credits through Native Energy to offset the energy used in the company-operated Experience Centers and Aveda-owned salons and institutes in New York City.[1]

---

[1]Aveda pays wind energy rates to support green e-certified wind power going into the utility grid from which it purchases electrical power; the company offsets use of natural gas power with wind energy credits.

Among many external recognitions, Aveda received the Corporate Wildlife Stewardship Award from the U.S. Fish and Wildlife Service in 2002, and was the first beauty company to achieve a Cradle to Cradle^{SM} charter (see MBDC, 2007) in 2009.

Aveda has been part of the Estée Lauder Companies, Inc., since its acquisition in 1997. The company employs about 2,700 people globally (approximately two thousand in the U.S.). Its products are currently sold in twenty-four countries.

Importance of the Organizational Mission

Aveda's corporate culture is best described as highly collaborative and relationship-driven. Like much of its customer base, Aveda's workforce can be characterized by a high sense of loyalty to the brand and company. Much of this phenomenon is tied to the corporate mission, which was inspired by Aveda's founder, Horst Rechelbacher, and formalized by Aveda employees in 1995 and permeates all aspects of an individual's experience as an Aveda employee:

> "Our mission at Aveda is to care for the world we live in, from the products we make to the ways in which we give back to society. At Aveda, we strive to set an example for environmental leadership and responsibility, not just in the world of beauty, but around the world."

This mission, with its emphasis on environmental leadership, is integral to the business success of Aveda Corporation. Survey data from a 2006 brand equity study show that 91 percent of professionals and 40 percent of its consumers are aware of the company's mission, and 70 percent and 50 percent, respectively, regard it as very personally meaningful to themselves (Conseil, 2011). The mission thus informs all aspects of the company's business model, including decisions regarding vendors with whom it does business, the ingredients used in its products, partnerships with local and indigenous communities, as well as progressive HR initiatives that aim to achieve mission alignment among the company's workforce. This case study provides an overview of those HR initiatives and their role in achieving mission alignment at Aveda.

Incorporating the Mission into Human Resource Management

It is evident that at Aveda Corporation social and environmental leadership are integrated with business strategy. The company's mission, however, is not expressed only in its product offerings or operations. Rather, leadership views environmental and social responsibility as driven by employee capabilities, values, and volunteerism (Conseil, 2011). The company has realized that employee-driven environmental responsibility depends both on employees' environmental knowledge and skills, as well as on personality, attitudes, and values. Aveda thus relies on a comprehensive HR program that addresses both stable and trainable employee capabilities through recruitment, selection, training, and performance management. In this way, the human resource function plays a central role in fulfilling the company mission.

Recruitment and Selection

As in any business organization, the first task of the human resource function is to recruit and select job candidates who possess the necessary knowledge, skills, and abilities to fulfill their *core job responsibilities.* However, because of the centrality of the company's mission, recruitment and selection at Aveda has a dual purpose: attract and identify job candidates who will be good at their jobs and at the same time will incorporate the environmental mission into their daily responsibilities and decision making. Both aspects are important, as Aveda leadership views highly qualified and mission-aligned employees as vital to the future success of the organization. Currently, the mission-focused components of the hiring process at Aveda rely on semi-structured interviews that include questions that may help determine a candidate's ability to be mission aligned in the workplace.

Employee Orientation

The recruitment and selection process at Aveda is aimed at identifying candidates who are open and receptive to the company's mission and who possess the requisite knowledge, skills, abilities, and other characteristics required to perform core tasks of their jobs as well as to fulfill Aveda's mission of environmental responsibility. Such recruitment and selection of environmentally responsible individuals is the first step in ensuring a mission-aligned workforce. Living the Aveda mission in all aspects of the job, however, also requires in-depth knowledge of the organization, its environmental policies and procedures, as well as other sustainability-related knowledge and skills that new hires need to acquire once on the job. For this purpose, Aveda's regular employee orientation programs also include an extensive component targeted at communicating the company's culture of sustainability and environmental responsibility, as well as relevant policies and procedures.

For new hires in corporate (non-retail) functions, Aveda conducts bi-weekly orientation sessions that include videos, policy reviews, and in-person presentations and education conducted by the company's Earth and Community Care Team. In addition to information that is part of most employee orientation programs (new hire paperwork, information on benefits, health, and safety, etc.), new employees at Aveda receive copies of the company's Green Ingredient Policy and Sustainability Policy, which are carefully reviewed as part of the session. Like most meetings at Aveda, this orientation starts with reciting the company's mission. Employees are expected to engage in business practices that are aligned with the mission and abide by the Green Ingredient and Sustainability Policies at all times.

The Earth and Community Care Team then educates employees on Aveda stakeholders and their interconnectedness in pursuing environmental sustainability—team members, guests, suppliers, indigenous and traditional communities, local communities, partner organizations and institutes, and global partners. The orientation also includes a review of plant-based ingredients, product packaging, and how each supports environmental sustainability. It concludes with education on basic principles of waste reduction, reuse, and recycling.

Retail employees receive a similar orientation upon hire. This program is comprehensive (spanning more than two work days) and provides in-store employees with knowledge regarding the company's business practices, so every in-store employee can educate Aveda's guests and customers on the company's mission, environmental performance, and benefits of its products.

Training

Aveda long recognized that knowledge on relevant processes and procedures is a necessary precondition for behaving in an environmentally responsible way at work. The orientation programs described above are comprehensive. However, these initiatives are truly *orientation* programs for new hires. Even though they convey all necessary knowledge of policies and procedures (as well as basic principles of environmental responsibility that every employee is expected to be aware of), they are not the only interventions targeted at increasing employees' knowledge in this domain. In addition to the company's environmental policies, Aveda employees are also asked to understand broader environmental issues such as water scarcity, climate change, organic ingredients and food, sustainable farming practices, energy conservation, recycling, and other environmental initiatives that relate to doing business at Aveda. Thus, in addition to new hire orientation and regular on-the-job training, Aveda maintains three special initiatives for training its employees on these issues and to reinforce the role of the mission in its business operations. The company also offers a similar, special immersive program for external stakeholders.

Material Use Toolkit. This is a three-hour workshop designed for employees who are directly or indirectly responsible for purchasing, specifying, developing, designing, and/or choosing materials, products, accessories, supplies, or equipment for Aveda. Its purpose is to provide information to ensure that employees' purchase and event planning decisions align with and support the Aveda mission while embracing brand authenticity. The workshop includes a presentation, a small group activity, and distribution of a printed resource guide.

Force of Nature. In addition to the Material Use Toolkit workshop, which is tailored to employees with purchasing or product development roles, Aveda offers a Force of Nature course through its Department of Earth and Community Care, which all employees are eligible to enroll in. The purpose of this course is educational but broader in scope, covering the topics of sustainability, global environmental issues, and Aveda's role in furthering these issues. As part of the Force of Nature course, participants explore what they can do in their daily work and personal lives to be stewards of the Earth. This program is being updated.

Full Circle. Aveda's Full Circle program is an in-depth, high-level training that intensifies employees' knowledge and awareness of the company's history and culture, which results in environmental stewardship. All employees are eligible, but participation is by invitation. The program occurs approximately twice a year and lasts three days. Presenters include organizational leaders, such as President Dominique Conseil, who speak on the company's history and foundation in its mission, botanical ingredients, and naturally inspired products, and the role of Aveda's Earth Month and Community Care initiatives. As part of this training, employees also learn about global sourcing ("soil to bottle") and company strategies for research and development, global communications, and marketing.

The company also provides this training (with slight modifications) to external customers. This three-day course occurs twice a year and is targeted at invited guests, such as distributors and other important stakeholders. High-level speakers address topics similar to those in the employee Full Circle program, but targeted to an external audience. Speakers provide an overview of the brand, its products and spa philosophies, the role of Earth and Community Care, and community sourcing. In addition, guests tour salons and Aveda's Institutes, and have the opportunity to receive signature services and participate in Aveda wellness rituals to learn more about what the company offers.

Performance Management

In addition to recruitment, selection, orientation, and training, Aveda's mission of environmental leadership is reinforced through performance management. First, the mission is integrated into the regular performance appraisal process in order to reward and incentivize outstanding environmental performance systematically. In addition, performance management at Aveda also includes special recognition of employees who display exceptional environmental stewardship through two different awards that recognize contributions to the organization's mission.

Performance appraisals. Aveda employees undergo standardized performance reviews on an annual basis. The company has long used this process to encourage employees to follow sustainable business practices. In the past, supervisors evaluated their employees' contributions on more than a dozen "success factors" that applied across Aveda job families. One of these central performance dimensions assessed each employee's contribution to "living and growing the Aveda mission." A recent harmonization of HR processes across Estee Lauder Companies has resulted in revised performance appraisal instruments. Aveda used this opportunity to intensify and further differentiate the assessment of employees' contribution to the Aveda mission. Specifically, the current performance appraisal process distinguishes between social and environmental responsibility and further defines outstanding mission-aligned performance.

Both exempt and some non-exempt employees are evaluated on three separate aspects of the mission. Supervisors evaluate the degree to which employees meet expectations with regard to "gives back to society," "cares for the world we live in," and "sets an example for environmental leadership and responsibility." The first describes social volunteerism and participation in corporate initiatives (including environmental ones, such as Earth Month, for example). The second aspect describes employees' respect for themselves, others, and the planet and also assesses initiative to improve work processes to further the mission. The final aspect reflects employees' tendency to make business decisions that are aligned with the company's environmental mission and the degree to which they inspire others to live and work in accordance with it.

In this manner, Aveda encourages and rewards mission-aligned performance among all employees on a regular basis. However, the company also incentivizes outstanding and exceptional environmental performance with special awards.

Employee awards. The Global Steward Award was begun in 2003 to recognize employees who lead by example in supporting the company's mission and sustainable practices. Any employee is eligible; nominations are submitted to and reviewed by the company's Earth and Community Care Team. Recipients must demonstrate a commitment to the Aveda mission and meet at least one of the following criteria: take initiative on behalf of the planet, seek innovative environmental solutions, find ways to save money and the planet, create ways to reduce waste, utilize all eight company-sponsored volunteer hours for service in the community, lead team volunteer efforts or participate in Aveda volunteer initiatives, regularly volunteer in the community above and beyond the eight paid volunteer hours, identify risk reduction opportunities, take initiative, and seek innovative solutions to address safety. Winners of the award receive recognition from the company president and vice president of Earth and Community Care and are announced to the entire Aveda Network (including affiliated institutes, salons, and spas). To date, thirty-nine Global Steward awards have been awarded to Aveda employees.

The Aveda Flower Award was begun in 2001 to recognize outstanding employees who are mission oriented and also display high job performance in other key areas (for example, team building, innovation, exceeding aggressive targets). It is not purely an environmental performance award, but incorporates mission alignment as one of its crucial evaluation criteria. The award is highly competitive and aspirational in nature, rewarding employees who "move the human spirit to a higher level." Employees must demonstrate extraordinary behaviors supporting the Aveda mission; to date, forty-six awards have been presented to Aveda employees.

Summary

Aveda Corporation was founded with the goal of providing products that are better for beauty professionals, their guests, and the planet they live on. Because of its deep-rooted tradition of environmental responsibility, Aveda has always understood the decisive role that employees and human resources play in supporting this mission. Aveda has had a head start in recognizing employees as the source of socio-environmental responsibility, and thus has a long tradition of incorporating its company mission into its HR processes. Contrary to some expectations, these efforts have not waned, but rather intensified with acquisition of the company by the Estee Lauder Companies in 1997. As a result, the company has one of the most comprehensive HR programs for environmental mission alignment that spans all aspects of the human resource function.

This short case study outlined only some of Aveda's initiatives in recruitment, selection, orientation, training, and performance management to encourage environmental responsibility among its employees. These efforts lay the foundation for developing, producing, and distributing products that not only contribute to sustaining the planet, but that also further the well-being of the people who make and use them. Aveda continues to invest in its employees to remain a leading source of responsible innovation in the beauty industry.

References

Aveda. (2010). Earth and community care report 2009–2010. www .aveda.com/aboutaveda/ceres/2010/

Coalition for Environmentally Responsible Economies (CERES). (2010). The 21st century corporation: The CERES roadmap for sustainability. www.ceres.org/resources/reports/ceres-roadmap-to -sustainability-2010

Conseil, D. N. (2011). Employee-based socio-environmental responsibility. Keynote address at the Thursday Theme Track of the annual conference of the Society for Industrial and Organizational Psychology, Chicago, Illinois.

MBDC. (2007). Cradle to cradle[SM] certification program: Version 2.1.1. http://epea-hamburg.org/fileadmin/downloads/allgemeines/ Outline_CertificationV2_1_1.pdf.

CHAPTER FIFTEEN

Environmental Sustainability Initiatives in Ugandan Light Industry

Daniel Manitsky
and Patrice Murphy

It is a common misconception that environmental concerns are difficult to address in situations of acute economic pressure—for example, in developing countries. However, recent projects in Uganda illustrate the capacity of organizations to adopt sustainable environmental practices with minimal resources, and to do so in a way that aligns the environmental outcomes with better economic, work safety, and social outcomes. The key to cost-effective environmental action in these situations is finding ways to more fully engage the creativity and imagination of employees at all levels of an organization—from the CEO to front-line staff. OD professionals can facilitate such efforts by paying close attention to how initiatives are structured, ensuring that efforts focus on concrete ambitious results, that they are defined in strategic and linguistic terms familiar within the organization, and that they provide developmental opportunities for both the organization and staff members.

The projects outlined here used the Rapid Results approach, a methodology in which small projects produce breakthrough results within one hundred days and fuel sustainable impact. The projects themselves were scoped to address a larger problem on a local scale. Workers engaged in these Rapid Results Initiatives

(RRIs) developed novel solutions and process innovations, as well as the confidence needed to build off the initial success and tackle other organizational challenges.*

The Rapid Results approach is based on the premise that the fundamental engine of change is human motivation and confidence—the courage to take a first step, to move boldly into collective action with a commitment to achieve a seemingly impossible result. Practitioner experience has shown over and over again that this psychological frame is so powerful it can enable solutions to the most vexing problems. Once leaders discover how to tap into this engine of change, great capacity for achievement is unleashed. Then, and only then, can leaders make full use of the other elements of change such as money, analysis, equipment, training, planning, evaluation and so on (Aiken & Keller, 2009; Armenakis & Harris, 2009; Beer & Nohria, 2000).

Background

The RRIs described here were implemented during 2008 and 2009 by Enterprise Uganda (EUg), a public-private institution helping entrepreneurs start small and medium sized enterprises as well as strengthen existing ones. In 2008, the World Bank Institute (WBI) offered to help EUg expand its services to include environmental sustainability support. This work largely focused on helping local businesses improve environmental and social responsibility impacts by facilitating the exchange of local good practices and on sharing knowledge about appropriate technical inputs. Working together, EUg and WBI conducted a series of workshops that built the Ugandan business community's understanding of the need for greater environmental sustainability and

---

*The lessons and insights expressed in this chapter arise from the collective experience of all our colleagues who work daily with the rapid results approach, both at the Rapid Results Institute and Schaffer Consulting. Any errors or omissions in this account are, of course, the responsibility of the authors. For more detail on the scalability of the rapid results approach on issues as diverse as corporate turnaround and growth, agricultural development and HIV/AIDS prevention, see Chapters 5 and 9 of *Rapid Results! How 100-Day Projects Build the Capacity for Large-Scale Change* by R.H. Schaffer and R.N. Ashkenas. (San Francisco: Jossey-Bass, 2005)

helped individual companies identify ways they could make a difference.

The initial support was highly successful in building interest in environmental action among small and medium enterprises. However, early on, EUg and WBI began to see hesitancy among many companies when it came to moving into action in their workplaces. This was consistent with what WBI staff had observed within previous social and environmental workplace programs. Many programs started well, but struggled when it came time for program participants to translate new knowledge and awareness into results on the ground.

The reasons for this hesitancy were several. First, with narrow profit margins, limited access to capital, and generally low workforce education, many participants thought their organizations would not be able to design and implement the needed process changes. Second, participants anticipated difficulty changing the behaviors and attitudes of individual employees. Previous "social-responsibility" projects, including HIV prevention and gender sensitivity, had stalled in the face of ingrained behaviors and beliefs. Participants quickly saw that improving environmental sustainability would require similar types of change. Finally, many participants also foresaw challenges getting sufficient levels of buy-in from fellow senior managers and CEOs. Given that many improvements in environmental performance rested on obtaining authorization for policy and process changes, getting active support from senior leaders would be essential.

EUg also had its own concerns about how to support "client" companies. It quickly began to see a need for highly specialized (and expensive) technical advisors in areas such as waste management, energy efficiency, and air-quality control. The potential cost of such advisors far outweighed the value of the environmental impact they could produce in relatively small enterprises.

Not wanting to see their current program suffer a fate similar to previous projects, WBI and EUg searched for ways to address participants' concerns while ensuring the overall effort remained cost-effective. Soon they happened upon a way that would allow EUg to play a catalytic role—helping companies overcome their hesitancy while minimizing the costs associated with its support.

The Change Management Approach

EUg and WBI eventually decided to introduce to participating companies the idea of using the Rapid Results approach. The approach appealed to EUg because it focused less on outside experts and more on using facilitative consulting techniques to help companies better leverage the knowledge and creativity that existed within their organizations. This would help EUg minimize the need for expensive technical consultants, thus allowing them a way to provide support in a way that was both cost-effective and sustainable within their existing service-delivery model.

To begin the Rapid Results process, EUg partnered with the Rapid Results Institute. With financial support from WBI and the African Capacity Building Foundation, EUg and the Rapid Results Institute gathered a group of ten companies from those that had participated in previous meetings. Several companies were recruited proactively, due to their high profile or the particularly serious nature of their environmental challenges. Others showed up on their own, in response to an invitation to attend a workshop on using the Rapid Results approach to improve environmental sustainability.

Within ten days, EUg and the Institute launched nine company-specific RRIs, seven of which were environmentally focused. A list of participating enterprises is included in Table 15.1. Over the next one hundred days, five of the environmental RRI teams achieved or exceeded their goals—producing not only significant and sustainable improvements to the environment, but also other important improvements to profitability, worker health, and community relations. In many cases, the RRIs also served as a catalyst for improved teamwork and communication within the companies. In purely economic terms, the increased annual profitability of the five companies easily exceeded the cost of the OD coaching services provided by EUg and the Institute.

In the following sections, we provide a short description of the seven environmental projects and then examine the characteristics of the change management intervention, the factors that drove success or failure, and the implications for human resource professionals who wish to drive rapid, sustainable shifts in environmental practices.

Table 15.1. Summary of Ugandan Enterprises

Company	Industry	Type	Size[a]
Leather Industries of Uganda	Tannery	For-Profit Private Company	Large
Numa Feeds Ltd.	Food/Animal Feed	For-Profit Private Company	Small
Igara Growers Tea Factory	Agribusiness/ Tea	Cooperative	Medium
Kampala Farmers Association	Butchery	Cooperative	Medium
Roofings Ltd.	Light Industry/ Construction Materials	For-Profit Private Company	Large
Cooper Shoe Factory	Shoes/Apparel and Vocational Training	Blended Non-Profit/For-Profit	Medium
Kampala Women's Cooperative	Women's Accessories	Cooperative	Small

Note: The names of some companies have been changed. [a] = Based on number of employees; small: 1 to 20, medium: 20 to 100, large: more than 100.

Seven Environmental Initiatives

The seven environmental projects covered issues as diverse as heavy metal contamination, air quality, fuel consumption, biological waste run-off, and reforestation.

Reducing Heavy Metal Contamination of Wastewater

Less than half a mile from the source of the Nile lies Leather Industries of Uganda, one of Uganda's largest tanneries. The tanning process creates wastewater typically contaminated by high concentrations of the dangerous heavy metal chromium. The obvious environmental issues were felt not only by workers and others nearby, but potentially by the broader eco-system and communities fed by the Nile. In the course of their first one-hundred-day Rapid Results Initiative, a tannery team reduced by 40 percent the amount of chromium in their wastewater using their existing technology. Since then, the team has continued to tweak the system to drive chromium levels down to just 0.001. mg/l, an astonishing 99 percent reduction from pre-RRI levels. This was accomplished with minimal investment and only negligible increase in operating costs.

Controlling Indoor Air Pollution

At a grain milling company called Numa Feeds, the process of pulverizing grain released dust that was a significant source of indoor air pollution—a hazard to worker health. Measuring air quality is difficult without expensive equipment. Consequently, the Rapid Results team came up with an easy-to-measure alternative: reduce the measured weight of grain "lost" during the milling process, since this primarily ends up as air-borne dust. Within one hundred days, this RRI halved the amount of grain lost, with a corresponding improvement in air quality. Since then, the organization has maintained the improvement and continued to track grain loss, both as a proxy for air pollution and as a cost control method. Apart from improved working conditions for its workers, the company achieved annualized savings equal to the salary of two employees.

Reducing Use of Firewood Fuel

At Igara Growers Tea Factory, workers convert raw tea into tea powder using a boiling process. Firewood is the main fuel for the boiler system. The company wanted to reduce the amount of firewood used to generate each kilogram of tea powder. Workers who formed a Rapid Result Initiative team increased Igara's fuel efficiency by 20 percent in one hundred days, lifting the amount of tea produced per cubic meter of firewood from a monthly average of 368 cubic kilograms to 440 cubic kilograms. After the one-hundred-day period of the RRI, the team further improved the system they developed, achieving a yearly average of 530 cubic kilograms—a 44 percent increase in efficiency overall.

Managing Biological Waste Run-Off

Even small slaughterhouses face critical waste-management problems. The Kampala Farmers Association used an RRI to manage biological waste from the slaughtering process, especially cow dung and offal. Like all RRIs, they focused on taking a practical, local view of the problem—in this case, reducing the number of times the company's dung trench overflowed and reducing the amount of dung on the slaughterhouse floor. Through employee training, process changes, and minor infrastructure improvements, the team reached its goal of preventing overflow of the dung trench and significantly reduced the amount of dung present in the environment. One year later, the company continued to use the waste management practices developed during the RRI. Additionally, Kishita shifted from seeing the waste as valueless to a potentially value-added asset. Whereas previously Kishita paid a hauler to cart away the waste, local farmers now remove dung for free to use as organic fertilizer.

Reforestation

Ugandan companies recently launched a nationwide campaign to plant one billion trees. In support of this program, the company Roofings Ltd. had for several years donated seedlings and instructional materials to community groups, non-profits, and schools across Uganda. However, the results from this collaboration were often disappointing: supplies were not used in a timely fashion, follow-up watering and tree care was not coordinated, trees died. Roofings wanted to increase the impact of its donations by finding a way to partner more effectively with recipients. The company agreed to support a Rapid Results team based in a nearby public school. Together, Roofings management and the school's head teacher challenged a team of students to plant and ensure the healthy growth of 125 seedling trees over 120 days. The goal setting and work planning were done by school students, providing the opportunity to study math, biology, and life-planning skills. By the end of the RRI, 125 trees were firmly planted and growing in the soil of the school, providing shade, fruit for much-needed nutrition, and future learning opportunities for students.

Additionally, it provided Roofings with a model for how to partner more successfully with other community groups.

In each of the five successful cases, the Rapid Results Initiative teams achieved a marked improvement in environment sustainability using the technology and human capability that were already available to the organization. However, two of the seven RRIs were not successful and failed to produce significant environmental results or insights into how such results could be produced in the future.

Converting Waste into Sales

Cooper Shoe Factory is a non-profit, largely self-financing technical training school. The organization trains Ugandans in the art of making shoes and other leather goods, which provide a significant source of revenue. To help increase profits while minimizing the environmental impact of its activities, the organization launched an RRI focused on expanding its product range to include goods made from leather scraps and other material wastes generated in the production of shoes. These new products were to include key chains, cell-phone holders, and other small accessories. However, after coming up with an initial one-hundred-day goal and work plan, the team's energy quickly dropped. The team was not able to establish a regular rhythm for its meetings and eventually stopped meeting altogether after struggling to successfully overcome several initial obstacles. Based on these facts, the EUg advised the senior managers to suspend the RRI approximately one month after its launch.

Transforming Plastic into Supplemental Income

The Kampala Women's Cooperative also wanted to expand sales of the belts and purses they make from plastic waste produced by surrounding factories. Co-op members, mostly marginalized women, weave small bands of plastic together into innovative and colorful designs. The co-op brought together its most active weavers for an RRI aimed at increasing their presence in areas frequented by tourists. While the team put significant energy into the work planning and strategy, team members quickly found that implementing the plan required a level of leadership and coordination they simply did not have at that time. After six weeks of struggling, the team decided to suspend their RRI.

Looking at these seven projects, launched together, it is interesting to examine the organization development interventions that enabled the majority of teams to unleash impressive results within a few months and then ,sustain and even extended them afterward. In particular we examine what determined success in these companies, while leading to unsatisfactory results in others.

The Intervention: Driving for Rapid Results in Environmental Initiatives

The Rapid Results approach is a very simple process built upon the basic unit of the Rapid Results Initiative. The RRI is a temporary project structure designed as a mini–organization development effort, with a triple focus on achieving results, generating learning about the organization's change dynamics, and developing the management capacities of its staff. The general approach is modular: RRIs can be launched as single projects or combined to drive large scale change. The life cycle of a typical Rapid Results Initiative is shown in Figure 15.1.

Shape

First is a short period in which change leaders, project sponsors, and organization development coaches work together to define an area for focused effort. This could arise from the organization's strategy, a compelling opportunity, an urgent problem, or some other change driver. Sponsors shape an executable challenge for the RRI team, providing guidance as to where a result is needed and any helpful intuition they may have about the solution space, for example:

> To create a context for the Ugandan environmental RRIs, the coach assigned to each company began by helping the sponsoring senior managers scope the opportunity area they had identified during the first round of WBI-sponsored meetings. These coaches

Figure 15.1. Phases of the Rapid Results Cycle

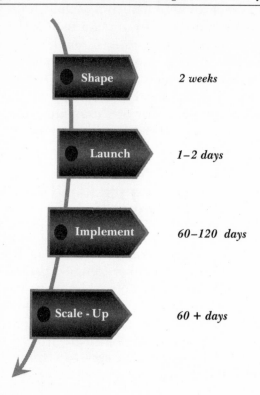

also helped senior managers select a team leader and team members from the organization's front-line staff. Coaches also helped the sponsors articulate the environmental improvement they wanted to see: Less firewood burned, less contamination of wastewater, and so on. The sponsors communicated the challenge in a short assignment letter that commissioned the team to deliver a measurable result in about one hundred days.

Launch

The coach then brings the team together at a formal launch event, usually lasting one or two days. The coach helps the team to carve out a goal that represents a real result in the area of opportunity that can be achieved within 60 to 120 days and shape a work plan for achieving that result. There are two critical distinctions here. One is that the goal represents a measurable, compelling *result*, rather than activities, analyses, or preparations. The other distinction is that the team *sets its own goal* at a level that is challenging enough to stimulate innovation and experimentation. If the team is relaxed and confident that the goal is readily achievable using the current system, then it is not enough of a stretch. The coach encourages the team to push itself into its own discomfort, taking on ownership of the challenge and accountability for delivering the result. For example:

> At the start of the RRI at Igara Tea, the sponsor challenged the team to reduce firewood consumption, then left the room. The team of front-line staff then spent two hours discussing how the work flowed and brainstorming ideas to increase efficiency of the boiler system. The coach encouraged them to aim high. At the end of the day, they reviewed the goal with their sponsor, and ultimately settled on the goal of increasing the amount of tea produced per cubic meter of firewood by 25 percent. This was based on their own instinct about the challenge ahead, using language and metrics with which they were most comfortable.

Implement

After the launch meeting, the team is in the driver's seat during an implementation phase that lasts 60 to 120 days. The coach supports the team, especially the team leader, as they experiment with ideas and struggle to overcome barriers. The coach also helps the team prepare for at least two major review points to report on progress and results to the sponsor. Half-way through the RRI, the team meets for a mid-point review to check for traction against goals and team learning. At project completion, the team has a final review to report and celebrate results, share the team's learning, and present their ideas and recommendations on how to sustain results over time. For example:

> The Igara RRI team held regular review sessions with the sponsor—sometimes at monthly intervals, sometimes on a fortnightly basis. During the review sessions, teams would report on progress against their goal as well as discuss any significant process changes and/or process-related lessons learned. Teams also used these meetings to ask for support in recruiting/co-opting stakeholders from other parts of the organization and for

advice on particularly significant strategic decisions. The team's coach supported the team and senior managers throughout, helping them define challenges, brainstorm solutions, and ensure that senior leaders did not provide too much, or too little, guidance to the team. By the end of the project, the team had transformed their workflow and developed organization-wide momentum for continued work in the selected focus area.

Scale-Up

Once the team's work is done, the sponsor and other change leaders consider the scale-up opportunities, taking into account the team's insights. This can include continuing to work in the same challenge area, turning attention to a related challenge or a new issue, extending the experiment to other locations or customer segments, or "snowballing" the best practice insights to other work groups for adoption or further development and discovery. In addition, RRIs often reveal supporting activities such as training or system improvements that are needed across locations. Organizations and communities, large and small, have built major transformations on RRIs that started as a trickle and scaled up to an enterprise, regional, or national level. For example:

> At day one hundred Igara's Rapid Results team formally reported their innovations and results, sharing both the successful and unsuccessful experiments they implemented during the RRI. Additionally, they discussed how to leverage these lessons learned, as well as the RRI process, to achieve similar reductions in the use of other inputs (water, gasoline, electricity). At the end of the end-term review, the team, with support from senior leaders, decided that there was still more work to do on the firewood front, and they launched another one-hundred-day initiative, this time focused on achieving a further 25 percent increase in the amount of tea produced per cubic meter of firewood.

Key Determinants of Success

As the preceding outline shows, the Rapid Results approach is beguilingly simple: break down a complex challenge into bite-size chunks, commission a front-line team, insist on accountability for a significant stretch result (and not preparations), then get out of their way while they innovate and deliver.

Simple? Yes. Easy? Not necessarily. The power of the approach lies in carefully crafting the conditions for success, a task that typically falls to an OD coach or consultant working with a leader in the organization. The Ugandan environmental RRIs benefited from attention to a small number of critical elements.

Build Buy-In by Linking Environmental Concerns to Existing Strategy

Making progress on environmental issues almost always requires changes to long-held customs, procedures, and ways of thinking. Front-line staff can be reluctant to truly commit their time and creativity to environmental efforts if there is no support for experimentation and innovation from senior managers. Indeed, an inability to obtain adequate buy-in from senior management was the main reason two of the seven environmental RRIs did not achieve significant results. It can be difficult to get senior leaders to commit to the cause of environmental sustainability. This may stem from a lack of connection between environmental sustainability and the health of the business. The OD coach can address this risk by helping leaders see and articulate the challenge for an environmental RRI in terms that closely connect the environmental result with the company's core strategies. Other senior managers may avoid paying attention to environmental concerns because they lie outside their intellectual and professional frame of reference. Trained as accountants, salespersons, or experts in a particular sector of the economy, many are not familiar with concepts and terminology associated with environment work. OD professionals can address this risk by paying close attention to "translating" environmental programs, using vocabulary and concepts that are in common usage within the business.

At Igara Tea, for example, senior managers actively supported the team's environmental work, but only after it was structured in a way that closely linked it to their main concerns: improving efficiency of the company's operations. While the company is socially conscious—it is a certified fair trade provider—managers had not put much attention to environmental issues because concepts such as global warming and carbon footprint did not relate to them as corporate managers. Once these concepts were recast in terms of reducing the consumption of firewood, an expensive raw material, they become focused and very supportive of environmental sustainability efforts. During and after the one-hundred-day RRI, senior managers regularly checked in with the team, providing support and ensuring accountability for results.

Linking environmental concerns to the business's existing strategy and operations can also increase staff motivation for change on an issue that management has not been able to sell successfully. Managers at Numa Feeds had long been concerned by the negative health effect of the mill's poor air quality. They had even equipped staff with personal air filters, which most employees refused to wear. Staff grew accustomed to the conditions. They complained that the masks were uncomfortable. They also did not perceive indoor air pollution to be a real issue, since most would not observe health problems until years later. Surprisingly, this tolerance of air pollution quickly changed when the problem was reframed as a matter of controlling costs by reducing product lost during the manufacturing process. With a more familiar and recognizable focus to their work, employees quickly became motivated, contributing a host of process changes that eventually were key to the RRI's success.

The experiences at Igara and Numa contrast sharply with those at Cooper Shoes. At Cooper, senior managers provided little written or verbal support to the team. In discussions as to whether the company wanted to continue the RRI after a slow start, senior managers admitted that, while the team's goal was a good idea and might fit with the organization's long-term strategy, there were other more pressing matters of concern for the company. Without a close linkage to management's immediate concerns, the team members did not get the institutional or personal support needed for them to feel empowered and motivated to take risks and try creative solutions to obstacles. When the RRI hit its first roadblock, the team's energy quickly flagged.

In retrospect, a more substantive conversation with senior management might have revealed the need to forge a closer connection between environmental sustainability and the company's performance priorities. For example, instead of developing and selling new products (a time-consuming and relatively risky endeavor), the environmental RRI could have focused on increasing the number of shoes produced per yard of raw leather. Such a goal would undoubtedly have decreased the organization's environmental footprint and improved its bottom line, albeit less than the new product goal the team had decided to pursue. Nevertheless, senior management support for a less ambitious goal may have led to greater success.

Build Confidence with Rapid Success

Generating buy-in among senior managers and staff can be especially difficult for organizations that do not already have a long track record of environmental results. Without a history of success, senior managers will have less confidence in the ability of their organization, and possibly themselves, to achieve meaningful impact. Front-line staff may have similar doubts. Without this confidence, an organization may hesitate to invest money or time in the effort. OD professionals can combat this by structuring initiatives to produce visible, confidence-building results early on. Such results provide the psychological motivation and business justification for continued effort and attention (Collins, 2001; Eisenhardt & Brown, 1997; Kotter, 1995; Schaffer & Thomson, 1992).

This was the case with Leather Industries of Uganda. At first, the organization was highly skeptical that it could improve its environmental performance without significant capital investment. As results came in showing declining chromium levels, the team members became much more confident and began to offer more ideas. Senior management, who were at first reluctant to trust such an important matter to less-educated staff, became more open to the team's ideas and allowed staff more leeway in implementing them. This same dynamic was observed in the other organizations involved in the environmental RRIs. The team's experience of success produced a noticeable lift in staff confidence and the trust they enjoyed from senior managers. The trust-building also extends to HR personnel, who may come from outside the department that is the focus of environmental work.

Producing early, concrete results can build trust in the coach's ability to help and create the momentum and confidence needed for long-term success.

When using this technique, OD professionals should keep in mind two key caveats. First, they should keep in mind that a strategy of obtaining short-term, concrete results is more effective when it is not merely a "quick wins" strategy. Quick wins are frequently superficial and temporary. In the context of environmental initiatives, fleeting or superficial results can actually backfire by giving rise to accusations of "greenwashing" and political correctness. Most importantly, focusing on easy results does not build the confidence of an organization to achieve difficult goals. To build true trust and confidence, results must be seen as compelling, a meaningful response to a real challenge.

Second, OD professionals should keep in mind the experience of the Kampala Women's Cooperative. One of the key reasons for the team's unsatisfactory performance was that its goal required leadership and management skills that were significantly beyond their capacity. While the team was initially excited by the goal they themselves had developed, it proved overwhelming for them. This situation led to a quick drop-off in energy and participation just a few weeks into their work plan.

Hence, while short-term stretch goals can help drive breakthroughs in performance in instances such as Leather Industries of Uganda, it is important to ensure that the goal is not so much of a stretch that it overwhelms employees and fails to motivate them. As a rule of thumb, OD professionals should help employees develop goals that are ambitious, but realistic. If it becomes evident that the goal is either too easy or too difficult, the team should be encouraged to adjust it.

Involve Everyone Who Needs to Own the Changes

Special attention also needs to be paid to ensuring that the right staff members are involved from the very beginning during the design of the environmental initiative. All of the RRIs were designed by a cross-section of operational staff directly involved in implementing the changes needed for improved environmental performance. Instead of an environmental task force or outside experts, each RRI goal and work plan was determined internally by those who would need to own the changes and the results. This not only allowed for greater diversity of ideas and innovations, but it also provided a venue for improving cross-department communication and collaboration—the absence of which lay at the root of many of the causes of poor environmental performance.

This was one of the main drivers of success at Kampala Farmers Association. Because the RR team had representatives from all stages of the slaughtering process, it was able to amass a list of small process changes that, in aggregate, produced significant impact. Similarly, at Igara Tea, the cross-functional team implemented many process changes across the operation, including how freshly cut tea leaves were transported to the factory, the storage of firewood, and the maintenance of insulation on pipes throughout the factory.

This contrasts with the unsuccessful RRIs at Cooper Shoes and the Kamapala Women's Cooperative. In both cases, the teams were relatively homogenous. At Cooper the team was made up of lower-level apprentices. The addition of one or two salespeople and/or more experienced craftspersons would have allowed the team to develop more ideas and give younger team members more confidence about engaging in creative thinking. Similarly, at the Women's Cooperative, where the team was made up entirely of weavers, the addition of a salesperson or marketer would have diversified the skill set and enabled the team to generate a wider range of ideas touching multiple facets of the production process.

Lessons and Implications

At first glance, this collection of cases from Uganda may seem to address issues quite different from those facing human resource professionals in large Western corporations. Hopefully, most readers will not be concerned about overflowing cow dung in the offices! However, the experiences highlight a few simple lessons relevant to anyone who is charged with stimulating and supporting shifts in human resource management for environmental sustainability.

An Urgent, Compelling Goal Breaks Through Psychological Barriers

In each case, the team responsible for the one-hundred-day result committed itself to achieving a goal that was, in its eyes, a dramatic step-up in performance. The degree of stretch that each team accepted for itself had to be enough to break the psychological barriers that often hold people back from re-thinking long-held habits. Truly committing themselves to an ambitious goal forced team members to confront the necessity for radical change.

Sustainable Performance Rests on Innovation

Initial breakthrough results were achieved not because people worked harder, but because the teams came up with—and implemented—specific product or process innovations. For example, in Igara Tea Factory, one of many changes made by the RRI team was to adjust how the firewood was cut. By changing the size of the firewood used in the boiler, the team achieved a longer burn time. The results did not occur by simply working harder in the same way as before. The organization may risk exhaustion if it attempts to sustain a higher level of effort indefinitely, without changes in the way work is being done. Guard against incremental goals that temporarily ratchet up worker effort.

Simple Measures Work Best

Simple, visible measures create a shared focus that everyone can rally around. Even complex results can be measured using simple indicators that everyone understands and can become excited about. Each RRI used an indicator that, while not always accurate to a scientific degree (Kampala Farmers Association's goal of not having the dung trench overflow), was nonetheless easy to see and understand for everyone in the company. Similar measures have been used in restaurants (number of bins filled with waste food) and offices (number of bins filled with waste paper). Simple measures also allow people to continue to measure and track progress, well after the formal RRI has ended. This increases the pool of people eager to champion the continued focus and drive further improvements. Hence, those designing environmental initiatives should be careful to balance the desire for scientific accuracy if it sacrifices employee motivation and engagement.

Sometimes managers are concerned at the potential for teams to "game" measures. Although gaming of measures is seen occasionally, we question whether it really matters. RRIs are not typically a basis for bonuses or even for regular compensation. They are not a regular part of the work structure. They are deliberately injected as temporary project structures that enable intensive periods of focused effort—creating the kind of "zest" that underpins breakthrough performance. Any manipulation of measures is likely to be accompanied by other more significant problems—lack of engagement and motivation to risk and to stretch. This is usually quite visible and can be addressed through sponsor engagement with the team. It is an easy matter for a sponsor to push back on the scope of a goal, the metrics chosen, the reliability of data collection, and the import of a reported result. The gaming of measures is, at most, a symptom of an underlying problem such as lack of commitment to the team's own goal or the RRI's learning objective. The critical thing is to encourage teams into a space of experimentation, risk taking, and stretch. Given that employers are almost never paying extra for the RRI, it could be argued that some gaming is tolerable, so long as teams are truly engaged in innovating for breakthrough performance.

Leaders Increase Engagement and Innovation by Delegating "Solution Making"

Senior leaders in each of these organizations challenged their people to make important environmental changes happen, but without specifying exactly *what* needed to change. Instead of determining the solutions themselves or hiring an outside expert do so, they left it up to a diverse but small team of front-line workers (Michaelson & Spiegel, 2010; Zhang & Bartol, 2010). By issuing a specific performance challenge such as "Reduce indoor air pollution significantly over the next one hundred days," they created a demand for solutions and made their employees accountable for supplying them. The performance challenge was paired with the freedom to experiment and try new ideas. This approach is called "delegated solution making." It leads to more creativity and innovation as well as greater pride and ownership of the end result. This ownership survives well beyond the one hundred days, motivating workers to sustain their result and expand on it over time.

Environmental Sustainability Can Be Achieved in Tandem with Other Objectives

The Ugandan RRI experience shows that efforts to reduce an organization's environmental footprint typically yield additional results in two related areas.

First, they frequently help reduce costs and increase profits. Making an explicit link between the environmental objective and other business objectives, such as lower cost, increased efficiency, or revenue growth, can secure immediate legitimacy and longer-term support for the environmental effort.

Additionally, any Rapid Result Initiative, including those targeting environmental outcomes, can be a means of developing staff. In all of the organizations that used RRIs, managers noticed significant upticks in levels of teamwork, creativity and delegated decision making among lower-level workers. By making your environmental sustainability projects exercises in delegated, result-focused project management, you can create opportunities for human resource development.

The Role of the OD Professional

We have touched previously on the role of OD professionals in guiding and implementing these organizational efforts. Here is a summary of the key points of leverage:

- OD professionals can generate initial buy-in and support from senior leaders and front-line staff by framing environmental efforts using language and terms that resonate linguistically and strategically within the organization.
- Once interest has been generated, OD staff can help translate initial interest into effective action by helping senior managers perform effectively as sponsors. This can include

assisting management sponsors in delegation of solution making, by identifying the opportunity or problem area, and then framing the assignment as a challenge for results rather than execution of a list of activities. This can also include helping sponsors be attentive to team dynamics, active in engaging other stakeholders, and open to securing resources for the team.

- To fully leverage the creative energies and existing knowledge of the organization, OD staff should also help senior managers create a temporary project structure that encourages cross-functional engagement and ownership by those who must own solutions in the short and the long term.

- To increase the probability of success on environmental initiatives and to enhance their ability to serve as a tool for organizational and staff development, OD professionals should be ready to provide on-the-ground project support, with appropriately skilled facilitation and coaching. Project teams often lack the skills needed to manage themselves toward an aggressive one-hundred-day goal. Providing support with simple team-management disciplines such as work planning, regular team meetings, and review sessions with project sponsors can be critical. This support, when properly delivered, can improve internal communication as well as the team and project management skills of staff and senior managers alike. These skills will likely pay benefits further down the line in areas beyond environmental performance.

- Finally, after achieving initial, sustainable success, OD professionals should help senior managers amplify the impact of the Rapid Results Initiative by focusing their attention on steps to institutionalize changes, promote cultural shifts, and leverage the confidence and engagement of staff.

Conclusion

Whether they are in a large multi-national corporation or a small locally owned business in a developing country, environmental initiatives can deliver value in many forms. The key to success is structuring such efforts so that they build an organization's capacity to leverage existing technology, knowledge, and creativity. To do this, OD practitioners must first help senior leaders see environmental impact in terms of concrete results that are closely linked to the organization's overall strategy and the day-to-day work experience of staff. Once senior leaders and staff see this connection, they can form temporary project structures that facilitate increased innovation, collaboration, and improved environmental results. The experience of striving—and succeeding—builds capacity, confidence, and trust throughout the organization. Ultimately, the experience of working together to accomplish tangible, compelling results fuels the organization's ability to pursue even more ambitious goals, both environmental and non-environmental.

References

Aiken, C., & Keller, S. (2009). The irrational side of change management. *The McKinsey Quarterly, (2)*, 101–109.

Armenakis, A. A., & Harris, S. G. (2009). Reflections: Our journey in organizational change research and practice. *Journal of Change Management, 9*(2), 127–142.

Beer, M., & Nohria, N. (2000). Resolving the tension between theory E and O of change (pp. 1–33). *Breaking the code of change.* Cambridge, MA: Harvard Business School Press.

Collins, J. (2001). The flywheel and the doom loop (pp. 164–187). In *From good to great: Why some companies make the leap and others don't.* New York: HarperCollins.

Eisenhardt, K. M., & Brown, S. L. (1997). The art of continuous change: Linking complexity theory and time-paced evolution in relentlessly shifting organizations. *Administrative Science Quarterly, 42*, 1–34.

Kotter, J. (1995, March/April). Leading change: Why transformation efforts fail. *Harvard Business Review*, pp. 59–67.

Michaelson, K., & Spiegel, M. (2010, Spring). Stop solving your business problems. *Leader to Leader*, pp. 52–59.

Schaffer, R. H., & Thomson, H. A. (1992, January/February). Succesful change programs begin with results. *Harvard Business Review*, pp. 80–89.

Zhang, X., & Bartol, K. M. (2010). Linking empowering leadership and employee creativity: The influence of psychological empowerment, intrinsic motivation, and creative process engagement. *Academy of Management Journal, 53*(1), 107–128.

CHAPTER SIXTEEN

Human Resource Development Initiatives for Managing Environmental Concerns at McDonald's UK

Julie Haddock-Millar,
Michael Müller-Camen,
and Derek Miles

In this chapter, we describe a research project carried out to improve our understanding of the potential contributions of human resource development (HRD) initiatives to environmental management. An increasing number of organizations have over the last decade committed themselves to reducing their negative impact on the environment. This is not only due to new laws, regulations, or stakeholder pressures (Delmas & Toffel, 2004), but also to an emerging business case for greener environmental management. In other words, it can make good business sense to be "green" (Ambec & Lanoie, 2008). In this context, it is suggested that green HRD now has to play a key role in improving the environmental performance of organizations (Fernandez, Junquera, & Ordiz, 2003). Green HRD can be defined as "a cyclic process of continuous development and transformation of self, others, and the organization, as prudent users of natural and man-made resources, aligning economic, environmental, and social growth, for present and future generations" (Haddock, Jeffrey, Miles, Müller-Camen, Yamin, Critten, & Hartog, 2009).

This McDonald's UK case-based research involved the study of three HRD initiatives, including the introduction of voluntary environmental champions, the development of an environmental educational module with an apprenticeship scheme, and a staff development trip to Costa Rica. Data was collected from multiple sources, including interviews, focus groups, company documents, and reports. The results demonstrate evidence of raised employee awareness around green issues as well as changes in restaurant operational practices positively impacting on environmental reporting statistics and altering of employee behavior.

McDonald's and the Environment

McDonald's opened its first restaurant in the UK in 1974, and now has over 1,200 restaurants serving around 2.5 million people every day and employing more than 85,000 people. Over 60 percent of restaurants in the UK are owned and operated by franchisees. McDonald's environmental vision is to maximise positive environmental impact through key stakeholder groups: suppliers, employees, and customers. In particular, the company aims to enable and support suppliers to use scale to make industry-changing positive moves, have the most environmentally empowered workforce in the UK, and use high street presence to help consumers change their behaviors (McDonald's Environment Department, 2009). This is an enormous undertaking, bearing in mind that all commercial activities cause some form of environmental impact, whether that is supplier, staff, or customer transportation, electricity, gas or water consumption, or waste and litter creation (Curtin, 2007). Moreover, all activities and their short- and long-term impact interweave operational practices and individual and organizational behaviors, presenting strategic and tactical challenges when attempting to bring about change. Some commercial enterprises have seen the benefit of establishing and maintaining their environmental credentials and "have been able to benefit by managing environmental issues sensitively, managing, protecting and maturing their reputation in the green world" (Curtin, 2007, p. 196).

Current Situation

McDonald's scale can impact on local and global communities, by working with hundreds of suppliers, employing thousands of staff, and serving millions of customers. Pressure to develop sustainable business practices comes from a variety of sources, including, among others, the UK government and European Union policies and practices. For example, the UK government published the UK sustainable development strategy, *Securing the Future*, which sets out a vision for sustainable consumption and production and promotes the following:

- Better products and services, which reduce the environmental impacts from the use of energy, resources, or hazardous substances;
- Cleaner, more efficient production processes, which strengthen competitiveness; and
- Shifts in consumption towards goods and services with lower impacts.

In line with the UK's sustainable development strategy, McDonald's UK has identified a number of opportunities to translate impact into positive results for all stakeholders, focusing on HRD initiatives that bring about changes in environmental practices, impacting on climate change, energy, recycling, litter, and responsible sourcing. Tackling negative media coverage and poor public perceptions around working for McDonald's, the last five years and arrival of David Fairhurst, chief people officer, Europe, has signaled an acceleration in people development activity in the UK, leading to awarding body status in January 2008 and achieving a Grade 2 (good) Ofsted rating in 2010, with several areas as Grade 1 (outstanding) for the Apprenticeship Program. The apprenticeship scheme is available to all employees, giving them an opportunity to develop job-specific skills acquired through workplace training and gain a nationally recognized qualification, a City and Guilds Apprenticeship in Hospitality.

A new range of learning pathways has been introduced, providing clear progression steps for all employees. Within each learning pathway is a specific training program, many resulting in nationally recognized qualifications, from adult certificates in math and English to Business Technical and Education Council (BTEC) qualifications and, more recently, a foundation degree in managing business operations for business managers with Manchester Metropolitan University. The aim is to provide employees with the knowledge, skills, and behaviors needed to develop and run a successful business, attracting and retaining a dedicated and motivated workforce. Furthermore, within the last two years the Environmental Department merged with the HR function and is now led by the vice president, people with responsibility for the delivery of HR, training, education, customer services, and environmental strategy at McDonald's.

Although the Environment and HR functions retain their separates titles, the newly combined efforts of two previously disparate functions signal a change in the organization's strategic approach. Indeed, it is the relationship between HRD initiatives and environmental practices that is at the core of this case study.

Research Approach

Our case-based research involved the study of the relationship between HRD initiatives and environmental sustainability within McDonald's UK. We gathered data from multiple sources, including interviews, focus groups, company documents, and reports. The purpose of the interviews and focus groups was to gather data relating to the feelings and opinions of a group of people involved in a common situation, discussing the same phenomenon, in this case the relationship between HRD initiatives and their impact on environmental sustainability (Collis & Hussey, 2009, p. 155).

The research commenced in September 2010 and was conducted over a two-month period. It was agreed with the organization that, in order to gain a range of perspectives, the research team would need to secure access to a vertical and horizontal slice of employees involved in both the strategic planning and development of human resource and environmental initiatives and the operational implementation of such initiatives at restaurant level. The respondents included the vice president of people, head of environment, environment consultant, operations manager, franchisee and business manager, first and second assistant restaurant managers, shift managers, and restaurant crew trainers.

It was also agreed that regional comparisons would be beneficial, potentially drawing out a range of challenges at a local and national level. Eight face-to-face interviews and one telephone interview were conducted with respondents in four locations. Three focus groups were held in Glasgow, Birmingham, and London with ten respondents each. The respondents' length of service with McDonald's varied between one year and twenty-three years, with the average length served standing at eight and a half years. The interview protocol can be viewed in Table 16.1.

On average, the one-to-one interviews lasted one and a half hours, and each focus group two hours. The transcripts were read several times to gain an overall feeling for the content. The data were analysed for meaning, which could then be clustered into significant themes, capturing and describing the essence of the respondents' experience in relation to the HRD initiatives, which were the focal subject of discussion (Marton, 1981, 1994). It is important to acknowledge the potential bias and environmental sensitivity presented by the respondents, as each respondent was either responsible for the creation or implementation of the HRD initiatives; therefore their responses may have been positively skewed toward an optimistic representation of impact and results. The next section explores strategic environmental and HRD challenges facing McDonald's UK at a national and local level that impact on HRD and environmental practices. The aims, objectives, design, development, and impact of the three HRD initiatives are also outlined.

Strategic Issues at the National and Local Levels

Respondents highlighted three strategic challenges for McDonald's UK, both at a national and local level: brand trust, current economic climate, and capacity. Brand trust was cited by seven respondents, one referring to brand trust as a global issue. Two respondents explained that consumers do not trust the McDonald's brand. When probed as to why this might be the case, respondents were not able to pinpoint one issue but instead referred to a number of contributory factors, including the image

Table 16.1. Interview Protocol

Personal Statement by the Interviewer

Interview Outline

Consent Form Discussion and Collection

Biographical Information

Current position in the organization

Number of years of experience in current position

Number of years of experience within the organization

Primary Questions

Strategic issues or challenges facing McDonald's at a national and local level

Main environmental challenges facing McDonald's at a national and local level and why

Main HRD challenges facing McDonald's at a national and local level in relation to the environmental issues and why

The relationship and fit between the human resource and environment departments

Provide two or three examples (initiatives) of how McDonald's is addressing these challenges

What was the general goal of the initiative?

What has been your involvement, if any, with the initiative?

What actions were taken to design, develop, implement, and evaluate the initiative?

The main costs and benefits of each HR initiative

What impact has the HR initiative had on environmental sustainability?

---

in part created by the documentary film, *Super Size Me* and the pressure consumers face to live a healthy lifestyle, prompting them to feel guilty when dining at a McDonald's restaurant.

Respondents also cited the current economic context as the key strategic issue McDonald's UK faces in the immediate future. In particular, respondents discussed consumers' shrinking disposable income and the inevitable forthcoming job cuts. Significant cuts have been introduced by the coalition government since coming into power in May 2010 in an attempt to reduce the UK deficit on £7.1 billion as of October 2010. Respondents explained that McDonald's had not suffered yet and that the business was in good health; however, there was no room for complacency. Investing in the business, re-imaging the restaurants, delivering first-class service, and delivering food quality were all cited as examples of how McDonald's is continuing to survive in such a turbulent environment. On the flip side, seven respondents noted that continued growth presents issues around capacity, which is also challenging. McDonald's now serves 40 percent more customers than three years ago, which puts a strain on the infrastructure and staff in restaurants.

Environmental and Human Resource Development Challenges

Three environmental challenges and four HRD challenges associated with environmental impact were raised. The environmental challenges described were uncertainty, infrastructure and the impact this has on restaurant processes and practices, and carbon footprint reduction. In established functions, there are tried-and-tested models. However, when tackling the environment, respondents did not have the same level of confidence, explaining that no one really knows how to tackle problematic issues and prioritize. One example given was around waste management: "On the one hand we've got advisers telling us get plastic out of your packaging and on the other hand we've got advisers telling us get as much plastic as possible into your packaging because of different philosophies about how you then handle your waste. So there is an argument that says you don't want plastic in your packaging because you want everything to be biodegradable and another argument that says if it is going to go in to landfill you want plastic because it locks the methane in." This particular example demonstrates uncertainty and the conflicting perspectives presented by a variety of advisers.

In addition, there is also uncertainty from a legislative perspective. Respondents are unclear about whether the government is going to impose a landfill ban on food or on plastic or whether they are going to ban incineration. One respondent stated that "the difficulty that we have from an environmental perspective is we are trialing things that we don't know if they are going to work or not, which is very counter-cultural. We normally trial things when we 95 percent know they are going to work. We are trying to second guess what the legislation is going to be when we don't really know and we are trying to work with science that is constantly shifting." McDonald's is currently trialing three different ways of disposing of waste so that, if the science or legislation changes, the business can respond and move quickly in one direction or another.

Respondents felt that the onus was on the government to stimulate the development of appropriate infrastructures to support businesses to reduce their environmental impact. Each region has a different waste policy and varying infrastructures, which present local challenges for business managers. McDonald's is a business built on consistency, implementing initiatives and delivering change that can be scaled at a national level. This is not possible to achieve if local authority practices vary throughout the country.

Respondents working within the head office function cited carbon footprint reduction within restaurants as a key strategic challenge, both at a national and local level, as the energy used in restaurants makes a significant contribution to McDonald's environmental impact. The HRD challenges they described were around training, development, engagement, and behavioral change. Respondents stated that one of the essential requirements of the business was to ensure staff had the tools needed to reduce their restaurant's environmental impact, whether technological solutions or staff training solutions. Addressing environmental concerns through the Environment and HR function, engaging staff, and instigating behavioral change were discussed at length with respondents. Over 50 percent of the respondents felt that engaging and embedding were the greatest HRD challenges, with employees facing ever-increasing targets and heightened expectations around the core fundamentals, such as service and quality. As yet, the environment is not deemed by the majority of respondents as a core key performance indicator and essential requirement; therefore the challenge is to raise the perceived importance of environmental impact reduction.

Human Resource Development Initiatives

When interviewed, respondents cited a number of HRD initiatives designed to tackle the organization's environmental impact. When asked to discuss two or three HRD initiatives in detail, respondents cited:

1. The introduction of a pilot voluntary role in restaurants: the Planet Champion.
2. The introduction of the Apprentice Key Skills Scheme and compulsory Environment Module.
3. A staff development visit to a coffee plantation in Costa Rica.

All respondents had direct experience of the first HRD initiative, either directly as a Planet Champion or indirectly as a pilot restaurant or region. Four respondents had direct experience of the Apprentice Key Skills Scheme and Environment Module as trainers or mentors. Only two respondents in the sample attended the staff development visit to Costa Rica.

The Planet Champion

The purpose of the Planet Champion was to "raise awareness of environment initiatives within restaurants feeding new ideas and insights back to head office and—hopefully—improve our (environmental) performance against some key measures" (McDonald's Environment Department, 2009). The overall aim of the initiative was to raise the profile of environment within restaurants and encourage staff to think—and act—in a way that is better for the restaurant and the planet. The voluntary role was introduced to staff in the summer of 2010. McDonald's hoped to recruit people who had the following motivational drivers to serve as Planet Champions:

- A desire to improve the environmental performance in their restaurants.
- A desire to gain experience of developing a new and important program for the business.
- A desire to make a difference—to create impact.

In July 2010, volunteer Planet Champions were invited to an introductory day in Manchester, UK, the purpose of which was to introduce the strategic vision, plan of action, operational tactics, role definition, and support processes. Approximately thirty members of staff attended the introductory day; attendees included crew trainers, shift managers, and assistant managers. Empirical research suggests that employees who feel their supervisors are supportive of environmental actions are more likely to try environmental initiatives than those who do not feel their supervisors use supportive behaviors (Ramus, 2002); therefore, pitching the voluntary role at a managerial level and recruiting individuals with drive and passion would have the greatest chance of success in restaurants. Volunteers were informed that each month over the summer period there would be a theme, which would provide a focus for their activities. The focus for July was recycling and cardboard; for August, the focus was waste and litter; for September, the focus was climate change and energy.

The operational tactics included measurement systems so that the volunteers would be able to understand their restaurant performance and the impact of their activities. Furthermore, volunteers were provided with details of activities for tackling each theme. During the recycling and cardboard focus, volunteers were encouraged to ensure staff had the knowledge to stack cardboard correctly and understand the impact correct stacking would have on their recycling figures. During the waste and litter focus, volunteers were encouraged to help colleagues understand the importance of litter collections and the impact litter has on the environment as well as on McDonald's reputation in the community. Staff created their own litter patrol chart detailing litter types, distance walked, and litter hotspots. During the climate change and energy focus, volunteers were encouraged to raise awareness of how much energy equipment uses with their restaurants, remind colleagues to put equipment on standby, and encourage colleagues to think "off" rather than "on."

Participating restaurants reported huge increases in cardboard recycling from 70 percent to 100 percent of cardboard recycled. Restaurants have also reported reductions in energy consumption: underlying electricity use in restaurants was reduced by 10 percent in 2009, additional reductions of 3 percent were made in 2010, and trial stores achieved an additional saving of £5 per store per week. Encouraging employees to put all restaurant grills on standby when not in use can save up to 20,000 tons of CO_2 per year, enough to fill 20,000 houses, and putting restaurant toasters on standby saves 30 percent of energy each year.

Support processes included email communication from the head office every two weeks, providing ideas/tips/information relevant to each monthly theme. The staff intranet website, called "ourlounge," comprised a green room for Planet Champions to share information among themselves. The environment team at head office were made available via email to answer questions and provide support. Finally, Planet Champions were encouraged to communicate directly with each other to share ideas and success stories.

The Planet Champion pilot was tested in a small number of restaurants from July to September 2010 before the decision was made to roll it out nationally. There were various tests to ensure it was designed to deliver the objectives and qualitative and quantitative data were analysed to evaluate the initiative. The initiative was rolled out nationally in January 2011 on a voluntary basis. Over 279 members of staff have attended training workshops in eight regional locations. The training workshops were delivered by the environment team, supported by the operations training function. The training gave Planet Champions the opportunity to understand the role requirements and expectations, participate in a range of practical activities to encourage engagement and enhance knowledge, and form a community of practice within their local region, creating a reflective structure to encourage and foster a learning and innovative culture (Brown & Duguid, 1991). The new Planet Champions are challenged to raise awareness and improve the environmental performance within their restaurants, supporting the implementation of new practices and processes, encouraging behavioral and cultural change within restaurants.

Apprentice Key Skills Scheme and Compulsory Environment Module

The purpose of the Apprenticeship Scheme is to recognize the value of skills learned and applied in the workplace, giving staff members the opportunity to start work, gain skills, and achieve a nationally recognized qualification. McDonald's UK invests over £30 million in training and development each year.

The Apprenticeship Scheme was launched in 2009. The course takes eight to twelve months to complete. More than five thousand staff members have completed the apprenticeship, gaining their nationally recognized qualification in hospitality, and there are an additional eight thousand employees currently studying. Respondents stated that staff turnover is now the lowest it has ever been, which they claim is a direct result of employee engagement, training, and development. Demonstrating to employees a transparent career development route with accredited qualifications has been instrumental in the record staff retention figures. The European chief people officer, Fairhurst, recently commented, "At McDonald's, we provide a learning ladder that our people can ascend while they work. There's no longer a need to choose between education and employment—people want to study at a stage in their life when it's convenient for them. Our full range of education programs increases productivity, efficiency, and staff confidence and staff turnover is now lower than it's ever been" (www.mcdonalds.co.uk/about-us/latest-news/latest-news.shtml).

The Environment Module focuses on knowledge, skills, and behaviors. This compulsory training module for apprentices requires them to complete a project related to either energy or litter. Activities include: identify and record energy saving actions; calculate the running costs of all low energy light bulbs in the restaurant for one day; calculate the cost per week of running individual pieces of restaurant equipment; and calculate the ratio of running a grill for an hour in use compared to an hour in standby.

A Staff Development Visit to a Coffee Plantation in Costa Rica

The purpose of the project was to raise awareness of sustainable business practices. More specifically, the trip was designed to improve staff members' understanding of the impact of coffee plantation practices from a local perspective and show them how sustainable farming can help local families, McDonald's staff, and customers.

The staff development visit involved a variety of activities including, among others: exposure to scientific projects involving investigating carbon emissions and pollution; coverage of the practices and certification of the Rainforest Alliance; and experience of coffee production processes and their impact on the environment. Upon returning to the UK, participants are "environmental and coffee ambassadors," promoting positive supplier environmental practices and their impact throughout the supply chain. The personal impact of the development visit on the two respondents was striking. Respondents described the experience as "life changing," "truly inspirational," and "amazing"; however, the wider impact was much more difficult to quantify. The project cost was significant: 1,500 staff members applied and eight were selected to go to Costa Rica. The project generated significant enthusiasm and energy for those directly involved; however, for the 1,492 members of staff who were not selected, the impact may have been lost.

The Merged Environment and Human Resource Function

During the last five years, the Environment Department migrated between a number of different functional areas, settling into the HR function approximately two years ago. The final move was initiated on the basis that sound environmental management and performance depend largely upon the three C's that drive employee engagement: people commitment, competence, and confidence (Fairhurst, 2009, p. 67).

Commitment is about the sharing of the core vision and values, *competence* is concerned with the development of skills and knowledge, and *confidence* is about having self-belief, the confidence to attempt, execute, and deliver. All respondents were asked about the "fit" between the environment and HR function and whether or not the respondents perceived and experienced a connection between the two. All respondents, excluding one, felt that there was a natural fit and synonymous relationship between the environment and HR function, citing "I think it fits perfectly" and "the environment is about behaviors so it should sit within the human resource function."

Four respondents thought that the environment and HR function had always been merged and that it was not a recent change. Respondents felt that, by making the environment part of the people initiatives, the business has more engaged employees. For the first time, McDonald's ViewPoint survey, which measures staff engagement, asked managers and crew whether they believe that McDonald's is committed to working toward reducing its environmental impact. Of all staff surveyed, 94 percent agreed that McDonald's is committed to working toward reducing its environmental impact, underpinning McDonald's human resource strategic vision that the three drivers of employee engagement are commitment, confidence, and competence.

Respondents' Personal Behaviors

The research team explored respondents' personal behaviors in relation to environmental practices and, in particular, how, if at all, they had been influenced by McDonald's initiatives. Muster and Schrader (2011, p. 141) consider the employees in their twofold role as producers and consumers and how environmentally relevant attitudes and behaviors result from work practice and private life.

The respondents interviewed were asked to reflect upon how, if at all, their personal behaviors had changed as a result of the organization's focus on the environment, in an attempt to ascertain the impact of work practice on personal practice. Respondents cited a range of examples, including an increased focus on recycling, energy consumption reduction, and using fewer kitchen electrical appliances. When probed more deeply about the catalyst for the changes in personal behaviors and practices, five respondents alluded to changes in recycling practices at a local level, instigated by the local authority waste collection and disposal departments. At a more senior level, respondents discussed the importance of role modeling positive environmental behaviors and practices. One respondent stated, "When you talk about it at work and you are trying to get one hundred employees to buy into something, unless you believe it yourself you can come across as a fraud. Lack of sincerity can be sought out very quickly by people."

One of the most significant findings was the increased level of pride and motivation in members of staff involved in the HRD initiatives. Reflecting upon the research results, a senior head office member of staff commented: "One of the things that we did not anticipate from it was the people element, and a lot that came out in your research was the fact that they felt more motivated and they felt it was something that they could put on their CV." Some members of staff made the connection between increased knowledge and skills development and the opportunity HRD initiatives gave them to enhance their personal and professional portfolio of experience, which they could then utilize to develop their career pathways.

Lessons Learned

The research team interviewed the McDonald's environmental consultant in March 2011, following the UK national rollout in January 2011. The respondent was able to share the feedback gathered from the pilot volunteer Planet Champions, which helped frame and shape the approach and content of the rollout program that is the primary focus of this chapter. The respondent was also able to share specific outcomes and perceived or direct impact on both the Planet Champions and the restaurant commercial results. Four key lessons informed the rollout, linked to commitment, competence, and confidence:

1. Clearly defined expectations.
2. Strategic integration of activities created to tackle environmental issues.
3. HR systems and processes aligned to environmental performance.
4. The development of a workplace community of practice.

Clearly Defined Expectations

The feedback from Planet Champions indicated that some were unclear about the purpose of the role, remittance of the role, and the amount of autonomy they had to innovate. Many champions had the necessary knowledge, skills, and abilities to engage with their teams, which can be a prerequisite to developing green behaviors (Mischel & Shoda, 1995), but they felt reluctant because they were unclear about the expectations of the organization or their business manager. The impact of this lack of clarity was that some champions lacked the confidence to fully engage in the role, while others were spending up to twenty hours per week, in addition to their usual working hours, creating and developing supporting materials for the centrally driven initiatives.

To address this problem during the rollout, Planet Champions were given a clear explanation around the aim of the role and the two main focus areas. The first is to raise understanding around the type of environmental initiatives underway in restaurants and why they are important. The second focus is to energize and encourage staff to participate in the organized environmental activities. While the scope of the role was clearly defined, however, it was emphasized that there is flexibility depending on the individual's interests and the business manager's directives. At this stage, Planet Champions are not expected to develop new or restaurant-specific projects, but rather integrate and embed the centrally driven environmental initiatives. Ensuring understanding at this early stage of the rollout provides Planet Champions with the job role knowledge (competence) to engage with their restaurant teams (confidence).

Strategic Integration of Activities Created to Tackle Environmental Issues

The greatest challenge identified by the respondents was embedding sound environmental practices into everyday life, rather than it being an additional activity. Business managers describe juggling numerous targets and operational activities and that if a new activity is added that is not part of the strategic approach or core operational scheme, it drops off the agenda. Indeed, Brio, Fernandez, and Junquera (2007) found that the strategic integration of environmental activities has a strong influence on companies' environmental performance. Embedding environmental activities through the people tactics achieves far better buy-in than adding it as an optional activity.

The barrier around the integration of practice and operating activities was addressed in the rollout. McDonald's restaurants are given a marketing calendar that outlines the key promotional activities planned for the year. When new environmental-impact-reducing activities are launched in restaurants, they are linked to the corporate marketing calendar. The purpose of linking activities to the marketing calendar is threefold: to retain operational relevance, to allow Planet Champions to plan in advance through fixed dates, and to allow activities to be themed with promotions. The underlying driver is the desire to ensure the environment is integrated into the core activities of the business, linking marketing, operations, HRM, and the environment. With this approach, Planet Champions and their teams are able to understand the relationship between the core operational activities and levers that drive environmental management (competence). This enhanced understanding gives Planet Champions the ability to describe the activities, their rationale, and the impact with their restaurant teams (confidence).

HR Systems and Processes Aligned to Environmental Performance

McDonald's is a results-focused business, and employee pay reviews and bonuses are based on performance. Interviews conducted with pilot Planet Champions revealed employees' keenness to measure restaurants' environmental performance. Staff are comfortable with key performance indicators; they understand why they are needed and how they can be achieved. Champions want to be recognized and rewarded for their efforts, although this did not necessarily require a financial reward framework. The environment team are now implementing a recognition and reward structure in response to the feedback. This will include providing opportunities for operations managers and business directors to formally engage with the champions. This will enhance levels of commitment, reinforcing the behaviors that drive environmental performance.

The Development of a Workplace Community of Practice

A number of champions indicated a strong desire to develop network connections so they could more easily engage with colleagues at all levels of the business, share practices and innovations, tackle in-store challenges, and stay abreast of developments, further enhancing their competence and confidence. It is noted that the development of a network may not appeal to all champions. Those who are highly motivated and nominate themselves for the voluntary role would undoubtedly participate fully, but those champions who were nominated or selected by their business managers might not be as enthusiastic. Participation and levels of learning in networks associated with environmental improvement was addressed by Millard (2011), who found a connection between levels of learning and the voluntary nature of participants. Although the champions did not refer directly to the term "community of practice," they presented a desire to work toward a joint enterprise, mutually engaging with their colleagues and sharing a repertoire of communal resources (Wenger, 1998). Encouraging individuals to take ownership for their changing behaviors, skills, and knowledge is essential. In response to the feedback, the environment team have provided a variety of links to encourage such practice.

The champions are provided with a virtual meeting space on ourlounge.co.uk, which has the dual purpose of providing information and enabling others to share information. The environment team are on hand to answer questions and provide support, and champions receive regular emails. Planet Champions are also encouraged to share ideas and challenges with other champions on a forum within the Planet People pages of ourlounge.co.uk. The environment team were able to utilize the feedback conducted by the research team to further shape the People Planet rollout. One respondent stated that the research enabled her to reflect on a number of success stories and the drivers for change and consider how others could be supported to comparable results.

Conclusion

Facilitating the creation of a green HRD culture will involve moving toward a community of purpose, emphasising shared values, health of the individual, organization, and community, consciousness of our ecological actions, and the guiding principles of fairness and duty of care toward ourselves and everyone around us. The McDonald's case study demonstrates a shift in momentum toward the creation of such a culture, aligning strategic and operational tactics through the environment and HR function, developing HR systems and processes, valuing and rewarding environmental improvements, encouraging the sharing of knowledge, and strengthening of communication networks through local, regional, and virtual communities of practice, and, perhaps most importantly, responding to employee feedback and the changing environmental challenges.

It is hoped that the research questions of this study are relevant to the design and implementation of future case studies, particularly contrasting companies within the food retailing sector with comparable strategic and operational issues. However, it is accepted that this research represents one case study and, as such, the full extent of the results cannot directly be transferred but merely give an indication of the types of HRD initiatives that might directly or indirectly positively impact environmental practices and performance. Furthermore, environmental policy contexts differ significantly, and thus there is a need to explore the impact of national institutional contexts on green HRD policies and practices.

Bibliography

A Framework for Environmental Behaviours Report 2008. Retrieved from www.defra.gov.uk/evidence/social/behaviour/documents/behaviours-jan08-report.pdf.

Ambec, S., & Lanoie, P. (2008). Does it pay to be green? A systematic overview. *Academy of Management Perspectives, 22*(4), 45–62.

Brio, J. A., Fernandez, E., & Junquera, B. (2007). Management of employee involvement in achieving an environmental action-based competitive advantage: An empirical study. *The International Journal of HRM, 18*(4), 491–522.

Brown, J. S., & Duguid, P. (1991). Organizational learning and communities-of-practice: Toward a unified view of working, learning, and innovation. *Organization Science, 2*(1), 40–57. [Special Issue: *Organizational learning: Papers in honor of (and by) James G. March.*]

Colaizzi, P. F. (1978). Psychological research as the phenomenologist views it. In R. Valle & A. King (Eds.), *Existential phenomenological alternatives in psychology* (pp. 48–71). New York: Oxford University Press.

Collis, J., & Hussey, R. (2009). *Business research* (3rd ed.). Basingstoke, UK: Palgrave Macmillan.

Curtin, T. (2007). *Managing green issues* (2nd ed.). Basingstoke, UK: Palgrave Macmillan, p. 196.

Delmas, M., & Toffel, M. W. (2004). Stakeholders and environmental management practices: An institutional framework. *Business Strategy and the Environment, 13*(4), 209–222.

Fairhurst, D. (2009). *Words from the "whys": An exploration of 21st century HR practice.* London: Haymarket Business Media, p. 67.

Fernandez, E., Junquera, B., & Ordiz, M. (2003). Organizational culture and human resources in the environmental issue. *International Journal of Human Resource Management, 14*(4), 634–656.

Haddock, J. A., Jeffrey, J., Miles, D., Müller-Camen, M., Yamin, A., Critten, P., & Hartog, M. (2009). Green HRD: The potential contribution of HRD concepts and theories to environmental management. Presented at the 6th International Conference of the Dutch HRM Network, *Capitalizing on diversity in HRM research.* Vrije Universiteit, Amsterdam.

Marton, F. (1981). Phenomenography: Describing conceptions of the world around us. *Instructional Science, 2,* 177–200.

Marton, F. (1994). Phenomenography. In T. Hussen & T. N. Postlethwaite (Eds.), *The international encyclopaedia of education.* London: Pergamon Press, pp. 4424–4429.

McDonald's Environment Department. (2009). *Easy EC Guide (Company Guide).* London: Environment Department.

Millard, D. (2011). Management learning and the greening of SMEs: Moving beyond problem-solving. *Zeitschrift fur Personalforschung, 25*(2), 178–195.

Mischel, W., & Shoda, Y. (1995). A cognitive-affective system theory of personality: Reconceptualizing situations, dispositions, dynamics, and invariance in personality structure. *Psychological Review, 102,* 246–268.

Muster, V., & Schrader, U. (2011). Green work-life balance: A new perspective for green HRM, *Zeitschrift fur Personalforschung, 25*(2), 140–156.

Ramus, C. A. (2001). Organizational support for employees: Encouraging creative ideas for environmental sustainability. *California Management Review, 33*(3), 85–105.

Ramus, C. A. (2002). Encouraging innovative environmental actions: What companies and managers must do. *Journal of World Business, 37,* 51–164.

Securing the future—The UK government sustainable development strategy (2005, March). Retrieved from www.defra.gov.uk/environment/ business/reporting/pdf/envkpi-guidelines.pdf.

Wenger, E. (1998). *Communities of practice: Learning as a social system.* Cambridge, UK: Cambridge University Press.

CHAPTER SEVENTEEN

Environmental Sustainability and Organization Sensing at Procter & Gamble

Andrew Biga,
Stephan Dilchert,
A. Silke McCance,
Robert E. Gibby,
and Anne Doyle Oudersluys

The Company

Procter & Gamble (P&G) is a multi-national corporation with headquarters in Cincinnati, Ohio. The company has one of the strongest portfolios of trusted, quality, leadership brands in consumer goods, including twenty-three brands that generate more than $1 billion and twenty brands that generate more than $500 million in annual sales each. Procter & Gamble's products are sold in more than 180 countries, primarily through mass merchandisers, grocery stores, drug stores, and "high frequency stores"—neighborhood shops that serve many consumers in developing markets. Its brands include household names such as Pampers®, Tide®, Ariel®, Always®, Whisper®, Pantene®, Mach3®, Bounty®, Dawn®, Gain®, Pringles®, Charmin®, Downy®, Lenor®, Iams®, Crest®, Oral-B®, Duracell®, Olay®, Head & Shoulders®, Wella®, Gillette®, Braun®, Fusion®, Ace®, Febreze®, and Ambi

Pur®. The fifty leadership brands account for 90 percent of sales and more than 90 percent of the company's profit. Procter & Gamble has a strong history of product innovation, including for environmental sustainability. Growing responsibly compels P&G to continually seek improvements in the design, manufacture, and delivery of products. Because of their products' ubiquity, product-driven environmental sustainability initiatives at P&G generate large scale: 4.4 billion times a day, P&G brands touch the lives of people around the world.

P&G focuses on sustainability as part of the company's purpose to touch and improve lives. Its environmental sustainability efforts have a long history dating back to the 1950s, when P&G first started evaluating the levels of surfactants in rivers. In the 1960s it began developing biodegradability tests, and in the 1970s P&G conducted the first environmental audit of one of its plants. In addition to its environmental sustainability impact through continued product and operations improvement, Procter & Gamble also has a wide reach through the environmentally relevant behaviors of its workforce. The P&G community includes employees representing over 145 nationalities. With operations in about eighty countries, P&G brands are available in more than 180 countries worldwide. The company's employee sustainability strategy is to engage and equip all of its employees to build sustainability thinking and practices into their everyday work by making sustainability a top-of-mind issue. This case study provides a brief overview of P&G's sustainability efforts in general and illustrates how the company uses organizational surveys as a pulse check on employee engagement and its link to environmental sustainability behaviors in the workplace.

Environmental Sustainability at P&G

Procter & Gamble's environmental sustainability efforts primarily focus on its operations and products. Employees are the most essential group to deliver these efforts. For products, employees develop the formulations, design the packaging, and create consumer awareness and education. Within operations, employees design manufacturing processes, run the equipment, and manage the product logistics. Each of these areas presents many opportunities for employees to implement environmental sustainability improvements. Here, we provide a brief overview of operations- and products-focused environmental sustainability initiatives before discussing the role of employees and organization sensing in P&G's environmental sustainability efforts.

Procter & Gamble has had great success in reducing the environmental footprint of its operations, reporting a 52 percent reduction in energy consumption, 53 percent reduction in CO_2 emissions, 61 percent reduction in disposed waste, and 58 percent reduction in water consumption from July 2002 through June 2011. In 2010, P&G added additional goals to reach by the year 2020 to further improve the footprint of its operations. The goals include a 20 percent reduction in truck transportation, powering its plants with 30 percent renewable energy, and sending less than 0.5 percent of manufacturing waste to landfills.

Procter & Gamble employs a science-based tool, called the Life Cycle Assessment, to make products more environmentally sustainable. This method analyzes the footprint of a given product throughout its entire life cycle (raw materials, manufacturing, transportation, consumer use, and disposal). This approach helps the company focus on where it can make the most impact with regard to its products. Based on findings from life cycle assessments of P&G's product categories, a number of recent company efforts have focused on rethinking raw materials and how products are designed and formulated to reduce material use, energy required for production, and waste.

For example, to reduce the waste from its products, Procter & Gamble continually looks for opportunities to reduce packaging while maintaining consumer needs and product integrity. Packaging sustainability experts work on every category of the business and look at packaging efforts systemically. Between 2006 and 2009, improvements made company-wide resulted in 136,000 metric tons of packaging material avoidance. Procter & Gamble is also shifting some petroleum-based materials to sustainably-sourced renewable sources, with several efforts under way. The goal in these efforts is to find ways to deliver significant sustainability improvement without asking the consumer to make trade-offs in performance or value. This section highlights only a few illustrative examples.

Laundry compaction. After innovating to convert parts of its liquid laundry detergent portfolio to a "2X" concentrated formulation, P&G now uses less water, generates less emissions and packaging, and has less environmental impact due to product shipping.

Ariel Turn to 30° C campaign. The life cycle assessment of laundry detergent revealed that one step consumed far more energy than any other: the heating of wash water during its use in consumers' homes. By developing the technology behind Ariel Cool Clean and spreading the word, P&G gave consumers in the UK the opportunity to reduce household electricity consumption—with no tradeoff in performance.

Olay packaging. By moving from bulky plastic "clam shells" to trapped blister-based designs, Olay reduced millions of pounds of plastic packaging. At the same time, the new packaging is now much easier for consumers to open at home.

Gillette Fusion. P&G partnered with Be Green® Packaging, a molded fiber supplier, to develop a breakthrough package for the Fusion ProGlide in Western Europe, resulting in a 57 percent reduction in plastic, 20 percent reduction in gross weight, and a 100 percent removal of polyvinyl chloride (PVC).

The Role of Organization Sensing

Employees play a central role in Procter & Gamble's corporate strategy, as they are the source for product innovation and the driving force behind environmental sustainability programs. For nearly eighty years, P&G has conducted surveys to understand what employees think and how they feel about the company, their work, and their careers. This longstanding tradition is one very important way that P&G leaders stay in touch with each employee and the needs of the organization. In recent years, "organization sensing" has also included P&G's social and environmental sustainability efforts, in order to evaluate their role in and effect on a variety of work-related behaviors and outcomes. The company is striving to be, and continues to be, recognized internally and externally as an employer of choice—a company that is broadly acknowledged as the place to be, a workplace where employees give their best performance, that attracts the best and brightest, and retains them. The annual employee opinion survey is used as a "pulse check" on how the company is doing in this regard. Here, we briefly describe this survey effort and summarize selected results that show a direct link between corporate environmental sustainability goals and employee attitudes and behaviors. Data from P&G's employee survey show that knowledge of the company's sustainability goals is positively related to employees' pro-environmental behaviors. Moreover, employees who report higher overall engagement (job involvement, empowerment, satisfaction, and affective commitment) are more likely to engage in pro-environmental behaviors on the job.

The P&G Survey Program

Over the years, P&G has approached organization sensing using employee surveys in a variety of ways. As the company has expanded globally, the complexity of organizations and sensing metrics tended to increase as well. To address the organization's need for sensing, multiple surveys across business units, functions, and regions were deployed. These surveys measured similar constructs and were often fielded by the same employees, creating redundancy for the survey administrators and alignment issues for action. In 2005, a revised, integrative survey (the "P&G Survey") was launched to leverage scale and be the single, annual culture survey for the company. Providing common measurement for the entire company, the P&G Survey program simplified the company's sensing efforts and cut cost and time, as all reachable employees are provided with the opportunity to complete a common survey once a year.

Based on the company's "employer of choice" model, the P&G Survey is a comprehensive engagement survey that measures twenty factors (e.g., meaningfulness of work, relationships with colleagues and supervisors, satisfaction with various aspects of the job, and culture). Development of the employer of choice model was based on three streams of research: (1) existing internal surveys in various business units, functions, and regions; (2) external surveys that P&G participates in each year; and (3) information gathered from the company's global recruiting organization. A group of subject-matter experts defined the initial factor structure for the survey with regard to what it means to be an "employer of choice." The factor structure is refined each year using confirmatory methods, but its core elements have remained stable.

To continue meeting the organization's sensing needs in a changing world, new survey questions and categories are developed and integrated into the survey program. These include the issue of environmental sustainability, which was first introduced in 2009. The new survey content (which was expanded in 2010 and 2011) assesses employee attitudes toward corporate-wide environmental sustainability goals and strategies. It also includes a pro-environmental work behavior checklist developed by a team of academicians. This "employee green behaviors" checklist is based on an empirically developed model of environmentally sustainable employee behaviors and covers sixteen different aspects of sustainability at work (Ones & Dilchert, 2009, 2010).

Using HR Survey Results to Drive Sustainable Action

Environmental sustainability–related survey results are used at P&G to drive action in several ways. First, descriptive statistics are used to understand baseline measures and determine year-to-year progress at the company. Second, scores are aggregated at the worksite level and linked to other sources of data to determine whether focused environmental sustainability efforts are making a difference. This way, P&G is also able to determine which populations are most impacted by company-wide environmental sustainability initiatives. Third, results are tied to a variety of other survey scales (such as organizational support and employee commitment to the organization). Below, we provide two examples of how this data can be leveraged to gain insight into environmental sustainability in the workplace.

Linking sustainability goal knowledge to organizational commitment and on-the-job behaviors. Using data from the 2009 P&G survey, we explored the linkages between employees' knowledge and acceptance of the company's sustainability goals and their own work behaviors and attitudes. (Results were presented at the 2010 SIOP conference; Dilchert, Ones, Biga, & Gibby, 2010.) Specifically, we tested the relationship between individuals' knowledge and acceptance of P&G's sustainability goals and their participation in company-sponsored sustainability efforts. Following prevailing models in the employee engagement literature (cf. Meyer, Stanley, Herscovitch, & Topolnytsky, 2002), we also tested whether the link between sustainability goal knowledge and on-the-job behaviors is mediated by employees' organizational commitment.

Knowledge and acceptance of organizational sustainability goals is perhaps the most fundamental step toward increasing participation in pro-environmental efforts in the workplace. *Knowledge* of organizational goals is a necessary condition for goal acceptance and pursuant effort toward goal attainment. *Acceptance* of goals is also crucial in goal-directed behavior, because without acceptance there can be no goal commitment. The link between knowledge and acceptance of an organization's sustainability goals and employees' behaviors may not be a direct one, however. Whether knowledge of assigned goals results in desired behavior might depend on how committed employees are to the organization. Affective commitment is characterized by "a strong belief in and acceptance of the organizational goals and values" (Porter, Steers, Mowday, & Boulian, 1974). Based on the literature linking organizational commitment to employee behaviors, affective organizational commitment might be an important mediating mechanism of the sustainability goal acceptance-employee sustainability relationship. Meyer, Stanley, Herscovitch, and Topolnytsky's (2002) popular model postulates that affective commitment leads to three types of employee behaviors and outcomes: turnover intentions, employee well-being, and on-the-job behavior (in our case, individual sustainability efforts).[1] Data from the P&G survey allowed us to not only investigate the link between organizational sustainability goals and employee behaviors, but also the possible mediating role of affective commitment.[2]

---

[1]Because Meyer, Stanley, Herscovitch, and Topolnytsky's (2002) model also includes turnover intentions and employee well-being as possible outcome variables, we included the respective scales from the P&G survey in our analyses as well, even though they were not the focal point of this investigation. Turnover intentions were measured with two items and personal well-being with three items.

[2]The often hypothesized mediating role of affective commitment was confirmed for the relationship between sustainability goal knowledge with turnover intentions (full mediation) and employee well-being (partial mediation).

Figure 17.1. Possible (Mediated) Relationships Between Sustainability Goal Knowledge and Acceptance and Employee Behaviors and Outcomes

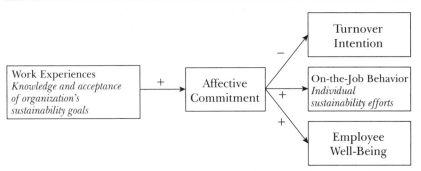

Based on Meyer, Stanley, Herscovitch, and Topolnytsky's (2002) Hypotheses.

In 2009, the P&G survey questions that relate to environmental sustainability were answered by a subsample of more than twelve thousand employees across all organizational levels working in about eighty countries. Knowledge and acceptance of P&G's sustainability goals was assessed with two items (internal consistency reliability $\alpha = .76$) and affective commitment was measured with a five-item scale ($\alpha = .85$). Employees' individual sustainability behaviors on the job were measured using a five-item checklist that corresponded to efforts specifically encouraged by P&G (recycling, reducing printer use, participating in Earth Day activities). We were interested in the relationships between the variables at the construct level (unhampered by measurement error), and thus corrected observed correlations for attenuation due to unreliability in measures. The resulting matrix of true-score correlations can be used to conduct a series of multiple regressions for each of the relationships (see Figure 17.1) and to test for the potential mediating effects of affective commitment (cf. Baron & Kenny, 1986).

Results confirmed that relationships were in the expected directions: knowledge and acceptance of organizational sustainability goals related positively to employees' environmentally sustainable behaviors ($\rho = .36$), well-being ($\rho = .33$), and negatively to turnover intentions ($\rho = -.16$). It also related strongly to affective organizational commitment ($\rho = .40$). The multiple regression-based mediator analyses revealed that the relationship between knowing and accepting organizationally assigned sustainability goals and individual sustainability was *not* mediated by affective commitment. Employees who indicate higher awareness and higher acceptance of the company's sustainability goals are also more likely to engage in environmental sustainability efforts on the job. The link between these variables is a *direct* one, and not dependent on employees' affective commitment to the organization.

Linking employee engagement to pro-environmental behaviors on the job. Our second example provides a closer look at the link between employee engagement and pro-environmental behaviors by broadening criterion measurement and including a larger variety of engagement variables. *Employee engagement* is often used to refer to a multitude of different constructs, both those that are dispositional in nature (for example, positive affect) and those that reflect a psychological state (for example, organizational commitment or job involvement; see Macey & Schneider, 2008). Many organizations regard the latter as focal variables of interest, because employee attitudes such as job involvement, satisfaction, and commitment—even if they partially have dispositional antecedents (cf. Dalal, Brummel, Wee, & Thomas, 2008)—can be manipulated through organizational interventions. Our question was whether employees who are more involved in their work, who feel more empowered and satisfied, and who experience more affective commitment to the organization are also more likely to behave in a manner congruent with the company's environmental sustainability strategy. If these aspects of employee engagement display a positive link to employee green behaviors, this would provide yet another incentive for a sustainability-minded organization to actively foster employee engagement.

To answer this question, we used data on more than eight thousand employees from the 2011 P&G survey, again spanning all hierarchical levels and nearly all of the company's international locations. We operationalized employee engagement using five different measures that reflect the relevant constructs identified in reviews of the engagement literature (see Macey & Schneider, 2008): Job involvement (five items; Cronbach's alpha = .89), empowerment (three items, $\alpha = .74$), satisfaction with compensation (five items, α = .83) and commendations (one item), as well as affective organizational commitment (three items, α = .88). The sum of these scores was used as an overall employee engagement measure; the seventeen-item scale had excellent reliability (alpha = .92).

In 2011, employees' pro-environmental on-the-job behaviors were assessed using a fifteen-item inventory based on the empirically derived "Green Five" taxonomy (Ones & Dilchert, 2009, 2010).[3] Employees were presented with a wider range of environmentally sustainable work behaviors (not only those specifically endorsed by P&G), for which they indicated the frequency with which they had engaged in each during the last twelve months on the job. This form of the scale yields an overall *employee green behavior* score (fifteen items, alpha = .90), and the two facet scores *working sustainably* (five items, α = .81) and *conserving* (five items; α = .73).

Results indicate that employee engagement relates to individuals' pro-environmental behaviors on the job. Observed correlations for the total sample were .25 (for working sustainably), .29 (conserving behaviors), and .31 (overall employee green behaviors). Construct-level relationships (corrected for measurement error) ranged from .29 to .35. Table 17.1 presents these results separately for P&G employees of different organizational tenure.

These findings bode well for organizational efforts geared toward fostering environmental sustainability through interventions that target employee engagement. Employees who are more involved in their work, satisfied with their jobs, and committed to their organization are also more likely to display pro-environmental behaviors on the job. Furthermore, this effect is not limited to any specific tenure group. Even though certain aspects of employee engagement have been shown to have a complex association with organizational tenure, which can moderate the relationship with important outcome variables (for example, see Wright & Bonett, 2002, for organizational

---

[3]Facet scores for additional subdomains (avoiding harm, taking initiative, and influencing others) are available for a longer form of this measure.

Table 17.1. Relationship Between Employee Engagement and Employee Green Behaviors

Tenure Group	EGB (overall)		Working Sustainably		Conserving Behaviors	
Total sample		.34		.29		.35
<1 year		.32		.27		.36
1–3 years		.31		.28		.32
4–5 years		.33		.29		.35
6–10 years		.34		.29		.34
11–15 years		.33		.25		.32
16–20 years		.37		.32		.40
>20 years		.38		.31		.36

Note: EGB = Employee green behaviors. Sample sizes for the individual tenure groups ranged from 603 to 1,344. 95 percent confidence intervals for all effects exclude zero.

commitment), the relationship with pro-environmental behaviors remains consistent across the different lengths of individuals' careers. Both new and experienced employees can be equally mobilized to foster environmental sustainability through employee engagement.

Future of Environmental Sustainability Research at P&G

The future of environmental sustainability research and practice needs to focus on understanding the connections between employee behavior and metrics that make a difference in improving a company's ecological footprint. The true measure of organizational research is the action taken from it. A critical step in P&G's research effort is to understand the impact of specific employee behaviors on quantifiable environmental outcomes. By examining how each category of employee behavior relates to hard outcomes (for example, waste reduction), P&G will be able to take even larger steps toward achieving its sustainability goals. This research will undoubtedly change how the organization views pro-environmental employee behaviors and, ultimately, the initiatives that promote these behaviors.

Creating a digital feedback loop that links such sensing data to data gathered from other sources (for example, plant outputs) is an evolution of this process. Automating these processes and systems, along with the analytics necessary to infer the appropriate conclusions, would enable the company to monitor progress essentially in real time. This digitization process also spans domains of organization sensing beyond environmental sustainability. The ability to make smarter, faster decisions is a common objective across research areas.

At P&G, the focus of environmental sustainability efforts is on improvements that matter, in order to maximize the organization's positive impact. Environmental sustainability at P&G is fully integrated into its growth strategy of improving more consumers' lives, in more parts of the world, more completely. In order to responsibly achieve its goals, the company must grow sustainably. This commitment begins with the company's purpose, values, and principles, in which environmental sustainability is embedded, and manifests itself in a systemic and long-term approach supported by empirically driven, cutting-edge research.

References

Baron, R. M., & Kenny, D. A. (1986). The moderator-mediator variable distinction in social psychological research. *Journal of Personality and Social Psychology, 51*, 1173–1182.

Dalal, R. S., Brummel, B. J., Wee, S., & Thomas, L. L. (2008). Defining employee engagement for productive research and practice. *Industrial and Organizational Psychology: Perspectives on Science and Practice, 1*, 52–55.

Dilchert, S., Ones, D. S., Biga, A., & Gibby, R. E. (2010, April). Organizational sustainability goals and individual sustainability and other on-the-job outcomes. In D. S. Ones & S. Dilchert (Chairs), *Shades of green: Individual differences in environmentally responsible employee behaviors.* Symposium conducted at the annual conference of the Society for Industrial and Organizational Psychology, Atlanta, Georgia.

Macey, W. H., & Schneider, B. (2008). The meaning of employee engagement. *Industrial and Organizational Psychology: Perspectives on Science and Practice, 1,* 3–30.

Meyer, J. P., Stanley, D. J., Herscovitch, L., & Topolnytsky, L. (2002). Affective, continuance, and normative commitment to the organization: A meta-analysis of antecedents, correlates, and consequences. *Journal of Vocational Behavior, 61,* 20–52.

Ones, D. S., & Dilchert, S. (2009, August). Green behaviors of workers: A taxonomy for the green economy. In S. Dilchert & D. S. Ones (Chairs), *Environmentally friendly worker behaviors, senior leader wrongdoing, and national level outcomes.* Symposium conducted at the annual meeting of the Academy of Management, Chicago, Illinois.

Ones, D. S., & Dilchert, S. (2010, April). A taxonomy of green behaviors among employees. In D. S. Ones & S. Dilchert (Chairs), *Shades of green: Individual differences in environmentally responsible employee behaviors.* Symposium conducted at the annual conference of the Society for Industrial and Organizational Psychology, Atlanta, Georgia.

Porter, L. W., Steers, R. M., Mowday, R. T., & Boulian, P. V. (1974). Organizational commitment, job satisfaction, and turnover among psychiatric technicians. *Journal of Applied Psychology, 59,* 603–609.

Wright, T. A., & Bonett, D. G. (2002). The moderating effects of employee tenure on the relation between organizational commitment and job performance: A meta-analysis. *Journal of Applied Psychology, 87,* 1183–1190.

CHAPTER EIGHTEEN

Sustainability in Coffee Sourcing and Implications for Employee Engagement at Caribou Coffee

John P. Muros,
Kevin Impelman,
and Lewis Hollweg

Caribou Coffee offers its customers gourmet coffee and espresso-based beverages, as well as specialty teas, baked goods, and whole bean coffee. The company employs more than six thousand people from more than five hundred national and international locations. For years, Caribou Coffee has made concerted efforts to promote sustainability in many forms, including environmental, economic, and social sustainability in ecosystems and communities. Its ongoing partnership with the Rainforest Alliance

We wish to acknowledge the efforts of Belinda K. Smith, M.S., who was instrumental in preparing, running, and reporting on the data analyses that informed this research. We would also like to thank Chad Trewick, Karen McBride, Alfredo Martel, and Dan Lee, who shared openly about Caribou's sustainability efforts and provided very helpful feedback on an earlier version of this chapter. Further, we are grateful to Mike Tattersfield, who opened the door to us so we could learn more about Caribou's initiatives.

program enables Caribou Coffee to source its coffee beans from sustainable coffee farms. Recently, the company committed to procuring 100 percent of its coffee from Rainforest Alliance–certified coffee farms by the end of 2011. This goal is unique for the industry. In the spring of 2010, Caribou engaged in a marketing and human resource training initiative designed to spread the word about this program, promote greater knowledge and awareness of Caribou's sustainability commitments, and generate enthusiasm and dialogue among employees and customers about sustainability. This chapter describes the context for embarking on this initiative, as well as Caribou's specific approach for increasing knowledge, awareness, enthusiasm, and communication about its sustainability efforts. We conclude by offering perspectives on Caribou's efforts and guidance to other organizations that are informed by the literature and empirical data analyses.

Company Background

Founded in 1992, Caribou Coffee offers its customers high-quality gourmet coffee and espresso-based beverages, as well as specialty teas, baked goods, whole bean coffee, branded merchandise, and related products. In addition, Caribou sells its products to club stores, grocery stores, mass merchandisers, office coffee providers, airlines, hotels, sports and entertainment venues, college campuses, and other commercial customers. The company also licenses third parties to use the Caribou Coffee brand on quality food and merchandise items.

From its conception, the company has woven a certain harmony with nature into its narrative and mission, as exemplified by this account of the company's origins:

> "In 1990, during an adventure through the Alaskan wilderness, our founders journeyed to the top of Sable Mountain. After a strenuous climb, they reached the summit and were rewarded with a sensational view: the boundless mountains, a clear blue sky, and a herd of caribou thundering through the valley. That was truly the 'aha' moment. The breathtaking panoramic view became the entrepreneurial vision for Caribou Coffee—a company that believes excellence is a product of hard work, and that life is too short for anything else." (Caribou Coffee, 2010)

Caribou is now headquartered in Minneapolis, Minnesota. They employ more than six thousand people and are the second-largest company-owned gourmet coffeehouse operator in the United States (based on the number of coffeehouses). As of July 4, 2010, Caribou Coffee has grown to include 411 company-owned coffeehouses and 128 franchised and licensed locations. They have locations in sixteen U.S. states and the District of Columbia, as well as in Kuwait, Bahrain, Jordan, and the Republic of Korea. For 2009, Caribou reported revenues of $262 million.

Caribou's leadership has long been interested in staying attuned to its workforce. As one means of doing so, the company has partnered with Batrus Hollweg International (BHI) since 2003 to conduct an employee satisfaction survey. The survey enables employees to share their perceptions of initiatives driven by the company overall and their individual managers in particular. Most of the survey's respondents (94 to 96 percent) are either hourly employees or store managers based in Caribou's customer-facing stores. From this survey, Caribou's leadership has obtained useful insights into how engaged their employees are, as well as whether the values they are trying to promote in the organization are coming through clearly to their people. As shown in Table 18.1, Caribou's leadership has done well over the years in ensuring that employees are clear on the company's mission and core values.

Commitment to Sustainability

One of Caribou's core values is called Commitment to Our Community, which reflects Caribou's dedication to minimizing its environmental footprint and being a positive, responsible presence in its local geographies and the broader global community. In short, it represents their view of *sustainability*, but of note is that Caribou takes a multidimensional view of this concept. The term sustainability is often used in reference to environmental issues (Huffman, Watrous-Rodriguez, Henning, & Berry, 2009), but as Campbell and Campbell (2005) noted, it is actually a broader term that "refers to the ability of a system to survive for some specified time" and can be applied to a range of activities beyond

Table 18.1. Response Trends for Mission/Core Values Items Across Survey Years

	2007	2008	2010	2010
	I Clearly Understand the Mission of Caribou Coffee	I Clearly Understand the Mission of Caribou Coffee	The Leadership at Caribou Coffee Emphasizes the Importance of Our Core Values	I Clearly Understand the Core Values of Caribou Coffee
Number of Respondents	4,761	4,079	3,937	3,937
Positive (Agree or Strongly Agree)	97%	97%	81%	95%
Neutral (Neither Agree nor Disagree)	2%	2%	12%	4%
Negative (Strongly Disagree or Disagree)	1%	1%	7%	1%

just environmentally friendly behaviors (for example, agriculture, property development, society).

As Caribou defines it, *sustainability* is made up of environmental, economic, and social components. *Environmental sustainability* includes practices such as teaching farmers to manage their lands responsibly, reforesting lands with native species, and helping to conserve wildlife, rainforests, and natural resources. *Economic sustainability* includes practices such as teaching farmers how to run a business, helping farmers control costs and improve quality, and ensuring that workers receive decent wages. *Social sustainability* includes practices such as improved housing, improved working hours and conditions, and reasonable access for workers and their families to education, clean water, and medical care. This more robust conception of sustainability transcends the "three R's" (reduce, reuse, recycle) that most think of when they consider "green" initiatives. Rather, it represents a more comprehensive approach that, while still inclusive of the three R's, pushes into areas that promote broader survival for nature, people, and Caribou's business.

A ready way for Caribou to express its commitment to sustainability emerged from its coffee sourcing processes. As a gourmet coffee provider, Caribou procures its coffee beans, the very backbone of its business, from coffee farmers around the world, including those located in Central and South America, East Africa, the Middle East, and Southeast Asia. The special nature of the coffee beans it uses requires Caribou to work with many smaller scale coffee farming operations. A risk inherent in dealing with smaller operations is their volatility. Market pressures drive the price of coffee up and down, and smaller farmers are often unable to weather tough economic cycles that cut into their revenues, sometimes driving them out of business. As a result, Caribou sought to fortify a stable roster of steady suppliers through increased sustainability efforts, with hopes of improving its ability to predict prices, control its procurement costs, and turn the profits needed to drive its success as a business.

A Partnership for Sustainability

In 2005, Caribou Coffee began a partnership with The Rainforest Alliance as a way of simultaneously addressing its desires to operate in an environmentally sustainable manner while also ensuring a healthy supply chain for its coffee beans. Other partnerships were available at the time, but none was a solid fit for Caribou's more comprehensive definition of sustainability. For example, the USDA Organic Program ensures that products such as coffee are grown without the use of pesticides or other chemicals. Although an important component of environmental sustainability, Caribou felt the USDA Organic Program lacked an approach to improving economic and social sustainability. Comparatively, the Fair Trade Certified Program works with coffee cooperatives to ensure that their trading practices are responsible. Although this was appealing to Caribou as a means of enhancing economic sustainability, it lacked some of the social and environmental sustainability components that Caribou desired. Worth noting is that some of Caribou's competitors (for example, Starbucks) have successfully embraced these programs. Still, Caribou sought a way of differentiating itself from its competitors based on its strong core values around sustainability.

The Rainforest Alliance (RA) offered Caribou a unique means of expressing its sustainability values while helping its business. It is a certification program that promotes sustainable agricultural practices (Rainforest Alliance, 2010). RA works with farmers to ensure compliance with standards that protect wildlife, wild lands, workers' rights, and local communities. More specifically, RA-certified farmers engage in practices that reduce waste, water use, soil erosion, water pollution, and damage to environmental and human health. At the same time, RA certification ensures that farms operate more efficiently, profitably, and competitively; it strives to improve working and living conditions for farmers and their families; and it encourages collaboration between farmers and conservationists to protect the biodiversity and habitats of local flora and fauna.

The RA certification process is a rigorous one that begins with an expert consultation to help farmers identify the strengths and weaknesses of their operations, as well as outline the steps needed to bring their farms into compliance with RA standards. When the farmer is ready, a team of RA specialists evaluates compliance and creates a report that is independently reviewed by a committee of outside experts. Those who pass are awarded the RA seal of approval and have permission to display it; those who do not pass may continue refining their operations and request reevaluations as desired.

As it relates to coffee farming, the "Rainforest Alliance Certified seal is a guarantee that coffee is grown on farms where forests are protected; rivers, soils, and wildlife are conserved; and workers are treated with respect, paid decent wages, properly equipped, and given access to education and medical care" (www.rainforest-alliance.org/agriculture.cfm?id=coffee). In particular, a distinction is made between "modernized" coffee farming and "agroforestry." The "modernized" approach is one in which "the sheltering forest is cleared, and coffee bushes are packed in dense hedgerows and doused with agrochemicals. These monoculture farms produce more beans, but at a tremendous environmental cost." By comparison, the "agroforestry" approach promotes "coffee forests" that serve as "bio-rich buffer zones for parks, protect watersheds, and serve as wildlife corridors. These 'coffee forests' are also important sources of firewood, construction materials, medicinal plants, fruits, flowers, honey, and other goods. Many farms in the certification program protect native forest reserves and community water supplies."

In sum, the Rainforest Alliance certification program enabled Caribou Coffee to express its core value of Commitment to Our Community in the most comprehensive way available. By supporting and encouraging its coffee farmers to become certified, the program allowed Caribou a vehicle for impacting the environmental, economic, and social sustainability of its local and global communities. This partnership has grown substantively since its inception in 2005, primarily through Caribou's commitment to increasing the percentage of its coffee supply that comes from Rainforest Alliance–certified farms. In 2007, Caribou Coffee initially committed to source 35 percent of its coffee supply from Rainforest Alliance–certified farms. However, it exceeded that goal in sourcing 49 percent of its coffee from certified farms in that same year. Realizing these objectives prompted CEO Mike Tattersfield to push the company for continued incremental progress in this domain. In 2008, 57 percent of Caribou's coffee came from certified farms, and in 2009, that percentage grew to 67 percent. Caribou exceeded its goal of 85 percent for 2010, and by the end of 2011 the company began sourcing 100 percent of its coffee from Rainforest Alliance–certified farms. Caribou celebrated the accomplishment of its 100 percent Rainforest Alliance–certification goal by communicating its achievement both internally and externally, adding "100%" to its coffee labels, and developing two new, 100 percent certified coffee blends (Starlight and Eclipse, both of which received high-quality reviews from industry experts). At the time of this writing, Caribou plans to continue celebrating this achievement on an ongoing basis.

Caribou's commitment to sourcing 100 percent Rainforest Alliance–certified coffee is unique in the industry. According to a press release from April 7, 2010 (Kaiden, 2010), Caribou Coffee is the first major coffee retailer in the U.S. to set such a goal. Chad

Trewick, Caribou's senior director of coffee and tea, described Caribou's motivations for doing so: "Caribou Coffee recognizes that a good cup of coffee goes beyond taste—it starts with farming practices that are environmentally and socially responsible. One hundred percent certification is a very aggressive goal but one that we're proud to set. We're helping ensure that our customers get premium coffee and our sourcing partners benefit environmentally, socially, and economically." Tensie Whelan, president of the Rainforest Alliance, described the implications of Caribou's initiative: "Caribou Coffee's tremendous commitment to sourcing 100 percent of their coffee from Rainforest Alliance–certified farms will benefit the lives of thousands of farmers, farm workers, and their families. It will also help protect waterways and wildlife, conserve fragile ecosystems, and promote soil health. We hope other retailers will see Caribou's example and follow suit."

Understanding Internal Sustainability Perceptions

Given the unique, comprehensive nature of its commitment to Rainforest Alliance certification, Caribou Coffee sought to understand more about perceptions of the program by its employees. Senior leadership took pride in the idealized vision they had articulated, as well as the commitments they put behind that vision. In 2007, Caribou Coffee asked BHI to begin including sustainability in its employee satisfaction survey. The survey results for the sustainability items across 2007, 2008, and 2010 are provided in Table 18.2.

These results provide insight into how a sustainability initiative like the Rainforest Alliance certification commitment has been perceived by Caribou's employees (recall that between 94 and 96 percent of survey respondents come from customer-facing store positions (that is, hourly employees or store managers)). In general, employee perceptions of such initiatives over the years have been mostly positive, with some ambivalence and a minority contingent of employees having negative reactions to Caribou's efforts. The 2007 results seem likely to have been confounded by the double-barreled inclusion of sustainability and its impact on desires to stay with Caribou. That is, it is possible that employees may have actually perceived Caribou's sustainability efforts

Table 18.2. Response Trends and Correlations for Sustainability Items Across Survey Years

	2007	2008	2010	2010	2010
	Caribou Coffee's Sustainability Efforts Have an Impact on My Decision to Stay with the Organization	*I Feel Good About the Ways We Contribute to the Community*	*I Feel Good About the Ways We Contribute to the Community*	*I Feel That Caribou Acts Responsibly in Our Global Community*	*I Feel That Caribou Coffee Is Making a Positive Difference on Our Environment*
Number of Respondents	4,761	4,079	3,937	3,937	3,937
Positive (Agree or Strongly Agree)	57%	79%	71%	69%	63%
Neutral (Neither Agree nor Disagree)	30%	15%	22%	22%	23%
Negative (Strongly Disagree or Disagree)	13%	6%	7%	9%	14%
Correlations					
Engagement	.44	.54	.42	.38	.41
Intent to Stay Longer Than One Year	.33	.35	.35	.32	.33

positively, but those positive perceptions may not have been strong enough to motivate them to stay with Caribou, given the other factors that can impact employee decisions to stay (for example, availability of other opportunities, job dissatisfaction). The results from 2008 seem to have provided a clearer picture. Perceptions of Caribou's commitment to contributing to the community were notably more positive at 79 percent, also garnering fewer ambivalent (15 percent) or negative (6 percent) responses. The survey for 2010 saw Caribou breaking the items out to evaluate sustainability perceptions in three different ways: as a function of community contributions, global community responsibility, and positive environmental impact. Across all three items in 2010, perceptions were mostly positive, although there was a notable decrease in the community contributions item relative to the results in 2008. The items related to global community responsibility and positive environmental impact were new for 2010, so their interpretation is limited by a lack of comparable baseline information from prior years. Still, it is notable that they yielded fewer positive ratings and more ambivalent or negative ratings. Taken together, the distribution of responses over the years suggests that Caribou Coffee's employees perceive the company's impact as mostly positive, although there is room for improvement, at least in employee perceptions of Caribou's sustainability actions, if not in the scope and impact of the actions themselves.

The correlation results presented in Table 18.2 offer useful insights into the impact of these perceptions on outcomes of interest to Caribou Coffee. Employee engagement was measured using an eleven-item scale averaged across items ($\alpha = .89$; sample item: "I see a clear connection between my work and the success of the organization."). Intent to Stay Longer than One Year was measured using a single item: "I intend to work for Caribou Coffee for at least the next twelve months." The pattern of consistently moderate correlations with both outcomes suggests that employees who view Caribou as acting more sustainably to communities and the environment are more likely to be engaged in their work and more likely to want to stay with the company. Although the correlational nature of the data does not allow insight into the order of causality, the potential that sustainability perceptions may have positive impacts on employee engagement and turnover intentions is promising. Such an interpretation implies that organizations that make sustainability a component of their core values and substantively act on them will have employees who are more dedicated to the company's mission over time and more focused and energetic in its pursuit.

Spreading the Word

The survey results over the years suggested to Caribou's leadership that there was room for improvement in modifying its employees' perceptions of sustainability initiatives like the Rainforest Alliance certification commitment. The results further suggested the potential for increased engagement and reduced turnover by improving employee perceptions of such efforts. In addition, Caribou recognized that it may be able to achieve a competitive edge based on the unique, values-driven nature of its commitment. Other competitors were aligned with less comprehensive sustainability programs than Caribou. As such, if Caribou was able to spread the message that its sustainability commitments would benefit the environmental, economic, and social good, their standing in the eyes of the public and their customers would likely improve. Thus, Caribou created a communication initiative about their sustainability philosophy designed to accomplish three primary objectives:

1. Drive press coverage, primarily focused on "green" media to reinforce Caribou's commitment to Rainforest Alliance and environmental causes.
2. Build awareness, education, and excitement among team members (enabling communication to guests) around the Rainforest Alliance program and an upcoming launch of two new Rainforest Alliance–certified coffees.
3. Re-emphasize Caribou's commitment to sustainability and environmentally friendly causes.

Although the above could be viewed as a marketing initiative, closer inspection reveals that it was simultaneously an intervention designed to impact employee knowledge, awareness, attitudes, and acceptance around the company's Rainforest Alliance certification initiative. In other words, it was both an external marketing campaign (per Objectives 1 and 3) and an internal human resource (HR) intervention (per Objectives 2 and 3). A review of this initiative through a marketing lens is not the intent of this chapter, but a more in-depth discussion of the above activities as viewed through an HR intervention lens is warranted.

To accomplish these objectives, Caribou engaged in a number of key activities timed around Earth Day (April 22, 2010). Caribou's activities included the following:

- *Traditional team member education.* This was deployed as an online training module for Caribou employees to complete. It was designed to ensure their understanding of RA, as well as build awareness and enthusiasm for Caribou's 100 percent commitment to RA.
- *Internal communications.* This included reinforcement of Caribou's RA and sustainability messaging through a memo from senior leadership, Caribou's internal newsletter, "Hoof Prints," and a celebration meeting with Rainforest Alliance president Tensie Whelan.
- *Traditional PR.* These included electronic press kits, press releases from Caribou and the Rainforest Alliance, the sponsorship of a breakfast event at an industry meeting, and press interviews for key executives.
- *Social media.* These included posts on Facebook and Twitter that communicated Caribou's 100 percent Rainforest Alliance commitment, announced the launch of their two new RA certified coffees, and reinforced Caribou's broader commitment to sustainability.
- *Point-of-purchase displays in stores.* These included messages about the launch of Caribou's two new RA coffees and its 100 percent commitment to RA. They also included posters highlighting Caribou's commitment to RA and how the Rainforest Alliance differs from the Fair Trade program.

Online Training Module

Caribou created an interactive, graphically appealing training module that could be completed via the Internet. It was designed primarily to impact Objective 2 on the previous page by increasing

Caribou employees' knowledge of and excitement about the company's broader sustainability agenda and its Rainforest Alliance commitment in particular. In doing so, it also served to impact Objective 3 by emphasizing Caribou's commitment to sustainability causes.

To that end, the content was delivered graphically, verbally, and with voice-over narration that guided the trainee through an interactive experience. Participants were prompted to click on various graphics or images throughout the module as a way of advancing through the content. Reading requirements were kept to a minimum, displayed mostly in single paragraph blocks or single sentence bullets. The overall result was a visually appealing training module that was informative and fun without being too taxing. A sample screenshot is provided in Figure 18.1.

Across thirteen interactive pages, the content of the module itself covered a focused range of information germane to Caribou's sustainability agenda. After a single-page introduction,

Figure 18.1. Sample Screenshot of Caribou Coffee's Sustainability Training Module

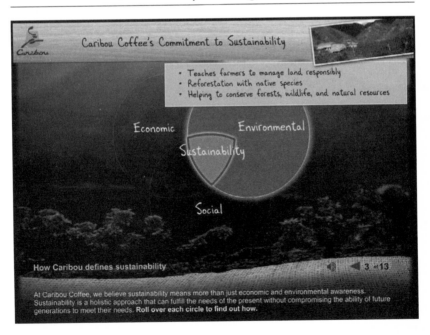

pages 2 and 3 articulated Caribou's definition of sustainability and its environmental, economic, and social components. Pages 4, 5, and 6 described Caribou's partnership with the Rainforest Alliance, providing more information about the Rainforest Alliance, as well as Caribou's history and future plans for the partnership. Pages 7 and 8 summarized the USDA Organic, Fair Trade, and Rainforest Alliance programs, and they described why Caribou deemed that the Rainforest Alliance was the right partner for its situation. Pages 9 and 10 briefly described some of Caribou's other partnerships with organizations that promote community health and prosperity (for example, Coffee Kids, Grounds for Health, Susan G. Komen for the Cure, and Project 7). Page 11 summarized the module's content and reiterated how each partnership fit into Caribou's comprehensive approach to promoting sustainability. Page 12 provided a knowledge assessment that enabled participants to take a brief quiz to test what they learned through the module. Page 13 prompted employees to consider their own sustainability goals and commit to something they felt was important. It also provided a phone number and an email address to enable employees to share the sustainability issues they felt were important with the corporate office.

Internal Communications

As described above, Caribou also put together a series of internal communications designed to build employee awareness, excitement, enthusiasm, and customer communication about the company's sustainability initiatives (Objective 2), as well as reinforce Caribou's commitment to sustainability (Objective 3).

The first of these was the March issue of Caribou's internal newsletter, "Hoof Prints." The newsletter typically contains a variety of messages about company initiatives, volunteer opportunities, benefits programs, and job openings and is distributed to Caribou employees electronically. The March issue featured a front-page article on Caribou's Rainforest Alliance commitment. The article announced Caribou's goal to sell only coffees that are 100 percent Rainforest Alliance–certified. It described the history of the partnership and Caribou's efforts in working with its coffee suppliers to encourage them to become certified. It also provided a bar graph detailing the percentages that Caribou had achieved over the years (49 percent in 2007) leading to its 100 percent commitment for 2011. The article ended with a question for readers: "Thought for the month . . . What are you 100 percent committed to?" The newsletter closed with a crossword puzzle on page 4 that included words and clues relevant to sustainability and the Rainforest Alliance.

The next internal communication came in the form of an electronic memo to employees from Caribou's CEO, Mike Tattersfield, and Chad Trewick, Caribou's senior director of coffee and tea. The memo itself was graphically designed to be visually appealing and thematically "green" (soothing color schemes, a tropical frog image). The content described the Rainforest Alliance program, as well as the many reasons and benefits for why Caribou committed to 100 percent supplier certification. It made a point to draw out Caribou's broader commitment to sustainability above and beyond the Rainforest Alliance program alone: "We realize there are several areas where we could do more and we want to! We've already formed teams to find ways we can become a more sustainable company and we'll continue to support organizations and partner with companies that share this mission. . . . we must invest in programs and products that support our local and global communities."

The following month, a celebration was held for employees in Minneapolis with Tensie Whelan, president of the Rainforest Alliance, featured as a guest speaker. Whelan typically spends most of her time in the field meeting with farmers or program supporters, but she shared that she was compelled to attend Caribou's celebration due to the "revolutionary" nature of Caribou's 100 percent commitment to Rainforest Alliance certification. The gathering was intended to be the celebration of a product launch for Caribou's two new RA-certified coffees. During the gathering, Whelan shared her perspectives on the impact of Caribou's commitment, and she participated in a town-hall-style question-and-answer session with employees as well.

The next month's issue of "Hoof Prints" contained additional content about Caribou's 100 percent Rainforest Alliance commitment. It featured an interview with Tensie Whelan that shared more information about the Rainforest Alliance, as well as discussed the history of its partnership with Caribou and its potential impact on the industry. On the same page, a variety of simple tips for "Living Green" were provided. The next page featured a message from CEO Mike Tattersfield in which he discussed Caribou's community-focused core values and challenged employees to consider how they might become more involved in their communities and connect better with customers. This message featured a photo of Tattersfield in his office standing next to his bicycle and wearing a full complement of bicycling gear. It featured the caption, "Mike T. gets ready to bike home thanks to the Jump Start the Journey Lacuna and Lakeshore Sales Contest." The copy that accompanied it was directly from Tattersfield and read as follows: "Kudos to our retail stores for selling 11,971 pounds of our new 100 percent Rainforest Alliance–certified coffees, Lacuna and Lakeshore, in just ten days! As promised, I put down the car keys and rode my bike to and from work (forty miles round trip) for five days. Thanks to great performance from our store teams, we achieved a significant bean sales goal and I personally got a high-octane jump start on my personal goal of biking or running one hundred miles a week!" The final page of the newsletter included a word-find puzzle to help reinforce sustainability-related terms.

Traditional PR, Social Media, and Store Displays

The activities described for Caribou's traditional PR, social media, and store display components of the campaign are more closely tied to the external marketing goal of driving press coverage (Objective 1). Still, they seem likely to have had some relevance and potential impact on building employee awareness, excitement, and customer communication (Objective 2), as well as reemphasizing Caribou's commitment to sustainability for employees (Objective 3). For one, employees were likely to have some exposure to the PR and social media campaigns, if not on their own, then through customer questions or comments about them. Additionally, the store displays seem likely to have had a passive impact on employees by their constant, visible presence, as well as a more active impact by stimulating customer questions and comments for employees.

Results of the Initiative

At the time of implementation, there were limited formal mechanisms in place for evaluating the results of this human resource intervention. Most of what is known is anecdotal in nature and must be qualified as such. Caribou did, however, track participation in the training module to a certain threshold. Their goal was to ensure that 80 percent or more employees participated, and two separate sources within Caribou confirmed that at least 80 percent (if not more) actually did take part in the online training. Field reports suggest that store employees were initially very excited by the messages conveyed in the campaign, and they reacted positively to the training module's format and content. Some field reports implied that employees were energized enough to talk with customers more frequently about the Rainforest Alliance Initiative.

Interestingly, Trewick shared that there was some slippage in the reported gains made by the intervention. An independent consulting partner of Caribou Coffee reported that employees in stores he visited were not as engaged by or communicating about the Rainforest Alliance commitment as expected a couple of months after the intervention. Trewick reported converging observations of his own, sharing that energy seemed to have waned after a short-term increase. He offered that some of this reduced enthusiasm may have arisen from having built greater employee awareness about sustainability issues through the intervention. Although reactions to the Rainforest Alliance commitment were not negative, Chad shared that employees were now more vocal about the day-to-day sustainability improvements they felt were needed. The Rainforest Alliance Initiative is rooted in coffee sourcing and procurement, which is many steps removed from the majority of Caribou's employees' daily experience in the stores. Comparatively, they see waste at the store level on a daily basis (trash volumes, energy usage, container and coffee waste) that is more salient and influential on their perceptions, especially once they have been primed to consider Caribou's environmental impacts. In short, employees may view Caribou as not doing enough to minimize its environmental footprint, and now that they have been provided signals that leadership is keenly interested in their perspectives on sustainability, they may be taking stronger positions about what they see as most important. Caribou does offer store-level recycling options in select stores and municipalities, and it has implemented a program to reduce energy usage through more energy-efficient lighting. Still, this may be a partial explanation for the greater ambivalence present in 2010's sustainability perceptions (see Table 18.2 presented earlier). Although the survey data were collected prior to this human resource intervention, employees may have already been noticing store-level environmental impacts and feeling a certain disconnect between Caribou's ongoing investment in the Rainforest Alliance program versus the day-to-day opportunities presented in their stores to further reduce Caribou's environmental impact.

Discussion and Integration of Observations

Although still quite small, there is a growing literature about organizational sustainability initiatives that is useful for placing Caribou Coffee's efforts into a broader context. This section will integrate Caribou's activities within recent scholarship on "green" efforts, as well as offer some perspectives based on additional analyses of the 2010 survey data presented previously.

Why Push for Sustainability?

What drives Caribou to pursue sustainability in their more complex formulation? Bansal and Roth's (2000) scholarship on the motives that prompt organizations to "go green" is helpful in classifying the primary drivers of Caribou's sustainability agenda. Bansal and Roth found three primary drivers for going green: (1) *competitiveness* (that is, going green to gain an edge against competitors); (2) *legitimation* (that is, going green to stay in compliance with regulations and avoid fines, penalties, and negative public perceptions); and (3) *ecological responsibility* (that is, going green because it's the right thing to do).

Descriptively speaking, Caribou's primary motive for sustainability appears to be ecological responsibility with some additional aspects of competitiveness. In terms of a legitimation motive, there are no industry requirements or legislative mandates requiring Caribou Coffee to pursue a sustainability program (as opposed to, say, industrial manufacturing companies, which are often more heavily regulated and monitored with regard to their environmental impact).

For Caribou, the competitiveness motive does not seem to be a primary driver based on Bansal and Roth's categorizations. If Caribou's motives were purely competitive, it could easily adopt a less comprehensive program (such as the USDA Organic or Fair Trade, embraced by some competitors) as a way of keeping pace with its competition. Aspects of a competitiveness motive do emerge, however, in Caribou's desire to make sure the public is aware of its commitment to Rainforest Alliance certification. It also stems from Caribou's desire to keep its business competitive by seeking a means to ensure the stability and consistency of its coffee supply and coffee suppliers. Still, what emerges from most of the messages Caribou sends about its Rainforest Alliance commitment is that it is has embarked on this journey because it is the right thing to do (ecological responsibility motive). The training modules, memos, and newsletters make frequent mention of the social benefits of Caribou's sustainability goals, the company's desire to change the world for the better, and its passion for taking care of the planet. This message appears to resonate given Caribou's long-standing reputation for being interested in sustainability. That is, it is not an about-face from a previously poor history with green interests, nor does it come across as an inauthentic reaction to a perceived trend. Rather, it fits well into Caribou's organizational DNA.

Ensuring a Positive Impact for Sustainability Programs

Harris and Crane (2002) conducted a study that shed light on the means by which organizations are able to go green, as well as the barriers they may face in doing so. Their study was based on a series of in-depth interviews the authors conducted with managers in various organizations. It provides vivid examples of the pitfalls that can emerge when trying to make a company greener. In particular, it offers a useful framework for evaluating Caribou's sustainability messaging and program implementations. Harris and Crane's work also yields recommendations that can facilitate the success of sustainability initiatives for a variety of organizations, including Caribou Coffee.

Messaging Recommendations and Observations

- *Make it clear that sustainability initiatives are fully supported by senior leadership.* Caribou appears to have done a nice job of this already, based on the survey results and its Rainforest Alliance communications. Part of this messaging includes reiterating that sustainability is not just a fad, but has been an enduring facet of Caribou's identity and core product.
- *Link organizational performance to sustainability issues.* A good example of this in Caribou's case is their sharing the message that Rainforest Alliance–certified coffee farmers will be more stable, consistent suppliers over time, which will help Caribou's supply chain be more predictable and profitable as a result. To more vividly illustrate this to employees, Caribou uses a specific coffee farming family as an example.
- *Emphasize long-term outcomes.* The positive impacts of sustainability initiatives happen across a longer time span than often more pressing business outcomes. As evidenced by this communication approach, Caribou has started to share frequent, consistent messages that remind employees that Caribou is about more than this quarter's profits alone, which seems to help its people keep perspective on the company's mission and core values.
- *Harness the power of symbols.* The inclusion of Mike Tattersfield's bicycling challenge in "Hoof Prints" is a good example of Caribou's use of symbolic gestures to reinforce the importance of sustainability from the top down.
- *Translate initiatives into actionable behaviors for employees.* It is common for lower-level employees to bring a more fragmented, skeptical view of idealized senior leadership directives. Thus, it is important to directly translate what initiatives mean to them in terms of their day-to-day behaviors. Caribou appears to offer some of this (for example, its "Living Green" tips in its May 2010 newsletter), but the company would be well-served by providing more

specific behavioral guidance and objectives within its
training modules.

Implementation Recommendations and Observations

- *Expect minor changes, not major impacts.* Making a company
more sustainable is a slow and painstaking cultural change,
so it is advisable to set modest, incremental expectations
internally and externally. The steady rise in Rainforest
Alliance sourcing percentage goals over the years is a good
example of Caribou's setting reasonable targets over an
extended period of time.
- *Make space for passionate individuals to carry
initiatives.* Sustainability initiatives seem to be well-served
when they have the feel of grassroots emergence. Allowing
enthusiastic insiders to drive aspects of the initiatives helps
employees link a potentially charismatic personality with what
could otherwise be a dry company directive. Caribou Coffee
benefits from having a CEO who is strongly inclined to
pursue a sustainability agenda, but the company still makes
space for passionate environmental advocates like Chad
Trewick to take leadership positions with its sustainability
programs.
- *Allow for geographic variations in sustainability
practices.* Surviving a winter in Minneapolis will yield uniquely
different sustainability ideas than making it through an
Atlanta summer. Caribou can likely better capitalize on
enthusiastic local employees by soliciting and empowering
them to devise their own sustainability approaches based on a
more intimate knowledge of their local environments.
- *Analyze the organization for competing business values.* It is
important to make sure competing interests have been
identified and addressed before launching sustainability
efforts. For instance, Caribou's stores are a mix of company-
owned and franchised locations. If noble, well-intentioned
sustainability initiatives from senior corporate leadership
result in increased costs and profit reductions to franchisees,
the programs are likely to falter. (Note that this issue was not
observed during this case study; it is offered solely for
illustrative purposes.)

Beyond Harris and Crane's (2002) ideas, other perspectives have recently emerged in I-O psychology. In general, there is a growing acknowledgement that green efforts must be a "team sport" that draws in people from a variety of company functions (DuBois & DuBois, 2010). Sustainability task forces made up of cross-functional experts seem to be growing in popularity as a way of facilitating a smoother conception and rollout of green efforts. In its early stages, the leadership team that drives Caribou's sustainability initiatives was cross-functional in nature (including its CEO, leaders from the coffee sourcing function, and independent consultants), but it was not comprehensive across all of the organization's functions. At the time of this writing, however, Caribou shared that the makeup of this team was evolving to be more representative across its business functions. Bringing together a diverse, functionally representative team helps to ensure that programs are well-thought-through so they don't have negative impacts on important parts of the business. It also helps to garner buy-in across functions to ensure that the initiatives aren't perceived as "someone else's agenda."

In particular, human resource professionals are especially important to involve in sustainability initiatives. There is a general trend to leave HR out of such processes, since most green initiatives rest within operational domains (DuBois & DuBois, 2010). Still, once the vision and values of such initiatives are communicated, most require some form of attitude and/or behavioral change on the part of employees. With its capabilities for influencing employee behavior through recruiting, hiring, onboarding, training, and performance appraisal, HR should be poised to contribute expertise that helps ensure the initiatives conceived by senior leadership are translated into actions taken by Caribou's people. Caribou has shared that it plans to include HR in these initiatives moving forward.

Two immediate examples from this case study emerge as ways that HR expertise and best practices could improve Caribou's sustainability initiatives. These are improvements that Caribou owns and appreciates, as they are committed to continuously developing these programs from "scrappy," grassroots efforts with limited resources into more fully realized initiatives with widespread organizational support. The first has to do with the training module Caribou created to inform employees about its sustainability agenda. The module itself was laudable. It was well-organized, visually appealing, interactive, easy to process, and engaging. Further, it helped move the user from passive information absorption to more active cognitive processing using the quiz and personal reflection prompts at the end (incidentally, this tactic was also employed in the newsletters through the inclusion of knowledge-reinforcing games and puzzles). In short, it effectively incorporated multiple best practices for virtual training design.

Where HR could have benefitted this effort, however, was in the broader design of the training intervention and its subsequent evaluation. For instance, consider the objective of building awareness, education, and excitement about sustainability that would enable guest communication. For one, each element of this objective could be broken out into measurable behavioral goals with different training approaches. The "education" component could be assessed by a test of declarative knowledge, whereas the guest communication component could be trained and assessed using role-playing exercises focused on sharing information about the Rainforest Alliance commitment accurately and compellingly.

On the other side of the training initiative, HR expertise and best practices could have put in place a mechanism for measuring the intervention's outcomes, perhaps grounded in Kirkpatrick's *reactions, learning, behavior,* and *results* framework (Kirkpatrick, 1994). Put simply, taking a more deliberate approach to this initiative with HR best practices in mind would increase the likelihood of more enduring attitude and behavioral changes for Caribou's employees. Doing so would also enable Caribou's leadership team to learn from and modify similar interventions over time based on a more robust approach to understanding the results of their training efforts.

The second way that HR expertise and best practices stand to benefit Caribou is through selection practices that improve the likelihood that employees will be engaged by sustainability initiatives in the first place. Similar to findings from the literature on job satisfaction, engagement is partially state-based and partially trait-based. That is, some people are naturally more inclined to

Table 18.3. Correlations from 2010 Survey Data

Variables	No. of Items	N	Mean	SD	α	1	2	3	4	5	6
1. Engageability index	15	3,777	3.8	0.7	.79						
2. Community item	1	3,953	3.9	0.9	–	.26					
3. Global item	1	3,953	3.8	1.0	–	.24	.69				
4. Environment item	1	3,953	3.7	1.1	–	.23	.67	.74			
5. Sustainability perceptions	3	3,953	3.8	0.9	.87	.27	.87	.90	.91		
6. Engagement index	11	3,953	3.9	0.7	.89	.27	.42	.38	.41	.45	
7. Intent to stay	1	3,953	4.0	1.1	–	.24	.35	.32	.33	.37	.37

be engaged by a given environment than others. BHI created a fifteen-item measure of this trait-based *engageability* that draws on an individual's confidence, self-efficacy, self-esteem, locus of control, people relations, and optimism ($\alpha = .79$; sample item: "I feel fully capable of completing any task ahead of me"). This measure was included with the other survey data in 2010 to better understand the role that engageability plays in engagement and other outcomes of interest to Caribou. Table 18.3 displays the intercorrelations between engageability, sustainability perceptions, engagement, and one's intent to stay with Caribou longer than one year. Based on the high intercorrelations among the individual sustainability items (variables 2, 3, and 4; $r = .69$, .67, and .74, respectively), a composite score for "sustainability perceptions" was created ($\alpha = .87$).

The data in Table 18.3 demonstrate that engageability, a trait-based construct, is a component of but not redundant with engagement, which is a function of the interaction of an individual with his or her environment ($r = .27$). Further, the data suggest that sustainability perceptions are related to employee engagement ($r = .45$) and employee intentions to stay with the company ($r = .37$). Thus, we wondered what portion of the variance in engagement and intentions to stay could be accounted for by the combination of engageability and sustainability perceptions. Put differently, would those who were more naturally engageable be more engaged and want to stay with the company longer if they felt more positively about Caribou's sustainability efforts?

To test this question, we split both the engageability data and the sustainability perceptions data into the Top 33 percent and Bottom 33 percent of respondents. This helped ensure our analyses compared only those groups who were most/least engageable or most positive/negative in their perceptions of Caribou's sustainability efforts. Given the large overall sample sizes, these splits still left us with a reasonable sample size for each subgroup (N's ranged from 312 to 1,064). ANOVA results revealed statistically significant main and interaction effects when engagement was the dependent variable ($F = 4.635$; $p < .05$), as well as when intent to stay longer than one year was the dependent variable ($F = 8.237$; $p < .01$).

Figures 18.2 and 18.3 illustrate the nature of the relationships that emerged from the data. Note that a score of 3 on

Figure 18.2. Effect of Engageability and Sustainability Perceptions on Engagement

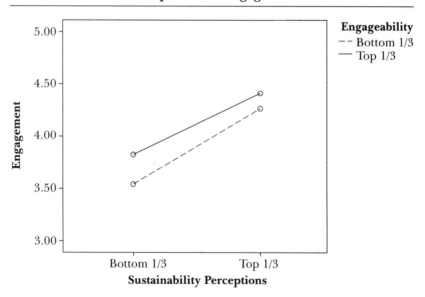

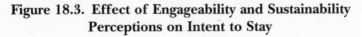

**Figure 18.3. Effect of Engageability and Sustainability
Perceptions on Intent to Stay**

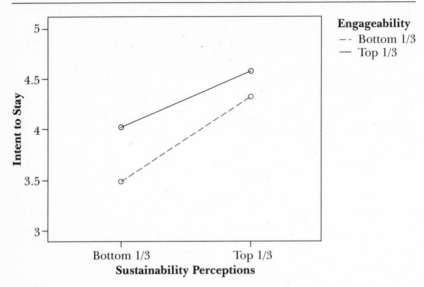

Engagement and Intent to Stay is equivalent to ambivalence (that is, a rating of "neither agree nor disagree"). By comparison, a score of 4 on Engagement and Intent to Stay is more positive (a rating of "Agree"). There is a main effect that shows that employees who see Caribou Coffee as a company that contributes to its local communities, acts responsibly on a global scale, and makes a positive difference on the environment (higher sustainability perceptions) are more engaged ($d = .92$; Figure 18.2). They are also more likely to stay with the company longer than one year ($d = .63$; Figure 18.3). Engageability plays an interactive role in these results, however. Employees who are by nature more engageable are more likely to be engaged by Caribou's sustainability efforts ($d = .10$; Figure 18.2). They are also more likely to stay with the company longer than one year compared to those who are less engageable ($d = .13$; Figure 18.3).

Thus, there are at least two avenues (stronger training design and revised selection practices) in which HR expertise and best practices could improve Caribou's likelihood of realizing greater impact from its noteworthy sustainability efforts. These analyses provide empirical support for the relatively unique idea of incorporating sustainability into employee selection practices. Perhaps because the greening of organizations is a fairly new idea, it seems that many organizations approach such efforts as an intervention to be carried out on the workforce as it currently exists (that is, training). The results we observed suggest that organizations can be more proactive in the future by including characteristics (for example, engageability, other attitudes, and relevant personality traits) that will facilitate the acceptance and adoption of sustainability initiatives in their selection processes.

More generally, it stands to reason that HR expertise and best practices could facilitate the implementation and adoption of sustainability initiatives across the talent management spectrum. For example, Bauer and Aiman-Smith (1996) describe research demonstrating that recruiting brochures highlighting environmentally friendly company policies can improve applicant reactions and their likelihood of accepting a job offer with the company. No doubt sustainability behaviors and objectives could also be woven into performance appraisals and promotions criteria as well. In sum, enabling HR professionals to contribute their capabilities to sustainability task forces will be an important means for ensuring the future success of such initiatives.

Summary and Conclusions

Caribou Coffee has long pursued the success and growth of its business while seeking to minimize its environmental impact. A certain eco-friendliness has always been a part of Caribou's identity, but the company renewed its commitment to a comprehensive approach to sustainability more recently. Through partnerships with sustainability-minded organizations like the Rainforest Alliance, Caribou is able to better realize its core values rooted in environmental and community welfare. These partnerships also provide Caribou with a competitive edge based on their uniqueness in the industry and the positive public perceptions they foster.

As described in this case study, Caribou has done commendable work in spreading the word about its sustainability initiatives. Further, the company has taken important measures to help promote knowledge and enthusiasm for such initiatives in its own workforce. A constructive critique of Caribou's efforts was offered based on academic scholarship and empirical data analyses. The work by Bansal and Roth (2000) provides a useful framework for analyzing one's organizational motives for going green in the first place. In addition, many of the findings reported by Harris and Crane (2002) are likely to benefit a variety of organizations that desire to go green. They will certainly benefit Caribou as it continues to revise and improve its efforts in this domain. Some key takeaways for other organizations embarking on their own sustainability initiatives are

- Ensure that sustainability efforts are led by a representative team of cross-functional experts.
- Include human resource professionals, who can bring critical expertise and best practices focused on people's attitudes, motivations, and behaviors.
- Explore and articulate the organization's motivations for going green.
- Think critically about the potential barriers that may inhibit sustainability efforts and attitudes, and then outline approaches that will minimize or negate their impact.
- Incorporate sustainability initiatives across the talent management spectrum, and consider including it as early on as recruiting and selection processes to attract people to the organization who will be more readily engaged by such efforts.

We believe that taking a more deliberate and proactive approach in these ways will facilitate the effective conception and execution of future sustainability initiatives for a wide variety of organizations.

References

Bansal, P., & Roth, K. (2000). Why companies go green: A model of ecological responsiveness. *Academy of Management Journal, 43*, 717–736.

Bauer, T. N., & Aiman-Smith, L. (1996). Green career choices: The influence of ecological stance on recruiting. *Journal of Business and Psychology, 10*, 445–458.

Campbell, J. E., & Campbell, D. E. (2005). Eco-I-O psychology? Expanding our goals to include sustainability. *The Industrial-Organizational Psychologist, 43*, 23–28.

Caribou Coffee. (2010). Statement on corporate website. Retrieved from www.cariboucoffee.com/page/1/company-info.jsp.

DuBois, C. L. Z., & DuBois, D. A. (2010). A call for I-O leadership in "going green." *The Industrial-Organizational Psychologist, 48*, 12–19.

Harris, L. C., & Crane, A. (2002). The greening of organizational culture: Management views on the depth, degree, and diffusion of change. *Journal of Organizational Change Management, 15*, 214–236.

Huffman, A. H., Watrous-Rodriguez, K. M., Henning, J. B., & Berry, J. (2009). "Working" through environmental issues: The role of the I-O psychologist. *The Industrial-Organizational Psychologist, 47*, 27–35.

Kaiden, E. (2010). Caribou Coffee first in U.S. with only sustainable coffee. Retrieved from http://phx.corporate-ir.net/phoenix.zhtml ?c=192910&p=irol-news.

Kirkpatrick, D. L. (1994). *Evaluating training programs: The four levels.* San Francisco: Berrett-Koehler.

Rainforest Alliance. (2010). Statement on organization's website. Retrieved from www.rainforest-alliance.org/agriculture.cfm?id =main.

Part Four

Future Directions

Part Four concludes this volume by asking readers to consider the implications of the preceding chapters for professionals and scholars working in the broad arena of human resource management.

Chapter 19, "Implications for HR and OD Professionals in the Future: Can I-O Principles and Practices Contribute to the Achievement of Corporate Environmental Sustainability?" by Leaetta Hough and Robert Muschewske presents thoughts about the new knowledge and skills that will be needed by I-O psychologists involved in corporate environmental initiatives and ideas for how we can ensure that our profession is prepared for the future opportunities and demands they will face.

Finally, Chapter 20, "Building Empirical Foundations to Inform the Future Practice of Environmental Sustainability" by Susan Jackson, describes the types of additional empirical evidence that would be useful for developing the science and practice of HRM in environmentally sustainable organizations. As this chapter makes clear, our progress toward improved environmental sustainability will be enhanced by collaborations that bring together the unique skills and insights of a wide range of scholars and practitioners.

CHAPTER NINETEEN

Implications for HR and OD Professionals in the Future

Can I-O Principles and Practices Contribute to the Achievement of Corporate Environmental Sustainability?

Leaetta M. Hough
and Robert C. Muschewske

Without question, the answer is a resounding "yes." During the past several decades, academics and practitioners in industrial and organizational (I-O) psychology have made tremendous advances in understanding the dynamics of leadership, managing organizational change, and implementing programs and systems that affect the behavior and performance of individuals, teams, and organizations. Looking beyond the current level of knowledge, we need to ask ourselves: What innovations in I-O psychology principles and practices will be important as organizations embrace corporate environmental sustainability? What new competencies do I-O academics and practitioners need to help organizations embrace and achieve this new focus?

Several of the chapters in this book illustrate how I-O principles and practices already have been instrumental in helping organizations and their members achieve smaller environmental footprints in the service of effective organizational performance. Leadership, education, assessment, recognition, and reinforcement—all are important. The programs and systems that I-O psychologists and practitioners design and implement to address organizational human resource management functions such as recruitment, selection, training, performance management, compensation, reward, and compensation systems are all central tools for organizational change. These are the toolkits that have been brought to bear to effect culture and organizational change in the past and can do so in the future. Several chapters in this book deal specifically with developing and implementing such systems to enhance environmental sustainability.

An excellent example is Chapter 10 by Van Velsor and Quinn, who describe the role of leadership in creating environmentally responsible organizations. They do an excellent job of describing many of the characteristics of leadership that have been derived from years of I-O practice and research in this critical area. They try to make the case that leadership for environmental sustainability is different from traditional leadership in that it "means producing leadership . . . in a context of significant novelty and complexity characterized by new and expanded value propositions, multi-faceted standards of success, shifting social contracts, a wide and diverse set of stakeholders with often competing interests, and multi-sector collaborations." They state that these are "challenges typically not dealt with in traditional organizational leadership frameworks." We disagree. These challenges and leadership characteristics seem to be very similar, if not identical, to the challenges faced by current business leaders in achieving a broad spectrum of key organizational change objectives. Van Velsor and Quinn also suggest that the three critical leadership tasks of setting direction, creating alignment, and building commitment for achieving environmental sustainability objectives are different from building commitment for other organizational objectives. Again, we disagree. We do, however, fully support the greater part of their chapter that nicely describes "Leadership Practices That Work." That these principles and practices are presented in the context of how to achieve corporate environmental sustainability objectives does not detract from their power in achieving other organizational objectives. The fact that these principles and practices can be utilized in achieving corporate environmental sustainability goals is a reminder to I-O psychologists that they may have important contributions to make to organizational initiatives in this area.

Many of the chapters in the book bring these leadership and organizational change practices to life by demonstrating how they have helped numerous organizations achieve environmental sustainability objectives. Johnson and Miller, in a fine case study presented in Chapter 14, describe how Aveda Corporation has achieved success since 1978 with an emphasis on environmental leadership that is "integral to the business success." The stated mission of Aveda is as follows: "Our mission at Aveda is to care for the world we live in, from the products we make to the ways in which we give back to society. At Aveda, we strive to set an example for environmental leadership and responsibility, not just in the world of beauty, but around the world."

Acquired in 1997, Aveda Corporation is now a wholly owned subsidiary of Estée Lauder Companies. It would be helpful to have current quantitative data describing Aveda's "business success," but that is difficult to obtain given how Estée Lauder reports its financial results. We take them at their word that their business model has led to "business success" as defined by accepted financial standards.

Johnson and Miller state that the "mission . . . informs all aspects of the company's business model, including decisions regarding vendors with whom it does business, the ingredients used in its products, partnerships with local and indigenous communities, as well as progressive HR initiatives that aim to achieve mission-alignment among the company's workforce." The case study they present focuses on the company's HR program that "addresses both stable and trainable employee capabilities through recruitment, selection, training, and performance management." The HR programs definitely appear to be based on practices developed on solid I-O principles.

It is exactly these principles and practices that are highlighted in several chapters that are being utilized by companies to change their behavior and their culture to bring about greater environmental sustainability. What new I-O principles and practices are needed? Our point of view is simply that more organizations need to bring existing principles and practices to bear to create greater environmental sustainability.

Industrial and organizational psychology practitioners are often brought into organizations to help address a variety of issues. The specific issues may change, but the principles do not. Principles improve as a result of building knowledge about individual and organizational behavior, and although greater knowledge might be developed while working in the context of an organization that embraces environmental sustainability, it might just as well have been developed in service of any other organizational objective. Such organizational objectives have included productivity, performance, adaptability, and innovation, among others. These are criterion domains that have benefited from I-O psychology's unique knowledge, tools, and practices. Likewise, it is building more knowledge (better science and better practice) in general that will increase I-O's ability to have greater impact in the area of environmental sustainability. Environmental sustainability is simply another criterion domain in which the science and practice of I-O psychology are relevant.

We must pause to address an issue that concerned us as we read the chapters in this book. Mesmer-Magnus, Viswesvaran, and Wiernik (Chapter 7) correctly state that "the objective of organizations involves generating value for their stakeholders." They are indeed correct. Increasing stakeholder value—or to use the current buzzword, corporate sustainability—requires leaders and organizations to achieve both short- and long-term financial success. Corporate sustainability or the creation of shareholder value involves the development and implementation of business strategies that achieve competitive advantage by embracing opportunities and managing risks derived from economic, environmental, and social developments. Each of these three is critical to corporate sustainability or the creation of shareholder value. The concern we noted above comes from our sense that a number of the chapter authors have elevated environmental sustainability to a preeminent position or objective over corporate sustainability or the creation of shareholder value. Such cannot be the case. Corporate sustainability or the creation of long-term shareholder value can only be achieved when environmental sustainability objectives, along with economic and social objectives, are achieved. A primary focus on environmental sustainability objectives will not necessarily lead to corporate sustainability or the creation of shareholder value.

We need to be cognizant of the importance of a long-term focus on sustainability, both environmental and financial. We also need to acknowledge our values and political activism as distinct from scientific principles and scientific discoveries. Clearly, I-O can bring to bear expertise to create a better, more sustainable environment. This book highlights just how much the field of I-O can do to further that goal. Can we do more? Yes, of course. What more do we need to know to do better?

Let's return to a case study. According to Johnson and Miller (Chapter 14), environmental sustainability is embedded in Aveda's HR management programs, including recruitment, selection, employee orientation, training, performance appraisal, compensation, and awards. Environmental sustainability activities and language touch virtually all of Aveda's physical and human resource management. Our point though is that, in developing the HR management programs to highlight environmental sustainability, no new I-O principles or practices are needed. For example, in addition to the efforts described in Chapter 14, Aveda has developed a new proprietary, standardized, multi-dimensional assessment tool specifically designed to assess "environmental attitudes, attributes, and sustainability-relevant traits" that have been shown to relate to environmental responsibility at the company (Conseil, 2010). Although no new measurement strategies were utilized and no new statistics were invented to analyze the data, a useful test was added to the catalog of psychological measures. As the lead author of this chapter has repeatedly demonstrated, prediction of different criteria (such as technical proficiency, training success, irresponsible behavior, sales effectiveness, combat effectiveness, teamwork, and creativity) call for different sets of predictor constructs (Hough, 1992). It appears that the criterion of employees' environmental sustainability performance was modeled and matched to appropriate individual differences-based predictors in this way. The new application involves the specification of environmental sustainability predictors for employee selection. This is good I-O science and practice applied to a new criterion domain.

The beauty of applying scientific principles is that they can be applied regardless of the criterion domain studied and context in which they take place. Environmental sustainability provides a new context to organizational behavior. Industrial and organizational psychology science and practice can successfully be applied to influence employee behaviors targeted at environmental sustainability, a new criterion domain for our field.

Similarly, any time that a new training or educational program is developed, content is needed. Yes, new content is needed to train people to impart environmental sustainability knowledge and skills, but that is true for all training programs designed to develop any new skill or knowledge. New content is needed, but principles of learning and training need not be new. I-O psychology is not about specific content for HR programs. It is about bringing to bear principles from many psychological disciplines, to name a few—social psychology, developmental psychology, differential psychology, experimental psychology, measurement and statistics, learning—to address real-life issues and problems. I-O psychology's training interventions draw from all of these areas to bring about change in different behavioral domains, such as teamwork, interpersonal interactions, and stress management, to name a few. Training programs for environmental sustainability constitute an addition to such approaches.

Principles of leadership are also relevant regardless of the context. Yes, situations and contexts can moderate relationships between independent variables and dependent variables, but environmental sustainability is not likely a moderating variable. Regardless of the specific context in which advances in understanding leadership are made, the principles generalize. That is the beauty of useful principles—they generalize.

Let us examine the groundbreaking work by Ones and Dilchert described in Chapter 5 that helps us understand the specific behaviors leaders and organizations need to reinforce and that need to be embedded in organizational change efforts to achieve environmental sustainability. Ones and Dilchert used a proven technique, critical incident methodology (Flanagan, 1954; Smith & Kendall, 1963), to identify the behaviors and dimensions underlying the behaviors. Although no new principles or practices were involved in advancing the knowledge base specific to elucidating green behavior, the specific content is new and important, as it specifies a new criterion domain.

Not so long ago the mantra was rapid change—the only thing we were confident of was that things would change. Organizations needed to understand "adaptability," what it meant as a criterion or dependent variable. Organizations needed to understand it so they could recruit, hire, and train people to adapt to the rapid change. Pulakos and her colleagues (Pulakos, Arad, Donovan, & Plamondon, 2000; Pulakos, Schmitt, Dorsey, Arad, Hedge, & Borman, 2002) used critical incident methodology to define the behaviors and dimensionality of adaptability. Again, I-O science and practice advanced the knowledge base and helped organizations deal with rapid change, but it did not require new I-O principles or practices.

An area to which I-O psychology lays claim is job or work analysis, an area that no chapter addressed, at least not in any depth. Is this an area in which new knowledge is needed to advance I-O's impact on an organization's achieving environmental sustainability? Let us examine the evidence.

In an audaciously titled presentation, "How Job Analysis Can Help Save the Environment," Anderson, Giumetti, and Harvey (2009) propose that to change the environmental impact of work we need to describe it. They suggest the impacts of interest to measure are natural resources, water footprint, electricity footprint, other energy resources footprint, greenhouse gas emissions, solid waste (non-hazardous), hazardous wastes, and air pollutants. They suggest (a) gathering facilities data and production data; (b) calculating an environmental impact; and (c) adding the information to the O*NET database. This would provide for a baseline against which employers could compare their jobs with the national average. Essentially, they suggest a strategy that allows employers to conduct an audit of their environmental impact through job analysis. This is innovative, but it does not require any advance in I-O science or its methodologies to implement. It does suggest a different practice for using I-O principles and methods.

The National Center for O*NET Development used job/work analysis methods to review and update the occupations in the O*NET system for describing work and worker requirements to address the greening of the world of work (Dierdorff, Norton, Drewes, Kroustalis, Rivkin, & Lewis, 2009). They identified several new and emerging occupations as well as changes in some existing occupations. New I-O psychology principles and practices were unnecessary. Instead, they used tried and proven techniques to revise the database and improve the description of work and worker requirements.

This again illustrates our main point. Existing I-O principles and practices can, indeed, contribute to the achievement of corporate environmental sustainability. The case studies presented in this book are a testament to the power of these capabilities in achieving environmental sustainability objectives in a wide variety of settings. Our science and practice make advances every day, and they should be used to enhance environmental sustainability. Likewise, any advances that occur as I-O psychologists engage in enhancing environmental sustainability should be applied elsewhere.

At the beginning of this chapter we raised an important question: "What innovations in I-O psychology principles and practices will be important as organizations embrace corporate environmental sustainability?" Our sense is that major innovations leading to increased levels of environmental sustainability will not come from the field of I-O psychology per se. Rather, they will come from an engaged and committed workforce responding to a compelling vision communicated by business leaders that new ways to achieve shareholder value through improved environmental sustainability methodologies must be found. Ambec and Lanoie, in their excellent chapter (Chapter 2), identify five ways that companies can gain competitive advantage through environmental sustainability efforts. Those strategies need to be amplified and new ones identified. In that process, the principles and practices of I-O psychology are strategically important. Environmental sustainability is a new frontier in which the principles and practices of I-O psychology can help organizations and their leaders succeed.

References

Anderson, L. E., Giumetti, G. W., & Harvey, J. L. (2009, April). How job analysis can help save the environment. Paper presented at the 24th Annual Convention of the Society for Industrial and Organizational Psychology, New Orleans, Louisiana.

Conseil, D. (2010, November). *Aveda—from profitable sufficiency to profitable sufficiencies.* Keynote address at the annual international conference on business and sustainability, Portland State University, Portland, Oregon. Retrieved February 1, 2012, from http://www.sba.pdx.edu/sustainabilityconference10/presentations/Dominique%20Conseil%20110410.pdf

Dierdorff, E. C., Norton, J. J., Drewes, D. W., Kroustalis, C. M., Rivkin, D., & Lewis, P. (2009). *Greening of the world of work: Implications for O*NET®-SOC and new and emerging occupations.* Raleigh, NC: National Center for O*NET Development.

Flanagan, J. C. (1954). The critical incident technique. *Psychological Bulletin, 51,* 327–358.

Hough, L. M. (1992). The "big five" personality variables—construct confusion: Description versus prediction. *Human Performance, 5,* 139–155.

Pulakos, E. D., Arad, S., Donovan, M. A., & Plamondon, K. E. (2002). Adaptability in the workplace: Development of a taxonomy of adaptive performance. *Journal of Applied Psychology, 85,* 612–624.

Pulakos, E. D., Schmitt, N., Dorsey, D. W., Arad, S., Hedge, J. W., & Borman, W. C. (2002). Predicting adaptive performance: Further tests of a model of adaptability. *Human Performance, 15,* 299–324.

Smith, P. C., & Kendall, L. M. (1963). Retranslation of expectations: An approach to the construction of unambiguous anchors for rating scales. *Journal of Applied Psychology, 47,* 149–155.

CHAPTER TWENTY

Building Empirical Foundations to Inform the Future Practice of Environmental Sustainability

Susan E. Jackson

To successfully tackle the challenge of achieving environmental sustainability, employers must improve their understanding of how people feel and think about their environmental responsibilities. To date, few human resource (HR) scholars or practitioners are focused on this important issue (Huffman, Watrous-Rodriguez, Henning, & Berry, 2009; Jackson & Seo, 2010; Renwick, Redman, & Maguire, 2008).

Addressing the immediate needs of organizations requires research that provides insights about how to effectively use specific human resource management (HRM) and human resource development (HRD) practices—staffing, training, individual and organizational development, performance measurement and feedback, rewards and recognition, and change management—to implement environmental sustainability. In this chapter, the term *workforce management* is used to refer to the full array of available HRM and HRD tools. Mounting pressure to advance our understanding of environmental sustainability creates new opportunities for problem-focused workforce management research that yields new insights and knowledge for managers to apply as they strive toward improved environmental sustainability.

A Strategic Perspective as the Starting Point

To maximize the practical usefulness of future research, HR scholars may find it useful to adopt a strategic perspective as a means for attracting the support of managers (for a recent overview of this large body of work, see Jackson, Schuler, Lepak, & Tarique, 2012). Two noteworthy assumptions of the strategic HR perspective are

1. Effective workforce management practices are aligned with the business strategy and organization context.
2. Effective workforce management practices are aligned to form a coherent and internally consistent system.

Aligning Environmental Initiatives with Business Strategy and Organizational Context

In the past, the strategic perspective has emphasized the importance of monetary costs and monetary returns, thereby elevating the interests of shareholders and other owners when evaluating the effectiveness of workplace management practices. Going forward, the traditional focus on financial performance measures is likely to broaden as firms recognize that long-term survival depends on the ability to successfully address a variety of environmental threats and leverage new opportunities for growing their businesses. Increasingly, environmental performance metrics are gaining legitimacy among investors, corporate boards, regulators, and consumers as bottom-line indicators of organizational performance.

The array of ecological performance metrics used by organizations includes those used to address government regulations and ensure compliance with industry standards, those assessed by third parties for verification and public reporting, and those most closely watched by consumers and the general public. In addition, as described by Ones and Dilchert (Chapter 5, this volume), rapid advances are being made in the development of behavioral measures to assess the environmental performance of individuals. The availability of these metrics, which address multiple levels of analysis, provide a foundation for building the behavioral cause-and-effect models needed to guide the design of HR systems that are tailored to environmental goals.

The environmental practices that are most effective in a particular firm may depend on the firm's particular reasons and strategic plan for achieving environmental sustainability (Ambec & Lanoie, Chapter 2, this volume). Successful strategy implementation requires an understanding of the role requirements of HR professionals (Staffelbach, Brugger & Bäbler, Chapter 3, this volume) and the appropriate use of workplace practices that address the firm's strategic imperatives. Successful organizational change also involves recognizing and taking into account an organization's current state. For firms that are in the early stages of pursuing environmental sustainability, employee training and reliance on volunteer environmental champions may be sufficient for attaining the organization's initial environmental goals. Subsequently, however, changes in performance management practices and leadership competencies may be needed for continued advancement toward environmental sustainability goals (see Haddock-Millar, Müller-Camen, & Miles, Chapter 16, this volume; Muros, Impelman, & Hollweg, Chapter 18, this volume).

In order to conduct rigorous evaluations of the effectiveness of various HRM and HRD practices, new frameworks are needed for describing and measuring the social and psychological conditions such practices seek to alter. In addition to specific individual green work behaviors, examples of other measures that would be useful include metrics for assessing the leadership competencies needed to create improvements in environmental performance, metrics for assessing the environmental knowledge and attitudes of employees, and new approaches for gauging employee engagement and commitment to environmental initiatives.

Internal Alignment Among Workforce Management Practices

The effectiveness of specific workplace practices depends partly on how well they are aligned with other elements of the total workforce management system, including activities typically labeled HRM and HRD. All HRM and HRD practices need to work in tandem; they should reinforce and complement each other. As an organization's environmental goals and aspirations evolve, components of HRM and HRD need to evolve and change also. Designing and maintaining an internally coherent workplace management system that supports the organization's aspirations and goals is the primary responsibility of senior human resource professionals.

A Problem-Focused Agenda for Research on Workforce Management and Environmental Sustainability

HR scholars may recognize the need for internally consistent workforce management practices, but often they focus their research efforts on just one or two elements of the total system. Following the logic of "basic science," they search for fundamental principles that apply across contexts. But this approach seldom produces clear answers to the questions that practicing managers must answer in order to solve specific problems.

Problem-focused research that specifically aims to improve the environmental sustainability of organizations may be more useful for producing applicable knowledge. A problem-focused approach shifts the goal of research from finding universal principles to identifying approaches that are useful for achieving specific outcomes—such as reducing the organization's environmental footprint through greater recycling, reduced energy use, technical innovations, and so forth.

The practical challenge of aligning elements of the workforce management system might be less daunting if scholars conducted research that was specifically aimed at providing solutions to organizations striving to achieve environmental sustainability. For such a problem-solving approach to gain traction, however, may require a shift in the criteria scholars use to evaluate the quality of research, putting less emphasis on theory testing as the primary goal and increasing the value assigned to research that generates clear recommendations for effective practice.

What questions might future research address in an effort to help organizations achieve environmental sustainability? Let's consider some possibilities.

Focus on Implementation Issues

Currently, HR scholarship emphasizes content and design issues, while mostly ignoring the question of implementation. The dominant paradigm assumes that best practices that are useful in a wide range of settings can be identified and, when such practices are identified, they will be adopted by practitioners. But we have ample evidence that this assumption is not valid (for example, Rynes, Giluk & Brown, 2007). Furthermore, for various reasons, HR practitioners seldom start with a blank slate and then design a "scientifically valid" and complete HR system that they can simply impose on the workforce. Instead, HR practitioners strive to understand the objectives of line managers, negotiate solutions that optimize results against multiple and sometimes conflicting goals, introduce changes while at the same time sustaining a sense of continuity, respond to signals that suggest current conditions are changing, and remain flexible enough to adjust to an unknown future.

A problem-focused approach to conducting research on workforce management and environmental sustainability would recognize that the focal question to address is: How can we use HRM and HRD activities to help our organization implement its environmental strategy? That is, how can we align the workforce management system—including both formal policies and the day-to-day practices of managers—to support progress toward improved environmental performance?

Achieving Alignment

Even firms that publicly declare their commitment to environmental sustainability vary greatly in the degree to which HRM and HRD practices are aligned with environmental management activities. Sometimes job analysis and design, competency modeling, selection, performance evaluation, training, and compensation appear to be unaffected by stated environmental management goals. In other firms, the influence of environmental imperatives can be seen across all aspects of the management system.

Managers' beliefs about which aspects of a workforce management system are most relevant for achieving environmental goals may partly explain the current gaps between stated environmental goals and management practices. An analysis of qualitative data from four Brazilian firms suggests that some practices (performance evaluation, rewards, and public recognition) were perceived as more important for achieving environmental sustainability (Jabbour, Santos, & Nagano, 2010). If such beliefs are widespread, it could explain why practices such as recruitment, socialization, on-boarding, training, and leadership development are not often modified to align them with changes in an organization's stance toward environmental sustainability. Which HRM and HRD practices are actually the most important, and/or the conditions in which they are the most important, is unknown.

The need for a more complete understanding of how to align an entire system of workforce management practices suggests several new research opportunities. Among the questions that such work might address are these:

- How can firms assess the extent to which alignment exists?
- What are some of the early warning signs that indicate the workforce management system is not well aligned?
- Are some evolutionary paths to alignment more effective than others? For example, is alignment of the workforce management system and environmental strategy best achieved by focusing first on performance evaluation and rewards? Or is the effectiveness of performance evaluation and rewards enhanced when the workforce is first prepared for these through extensive socialization and training?
- How can firms improve and speed up the process of aligning the workforce management system with other relevant systems involved in achieving environmental sustainability? Is it more effective to begin with voluntary efforts to create employee engagement? Do top executives really need to be onboard first, or can they be inspired by successful environmental performance results that are initiated and achieved through voluntary efforts at lower levels?
- Where in the organization (which functions, at what levels) are managers most likely to readily understand the value of aligning HRM and HRD practices with environmental goals

and become willing partners in change efforts? How can managers who are most likely to be willing and supportive partners be identified?

- What are the most common obstacles to achieving alignment between environmental strategies and workforce management practices? Do different environmental goals (for example, reducing carbon emissions versus eliminating waste) present different obstacles? How can those obstacles be managed?

Engaging Multiple Stakeholders

A salient feature of past strategic HR scholarship has been the priority given to investors as the stakeholders of primary concern. By focusing so much effort on demonstrating the economic value of HR systems, strategic HR scholarship has drawn substantial criticism from scholars who assert the value of addressing the interests of a wider set of stakeholders.

By attending to the concerns of multiple stakeholder groups, research at the intersection of HR and environmental sustainability offers an opportunity to reform and improve HR scholarship and practice. Generally, HR scholars and practitioners alike recognize the value of attending to the differing perspectives and knowledge bases that characterize subgroups of employees. Many members of the HR profession—especially research scholars—reflexively seek answers to questions that focus on differences among employees based on age, gender, education levels, and so forth (see Klein, D'Mello, & Wiernik, Chapter 6, this volume). Less automatic is fully considering the implications for HRM and HRD of the differing perspectives of stakeholders other than employees.

Numerous cases in this volume illustrate that efforts to achieve environmental sustainability often target changes in the attitudes and behaviors of employees *and* customers *and* the community *and* investors *and* the media. As Caribou Coffee learned, environmentally friendly product sourcing and marketing efforts may be ineffective if they occur in isolation from simultaneous efforts to align the environmental behaviors, attitudes, and knowledge of employees (see Muros, Impelman, & Hollweg, Chapter 18, this volume).

When environmental sustainability is the objective, alliance partners upstream (suppliers of raw materials, product manufacturers) and downstream (distributors, consumers) in the value chain are very important stakeholders also. An organization's effort to reduce its environmental footprint can succeed only if environmentally friendly practices are used throughout all stages of the lifecycle of its products and services. In addition, alliance partners may collaborate in their efforts to influence government and industry regulations, develop new industry standards for the environmental performance of new products, and shape educational and community practices. Thus, workforce management practices might appropriately target the employees of these strategic partners.

Daimler AG's approach to environmental sustainability reflects keen awareness of the value of stakeholder inclusiveness (see Deller, Schneiders, & Titzrath, Chapter 13, this volume). Indeed, their annual Sustainability Dialogue event specifically targets representatives of numerous stakeholder groups to obtain their input for use in establishing the company's goals and seek their collaboration in finding solutions that will help them achieve their environmental goals. Daimler's ten-year (2010 to 2020) sustainability plan reflects their stakeholders' preference for giving more emphasis to *environmental* sustainability issues (versus other social and governance issues that fall under the broader umbrella of sustainability). Daimler's Materiality Matrix is a systematic and practical tool for mapping the importance of various stakeholder concerns and evaluating how addressing those concerns fits with the firm's perception of strategically important issues.

Many HRM and HRD professionals understand that relationships with an array of stakeholders influence and can be influenced by the organization's HR system. Yet most of these other stakeholders are ignored when assessing the effectiveness of workforce management practices. As firms experience increased pressures for transparency around environmental practices, their HRM practices are exposed to greater scrutiny by all stakeholders. For example, approximately 20 percent of the content of the

Global Reporting Initiative addresses issues that fall within the domains of HRM and HRD. Thus, research that addresses the following questions would be of considerable practical use:

- How do various stakeholders evaluate whether stated environmental goals and aspirations are reflected in an organization's workforce management practices?
- What procedures and practices can organizations use to facilitate alignment between elements of the workforce management system and other activities that are visible to multiple stakeholders (marketing efforts, accounting practices, facilities management)?
- When audits of alliance partners yield negative results or indicate the need for change, what are some effective techniques for promoting change across an entire network of alliance partners?
- What are the consequences for the environmental attitudes and behaviors of employees, customers, and investors of perceived inconsistencies between the workplace management practices of alliance partners and the firm's own stated environmental goals and achievements?

Environmental Sustainability in the Global Context

As globalization progressed over time, it challenged firms around the world to develop management systems that are effective across locations with dissimilar laws, cultures, politics, economic conditions, and so on. Progress toward environmental sustainability requires understanding how such differences, which shift over time, influence environmental attitudes and behaviors.

Despite wide variation in the institutional environments that influence HR systems (for example, Florkowski, 2006), HR systems around the world are converging and becoming more alike (Brewster, Mayrhofer, & Morley, 2004). As firms become more engaged in pursuing environmental sustainability goals, the pace of such convergence may quicken. McDonald's UK learned how to effectively change the behaviors of its UK employees and is now attempting to diffuse some of the practices that were effective in the UK to stores in other countries (Haddock-Millar,

Müller-Camen, & Miles, Chapter 16, this volume). Procter & Gamble (P&G) conducts surveys that assess the green attitudes and behaviors of employees spread across eighty countries (Biga, Dilchert, McCance, Gibby, & Oudersluys, Chapter 17, this volume). As P&G initiatives undertake to begin changing these attitudes and behaviors, the company will face the challenge of anticipating how employees in different countries are likely to respond to specific HRM and HRD practices.

The Rapid Results Institute's (RRI) experience using their standard approach to creating organizational change suggests that principles such as coaching, employee involvement, setting measurable goals to be achieved within a short time frame, delegating responsibility for solutions to small teams, and ensuring rapid success against the goals can be effective across a wide range of cultures (Manitsky & Murphy, Chapter 15, this volume). Nevertheless, it is likely that RRI's success is partly due to the deep tacit cultural knowledge that their coaches bring to this work. Is it possible to identify the specific cultural knowledge needed in order to succeed in adapting a seemingly "standard" intervention to differing cultural contexts? Many large multinational companies are facing such a challenge, creating the need for new research that provides answers to questions such as:

- How do the environmental attitudes and behaviors of workers differ around the world? Where is convergence in environmental attitudes and behaviors most (least) evident?
- Which aspects of the institutional context (laws, culture, economy, etc.) are most strongly associated with the environmental attitudes and behaviors at work? And what are the implications of such differences for human resource management for firms with operations, markets, and alliance partners distributed around the world?
- How do international differences influence the way employees (and other stakeholders) react to specific HRM and HRD efforts aimed at environmental sustainability?
- If company-wide convergence of attitudes and behaviors is desired, what processes might be used by employers striving to achieve it?

Organizational Learning

As organizations embark on the journey to environmental sustainability, their change efforts reflect their current change management capabilities. Over time and with experience, some organizations have developed a greater capacity for change. Research that sheds light on how organizations develop and maintain their change management capabilities could help organizations evolve toward environmental sustainability more quickly, for long-lasting results.

It seems likely that past experiences in creating organizational change—whether successful or unsuccessful—can help an organization prepare for future change efforts. For example, prior efforts to implement total quality management or customer service initiatives may have prepared some organizations for current change initiatives aimed at environmental sustainability. Organizations that emerged successful in the face of increased pressures for better quality products and customer service may have developed a cadre of leaders with the competencies needed to effect change in response to recent environmental pressures (see Van Velsor & Quinn, Chapter 10, this volume). And earlier experiences may have taught change agents the value of practices such as rigorously analyzing specific attitudes and behaviors that are relevant to implementing environmental initiatives, establishing specific goals, conducting small-scale pilot projects, and using simple metrics to monitor and evaluate progress. As described in Chapter 16, McDonald's UK environmental sustainability success now is partly due to the company's long history of implementing organizational change in response to changing external conditions. Caribou Coffee (that is, front-line employees and managers), by contrast, has less experience with driving change through HRM initiatives, so it is likely to encounter more and different obstacles and move more slowly toward success.

The 2010 SHRM survey assessing sustainability efforts revealed wide variation in how firms are addressing environmental issues (see Schmit, Fegley, Esen, Schramm, & Tomasetti, Chapter 4, this volume). It clearly shows that some practices are more widespread than others. Differences in approaches include fundamental decisions about who takes responsibility for the strategy, methods used to engage employees, and specific activities like collecting dona-tions to aid victims of environmental disasters, monitoring the company's environmental impact, and promoting the use of low-carbon transportation. What is not yet understood, however, is whether some of these practices are more (less) effective at different stages of an organization's sustainability journey.

Organizational change efforts—including those associated with addressing environmental issues—often employ education and training programs to communicate organizational values, inform employees about the changes being introduced by the organization (for example, changes in performance evaluation criteria), and improve employee competencies that are believed to be relevant to the upcoming changes (see National Environ-mental Education Foundation, 2009). How effective are such efforts in creating a cultural change that supports environmental sustainability? Research on training programs designed to change employees' attitudes has found that such programs seldom succeed in creating organizational change (see Kulik & Rober-son, 2008, who studied diversity training programs). Others have concluded that it is more effective to hold managers accountable for meeting measurable goals (Kalev, Dobbins, & Kelly, 2006).

Alternatively, training programs may be most effective during the early phases of pursuing environmental sustainability, and then become less important after a solid base of knowledge has been built up—perhaps across an entire industry (see Wagner, 2011). Perhaps neither of these approaches is likely to be as effec-tive as attracting employees who are personally committed to environmental sustainability when they are hired. Perhaps the effectiveness of training and incentives is more effective when accompanied by on-boarding and socialization "best practices" such as those described by Bauer, Erdogan, and Taylor (Chapter 9, this volume), which are designed to lay a foundation for sub-sequent HRM and HRD efforts to promote environmentally friendly employee actions. Subsequently, efforts to elicit employee commitment, retain employees, and minimize voluntary turnover may ensure greater returns on the investments made to develop a pro-environment workforce (see Mesmer-Magnus, Viswesvaran, & Wiernik, Chapter 7, this volume).

Future research could begin to develop new knowledge about how best to design learning opportunities that extend over long periods of time, generate intrinsic interest, and lead to desired behavioral change throughout the organization (see Millar, 2011). Practical knowledge is needed concerning questions such as:

- What types of activities are most effective in stimulating employees' desire to learn and promote active employee engagement in environmental issues?
- Is repeated and regularized involvement is such activities for short periods of time more effective than intense immersion for one or two days?
- What percentage of the workforce needs to participate in order for their experiences to disseminate and influence nonparticipants? Does the answer depend on who participates, for example, does participation of higher-level executives speed up or slow down the diffusion process?
- What types of activities stimulate the formation of social networks that serve as conduits for peer-to-peer learning and influence?
- What steps can be taken to leverage individual learning to advance organizational learning?

Toward Environmental Engagement

An effective workforce management system creates a setting in which employees' behaviors are directed toward achieving strategic targets such as energy efficiency, waste reduction, zero emissions, and other sustainability goals. But is tinkering with elements of the HR system sufficient to ignite the full potential of an organization's workforce? Will the current, rather bureaucratic, top-down approach to HRM be adequate?

Employees learn behavioral norms by attending to the actions of others and the consequences associated with those actions. The actions of peers and those in supervisory and leadership positions, and the consequences associated with those actions, matter. But employees are self-directed, too. Employers who seek to develop more engaging workplaces recognize that employees' feelings about the organizations where they work influence a wide range of discretionary behaviors. According to a recent survey of Canadian firms, employee engagement is associated with more positive views of a company's reputation for corporate social responsibility. One interpretation of the study's findings is that employers who invest in socially responsible management practices (including recycling, reduced business travel, and community involvement) reap a return that is paid back in the form of more responsible environmental behaviors (Hall, 2010).

Effective environmental initiatives will surely include some traditional HRM practices—including socialization, training, and performance management. But the novel, experiential practices also have great appeal and may be more effective in creating a truly engaged workforce. At companies like Google and Intel, employee gardens have been established on company grounds. Although they were introduced as an employee perk rather than for educational purposes, with a little imagination, employee gardening activities could be developed into educational experiences that teach principles of environmental sustainability. Perhaps supporting employees' voluntary participation in environmental activities that are only weakly associated with their work will prove to be more effective as a means for leveraging the human desire for self-determination, compared to more formal programs and schemes designed to push employees toward more environmentally responsible behavior on the job.

Many organizations already understand the power of passion. At Sherwin-Williams, the passion of environmental "true believers" helped convince executives to develop their EcoVision, which in turn relies heavily on the continued dedication of such employees (see DuBois, Chapter 12, this volume). At 3M, the passion of executives and employees at all levels throughout the organization drives and sustains that company's culture of environmental sustainability (see Paul & Nilan, Chapter 11, this volume). Thus, perhaps the most significant question to address is

- How can the free will and idiosyncratic interests of employees be addressed and leveraged by employers as they strive to engage the hearts and minds of employees for the purpose of achieving environmental sustainability?

Conclusion

Achieving environmental sustainability will not be easy. There are no quick fixes for this complex challenge. Recognizing the need for action is the first important step toward finding solutions, and many organizations have taken that step during the past decade. Now the time has come for HRM and HRD practitioners and scholars alike to demonstrate that they can contribute to the success of environmental sustainability initiatives in the workplace. Environmental interventions can influence an organization's internal operations, supply chain, distribution processes, marketing efforts, customer behaviors, and so on. To be maximally useful, future research should reflect and address these interdependencies; it will involve stepping out of narrow knowledge silos and working in multidisciplinary teams of experts.

Nor is it likely that the most useful new insights will flow from one-shot, short-term, or highly focused interventions—that is, the types of interventions that lend themselves to publication in scholarly journals. Collaborative efforts that cut across functional, disciplinary, and organizational boundaries and extend over substantial periods of time will be required to effect change and document the outcomes (see Fairfield, Harmon, & Behson, 2009; Harris & Crane, 2002).

Multi-level complexity also must be addressed. At the individual level of analysis, we seek to understand and perhaps alter the attitudes and behaviors of individuals who often are embedded in a larger organization, which itself is interdependent with other organizations that influence its environmental footprint. Employees' attitudes and behaviors also are shaped by a variety of relationships with people in other organizations and community groups (schools, professional associations, talent agencies, political groups, and so on). Such complexity presents challenges when conducting research, but tackling such challenges may also contribute to the development of enriched theoretical models, creative research methodologies, and knowledge that can be readily applied to achieve specific outcomes.

Many leaders in this new arena contributed to this volume with hope of inspiring you to consider how you can contribute to the creation and diffusion of new knowledge that contributes to achieving environmental sustainable organizations within the foreseeable future. We all look forward to seeing the results of this effort!

References

Brewster, C., Mayrhofer, W., & Morley, M. (2004). *Human resource management in Europe: Evidence of convergence?* Burlington, MA: Elsevier Butterworth-Heinemann.

Florkowski, G. F. (2006). *Global legal systems.* London: Routledge.

Fairfield, K. D., Harmon, J. I., & Behson, S. J. (2009, June). A model and comparative analysis of organizational sustainability strategy: Antecedents and performance outcomes perceived by U. S. and non-U.S. based managers. Presented at the International Eastern Academy of Management Conference, Rio de Janeiro, Brazil.

Hall, R. (2010). CSR is well worth the investment. *CAmagazine.* Retrieved from www.camagazine.com.

Harris, L. C., & Crane, A. (2002). The greening of organizational culture: Management views on the depth, degree and diffusion of change. *Journal of Organizational Change Management, 15*(3), 214–234.

Huffman, A. H., Watrous-Rodriguez, K. M., Henning, J. B., & Berry, J. (2009, October). "Working" through environmental issues: The role of the I/O psychologist. *The Industrial-Organizational Psychologist, 47,* 27–35.

Jabbour, J. C., Santos, F. C. A., & Nagano, M. S. (2010). Contributions of HRM throughout the stages of environmental management: Methodological triangulation applied to companies in Brazil. *Journal of International Human Resource Management, 21,* 1049–1089.

Jackson, S. E., & Seo, J. (2010, Winter). The greening of strategic HRM scholarship. *Organizational Management Journal, 7,* 278–290.

Jackson, S. E., Schuler, R. S., Lepak, D., & Tarique, I. (2012). Human resource management practice and scholarship: A North American perspective. In C. Brewster & W. Mayrhofer (Eds.), *Handbook of research in comparative human resource management* (pp. 451–477). Cheltenham, UK: Edward Elgar Publishing.

Kalev, A., Dobbins, F., & Kelly, E. (2006). Best practices or best guesses: Diversity management and the remediation of inequality. *American Sociological Review, 71,* 589–917.

Kulik, C. T., & Roberson, L. (2008). Diversity initiative effectiveness: What organizations can (and cannot) expect from diversity recruitment, diversity training, and formal mentoring programs. In

A. P. Brief (Ed.), *Diversity at work* (pp. 265–317). Cambridge, UK: Cambridge University Press.

Millar, J. (2011). Management learning and the greening of SMEs: Beyond problem-solving. *Zeitschrift für Personalforschung (German Journal of Research in Human Resource Management), 25*(2), 178–195.

National Environmental Education Foundation. (2009). *The engaged organization: Corporate employee environmental education survey and case study findings.* Washington, DC: National Environmental Education Foundation.

Renwick, D. W. S., Redman, T., & Maguire, S. (in press). Green human resource management: A review and research agenda. *International Journal of Human Resource Management.*

Rynes, S. L., Giluk, T. L., & Brown, K. B. (2007). The very separate worlds of academic and practitioner periodicals in human resource management: Implications for evidence-based management. *Academy of Management Journal, 50,* 987–1008.

Wagner, M. (2011). Environmental management activities and HRM in German manufacturing firms: Incidence, determinants, and outcomes. *Zeitschrift für Personalforschung, (German Journal of Research in Human Resource Management), 25*(2), 157–177.

Name Index

Subject Index

Page references followed by *fig* indicate an illustrated figure; followed by *t* indicate a table.

A

DATE DUE

BRODART, CO.

Cat. No. 23-221